DIRECTING OPERATIONS:

BRITISH CORPS COMMAND ON THE
WESTERN FRONT 1914-18

DIRECTING OPERATIONS

BRITISH CORPS COMMAND ON THE WESTERN FRONT 1914-18

by

Andy Simpson

SPELLMOUNT

To my Parents

British Library Cataloguing in Publication Data:
A catalogue record for this book is available
from the British Library

Copyright © Andy Simpson 2006

ISBN 1-86227-292-1

First published in the UK in 2006 by
Spellmount Limited
The Mill, Brimscombe Port
Stroud, Gloucestershire. GL5 2QG

Tel: 01453 883300
Fax: 01453 883233
E-mail: enquiries@spellmount.com
Website: www.spellmount.com

1 3 5 7 9 8 6 4 2

The right of Andy Simpson to be identified
as the author of this work has been asserted by him
in accordance with the Copyright, Designs
and Patents Act 1988

Printed in Great Britain by
Oaklands Book Services
Stonehouse, Gloucestershire GL10 3RQ

Contents

Acknowledgements

Firstly, I would like to thank my Ph.D. supervisor, Professor David French, without whose considerable help and guidance the thesis from which this book is derived could not have been written. His generosity with his time and advice and his thoroughness and speed in reading and commenting on draught chapters and the final thesis went well beyond the call of duty. In addition, the following (in alphabetical order, not necessarily order of merit) have made helpful suggestions and comments during the lengthy production process: Dr. John Bourne, Mr. Tony Cowan, Dr. Bryn Hammond, Mr. Chris McCarthy, Dr. Krisztina Robert and Professor Gary Sheffield. As ever, any mistakes or oversights are mine alone. I owe a special debt to my wife, Krisztina Robert, for her help and support, and also to my parents for theirs, as well as their generosity and encouragement over many years. In addition, I must mention with thanks the assistance given to me by a number of financial institutions and software testing consultancies in the City of London.

I would also like to thank the following institutions and their staffs for their kind assistance: the Imperial War Museum; the National Army Museum; Churchill College, Cambridge; the British Library; the National Library of Scotland; the Liddell Hart Centre for Military Archives; Durham County Record Office; Staffordshire County Record Office and West Sussex County Record Office.

Acronyms and Glossary

A&QMG – Adjutant and Quartermaster-General.

ADC – Aide de Camp.

AG – Adjutant-General.

AHQ – Army Headquarters.

AIF – Australian Imperial Force.

ANZAC – Australia and New Zealand Corps.

APM – Assistant Provost Marshal

ASC – Army Service Corps.

BEF – British Expeditionary Force.

BGGS – Brigadier-General, General Staff (the chief staff officer of a corps).

BG (O) – Brigadier-General (Operations) at GHQ.

BGRA – Brigadier General, Royal Artillery (the term by which the GOCRA was known until approximately late 1915).

C2 – In modern military parlance, Command and Control.

C3 – In modern military parlance, Command, Control and Communications.

CBSO – Counter-Battery Staff Officer (attached to corps artillery HQ).

CEF – Canadian Expeditionary Force.

CGS – Chief of the General Staff (the chief staff officer at GHQ).

CHA – Commander, Heavy Artillery (at corps level).

C-in-C – Commander in Chief.

CIGS – Chief of the Imperial General Staff.

CMGO – Corps Machine-Gun Officer.

COS – Chief of Staff (a generic term for the chief staff officer at any level of command).

CRA – Commander, Royal Artillery (the usual term for a divisional artillery commander).

CRE – Commander, Royal Engineers of any formation from division to Army.

DA&QMG – Deputy Adjutant and Quartermaster General (the chief administrative staff officer of a corps or Army).

DD Signals – Deputy Director of Signals (senior signals officer of an Army).

DGT – Director-General of Transportation.

DGT Line – The administrative boundary between Army and corps.

DHQ – Divisional Headquarters.

DLI – Durham Light Infantry.

DMO – Director of Military Operations.

DMT – Director of Military Training.

DSD – Director of Staff Duties.

Eingreif division – A counter-attack division in the German 1917 defensive model.

FOO – Forward Observation Officer (artillery), placed to spot the fall of shot and report back to his battery.

GHQ – General Headquarters, the main Expeditionary Force staff.

GOC – General Officer Commanding.

GOCRA – General Officer Commanding, Royal Artillery (the usual term for a corps artillery commander from 1916).

GQG – Grand Quartier Général (the French and Belgian equivalent of GHQ).

GS – General Staff. The GS or 'G' branch of a staff was concerned with the planning and execution of operations.

GSO1, 2, 3 (I)/(O) – General Staff Officer, Grade 1, 2 or 3, belonging to the (Intelligence) or (Operations) branch of the Staff.

HAG – Heavy Artillery Group.

HAR – Heavy Artillery Reserve.

MEF – Mediterranean Expeditionary Force.

MGC – Machine-Gun Corps.

MGO – Machine-Gun Officer of a formation.

MGGS – Major-General, General Staff (the chief staff officer of an Army).

MGRA – Major-General, Royal Artillery (the adviser for that arm at Army HQ).

psc – Passed Staff College (and hence a trained staff officer).

QMG – Quartermaster-General.

RA – Royal Artillery.

RAF – Royal Air Force.

RE – Royal Engineers.

RFC – Royal Flying Corps.

RGA – Royal Garrison Artillery (heavy artillery).

Foreword

By Professor Gary Sheffield

We are not short of books on First World War British generals and generalship. For ninety years, the conduct of the war on the Western Front by the British Expeditionary Force (BEF) has been a hugely contentious issue. But for all the sound and fury, it is curious how little we know about so many important aspects of the subject. While there are numerous books on Douglas Haig, many other senior commanders have been neglected by writers. Those books that have appeared are of distinctly varying quality. In any case, a biographical approach tends to have its limitations. Exactly how these generals commanded, what they did from day to day, and how the various levels of command related to each other has remained surprisingly obscure. In short, there are significant gaps in our understanding of the BEF's practice of command.

This is in spite of the revolution in the study of the BEF in recent years. The 'lions led by donkeys' caricature has been thoroughly discredited, and replaced by a nuanced view of the transformation of the British army between 1914 and 1918. A small, colonially-orientated force developed into a large, sophisticated and technologically advanced army that played a primary role in defeating the German army in the Hundred Days campaign of 1918. However, much of this research has been directed at the top of the BEF – at the level of GHQ and Army – or much further down, looking at individual units. Curiously little attention has been paid to what might be called the middle-management of the BEF, command at brigade, divisional, and corps level. With two striking exceptions, the corps level of command has suffered from a particular degree of neglect. The Australian and Canadian Corps functioned as, in effect, national armies. Therefore it is not surprising that Australian and Canadian historians have been drawn to the study of these formations. At long last, Andy Simpson's masterly study redresses the balance by subjecting British corps to detailed analysis.

Directing Operations traces the development of the responsibility of corps during the First World War. In 1914, corps served an administrative function, as a post-box through which orders from GHQ would reach subordinate formations. In reality, in the confused fighting of August-September 1914 both Haig at I Corps and Smith-Dorrien at II Corps had a vital role as semi-independent commanders. Exactly what purpose a corps served was to be a matter of debate for some time to come. The centrality of artillery to success on the First World War battlefield ensured, during 1915, that corps acquired greater significance as a means of co-ordinating firepower. But as Andy Simpson shows, during the battle of the Somme in 1916 the two principal Army commanders used corps in very different ways. Hubert Gough continued to use corps as post-boxes, as a way of delivering his prescriptive instructions to divisions, and he liked to breathe down the necks of his corps commanders during operations. Henry Rawlinson, by contrast, had a more relaxed approach, allowing corps greater latitude to discuss and debate orders, and conduct operations.

As with so many other aspects of the development of the BEF, the Battle of the Somme was a watershed. From 1917 onwards corps played a vital role in planning and executing operations, within a context of increasing devolution of responsibility to the divisional level. This reflected, among other things, the increasing competence and sophistication of commanders and staff. As Dr Simpson convincingly argues, by the second half of 1918 the flexibility of the command structure – along with effective logistic provision and an abundance of guns and ammunition – allowed the BEF to achieve a high operational tempo. In the period of trench warfare, initial success, even if it was on an impressive scale, as at the beginning of the battle of Arras in April 1917, inevitably became bogged down. In the Hundred Days, this problem was largely overcome. In contrast to the flawed methods employed by the Germans during their 1918 Spring Offensive, the BEF mounted a series of shallow but logistically sustainable advances backed by formidable concentrations of artillery. These attacks brought relentless pressure to bear along the entire front. Not the least of Andy Simpson's achievements lies in his delineation of the role of corps in bringing about and maintaining this high operational tempo.

Dr Simpson also succeeds in giving the anonymous corps level of command a human face. In a straightforward but effective chapter, he analyses the diaries of a number of corps commanders and finds out how they spent their time. They rode for exercise and to get from place to place; they entertained important visitors from Britain, to do business with subordinates or allies, or to gossip; they held conferences to plan operations; they commanded in battles. *Pace* Alan Clark and *Blackadder*, generals did not simply sit in comfortable chateaux, oblivious to the sufferings of their men. The corps commanders studied here did visit the front line. One, Walter Congreve, lost a hand to shellfire.

Directing Operations is an impressive work based on sustained archival research. Dr Simpson is rightly critical of previous historians who tended to rely on post-war anecdotal evidence, some of which might be described as gossip. He does not fall into this trap, instead using contemporary operational records held at the National Archives, supplemented by personal papers from sources such as the Imperial War Museum and the Liddell Hart Centre for Military Archives. Dr Simpson brings much-needed scholarly rigour to the subject. *Directing Operations* is undoubtedly one of the most significant books on the British army during the First World War to appear in recent years. It is a first-class piece of historical scholarship, written in an accessible style, with flashes of mordant wit. I look forward to seeing more from Andy Simpson's pen in the future.

Gary Sheffield   JSCSC, Shrivenham
Professor of Modern History   April 2006
King's College London

Introduction

This Introduction addresses three points: firstly, what the book sets out to demonstrate; secondly, how the operational role of British corps command on the Western Front is treated in the literature; and thirdly, to justify the sample of corps selected. The Australian and Canadian Corps are not included here, having a literature of their own (which is discussed below) and being special cases anyway. This was because their staff structures differed somewhat from British corps and, more importantly, they were usually composed of the same divisions, whereas British corps tended to have divisions rotated through them. Furthermore, in 1918 they retained the 12-battalion division when the British went down to nine battalions per division.

It should be noted that the term 'operational command' is not used in its modern sense (the level of command "concerned with the direction of military resources to achieve military strategic objectives"[1]). It is used in the way in which it was employed during the Great War, where it connoted operations involving any formation from a brigade upwards. Usually it will refer to corps- or Army-level operations, depending upon the context.

The object of this book is to assess how important the corps level of command on the Western Front was, and to establish what British corps did, and how they did it. An important part of this is to establish the doctrinal basis (if any) of the BEF's activities, for which some clarification of the term 'doctrine' is required. John Gooch defined doctrine as "a set of beliefs about the nature of war and the keys to success on the battlefield."[2] Brian Holden Reid observed that for much of the twentieth century the British Army lacked "a coherent doctrinal philosophy," though it was not lacking military thinkers. He argued that doctrine must establish an institutionalised, general framework for thought and action, rather than simply being a set of ideas, however widely disseminated.[3] The relevance of this point to thought in the British army is discussed later in this chapter.

A number of themes have emerged during this research. One is the continuity of thought in the British Army from before the war through to its conclusion, which was expressed by the application of *Field Service Regulations (1909) Part 1 (Operations)*, which will henceforth be referred to as *FSR I*. Although it might be thought that pre-war thinking would necessarily become obsolete during the military revolution which took place during the Great War, this was not the case, because of the way in which *FSR I* was designed to be used. At the 1913 General Staff conference, Colonel Whigham (a GSO1 under the DSD) raised the point that *FSR I* should state the principles under which the army should operate, and that these might therefore be omitted from training manuals. In reply, Br.-Gen. Du Cane (Staff Officer to the Inspector-General of the Forces) observed that the General Staff favoured the amplification of *FSR I*'s principles "to a certain extent in the manuals of the arms concerned..."[4] The point was further emphasised by Br.-Gen. Kiggell (the DSD), who said that:

> There is no doubt as to the danger which, I think, all admit, of laying down too much detail in official regulations. Human nature loves details of that sort to be laid down: it makes it very much easier for instructors in peace to be able to say, "You are wrong: there is the book," and it makes it very much easier for the pupil to be able to say, "Please, Sir, I think I am right; there is the book." But we know that the problems of war cannot be solved by rules, but by judgement based on a knowledge of general principles. To lay down rules would tend to cramp judgement, not to educate and strengthen it. For that reason our manuals aim at giving principles but avoid laying down methods.[5]

In other words, *FSR I* was a set of principles for application by trained and experienced officers, which specifically avoided going into too much detail, since those applying them should, through experience and training, know what detailed actions to perform within their framework. Indeed, Haig stated after his 1911 Indian Staff Tour that although the General Staff had been criticised for lacking a doctrine, this ignored the varying conditions under which the army might be required to act. Given that *FSR I* was written sometime between 1907 and 1909, when Haig was DSD (and as such, its sponsor) it is unsurprising that he felt that the level of detail was perfectly adequate. To make it more specific ran the risk of officers finding it to be sometimes inapplicable.[6] This reflected the general reluctance within the British army to accept a formal doctrine at the time, and also that its varied Imperial commitments meant that it was in a very different position from the German army, which knew that its next major war would be fought in Western and Central Europe and could therefore arrange its training and doctrine for that environment and set of enemies.[7]

On the basis of Reid's definition cited above, it is apparent that the BEF did not have a doctrine as such. It is also debateable whether the British army needed a formal doctrine in any case. Albert Palazzo has contended that for the BEF, its ethos (defined as "the characteristic spirit and the prevalent sentiment, taste, or opinion of a people, institution or system") worked better than a standardised doctrine, enabling the adoption of a flexible approach, owing to the varied nature of the challenges the army might have met before the war.[8] As a result, the BEF could absorb a huge increase in numbers and tremendous changes in technology and tactics without undergoing the sort of wholesale reorganisation which the Germans undertook, and which led to the adoption of the stormtroop tactics which played such an important part in Germany's defeat, notwithstanding their tactical utility.

The flexibility of *FSR I* was such that it remained applicable even during the enormous changes in the way in which the army waged war during the course of the conflict. This was most crucial in the volume of artillery employed and the techniques used to make it more effective, though new weapons were also introduced and worked into the conceptual framework of the army. How corps operated with all these is therefore an important part of assessing what it did. Indeed, as the need for greater control of artillery grew, the importance of corps grew. The Battle of the Somme saw the period of greatest intellectual confusion in the BEF, when it became apparent that the earlier assumption, that a hole could simply be blasted through the German defences, was incorrect. At this time corps had a more centralising role than before or after (though at all times operations were usually discussed with divisions and not simply imposed upon them). Once the lessons of the Somme had been digested, and confusion diminished, command became less centralised, as the new system of attack, expressed for the corps and divisional level in the pamphlet *SS135*, was worked into the procedures followed by the BEF. By September 1917, the style of attack was such that Army merely passed to corps the outline of what it had to do, and corps organised the whole operation, delegating to divisions as necessary. By the time of the Hundred Days, the command structure was sufficiently flexible for corps to leave divisions to get on with attacks with minimal supervision, unless a co-ordinated approach was especially required. At the same time, a sufficiency of artillery and improved staff work led to the tempo of the BEF's operations reaching a higher level than at any other time in the war. And though the role of corps was largely confined to executing Army's wishes, it is noteworthy that the 46th Division's storming of the Hindenburg Line was a IX Corps plan, suggested by it to Army. It should also be noted that the BEF improvised its fighting techniques; no-one trained corps commanders in a doctrine, since they were expected simply to apply *FSR I* to the new circumstances.

Another important aspect of the operational art as practised in the BEF during the Great War was tempo, which John Kiszely defined as "the rate or rhythm of activity relative to the enemy."[9] He went on to elaborate on the point, observing that high tempo allows a force "to move into a position of advantage relative to the enemy either to apply force, or to threaten the application of force, thus forcing a reaction which... [it] can exploit further. High tempo is achieved by a fast decision-action cycle..., by a high standard of tactical drills (thus reducing the need for orders) and by fast, mobile weapon-platforms." Though, as the last part of this quotation reveals, Kiszely was thinking of manoeuvre warfare, his ideas are applicable to the Great War, not least because "tempo is relevant only in comparison to our opponent." The tempo of the BEF's operations varied during the course of the war, as will be seen, and played a vital part in the last few months. In the Hundred Days the constant Allied (and particularly British) offensives kept the Germans off balance and unable to react swiftly enough to contain them; this was the first sustained period during which one side had higher tempo than the other since 1914.

The literature on the operational aspects of the Great War has been very ably discussed by Ian M. Brown.[10] He, as is customary, splits these studies into those ascribing the behaviour of the BEF to internal factors and those which stress external factors. The former group is characterised by an approach which examines the generals and the staff and finds them wanting; the latter by one which concentrates more on material or strategic factors, such as lack of artillery or the need to improvise a large army, blaming them for the problems the BEF suffered until the battles of the Hundred Days.

In addition to the division of the literature by its attitude to external and internal factors, it falls into two other groups, the 'old' and the 'new.' It appears that virtually everything published before Bidwell and Graham's *Fire-Power* was based on the Official History's narrative, with a leavening of formation histories to provide detail of operations, and a reworking of the early biographies, memoirs and published diaries of participants; the proportions of these ingredients varied according to whether the author was writing an operational account or a biography.[11] Before the Public Record Office files were opened in the late 1960s, these were virtually the only primary sources or (in the cases where, for example, Harington's biography of Plumer or Duff Cooper or Charteris on Haig were used) the nearest an author could get to them.[12] Naturally, they were interpreted according to the viewpoint of the historian. This led to the surprising coincidence that of the 22 works cited in John Terraine's *Douglas Haig: The Educated Soldier* (a stout defence of its subject), nine were also used (out of 16 works in the bibliography which were not unit histories) by Alan Clark in his polemical attack on all British Great War generals, *The Donkeys*.[13]

The 'new' literature in general has not analysed corps command in any depth. Bidwell and Graham's *Fire-Power* concentrated on tactical issues and debates before, during and after the Great War, and had little to say about corps command. Though *The Killing Ground*, by Professor T.H.E. Travers, dealt with the decision-making process in the BEF, both at the tactical and the strategic levels, it again did not particularly emphasise corps command, being more concerned with perceived internal problems at the GHQ and Army levels. Travers' next book, *How the War Was Won*, continued these themes, and contained more detailed operational analysis of the way in which he thought corps worked in late 1917 and 1918.[14] However, it is flawed in its basic premises, not least because Travers' assertion that officers who were not wholeheartedly pro-tank, to the satisfaction of the zealots of the tank corps, were 'traditionalists' is fallacious. Artillery techniques had become so complex by late 1917 that officers who put their faith in the infantry-artillery attack were necessarily technologically-minded. In fairness to Travers, however, it must be noted that together with *Fire-Power*, his work marked the beginning of the modern, archive-driven, scholarly approach to research on the operational aspects of the war. Travers' comments on command structure were complemented by those in *Doctrine and Dogma* and *Command or Control* by Martin Samuels, which also dealt with 1917 and 1918, though at a tactical and doctrinal level.[15] However, Samuels was not interested in corps. Prior's and Wilson's *Command on the Western Front*, as a study of one commander at corps and then Army level, is obviously not necessarily representative of corps commanders as a whole, though it is extremely valuable in showing how IV Corps and then Fourth Army operated under Sir Henry Rawlinson.[16] Their more recent *The Somme* did pay more attention to corps and their commanders than has been customary, but was concerned with the campaign as a whole, including its political aspects, rather than just one level of command.[17] Harris' study of the Hundred Days, *Amiens to the Armistice*, is also a valuable account and devoted more time to corps command than most other operational studies, but it nevertheless did not attempt a systematic analysis of how corps operated.[18] And in *Battle Tactics of the Western Front*, Paddy Griffith outlined the changes in command of the BEF's corps in an appendix, but otherwise left them alone.[19] *Seeking Victory on the Western Front*, by Albert Palazzo, had little to do with corps command, but is of particular interest because its author stressed the applicability of *FSR I* throughout the war owing to its place in the ethos of the BEF, as discussed above. The weakness of Palazzo's book (a study of chemical warfare in the BEF) is that it accepted the post facto reasoning of Haig's *Final Despatch* regarding his intentions during the war. Two books by Professor Ian Beckett – *Johnnie Gough, VC* and *First Ypres* – covered the activities of corps more thoroughly than is usually the case, but this is because they were largely concerned with fighting in 1914, before Armies had been formed and so corps commanders were more noticeable.[20]

Nikolas Gardner's *Trial by Fire* also dealt with 1914 and again corps was mentioned more than usual. However, its thesis is not entirely convincing, since it relied on Samuels' argument that the BEF practised a style of command which he termed 'umpiring'. Since this is based on the unproven assumption that the command style he perceived at Haig's GHQ and that of Sir Ian Hamilton at Gallipoli was practised at all levels of the BEF, it seems badly flawed. Indeed, the present study demonstrates the invalidity of Samuels' argument for corps.[21] Simon Robbins' *British Generalship on the Western Front, 1914-18: Defeat into Victory* is the exception to the rule as regards corps command, since as a survey of the high command of the BEF it does pay far more attention to corps than is the norm.[22]

Another variety of newer publications is those produced under the aegis of the Strategic and Combat Studies Institute. Gary Sheffield stressed the improvement in the BEF's communications systems as the war went on, in tandem with advances in 'C2'; these were most evident in the Hundred Days.[23] Geoffrey Till demonstrated the failure of delegated command at Gallipoli and the importance to Sir Ian Hamilton of his Chief of Staff being a graduate of the Staff College.[24] A striking point was made in a paper on naval warfare, where Andrew Gordon observed that though the term 'C3' seems to imply equalities between its components, in fact only command and control are equal. Communications are only a means to an end in providing effective 'C2', and another way of achieving this is through doctrine.[25]

The Dominion corps have a literature of their own, of which only the most modern works will be mentioned here. Three studies highlighted the role of the CEF. The first, *Surviving Trench Warfare* by Bill Rawling, was a clear account of the development of this formation and its use of technology during the war.[26] Ian M. Brown's article 'Not Glamorous, But Effective: The Canadian Corps and the Set-Piece Attack, 1917-1918' carried on Rawling's work, with particular reference to the development through 1917 and 1918 of the set-piece as practised by this formation.[27] Shane B. Schreiber's study of the Canadian Corps, *Shock Army of the British Empire*, was rather partisan in its attitude to its subject and at times peculiarly reliant upon Denis Winter's work. It was also heavily influenced by Travers, while attempting nevertheless to display the war-winning abilities of the Canadians.[28] The AIF has been dealt with in J.D. Millar's work, *A Study in the Limitations of Command*.[29] This argued that the role of corps command was inherently limited by virtue of its subordinate position to Army and GHQ, and Birdwood's freedom of action was therefore very restricted until his corps came under the command of Second Army in 1917. Millar accepted Travers' views regarding the top-down style of command in the BEF and referred to Birdwood's 'unquestioning deference to the command structure.' Because of the parameters imposed by the structure of the BEF, corps commanders could only operate as individuals when it came to asserting their personalities, and it was here, as a leader of men, that Birdwood excelled. However, in its generalisations about corps as a whole, this work suffers because of the limited sample with which it dealt, and it exaggerates the degree to which corps commanders were limited in their freedom of action.

Another category of writing with the potential for touching on corps command is the biographical. Such works were usually favourable to their subject (almost invariably an Army commander), and tended either to skip over their periods of corps command or to bestow upon them a degree of success in that position which appeared, once they became Army commanders, to be unavailable to their subordinates. Brian Gardner's *Allenby*, (the most competent attempt; Lawrence James' more recent work was marred by a failure to understand the primacy of artillery in the Great War, to rely excessively on anecdotal evidence and not even to understand the function of a creeping barrage) briefly made the point that his tenure as a corps commander "was a most unhappy period for Allenby, although more unhappy still for his troops."[30] But once their subject undertook the command of Third Army, neither Gardner nor James made more than passing reference to the corps under his command. In *The Congreves Father and Son*, Pamela Thornton and Lt.-Col. Fraser pointed out that they "rely for the most part on appreciations written by those with whom he [Sir Walter Congreve] was most intimately associated," which does not seem to indicate an especially objective approach.[31] Geoffrey Powell's *Plumer* made reference to the potentially limited role of the corps commander, and especially his lack of opportunity to change events once fighting had begun; but it also stressed that a corps commander could make an impact through careful preparation, planning, and training of troops.[32] However, after Plumer's appointment to Second Army, little mention was made of corps. Much the same can be said of Jeffrey Williams' *Byng of Vimy*, except that Byng's role in training the Canadian Corps was stressed more heavily, and he was credited with being ahead of his time in concentrating on small-unit tactics.[33] The only modern biography of a corps commander who rose no higher during the war is Sir John Baynes' work on Sir Ivor Maxse. However, it is largely a narrative, and apart from a stout (and convincing) defence of Maxse's conduct in March 1918, did not say much about corps.[34] Sir Aylmer Haldane, of VI Corps, wrote an autobiography in the 1940s, but it cast little light on the workings of corps command, though it was illuminating regarding his dislike of Allenby.[35]

It is important to note that Sir Basil Liddell Hart had a hand in many of the works of the 'internal school,' from Lloyd George's outstandingly biased *Memoirs* in the 1930s through to the '60s. He was also an assiduous collector and re-teller of gossip (a substantial amount of which was, ironically, provided over many years by Sir James Edmonds, whose Official

History is the greatest monument of the 'external school'). This has led to widespread acceptance, for example, of the phrase 'lions led by donkeys' as having been coined by German generals about their British counterparts in the Great War. However, this is simply what was passed to Clark by Liddell Hart during the two years they worked on *The Donkeys*, and the saying originated perhaps 45 years earlier.[36] Another example, with an even stronger emotional overtone, is the story of the GHQ officer who, on seeing the swampy battlefield at the end of Third Ypres, burst into tears, exclaiming "Good God, did we really send men to fight in that?" Liddell Hart obtained this from Edmonds in 1927 and used it in *The Real War*, though it subsequently found its way into other works as far apart in time as Lloyd George's *Memoirs* and, almost 30 years later, Leon Wolff's impassioned study of the Flanders campaign in 1917, *In Flanders Fields*.[37] In fact, these supposedly first-hand accounts were often simply gossip and have proved so pernicious and self-serving a form of evidence in Great War writing that they should be treated very cautiously. That Liddell Hart had his own agenda regarding the Great War generals has been pointed out by John J. Mearsheimer too, and while Sir James Edmonds is rightly regarded as an important source of information, it must not be forgotten that he was perfectly capable of also passing on the startling fact that Prince Albert's marriage to Queen Victoria was only permitted by Lord Melbourne because they were not really cousins at all. Albert, he asserted, was the bastard offspring of his supposed father's court bandmaster.[38] Therefore Edmonds' historical writing rather than his table-talk is referred to here and the temptation to denounce him as an unreliable gossip and then quote him anyway has been avoided. In general, this book relies upon non-anecdotal primary sources, principally the reports, memoranda, conference minutes, orders and other documents in corps, Army and GHQ War Diaries (though not the War Diaries themselves, which have greater potential for retrospective falsification).[39] This is perhaps a rather bloodless approach, but corps commanders as men were not extensively written about, and while one officer may have, for example, viewed Sir George M. Harper as an 'old ass,' another saw him as having the makings of a great general.[40] Chapter 8, however, is based solely upon the personal diaries of six corps commanders. Criticism of Travers is made not infrequently, because he is too often inclined to believe anecdotal evidence which suits his argument, but fails to verify it elsewhere, such as by reference to the General Staff papers of formations. The bibliography of *How the War Was Won* contains 30 references to CAB 45 files in the National Archives (i.e. largely anecdotal evidence relating to the writing of the OH) but only four to WO 95 (General Staff War Diary papers), though a number of other operational papers are cited. In the file CAB 45/185, evidence both refuting and confirming his argument nestles side by side. It is important to deal with what can be verified in the documents or corroborated by other, independently recorded anecdotes, rather than simply to relate retrospective tittle-tattle.

In recent years another strand has appeared in the historiography – the 'learning curve' debate. Amongst books which take a generally favourable view of the BEF's performance, it is argued that the BEF reached a peak of efficiency, both tactical and operational, in late 1918. The process by which it arrived at this point, starting from comparative ineffectiveness on 1st July 1916, is known as the 'learning curve'. Amongst its earliest exponents was Bill Rawling in *Surviving Trench Warfare*, the first chapter of which is entitled "The Learning Process Begins". In *Command on the Western Front* Prior and Wilson highlighted the process for Sir Henry Rawlinson at Fourth Army, and also some of the problems in interpreting what went on, since at the Army level of command at least, the learning curve seems to have been neither smooth nor uninterrupted. Paddy Griffith began to make the case for the BEF as whole in *Battle Tactics of the Western Front* and was the first to point out the importance of the SS series of pamphlets. The present author's *The Evolution of Victory* was an early, popular, contribution to the genre.[41] Gary Sheffield's *Forgotten Victory* put across the concept of the learning curve while debunking many of the myths put forward by the 'Lions led by donkeys' school of thought.[42] His *The Somme* was the first study of a major battle written with the development of the curve in mind (Harris and Barr's *Amiens to the Armistice* dealing with its culmination). Albert Palazzo has examined the learning curve from the point of view of chemical warfare.[43] And Simon Robbins' *British Generalship on the Western Front* has demonstrated the operation of the learning process amongst the BEF's high command. More research needs to be done on the learning curve, however. It seems likely that the rate of new ideas spreading across the BEF varied, and that there was a different curve (if indeed it was a curve, in terms of constant progression) for each level of command. Sheffield and Todman's (eds.) *Command and Control on the Western Front* made a start on this. Perhaps formations with a high turnover of commanders needed to learn a set of tactics more than once. How information was disseminated is also a problem. And since to some extent, the learning curve represents a response to changes in German defensive tactics, research needs to be concerned with how the BEF was eventually able to change faster than the Germans could change to counter its tactics. This book outlines the development of the learning curve at the corps level of command, as well as putting forward the ideas that the SS pamphlets were essential in its evolution, and that *FSR I* was applicable throughout the war, owing to its adaptable nature It also provides the first analysis of the day-to-day job of generalship in the First World War.

The process of selecting a range of corps to study necessarily involved ensuring that those chosen were reasonably typical of the British corps serving on the Western Front as a whole. Firstly, it was necessary to assess in which major operations they took part, as compared to the body of corps as a whole. Secondly, the commanders of the corps short-listed should themselves have been representative of corps commanders as a whole.

By way of a yardstick, I Corps, as the prewar Aldershot Command and the corps most likely early in the war to apply the principles of *FSR I* (given that Haig was responsible as DSD for supervising the writing of them and commanded I Corps at the beginning of the war) was selected automatically. Corps deliberately omitted were as follows: II and III since, together with I Corps, they constituted the original BEF (this is somewhat arbitrarily defined as corps seeing action before the First Battle of Ypres); XII and XVI since their service was effectively confined to Salonika; XX and XXI since their service was confined to Palestine; XXII since it was to some extent II ANZAC under another name; XXIII since it was Home Forces only; and XXIV since it only existed as the rump of a corps staff for ten days in Cairo.

The table below shows the major operations undertaken by the BEF and those corps participating which have not already been excluded; the offensives in 1915 are omitted since only IV and IX Corps took part. In the Final Advance column, an asterisk against a corps number indicates that it participated in the storming of the Hindenburg Line. From this, it was decided that the following corps should be shortlisted in addition to I Corps, subject to further selection through the other criteria given above: V, VII, VIII, X, XIII, XVIII. VIII and XVIII Corps, it will be noted, had less operational experience than the others in the list. Nevertheless they were deemed worthy of inclusion since VIII and XIII could usefully be compared as exemplifying extremes of success and failure on the first day of the Somme; and, although XVIII was atypical in being commanded by Sir Ivor Maxse, his influence on that corps must nevertheless be of interest. In addition, XVIII Corps staff was merged with VIII Corps staff in July 1918. Other corps were also used where it was felt that their inclusion significantly added to the relevant chapter or chapters.

Somme	Arras	Messines	Third Ypres	Cambrai	March Retreat	Lys	Final Advance
				IV	IV		IV*
V	V		V	V	V		V*
	VI			VI	VI		VI*
VII	VII			VII	VII		
VIII							VIII
		IX	IX			IX	IX*
X		X	X				X
XI						XI	XI

Somme	Arras	Messines	Third Ypres	Cambrai	March Retreat	Lys	Final Advance
XIII	XIII				XIII		XIII*
XIV			XIV				
XV							XV
	XVII				XVII		XVII*
			XVIII		XVIII		
			XIX		XIX		XIX

As to the typicality of the commanders of these corps, a problem arises immediately. Across 47 corps GOCs on the Western Front as a whole, 19% (9) were cavalrymen, 60% (28) infantry, 4% (2) engineers and 17% (8) artillerymen. Of the 19 GOCs of the shortlist, 32% (6) were cavalrymen, 47% (9) infantry, 5% (1) engineers and 16% (3) artillerymen. In other words, the cavalry are over-represented, principally at the expense of the infantry. However, other factors need to be borne in mind. Firstly, each commander's length of service as a GOC must be considered, since a short period of command would imply that they had less impact on their corps. The average length of a corps commander's tenure was 423 days; however, of I Corps' six GOCs, four had command for less than half this time and another for just over half. Similarly, of V Corps' five GOCs, three had command for less than half this time and another for just over half. Since these two corps had as GOCs four out of six cavalrymen it would seem that cavalrymen had command for short periods. So although the cavalry are over-represented numerically, they can be assumed to have been (on average) less influential as corps commanders. Furthermore, the most significant period in the evolution of operational art might arguably be defined as that between mid-1916 and mid-1918 (i.e. the development of shooting off the map, the use of Fuze 106 etc. for the artillery and small-unit infiltration tactics for the infantry), well before which Gough, Haig and Allenby (i.e. 50% of the cavalrymen) had moved on to higher things. Secondly, of GOCs as a whole, 68.09% passed Staff College; of the sample, 68.42% did so, so in this respect the sample is representative. Therefore it appears to be safe to use the sample of I, V, VII, VIII, X, XIII, and XVIII Corps without the risk of receiving a distorted view of British corps on the Western Front.

The chapters which follow are in chronological sequence. Chapter 1 deals with Sir Douglas Haig's ideas as expressed in *FSR I* and his *Final Despatch*, and how they were applied when he was GOC I Corps in 1914 and then GOC First Army, under which I Corps operated, in 1915. The question of the tempo of operations in 1914-15 is also examined, as are changes in the function of corps in that period. Chapter 2 is concerned with how corps functioned during the Battle of the Somme (again, looking particularly at the relevance of *FSR I* and the tempo of operations). It also outlines the changes in the status of the corps artillery adviser in early 1916 and their effects, and examines the relationship between corps and Army and corps and division during the campaign. Chapter 3 is devoted to the set-piece battles of the first part of 1917, Arras and Messines, adopting much the same approach as Chapter 2. However, at this point the lessons of the Somme began to be disseminated through the *SS* pamphlets (in conjunction with *FSR I*) and especially, for the purposes of this book, *SS135*, so their application is crucial to the argument of the chapter. The planning and execution of the Third Battle of Ypres are dealt with in Chapter 4, as before focusing on the use of *FSR I* and the *SS* pamphlets, and the relationships between corps and the formations above and below. The stereotyping of attacks from September 1917 onwards, with Army delegating the organisation to corps, is a central theme. Chapter 5 is concerned with the planning and execution of the Battle of Cambrai, again noting the impact of tempo, *FSR I* and the pamphlets and the relationships between corps, Army and division. The essentially conventional nature of the preparation of the attack, basing ideas on lessons learnt earlier in the year is also brought out. Chapters 6 and 7 deal with 1918, the first concerning itself with the period in the first half of the year when the BEF was on the defensive and the second with the Hundred Days. Again, the application of prewar principles is stressed, but the learning process during the war is also studied; lessons learnt at Cambrai in mobile warfare were applied in March and April, refined afterwards and used in their modified form in the Final Advance. And the impact of tempo is perhaps more evident in 1918 than at any other time in the war; in the first half of the year, the Germans had higher tempo than the BEF, but in the Hundred Days the reverse was true. Chapter 8 looks at the job of the corps commander, pointing out the principles on which it was based and however these generals went about their work. Lastly, the Conclusion brings together the themes of continuity with prewar ideas, tempo of operations and the changing relationships between corps and Army and corps and division and gives a general view of the importance of British corps command in the BEF.

NOTES

1 *British Defence Doctrine. Joint Warfare Publication (JWP) 0-01* (London, MOD, 1996), 1.9.

2 Gooch, John, 'Military Doctrine and Military History' in Gooch, John (ed.) *The Origins of Contemporary Doctrine* (The Strategic and Combat Studies Institute. The Occasional, No. 30, September 1997), 5.

3 Reid, Brian Holden, 'War Fighting Doctrine and the British Army' in Reid, Brian Holden, *A Doctrinal Perspective 1988-1998* (The Strategic and Combat

INTRODUCTION

Studies Institute. The Occasional, No. 33, May 1998), 12-28.

4 *Report on a Conference of General Staff Officers at the Royal Military College, 13th to 16th January, 1913*, 13. TNA:PRO, WO 279/48.

5 *Report on a Conference..., 13th to 16th January, 1913*, 17.

6 De Groot, Gerard, *Douglas Haig, 1861-1928*. (Unwin Hyman, 1988), 128. Terraine, John, *Douglas Haig, The Educated Soldier* (Hutchinson, 1963), 49.

7 The argument regarding the dislike of doctrine in the Edwardian army is made in 37-41 of Travers, T.H.E., *The Killing Ground: The British Army, the Western Front and the Emergence of Modern Warfare 1900-1918*. (Allen and Unwin, 1987).

8 Palazzo, Albert, *Seeking Victory on the Western Front. The British Army and Chemical Warfare in World War I*. (Lincoln, Nebraska and London: University of Nebraska Press, 2000), 8-27.

9 Kiszely, John 'The British Army and Approaches to Warfare since 1945' in Reid, Brian Holden (ed.) *Military Power. Land Warfare in Theory and Practice* (London and Portland, Oregon: Frank Cass, 1997), 180. The definition is expanded in the same author's 'Achieving High Tempo – New Challenges' in *Journal of the Royal United Services Institute for Defence Studies*, December 1999, 47-53.

10 Brown, Ian Malcolm, *British Logistics on the Western Front 1914-1919* (Westport, Connecticut and London: Praeger, 1998), 1-13.

11 Bidwell, Shelford and Graham, Dominic, *Fire-Power. British Army Weapons and Theories of War 1904-1945* (Allen and Unwin, 1982). Edmonds, Sir James E. and others, *History of the Great War: Military Operations, France and Belgium 1914-18*, 14 volumes plus appendices and maps (Macmillan and HMSO, 1922-48). Henceforth in this book, 'OH' with volume and page numbers.

12 Harington, General Sir Charles, *Plumer of Messines* (John Murray, 1935). Charteris, Br.-Gen. John, *Field-Marshal Earl Haig* (Cassell, 1929). Duff Cooper, Alfred, *Haig* (Faber and Faber, 1935).

13 Terraine, John, *Douglas Haig, The Educated Soldier* (Hutchinson, 1963), xi-xii. Clark, Alan, *The Donkeys* (Hutchinson, 1961), 209-10.

14 Travers, T.H.E., *How the War Was Won. Command and Technology in the British Army on the Western Front 1917-1918* (London and New York: Routledge, 1992).

15 Samuels, Martin, *Doctrine and Dogma. German and British Infantry Tactics in the First World War* (New York, Westport, Connecticut and London: Greenwood Press, 1992). *Command or Control: Command, Training and Tactics in the British and German Armies, 1888-1918* (London and Portland, Oregon: Frank Cass, 1995).

16 Prior, Robin, and Wilson, Trevor, *Command on the Western Front*, (Oxford and Cambridge Massachusetts: Blackwell, 1992).

17 Prior, Robin and Wilson, Trevor, *The Somme* (New Haven and London: Yale University Press, 2005).

18 Harris, J.P., with Barr, Niall, *Amiens to the Armistice. The BEF in the Hundred Days' Campaign, 8 August-11 November 1918*. (London and Washington: Brassey's 1998). This will henceforth be referred to as '*Amiens...*'

19 Griffith, Paddy, *Battle Tactics of the Western Front*, (New Haven and London: Yale University Press, 1994).

20 Beckett, Ian F.W., *Johnnie Gough, VC* (Tom Donovan, 1989) and *Ypres. The First*

Battle, 1914 (Harlow: Pearson Education, 2004).

21 Samuels, *Command or Control…*, 34-60.

22 Robbins, Simon, *British Generalship on the Western Front, 1914-18: Defeat into Victory* (London and Portland, Oregon: Frank Cass, 2004).

23 Sheffield, Gary, 'British High Command in the First World War: An Overview' in Sheffield, Gary and Till, Geoffrey (eds.), *Challenges of High Command in the Twentieth Century* (The Strategic and Combat Studies Institute. The Occasional, No. 38, December 1999), 15-25.

24 Till, Geoffrey, 'The Gallipoli Campaign: Command Performances' in ibid., 26-43.

25 Gordon, Andrew, 'Ratcatchers and Regulators at the Battle of Jutland' in ibid., 49.

26 Rawling, Bill, *Surviving Trench Warfare: Technology and the Canadian Corps 1914-1918* (Toronto, Buffalo and London: University of Toronto Press, 1992).

27 Brown, Ian M., 'Not Glamorous, But Effective: The Canadian Corps and the Set-Piece Attack, 1917-1918.' *Journal of Military History*, Volume 58 (July 1994), 421-44.

28 Schreiber, Shane B., *Shock Army of the British Empire. The Canadian Corps in the Last 100 Days of the Great War* (Westport, Connecticut and London: Praeger, 1997).

29 Millar, John Dermot, 'A Study in the Limitations of Command: General Sir William Birdwood and the AIF, 1914-1918' (Ph.D. thesis, University of New South Wales, 1993).

30 Gardner, Brian, *Allenby* (Cassell, 1965), 86-7. James, Lawrence, *Imperial Warrior* (Weidenfeld and Nicholson, 1993).

31 Thornton, Lt.-Col. L.H and Fraser, Pamela, *The Congreves, Father and Son* (John Murray, 1930), 154.

32 Powell, Geoffrey, *Plumer – The Soldier's General* (Leo Cooper, 1990).

33 Williams, Jeffrey, *Byng of Vimy. General and Governor General* (Leo Cooper, 1983).

34 Baynes, Sir John, *Far From a Donkey: The Life of General Sir Ivor Maxse* (London and Washington: Brassey's, 1995), 166-208.

35 Haldane, Sir Aylmer, *A Soldier's Saga* (Edinburgh and London: William Blackwood and Sons, 1948).

36 Baynes, *Far From a Donkey*, viii-ix.

37 Hart, Basil Liddell, *The Real War 1914-1918* (Faber and Faber, 1930), 367. The anecdote in its various forms is discussed and dismissed in Davies, Frank and Maddocks, Graham, *Bloody Red Tabs* (Leo Cooper, 1995), 18-21. They cite Lloyd George's *Memoirs*. See also Wolff, Leon, *In Flanders Fields* (London, New York, Toronto: Longmans, Green, 1958), 253. The original is in Liddell Hart diary for 7th October 1927. Liddell Hart Papers, LHCMA, KCL. 11/1927/17.

38 Talk with Sir James Edmonds, 14th July 1931. Liddell Hart Papers, Liddell Hart Centre for Military Archives (LHCMA), 11/1931/7. Mearsheimer, John J., *Liddell Hart and the Weight of History* (Ithaca, New York, and London: Cornell University Press, 1988), 53-83. This is one aspect of his argument not challenged by Azar Gat; see Gat, Azar, *British Armour Theory and the Rise of the Panzer Arm* (Macmillan, 2000). See also Danchev, Alex, *Alchemist of War. The Life of Basil Liddell Hart* (Phoenix, 1998), 76, 107, 162-4. For Edmonds and the Official History see Green, Andrew, *Writing the Great War. Sir James Edmonds*

and the Official Histories, 1915-1948 (London and Portland, Oregon: Frank Cass, 2003).

39 Prior, Robin and Wilson, Trevor, *Passchendaele: The Untold Story* (New Haven and London: Yale University Press, 1996), 218-9.

40 Travers, *How the War Was Won*, 6. Nicholson, Col. W.N., *Behind the Lines,* (Stevenage, Herts.: The Strong Oak Press with Tom Donovan Publishing, undated), 149.

41 Simpson, Andy, *The Evolution of Victory* (Tom Donovan, 1995).

42 Sheffield, Gary, *Forgotten Victory. The First World War: Myths and Realities* (Headline, 2001).

43 Palazzo, *Seeking Victory on the Western Front.*

CHAPTER 1

Field Service Regulations and Operational Doctrine in I Corps, 1914-15

This chapter is intended to show how *FSR I* was applied to the actions of the BEF's First Army Corps (hereafter referred to as 'I Corps') in the period from August 1914 to the end of 1915.

Firstly, it is necessary to explain what an army corps was, early in the First World War. A formation subordinate to an Army, it was usually commanded by a Lt.-Gen. and composed of a variable number of infantry or cavalry divisions or occasionally both.[1] The infantry division, consisting of three brigades of four battalions apiece, was at the time considered to be the basic tactical unit of all arms. Its war establishment was some 18,000 men, of whom 12,000 were infantry, 4,000 gunners (to serve seventy-six artillery pieces) and the rest divisional cavalry, engineers, signallers, medical staff and transport troops.[2] In British (rather than Australian or Canadian) corps, the only permanent members were the staff (i.e. those officers responsible for the administration and operations of the corps) and the 'corps troops,' who were engineers and the like, much as in a division. During the winter of 1914-15 (after the BEF had been split into two Armies), direct control of the heavy artillery hitherto controlled by divisions passed to Army, which allocated it back to the divisions as required. In addition, a Heavy Artillery Reserve (HAR), composed of five groups of newly arrived batteries (and later extended to cover all heavy artillery in the BEF), was formed. These were allocated by GHQ to corps or Armies, but were not under their direct command. However, for the Battle of Loos in September 1915, corps did take direct command of all their divisions' field artillery, as well as co-operating closely with their allotted HAR groups.[3] While being by no means a completely satisfactory solution to the problem of artillery control, this reflected the growing centralising influence of corps, as the BEF's artillery complement was expanded both absolutely and proportionately to the infantry. In the period under consideration, from consisting of two corps at the beginning, the BEF had expanded to seven[4] by the end of the year and thirteen (in three Armies) by the end of 1915.[5]

The BEF in August 1914 was commanded by Field-Marshal Sir John French, whose corps commanders were Lt.-Gen. Sir Douglas Haig and General Sir Horace Smith-Dorrien (I and II Corps, respectively; II Corps was initially commanded by Sir James Grierson, who died on 17th August). Each corps consisted of two infantry divisions, and in addition, the BEF had five brigades of cavalry. Although skeleton divisional staffs were maintained in peacetime, only the Aldershot Command, which in wartime corresponded to I Corps, had a peacetime corps staff, since according to the OH, the original intention had been that GHQ would deal directly with its divisions.[6] The OH asserts that only on mobilisation on 5th August was it decided that the BEF's organisation should conform more closely to that of the French army, and the corps tier of command added.

However, the army corps was not a new part of the British army's organisation; indeed, in his evidence to the Royal Commission on the South African War, Wolseley stated that since 1888 the Army had been organised to put into the field three Army corps, of which two were Regular and for use in overseas expeditions as required.[7] Until the Haldane reforms of 1906-8, the country was divided into six corps areas, although the composition of these corps differed from that adopted later. A Special Army Order of 4th March 1902 established them as each consisting of three divisions of two brigades.[8] But in 1904 the army corps areas were renamed 'Commands.' Some debate as to their composition then took place. Home forces were either to be organised in three army corps or six self-contained divisions. In the end, the latter won the day, since they were both "more suitable to the size and requirements of our army" and "more flexible than an army-corps organization." It was accepted that if corps were formed, they would have a permanent staff, but the QMG took the view that a corps could be more easily improvised than separate divisions.[9] In view of the staff problems the BEF at times faced as a result of officers' inexperience in that role, this was unfortunate.

From 1904 onwards, corps had moved into a kind of limbo. When the system of Commands was set up, the DMT raised at an Army Council meeting "the question whether the Aldershot force should not still be called an 'army-corps'." The CGS agreed, saying that "the objection commonly entertained to the use of the term, viz., that the corps does not really exist, does not apply in this case."[10] Neglect of corps as an institution continued, since at one of the conferences of General Staff Officers held at the Staff College, in January 1908, Br.-Gen. William Robertson (later CIGS, 1915-18) observed "that there was no headquarters organisation laid down in war establishments between that for a division and that for an army." The DSD, Maj.-Gen. Douglas Haig, replied that he had raised "a very important point" and that the matter "had been thrashed out, but had not yet been published... It was very important, for if we went to war, it would seem impossible for one man to command efficiently six divisions."[11] The problem was indeed addressed, as shown by the presence of two 'armies' below GHQ in the Expeditionary Force Tables of 1912 and 1914.[12]

However, corps as an institution was subject to terminological confusion, being referred to variously as 'corps,' 'army' or 'army corps.' After a Staff Tour in 1912, Lt.-Col. W.D. Bird wrote for the attention of the DSD that officers were not always aware "of the relationship and division of responsibility between General and Army Headquarters and this is not very clearly defined in the Staff Manual."[13] In response, another officer wrote in a minute for the DSD that this relationship was clear in *FSR I* Part 2, though "the Commandant, Staff College, thinks the term 'Army' misleading and would rather have 'Army Corps.'"[14] Although a marginal comment, presumably made by the DSD, stated that "The objections to the term Army Corps are, I think, considered stronger than the objections to 'Army,'" the discussion did not end there. After the Army Exercise of 1913, Lt.-Gen. Sir James Grierson wrote to the DMO that "The term 'Army Corps' should be substituted for 'Army' and 'Army Headquarters' for 'General Headquarters'."[15] Nevertheless, as late as November 1914, a senior officer in the field was still referring to 'Army' when he meant corps.[16] A clear statement of the Deputy DMO's perception of this troublesome body came in another minute to the DMO, when, with regard to problems of communications between GHQ (confusingly referred to as 'Army') and corps headquarters at the 1913 manoeuvres, it was clearly stated that corps was to act simply as a conduit or post-box, through which orders would pass on their way from GHQ to the divisions.[17] It can be seen, therefore, that officers seemed to be unable to decide how to refer to corps before the war and in some cases, even into its first few months. Indeed, the mobilization tables for the BEF had on the corps staff the "Officer i/c Army Signals."[18]

Before going on to discuss *FSR I*, it is necessary to explain its importance in the thinking of Sir Douglas Haig, since he was always a firm believer in its value, as well as being GOC of one of the original BEF's corps. Like those of many officers, Haig's ideas were tied in with then prevalent beliefs in the unchanging nature of war and in the human-centred battlefield. Then the application of *FSR I* in practice, and what it prescribed for the actions of corps, is examined.

Given that this book is intended to deal with the operational role of corps command in the BEF, the selection of a single corps in a limited period should be explained. I Corps has been selected as the principal subject for this chapter because it had the only pre-war corps staff in the British Army, and because it was commanded by Haig. On the first of these counts, it is, as the only regular corps, useful as a yardstick for comparisons with corps formed later. Although II, III and IV Corps were also initially composed of regular troops, their staffs were improvised at or near to the outbreak of war. On the second count, *FSR I* comprised the army's only official statement of military principles, if not actually doctrine, and its introduction was strongly supported by Haig. Consequently, I Corps' operations when directly commanded by him (until late December 1914), and when directly subordinate to him (as GOC, First Army in 1915), make a useful illustration of the application of *FSR I* in wartime.

It is not surprising to see that *FSR I* reflected Haig's thinking throughout the war. After the victory at Epéhy in September 1918, a colleague wrote to congratulate Haig. Part of his reply was illuminating: "Thanks to these gentlemen [his subordinates] and to their 'sound military knowledge built up by study and practise until it has become an instinct' and to... the principles of our Field Service Regulations Part I are our successes to be chiefly attributed."[19] In this passage, Haig's own quotation was from *FSR I*, Chapter 1, Section 1. His *Final Despatch* of 21st March 1919, was also revealing, stressing that wartime experience was not, in itself, enough for the army to have coped with the changing conditions of the Western Front and that prewar principles of command, staff work, and organisation had proved themselves.[20] Furthermore, he asserted, "As each war has certain special conditions, so some modifications of existing ideas and practices will be necessary, but if our principles are sound these will be few and unimportant."[21] In fact, the *Final Despatch* was a mixture of the old and the new. Notwithstanding the views expressed above, Haig also felt able, regarding tanks, machine-guns, mortars and the like, to state that "Every mechanical device so far produced is dependent for its most effective use upon the closest possible association with other arms, and particularly with infantry and artillery."[22] Given the limitations of communications systems and much machinery in the first two decades of the twentieth century, this was perfectly reasonable. However, the *Final Despatch* was written with a view to answering his critics and was very much based on post facto reasoning. Its sub-headings were themselves a sign of this, often referring to contentious areas: "The Extent of our Casualties;" "Why we Attacked Whenever Possible;" "The Value of Cavalry in Modern War;" and "The Value of Mechanical Contrivances."[23] Nevertheless, he obviously was prepared to accept innovation, or no tanks, for example, would have been used on the Western Front.

While Haig was by no means as hostile to new ideas as has sometimes been suggested, he felt obliged when producing the *Final Despatch* to fit new ideas into the existing framework of *FSR I*. Indeed, it seems that Haig's ideas were formed when he was studying at the Staff College in

4

1896-7, and that *FSR I* reflects the lessons he learned then.[24] He acquired a view of warfare, derived from study of Napoleon's campaigns and the first part of the Franco-Prussian War, as a process whose salient features were mobility and a definite structure and where battle would be decisive. Furthermore, the battle itself fell into four stages. The first was the preparatory, or 'wearing out' fight, designed to (2.) pull in the enemy reserves and leading to (3.) the decisive assault on the weakened enemy, which would lead in its turn to (4.) the phase of exploitation.[25] Naturally, he envisaged the last stage as the job of the cavalry; in the *Final Despatch* he alleged – not unreasonably – that had the Germans possessed a few cavalry divisions during their offensive of March 1918, "a wedge might have been driven between the French and British Armies."[26] Certainly a lack of mobile troops was one of the reasons for their failure.

That individual battles in the First World War tended neither to fit into this four-stage structure nor to be decisive, was side-stepped in the *Final Despatch*. Haig stated that the war could only be properly understood if the fighting from the Somme onwards was looked at as one long battle.[27] Then he demonstrated which parts of the war corresponded to the classic four phases. The first – deployment and manoeuvre – ended once trench warfare began. The wearing-down phase, in which "losses will necessarily be heavy on both sides" and the pulling in of the enemy's reserves, corresponded to the battles of 1916 and 1917; interestingly, he made no reference to 1915, at which time, of course, he was not Commander-in-Chief. Then, whether it was the result of "higher moral" (as opposed to "morale", though the two are related) or "greater... tenacity" or even better generalship, the time came "when the other side will begin to weaken and the climax of the battle is reached."[28] His training of twenty-two years earlier showed itself as he compared the German offensives of 1918 to the last-ditch attack of Napoleon's Imperial Guard at Waterloo. This is convincing as a retrospective overview of the war, though it does not reflect Haig's own intentions as each successive breakthrough offensive was planned.

Haig's stress on 'higher moral' brings out the other important strand in his thinking, and one he had in common with many of his contemporaries. This was a belief in the importance of moral factors on the modern battlefield, and the consequent cult of the offensive. Given the firepower available, heavy casualties were inevitable, but the side with the greater moral force would prevail, and this would be the attackers; the defensive was held to be inherently morally inferior. Hence the *Final Despatch* stated that "a purely defensive attitude can never bring about a successful decision... decisive success in battle can be gained only by a vigorous offensive." Troops permitted to stand on the defensive would suffer a decline in their 'moral' and the battle would have been lost from the start.[29] This would seem reasonable, in view of the Social Darwinist ideas with which

Haig's generation were imbued. Troops on the defensive might well have lower morale than their opponents if the latter were, for example, better equipped or fed or rested. But perhaps more importantly, only through displaying courage or élan in the attack could the soldier display those moral characteristics which – in theory – made his 'race' fitter to survive than the defenders'.

However, perhaps Travers exaggerates the absurdity of the view that psychology is important on the battlefield; good generals usually pay attention to morale and attempt to nurture it (Field-Marshal Montgomery is a good example). Furthermore, given the willingness with which Haig embraced tanks and gas and even, at one point, a death ray, it seems unfair to say that the belief in the psychological battlefield led to new weapons being ignored.[30] Travers is right to say that new weapons were integrated with existing ideas to some extent, but this is not unreasonable; tanks and the like were indeed "incapable of effective independent action," as Haig asserted.[31]

The next question which must be answered is what *FSR I* prescribed for the conduct of modern war. As might be expected from the preceding discussion, those parts dealing with fighting and the characteristics of troops were permeated with Haig's views on the importance of moral factors; the first page of the first chapter contained the assertion that "Success in war depends more on moral than on physical qualities."[32] and went on to stress the importance of developing them, since "Skill cannot compensate for want of courage, energy, and determination." The remainder of Chapter 1, devoted to "The Fighting Troops and Their Characteristics," was a generally uncontroversial series of comments on the perceived capabilities of the arms of the service.

Chapter 2 – "Inter-Communication and Orders" – was a clear, detailed and sensible definition of the responsibilities of officers when framing and issuing orders and reports. It also contained one of the few mentions of corps in *FSR I*, in a table giving the authorised abbreviations for unit names to be used in communications.[33] However, corps was also noticeable by its absence from the following definition, given in a footnote: "A subordinate commander is any commander other than the commander-in-chief, *e.g.*, the commander of a division, of a cavalry brigade, of an infantry brigade... &c."[34] Given the way in which corps operated on the Western Front, the comments on orders were illuminating. They stressed the necessity for orders not to be too detailed, instead leaving the man on the spot to use his own initiative.[35] The concept of 'the man on the spot' was important in *FSR I* in determining how orders were to work in practice, but it was not clearly defined. However it would seem to have approximated to 'the nearest responsible subordinate of the officer issuing orders, to the site of the action.' This would necessarily vary according to circumstances (and the definition of responsibility), however, and by the end of 1915, corps commanders were increasingly encroaching upon their subordinates' freedom of action, though as will be seen, this tendency was later reversed.

The contents of the next chapter, "Movements by Land and Sea", are self-evident. Once again, corps was omitted from formations mentioned in one part, but included in others.[36] Later, however, it seemed that the position of divisional ammunition columns on a line of march was normally to be established by divisional commanders "but it may... be fixed by army corps or general headquarters."[37] However, this was very much an administrative function, as it was when it was stated that only the C-in-C or "an Army Corps Commander" could authorise the entrainment of horses unsaddled.[38] The following chapter, entitled "Quarters," contained no mention of corps, although the comment that "billeting areas may be allotted to armies or divisions" was somewhat ambiguous, given the confusion over the word 'army' at the time.[39]

FSR I did not explicitly mention the concept of tempo, but it is evident that Haig was aware of the need to seize the initiative in operations: "Success in... preliminary combats will retain for a commander the initiative he has gained... it will gain him strategic liberty of action, and will thereby enable him to act with certainty and impose his will on the enemy."[40] The battle would be fought by pinning the enemy down through superiority of fire and a series of preliminary assaults, designed to pull in his reserves, and then victory would be won by launching the decisive assault at a preselected point.[41] Higher tempo would be attained by pinning the enemy down and using up his reserves.

To summarise, then, it would seem that before the outbreak of the First World War, the corps was viewed as a formation which existed simply to help the Commander-in-Chief of the Expeditionary Force administer his six divisions by acting as a conduit for his orders.[42] Consequently, when the two corps of the BEF began operations in 1914, they did so in a relatively unimportant role. Their steady erosion of the responsibilities of divisions during 1915, especially in the handling of artillery, may therefore be assumed to have been the product of the pressure of events. Examination of the operations of I Corps during 1914-5 might also be expected to show a consistency of outlook, orientated towards *FSR I* and matching that of Haig as its commander and, later, immediate superior. Given the almost complete omission of corps from *FSR I*, operations could only be conducted by the corps commander applying *FSR I*'s principles, as expressed therein for divisional commanders, to his own position.

In the next part of this chapter, how *FSR I* was actually used in the field in 1914-15 will be examined. Before relating the Regulations to the actions undertaken by I Corps in the period under consideration, it is necessary to outline what types of action took place. These fell into the following categories: rearguard (the Retreat from Mons), offensive (the Battles of the Aisne,

Neuve Chapelle, Aubers Ridge, Festubert and Loos), encounter (the First Battle of Ypres) and defensive (again, First Ypres).

Turning first to the retreat from Mons, *FSR I* assumed that a rearguard was only necessary for a defeated force.[43] Part of the force was to be detached from the main body, in order to slow the advancing enemy and permit the former "to move in comparative safety and to recover order and *morale*."[44] In addition, a rearguard had to be composed of all arms.[45] I Corps complied with this, employing the 1st (Guards) Infantry Brigade, with cavalry and artillery support. In addition, flank guards were posted, in accordance with *FSR I*.[46] However, given that the Germans were known to be pursuing from the north and north-east, it seems odd that the western flank guard comprised an entire infantry brigade, while the eastern was only one battalion of infantry and a battery of field artillery.[47] Presumably the artillery was to use its range to hold the Germans off. Otherwise, Haig was in breach of *FSR I*'s dictum that "the strength, composition and dis-position" of such forces should be dictated by the position and strength of the enemy.[48] It should be noted that there was no question of the BEF having higher tempo than the Germans during the Retreat; the BEF had no option but to fall back, and on the whole (the Battle of Le Cateau being an obvious exception) the initiative was with the Germans. However, the BEF was prepared to fight at minimal notice, both at Mons and Le Cateau. Sir John French ordered the taking of positions for the former the night before the battle, and Sir Horace Smith-Dorrien only decided to fight at Le Cateau in the early hours of the day of battle.[49]

The First Battle of Ypres, the BEF's only experience of an encounter bat-tle and of large-scale defensive action in this period, was not intended to be a major engagement. The intention for I Corps was to attack what were perceived as weak German forces, before outflanking their main body. However, they ran into considerable opposition and were forced into a full-scale battle. At first, attempts to attack, and so to retain the initiative, were made, as advised by *FSR I* for an encounter battle.[50] However, the considerable German superiority in numbers meant that I Corps lost the initiative. The battle became a defensive action, in which the deployment of reserves was vital, much as prescribed by *FSR I*; even corps troops were used. Whenever possible, counter-attacks were made, which also conformed to *FSR I* for the defensive battle. However, while *FSR I* saw these as the prelude to a resumption of the offensive, the manpower was not available to do this. For the same reason there was not always a corps reserve available, although attempts were made to re-establish it when-ever possible.[51] Although this lack of reserves went against the precepts of *FSR I*, it was unavoidable, and adding to the reserve by strengthening the position held, so making it possible to reduce its garrison, was very much a part of *FSR I*'s defensive battle.[52] Hence, First Ypres was conducted very much in the style of *FSR I*, with slight modifications owing to the circumstances under which it was fought. For the purposes of assessing the speed with which the BEF prepared operations in 1914, only the initial phase of the battle, when Sir John French expected to advance to the north of Lille and beyond should be considered. The fighting after that was dictated by the Germans, as mentioned above, and the question of the British initiating any major operation was out of the question. But at the beginning of the battle, the BEF was still capable of mounting an attack at only a day's notice, as was demonstrated by II Corps between 11th and 20th October.[53] Since corps had little to do in organising the attack apart from passing on GHQ's orders to divisions, and there was no requirement for any level of command to draw up and co-ordinate the sort of complex fireplan for the artillery that became routine by the end of 1916, this swiftness is not surprising.

Turning to the offensive battle, I Corps had varied experience in the 1914-15 period. The four-stage battle mentioned before was the key to this type of action, and according to Haig's reasoning, this was the model for the Battles of the Aisne, Neuve Chapelle, Aubers, Festubert and Loos.

The Battle of the Aisne was preceded by the Battle of the Marne, which for I Corps was really a conventional advance against a retreating enemy. On the Aisne, all began in keeping with the tenets of *FSR I*; on 13th September, "the fighting troops having closed up, the advanced guards advanced to the river line."[54] The intention was to push cavalry patrols forward, with the formed up divisions behind ready to act on information received from them; this corresponded to the pre-battle deployment *FSR I* recommended.[55] Again, the BEF responded promptly to events; the attack was ordered on the previous day. High tempo was demonstrated by the slipping of the 11th Brigade across a damaged bridge over the Aisne in the early hours of the 13th, followed by a bayonet charge which caught the Germans in the area completely off balance and compelled their retirement.[56] As the fighting went on, Haig continued to act according to *FSR I*. On 14th September, he ordered the GOC 2nd Division, Monro, to set up a reserve.[57] Upon the Germans unexpectedly counter-attacking, this was invaluable, although the situation was for a time critical. As the German attacks weakened, and the French to the right of I Corps advanced, Haig moved on to the offensive. This began at sunset, but was soon repelled by heavy artillery and rifle fire. *FSR I* stated that the decisive attack should be made "in the greatest possible strength," which I Corps, advancing with tired troops, certainly lacked.[58] And it also said that the assault should be made when "superiority of fire" had been achieved.[59] That the attack failed owing to inferiority of fire indicates that Haig had convinced himself that he had the upper hand, because of the German counter-attacks weakening and the French advancing to his right.

As a consequence of this setback, "the Corps entrenched itself in close touch with the Algerian troops" to the right, which was in accordance with *FSR I*.[60] Haig described the position won as "an admirable pivot of manoeuvre for further offensive operations."[61] *FSR I* stated that a commander could, on occasion, take up a defensive posture, especially if he had specifically occupied a position for this purpose; "such a position has its true value as a pivot of manoeuvre."[62] But given that he had by no means deliberately selected the position in which his men found themselves, he was plainly making a virtue of necessity. Hence, he commented that after 14th September the impossibility of a further advance was realised, "and the line which had been gained by the 1st Corps as the result of an offensive battle had to be adapted for purposes of defence."[63] However, the line held was so long as to deprive him of a general reserve, and its right was subject to enfilade fire, both contrary to *FSR I*.[64] Haig permitted this state of affairs to continue because firstly, he viewed the position as a stepping stone for attacks later, and secondly, he needed to retain the ground to keep his right in alignment with his French neighbours.[65]

Naturally (from Haig's point of view), "in the fighting which followed [14th September] the British soldier soon established a moral superiority over the German." However, the latter's superiority in artillery meant that their fire had at first a considerable "moral effect," although this diminished with time. Nevertheless, on 16th September, Haig ordered a 20-minute bombardment of the German line by all the artillery in the corps, in order to undertake some form of offensive action to retain the initiative. Given the paltry artillery resources available to I Corps, this smacks of wishful thinking, as did his conclusions regarding the results: "from captured diaries and from statements of captured prisoners the bombardment achieved highly satisfactory results."[66] This fits *FSR I*'s view of the role of artillery in the offensive battle, where "artillery fire is to help the infantry maintain its mobility and offensive power."[67] It also indicates Haig's faith in the moral superiority of the British soldier, since he seemed to feel that although his own troops had become accustomed to enemy shelling, the Germans would not. However, it is apparent that neither side had higher tempo than the other by this time, and the time for quick attacks of the type launched on 13th September was past. The first trenches had been dug and the protagonists lacked the strength to evict each other from their respective defences. It was apparent to commanders that better results might be obtained by concentrating their efforts on their opponents' remaining flank, to the north.

Since as the battle went on, some of the departures from *FSR I* were corrected, for example, a new corps reserve being formed on 19th September, it is safe to say that I Corps' operations in the Battle of the Aisne were generally conducted according to *FSR I*.[68] Those occasions when it appears not to have been applied can be explained by lack of troops or by the over-optimism in the attack which often characterised Haig.

I Corps' next clear-cut offensive was its diversionary action in the Battle of Neuve Chapelle in March 1915, the main attack being undertaken by IV and the Indian Corps. By now, Haig was in charge of First Army and in overall command of the operation, and the GOC I Corps was Lt.-Gen. Sir C.C. Monro. The formation of Armies had little effect on the position of corps. GHQ issued a document on 29th December 1914, delineating its subordinate formations' new responsibilities and lines of communication. To some extent, the new Army headquarters were to act as an additional post-box; they were to send "to the Commander-in-Chief, the weekly report on operations which has hitherto been furnished by Corps Commanders…" and operational orders and reports were to be sent from GHQ to corps via Army, and vice versa.[69] However, "to avoid loss of time, Corps will send copies of all intelligence which they may get direct to G.H.Q. (intelligence);" the reverse was also true. This need not have indicated any acquisition of influence on the part of corps, but merely the application of common sense. Indeed, a similar memorandum, issued two days earlier by First Army to I Corps stated this explicitly. Interestingly, the same memorandum stated that "It is important to avoid turning the Army Headquarters into a 'Post Office' pure and simple."[70] The position of corps was unchanged, except that it now had two masters.

The attack near Givenchy in support of IV and the Indian Corps at Neuve Chapelle in March 1915 was the largest made by I Corps to date. Since trench warfare rendered redundant most of *FSR I*'s assumptions about an attack, reconnaissance by a cavalry screen or the manoeuvring of troops into an advantageous position (for example) being impossible, it is difficult to see how it could be applied at all. However, the Official Historian stated that for Neuve Chapelle, the deployment of troops and other preliminary stages of the battle were now carried out the night before, and the assault, which had been in the manuals the last stage of the attack, now became its first.[71] The question that arises, therefore, is whether what was done can be ascribed to the application of *FSR I* or simply to commanders using their own judgement in unfamiliar circumstances.

Efforts to grapple with the problems arising from the new conditions were made before the Neuve Chapelle attack. After conferences of divisional commanders with Monro on 15th and 18th February, his BGGS issued notes for guidance to them. These were copied from notes issued by Haig's MGGS to corps commanders on 16th February, and dealt with matters such as the assembly of assaulting troops before an attack and how to cross the British wire when attacking. In addition, "When we attack, machine guns and wire will probably give us more difficulty than anything else." and "our guns should practise destroying the enemy's wire." Some uncertainty regarding the latter action was displayed by the comment that "we must know exactly what our guns can do, so that we can make our plans."[72] None of this could be said to contravene *FSR I*, and Monro's hands-off style of management was certainly consonant with *FSR I*.[73] A further conference, just before the battle, was thoroughly conventional in tone. The notes stressed that the key to breaking the German line was "<u>offensive action</u> [underlined in original]." Consequently, commanders were "to carefully consider the <u>employment of their reserves</u>" to maintain momentum, though "at the same time, the principle of <u>securing ground already gained</u> must not be overlooked."[74] The stress on the offensive, the building up of the firing line and the principle of consolidation all belong in *FSR I*'s offensive battle.

Notwithstanding these good intentions, the subsidiary attack at Neuve Chapelle was a complete failure. Attempts to learn from the experience of the battle began soon after. A GHQ paper of 14th March took many of its ideas from *FSR I*, stating, for example, that now the infantry attack equated to "what our regulations call the final assault in battle."[75] However, the pre-eminence that the artillery later came to hold over other arms was beginning to emerge; the earlier uncertainty over its capabilities had gone. With regard to the feasibility of offensive operations, "Divisional and Army Corps Commanders will... be guided by the advice of their artillery and engineer advisors." The tasks of the artillery (the preparation of the attack and the support of the infantry assault) were explicitly laid out for the first time. Having gone on to detail the types and numbers of shells required to perform these tasks, it then observed that a preliminary bombardment would sacrifice surprise, and indicated how this problem might be overcome. In addition, the need for assistance from aircraft in artillery observation was stressed and its readership was reminded that meteorological conditions should be borne in mind upon opening fire.[76] After Neuve Chapelle, the high command was working with ideas partly drawn from *FSR I* and partly from experience, blending the two. However, it is also apparent that corps were still acting only as a medium of communication between GHQ, Army and divisions, rather than taking a more active role in operations.

The question of tempo does not really arise at Neuve Chapelle, since the BEF lacked the means to follow up any success it might have gained, as was the case with the main attack, which did catch the Germans off-balance. As regards time of preparation, Haig asked Sir Henry Rawlinson of IV Corps on 6th February to come up with a plan, though he was intending at that point to attack in less than a fortnight.[77] Nevertheless, it is clear that the need for artillery preparation was slowing things down considerably compared to 1914; 32 days elapsed between the start of planning and the attack, though Rawlinson's inability initially to come up with a plan which satisfied Haig also contributed to the delay, as did the need to give the ground time to dry out.

A little before I Corps' next attack, the Battle of Aubers Ridge (9th May 1915), two documents were issued by First Army. These were *Paper 'A'. General Instructions for the Attack* and *Paper 'B'. General Principles for the Attack*.[78] The latter was the more important as a statement of attack methods and was discussed at a First Army conference with corps and divisional commanders on 27th April.[79] Like its predecessors, it stressed the need for a vigorous offensive, that reserves should be kept well forward and that only success should be reinforced. In addition, reference was again made to the power of the artillery: "Infantry commanders must know the time table of artillery fire, and regulate their progress and time their assaults in accordance with it." The whole attack could be conducted to a precise timetable, dictated by the artillery, since the German positions could be precisely located beforehand, owing to the perceived accuracy of maps based on aerial photography (which were just coming into use). The assault would be given more teeth, too, since "field guns, trench mortars, machine guns, etc., must be pushed forward in close support of the attacking infantry." This sort of thinking was decidedly modern, though it under-estimated the problems of GHQ's cartographers when working from photographs.[80] However, as before, new ideas were plainly expected to work with old and the need for consolidation was addressed thus: "All ground gained will be secured (F.S.R. Part I, Sec. 105 (5))."[81] Another GHQ paper issued after Neuve Chapelle demonstrated this attitude again.[82] After stressing that the earlier battle showed the need for careful artillery preparation and the consolidation of the ground won, it went on to say that were the enemy reserves to be unavailable at the point of attack, the troops should be able to break into the German position and then roll up its flanks. This was to be achieved by a series of careful assaults, designed to force the enemy into expending his reserves in counter-attacks, and to be followed by the breakthrough at a different point. The root of this reasoning was clear: "We thus get the idea of two distinct operations which may be regarded respectively as the preparatory action and the decisive attack referred to in Field Service Regulations." And once the German reserves had been used elsewhere, it would be far easier to attain higher tempo at the point of the decisive attack.

The outcome of Aubers Ridge was just as disappointing for I Corps as Neuve Chapelle. After a short bombardment, the attack was made in two places, 6000 yards apart, the idea being that on penetrating the German line, the two assaulting forces would converge and cut a large number of German troops off. However, this also meant that the latter were perfectly positioned to enfilade the attackers, and given that the artillery lacked the firepower to suppress the defenders of the portions of line actually assaulted, still less the section between them, it is not surprising that no advances of importance were made. The British troops manning the line in the gap had been ordered to employ rifle fire to suppress enemy machine-gun and rifle fire in that area, in a ludicrously optimistic attempt (which followed *FSR I*) to make up for the lack of artillery and ammunition for what artillery there was.[83] However, what is most peculiar about the battle is that no attempt was made to make a preparatory attack in order to draw the German reserves in, notwithstanding the views expressed in the memo quoted above. The use of *FSR I* would seem at this time to have been inconsistent, reflecting a degree of confusion as to its application on the ground. And again, tempo was an irrelevance – the BEF's resources were still insufficient to make successive attacks with any chance of breaking the German line. Indeed, Haig had intended to make a fresh attack immediately after Neuve Chapelle, but stocks of artillery ammunition were too low. However, planning had begun for Aubers on 14th March, so it had a longer gestation period than its predecessor, at 56 days. This was partly because the date was set in advance by the French, and also because of the need to build up ammunition stocks. Unfortunately, the Germans used this period to strengthen their positions considerably.[84]

The next attack was the Battle of Festubert, beginning on 15th May. It was a more modest affair than Aubers, with an advance of 1000 yards being contemplated, rather than 3000 yards as at Aubers. Again, the assault was to be two-pronged, but the gap would this time be only 600 yards, and because the preliminary bombardment was to last for 36 hours it could more effectively deal with the German troops and defences along the whole front.[85] That the use of a hurricane bombardment, which had proved successful for IV Corps at Neuve Chapelle, was abandoned, was the result of its failure at Aubers Ridge. Success was to be achieved by "a deliberate bombardment," notwithstanding the loss of surprise.[86] Some trouble was taken to ensure that artillery fire was effective, both before and during the battle, I Corps ordering on the night of 16th May that reports as to the result of the bombardment were to be made to corps at 7am the next day. Monro would set the time of attack, but it would not be before 8am.[87] It is clear that nothing was to happen until he had assessed the effects of the artillery fire. A more deliberate approach to battle was beginning to emerge, and with it a more important role for corps command.

Notwithstanding this new approach in the sphere of gunnery, no new tactical notes were issued for the battle, and so it seems that it was conducted using the same mixture of old and new ideas as before. However, that the corps artillery commander (the BGRA) was beginning to make his presence felt was demonstrated in an order issued the next day, in which the dividing line between divisional artillery was specified and the heavy artillery was informed that it would engage targets selected by the BGRA.[88] As early as January, GHQ told formations that the BGRA was to be termed the CRA of the corps (though this appellation seems not to have been used much), he was to be given a Staff Captain and he would then "command such portions of the artillery as are not placed specifically under divisional commanders."[89] Although he might also command some divisional artillery, this applied principally to the 60-pounders, which soon ceased to be part of the divisional complement anyway, and the BGRA essentially remained an adviser. However, Festubert, presumably because it was a continuation of the Aubers plan (but with a longer bombardment), took only five days from 10th May to prepare.

Given that Festubert came tantalisingly close to success, the conclusion drawn was that with more men and guns and a longer bombardment, a breakthrough might be achieved. Planning for the Battle of Loos was undertaken on this basis. Even in the early stages, the commander of 1st Division was pointing out that a deliberate and accurate bombardment, lasting several days, was required.[90] In his report to First Army, summarising his and the GOC 1st Division's views, Monro explicitly stated that success rested upon finding good targets for the heavies and the factor of surprise.[91] However, there seems to have been some confusion in this plan; 1st Division's deliberate bombardment was bound to militate against the gaining of surprise.

In addition to the need for applying a greater weight of metal against the German lines, it had become clear during Festubert that artillery command and control required revision. At one point, the CRA of 7th Division had under him the artillery of the 7th, 51st and 1st Canadian Divisions, plus three independent brigades.[92] This was far too much for his staff of two officers to cope with.[93] Consequently, on 24th August 1915 "A Staff [of four officers] for 1st Corps Artillery was extemporised" and the BGRA was to control all the weapons used by I Corps in the forthcoming attack, though he took care to consult divisions as to the lifts of the barrages, in order to tie in with the infantry plan.[94] As a result of this reorganisation, I Corps issued a memorandum to its divisions on 10th September, requiring infantry officers to note the locations of loopholes, machine-gun emplacements and gun positions in the German lines, and having plotted them on a map, to send it on so that the necessary artillery treatment could be organised.[95] And in the IV Corps order for the attack, the "Corps Artillery Commander" was to detail part of the divisional artillery to follow up the infantry advance in order to provide close support, as well as sorting the assorted artillery available into a group for the support of each attacking division.[96] It should be noted, however, that IV Corps' policy was for these, once organised, to function in as decentralised a way as possible, without reference to corps.[97] Although counter-battery work on the entire First Army front was under the separate command of No. 1 Group, HAR, this reorganisation in the BGRA's favour again indicates that pressure of events was responsible for corps' taking over areas of prewar divisional responsibility.

This was, perhaps, not only in the sphere of artillery control. At a conference held at I Corps HQ on 25th August 1915, the GOC, now Lt.-Gen. Hubert Gough, drew the attention of his divisional commanders to various papers, "to be... brought particularly to the attention of battalion and company commanders."[98] Given that one of the documents was GHQ's *General Principles for the Attack*, it could be argued that corps was again acting as a post-box, but the insistence on divisional commanders telling their junior subordinates about the documents was far from the delegation of authority emphasised in *FSR I*. That this flexing of the muscles of corps command was to continue was shown on 6th October, when a memorandum was sent to the GOC 28th Division (Maj.-Gen. E.S. Bulfin) concerning orders issued by him to his brigade commanders. It concluded, after a number of stinging criticisms (made with an eye to the sections of *FSR I* regarding the framing of orders[99]), with a summary of the shortcomings perceived, which were that in some respects they were too detailed and in others, insufficiently so and furthermore omitted a number of points altogether.[100] That it was deemed necessary to rebuke the commander of a Regular division so sharply may reflect corps' view of the inadequacies of a staff improvised on the unit's formation.[101] *FSR I* was intended to be used by properly trained officers, and corps was compelled to centralise authority if subordinate formations lacked them, particularly on the staff. That the division was despatched to Salonika soon after reflected corps' view of its indispensability or otherwise. Haig recorded in his diary – stressing moral factors in no uncertain tones – that on 3rd October he saw Gough, who was unhappy since the 28th Division "failed to carry out his orders. They seem to me to be carrying on exactly like the Second Army... No initiative, no real offensive spirit. I reminded Gough that we'll win 'not by might, nor by power but by MY SPIRIT, saith the Lord of Hosts'."[102]

Although it was felt that a breakthrough could be achieved with more guns and a longer bombardment than at Festubert, the problem arose that the BEF did not possess sufficient artillery to do this. However, it was felt that gas would make up for the lack of firepower. The use of such a weapon would, at first sight, seem to have fallen well outside the realm of *FSR I*, but if the view was taken that it was employed, in effect, to strengthen the firing line, then traditionalists would have had no difficulty in accepting it. That Haig remained in the latter camp was demonstrated by his diary entry for 30th July; upon being asked how to win the war, he replied, "by applying the old principles to the present conditions." On the other hand, the entry for 16th September stated that gas would lead to decisive results in the forthcoming attack, while heavy casualties and minimal progress were to be expected if it were not used.[103] Haig's enthusiasm for gas, and its accommodation in the plan, are easily explained by his belief in it as a means of winning the fire-fight and so a decisive victory, and this demonstrates the potential of *FSR I* for flexible application.[104] Furthermore, although it is difficult to be precise on this point, it appears that responsibility for authorising the gas discharges on the day was delegated from Army to corps and thence to division, very much in the spirit of *FSR I*.[105]

The changes in thinking consequent upon Aubers Ridge and Festubert were demonstrated in a new version of April's *Paper 'B'*. Entitled *General Principles for the Attack*, it was in many respects a direct copy of the previous document.[106] However, the function of the preliminary bombardment, not present in *Paper 'B,'* was outlined under six separate headings, and it was stated that "The preliminary bombardment will be deliberate and carefully observed." Furthermore, the idea in May that "The artillery objective is... the whole position, with a view to destroying the hostile infantry" had been omitted by September. As before, old and new thinking were simultaneously being followed, with the difference in September that the key role of the artillery was recognised, and that it was necessary – on purely pragmatic grounds, rather than as part of any departure from existing principles – to supplement it with gas.

Again, given the weakness of the BEF in 1915, the possibility of attaining higher tempo than the Germans (even in conjunction with the French attacks in Artois) in the autumn of 1915 does not arise. Indeed, the preparation time for Loos was the longest yet, since Haig called a conference to initiate planning on 3rd July, 83 days before the attack.[107] This was in part because the aim of the offensive changed several times as the weeks went by and the ideas of Haig, Sir John French and Marshal Joffre (the French C-in-C) changed. In addition, the prevalent idea that a methodical and careful bombardment was required to breach the German defences led to a reduced sense of urgency amongst the planners. Rawlinson's diary does not give the impression that he felt any need to rush to prepare his scheme; indeed, he even had his BGGS changed in August.[108] And if corps felt the need to supervise divisions more closely than in 1914 (owing to the inexperience of their staffs), planning could not easily be delegated to them.

The failure at Loos, which at the time was largely blamed on GHQ's inability to get the two reserve divisions up to the front line in time, and their poor performance once they had arrived, led to further reassessment of how to make a successful attack. In the course of the recriminations regarding the reserves, Haig asserted that they failed because "they were new formations, and... both the [XI] corps and divisional staffs were recently formed..."[109] Plainly the inexperience of the new divisions arriving from Britain was a problem. The Official History cited two reports compiled immediately after the battle, the first of which stated that, owing to the increasing size of the BEF, staffs were neither well trained nor experienced and so were at times inefficient. The second made the more general point that the proportion of trained officers in the army was falling, and the newcomers required more definite instructions than were provided by *FSR I*.[110] In fact, *FSR I* and the training manuals intended to back it up were not at fault, but the officers applying them on the ground were simply too inexperienced to do so properly. Even before the war it had been recognised that this might be a problem. During the discussion of how *FSR I* was to be employed, at the 1913 Staff College meeting, Lt.-Col. Edmonds (GSO1, 4th Division) remarked that at a previous conference an Australian officer had said "that our training manuals required so much skilled interpretation that they were about as useful to the average Australian soldier as the cuneiform inscriptions on a Babylonian brick."[111] However, the view taken was that if anything had to change, it was not *FSR I*. Sir William Robertson, then CGS to Sir John French, issued a memorandum on 26th October 1915, which stressed that owing to the novel conditions of the Western Front and the number of new soldiers and new formations in the BEF, centralised training was required. Furthermore, this would to some extent deviate from the principles expounded in existing manuals (but not *FSR I*).[112] As a result of this, First Army issued a rather more conservative document, which can be taken as reflecting Sir Douglas Haig's views at this point.[113] It stated that while recent experience showed the need to emphasise some points more than before the war, on the whole, the principles in existing training manuals were sound. Nevertheless, it was necessary to devise a way by which instructors could themselves be trained, in order to disseminate new methods and to ensure that they were applied uniformly. Since *FSR I* Part 2 stated that the basic tactical unit of all arms was the division, it was at this level that the new training schools would be formed, and commanding officers were to be personally responsible for the training of their divisions, "assisted, controlled and supervised by the Corps and Army." It went on to outline whom the divisional schools should teach; these were junior officers and specialists (such as machine-gun officers); corps schools were to run signal classes only, and those not for wireless operators. This seems logical given the view of the division as the basic tactical unit of the army, notwithstanding corps' recent gains in the control of artillery. Most importantly, it also quoted *FSR I* on the relative importance of moral as opposed to physical qualities, and stressed that it was vital to develop "the moral and soldierly spirit of all ranks." In addition, to supplement *FSR I*, GHQ began to issue instructional pamphlets for the new warfare.[114]

The viewpoint of the most senior officers may well have been as expressed in a GHQ memorandum, which opined that the old problem of bringing reserves to bear at the right place at the right time was exacerbated by the absence of a flank to attack under current circumstances.[115] Nevertheless, it was felt, these did not alter the principles of warfare, which should not be rejected but simply applied correctly. Interestingly, this implied that none of the battles of 1915 was conducted using traditional principles, although there is evidence before each of a widespread belief that the forthcoming operation was in most respects 'normal.' Now it was felt that insufficient attention had been paid to drawing in the German reserves before the decisive assault, though perhaps comfortingly, apparently the French had made the same mistake. This idea of drawing in the enemy reserves was the key to British ideas on how to gain higher tempo at the point of assault. It does not seem excessive to say that this implication was a retrospective attempt to explain the repeated failures of the year. It was far easier to blame human error in the application of principles than to confront the issue that until the BEF had sufficient hardware and the right techniques for its use, and trained (or at least experienced) generals and Staff officers, the principles were an irrelevance. However, the situation was less clear-cut for corps and divisional commanders. The notes of a conference held by Gough on 20th December contained the mixture of old and new ideas so common in 1915. As *FSR I* prescribed, there would be an advanced guard which would move forward before the main assault, since "on the modern battlefield" it took two or three days before sufficient force had been built up to make the maximum effort. This is odd, given that the BEF's experience would appear to indicate that even if success were achieved on the first day of an attack, it would not be forthcoming later. The rest of the force would not attack – indeed, the troops would not even be deployed – "until a plan has been decided upon." This seems to indicate that Gough expected the Germans to give him time to devise such a plan in the middle of an offensive.[116] All this shows that the gulf between strategic and tactical thought was becoming increasingly wide by the close of 1915.

In conclusion, it seems that corps as a formation was viewed in the British Army as being relatively unimportant before the First World War, and this attitude persisted into 1915. Its functions were confined to easing the job of the C-in-C in controlling an increasing number of divisions, which were viewed as the basic tactical unit of the army. In that role, even after the creation of Armies within the BEF in December 1914, it was more or less explicit that corps was to act as a post-box for information and orders passing from GHQ to divisions and vice versa. However, as the artillery complement of the BEF grew, and its importance was realised, corps began to assume greater importance in the conduct of operations. Meanwhile, corps began to take a more centralising role in any case, since the improvised nature of most divisional staffs meant that they needed closer supervision than those of the original BEF. And another conse-quence of both the need for longer and heavier bombardments and of the inexperience of Staff officers was that, in general, the attacks of 1915 took far longer from inception to execution than had been the case in 1914. Partly for this reason and partly because of the lack of resources available to the BEF, there was no possibility of it attaining higher tempo than the Germans after the beginning of the Battle of the Aisne.

Throughout the period under consideration, I Corps was either commanded by, or its commander's immediate superior was, Sir Douglas Haig. As its main exponent during the period of army reform early in the century, it is not surprising that he took the view, both in 1914-15 and later, that *FSR I*, the ideas in which embodied his beliefs in the continuity of military principles and in the psychological battlefield, was always applicable to the fighting on the Western Front. Those relatively few occasions upon which he could be said to have diverged from it seem invariably to have been the result of manpower shortages or his incorrigible optimism when conducting an attack.

As trench warfare became established, Haig and other 'traditionally-minded' officers found it easy to cling to a traditional, *FSR I*-based model of warfare, simply by virtue of the way in which the Regulations were designed to be applied – as general, high-level principles. Indeed, it is perfectly reasonable to assert that they were applicable throughout the war, since they were always intended to be employed in conjunction with other manuals, and these were either replaced or supplemented by other publications and schemes of training by late 1915. Furthermore, *FSR I* was so unspecific as easily to permit new weapons and tactics to be incorporated into its framework with a minimum of mental gymnastics. This did not help the troops on the ground, who needed far more detailed training in the new warfare and weapons. The problems of, for example, battalion commanders, were tactical, and these *FSR I* was not designed to address, even while remaining perfectly and legitimately useable for the army's strategists. This helps to explain the belief of Haig and his colleagues in the possibility of a breakthrough throughout 1915 and later, even though at a tactical level, neither the weaponry nor the technology were available to achieve this until late 1917. For them, tactics were not a problem, or even a legitimate concern. For corps commanders the same was true, but their acquisition of responsibilities in the sphere of gunnery was by late 1915 beginning to place them in a position where they had to breach *FSR I* and become far more prescriptive in their handling of their subordinates.

NOTES

1 This could be none when the corps was in reserve, or as many as five or six.
2 These were organised into three brigades of 18-pounder guns (fifty-four light guns), one brigade of 4.5-inch howitzers (eighteen light howitzers) and one battery of 60-pounder guns (four heavy guns). See O.H., 1914 Volume 1, 7, and Farndale, General Sir Martin, *History of the Royal Regiment of Artillery: Western Front 1914-18* (RA Institution, 1986), 2. Henceforth referred to as 'Farndale, *Artillery*.'
3 O.H., 1915 Volume 2, 174-5., and Farndale, *Artillery*, 355.

4 These were the British I-IV and Cavalry Corps and the Indian and Indian Cavalry Corps.

5 These were the British I-VII, X, XI, XIII and Cavalry Corps, the Canadian Corps and the Indian Cavalry Corps.

6 O.H., 1914 Volume 1, 7. See *Mobilization Appointments. Part I. Expeditionary Force. 1st April, 1914.* The National Archives, Public Record Office (hereafter TNA:PRO), WO 33/611.

7 *Parliamentary Papers 1904.* Volume 40, 364. *Royal Commission on the South African War.* Evidence given by Wolseley on 27th November 1902.

8 *Minutes of Proceedings and Précis Prepared for the Army Council for the Year 1904,* 93., Précis No. 22. TNA:PRO, WO 163/9.

9 *Minutes of Proceedings and Précis Prepared for the Army Council for the Year 1906,* 58., Précis No. 278. TNA:PRO, WO 163/11.

10 *Minutes of Proceedings and Précis Prepared for the Army Council for the Year 1904,* 412-3., Précis No. 154. TNA:PRO, WO 163/9.

11 *Report on a Conference of General Staff Officers at the Staff College. 7th to 10th January, 1908,* 21 and 25. TNA:PRO, WO 279/18.

12 TNA:PRO, WO 33/606 and WO 33/660, respectively.

13 *Result of a Staff Tour, 25-6th March 1912.* Staff Manual, War, 1912. TNA:PRO, WO 32/4731.

14 Minute (26th April 1912) from R.D. Whigham to DSD, in Staff Manual, War, 1912. TNA:PRO, WO 32/4731.

15 Minute (3rd October 1913) from Sir James Grierson to DMO, in Staff Manual, War, 1912. TNA:PRO, WO 32/4731.

16 Entry for 6th November 1914, Rawlinson Diary, Churchill College Cambridge. RWLN 1/1.

17 Minute (1st October 1913) from G.M. Harper to DMO, in Staff Manual, War, 1912. TNA:PRO, WO 32/4731.

18 *Mobilization Tables.* TNA:PRO, WO 33/611.

19 Terraine, John., *To Win a War: 1918, The Year of Victory* (Sidgwick and Jackson, 1978), 150-1.

20 Boraston, Lt.-Col. J.H. (ed.), *Sir Douglas Haig's Despatches (December 1915-April 1919)* (Dent, 1919), 343. Henceforth 'Boraston, *Despatches.*'

21 Boraston, *Despatches,* 344.

22 Boraston, *Despatches* , 329.

23 Boraston, *Despatches* , 321-329.

24 Travers, *The Killing Ground.* See especially chapters 2, 3 and 4 for the development of Haig's views and chapters 2 and 3 for those of his contemporaries.

25 *FSR I,* 133-145.

26 Boraston, *Despatches,* 328.

27 Boraston, *Despatches,* 319.

28 Boraston, *Despatches,* 320.

29 Boraston, *Despatches,* 325.

30 For the death ray see Haig diary entry for 28th September 1916. TNA:PRO, WO 256/13.

31 Travers, *The Killing Ground.*, 75-7. Boraston, *Despatches,* 329-30. For the limitations of tanks see Childs, D.J., 'British Tanks 1915-18, Manufacture and

Employment' (Ph.D. thesis, Glasgow University, 1996), 155, 183.
32 *FSR I*, 13.
33 *FSR I*, 36.
34 *FSR I*, 32.
35 *FSR I*, 27-8.
36 *FSR I*, 54.
37 *FSR I*, 57.
38 *FSR I*, 65.
39 *FSR I*, 78.
40 *FSR I*, 133.
41 *FSR I*, 136.
42 It is ironic that in the event, the BEF went to France with only four divisions, a number which corps commanders frequently had under their control by 1916.
43 *FSR I*, 99.
44 *FSR I*, 99-100.
45 *FSR I*, 100.
46 *FSR I*, 99.
47 O.H., 1914 Volume 1, 206.
48 *FSR I*, 91.
49 O.H., 1914 Volume 1, 59, 135.
50 *FSR I*, 156.
51 I Corps War Diary for 3rd November 1914. TNA:PRO, WO 95/588.
52 *FSR I*, 150.
53 O.H., 1914 Volume 2, 76-86.
54 Report entitled *Operations of the Ist Corps on the River Aisne, 13th to 30th September, 1914* (henceforth *I Corps on the Aisne*) 3. TNA:PRO, WO 95/588.
55 O.H., 1914 Volume 1, 327. *FSR I*, 96. "The special duty of the van guard is reconnaissance. It will, therefore, be composed of the advanced guard mounted troops..."; *FSR I*, 134-6.
56 O.H., 1914 Volume 1, 325-6.
57 *I Corps on the Aisne*, 8. TNA:PRO, WO 95/588. And see *FSR I*, 131-161, passim for comments on reserves.
58 *FSR I*, 137.
59 *FSR I*, 144.
60 *I Corps on the Aisne*, 11. TNA:PRO, WO 95/588. *FSR I*, 142.
61 *I Corps on the Aisne*, 11. TNA:PRO, WO 95/588.
62 *FSR I*, 132.
63 *I Corps on the Aisne*, 12. TNA:PRO, WO 95/588.
64 *FSR I*, 146-7. "If the frontage occupied in battle is so great as to reduce the force kept in hand for the offensive much below half the total force available, the position may be considered too extended" And see *FSR I*, 147.
65 *I Corps on the Aisne*, 13. TNA:PRO, WO 95/588.
66 *I Corps on the Aisne*, 15.
67 *FSR I*, 140.
68 *I Corps on the Aisne*, 19. TNA:PRO, WO 95/588.
69 Memorandum entitled *Organization Of Armies. Instructions as to General System of Administration*, 29th December 1914. TNA:PRO, WO 95/25.

70 Memorandum entitled *Notes Regarding Staff Duties,* 27th December 1914. TNA:PRO, WO 95/589.

71 O.H., 1915 Volume 1, 81-2.

72 *1st Army No: G.S.37* and *1st Corps No: 195 (G),* 16th and 18th February 1915, respectively. TNA:PRO, WO 95/590.

73 *FSR I,* 27. With regard to the leadership or management styles practised in the BEF at this time, they seem to have been a curious mixture of the authoritarian and the democratic, with *FSR I* stressing the latter aspect of things. See Handy, Charles, *Understanding Organisations* (Penguin, 1993), 96-123.

74 *Notes at Conference on 5/3/15.* TNA:PRO, WO 95/590.

75 *2nd London Division , T.F. Scheme of Training for the Present when in Reserve,* quoting *1st Corps No: 236 (G),* which quoted *GHQ O.A. 042,* 14th March 1915. TNA:PRO, WO 95/590.

76 *2nd London Division , T.F. Scheme of Training…, Appendix "A".*

77 Prior and Wilson, *Command…,* 23.

78 *1st Army No. G.S.73(a),* 13th April 1915. TNA:PRO, WO 95/708.

79 *Conference, 1st Army, 27th April, at Bethune.* TNA:PRO, WO 95/708.

80 See Prior and Wilson, *Command…,* 39.

81 *1st Army No. G.S.73(a).*

82 Undated memo entitled *General Staff Notes on the Offensive.* TNA:PRO, WO 158/17.

83 *1st Army Operation Order No. 22,* 6th May 1915. TNA:PRO, WO 95/591.

84 O.H., 1915 Volume 2, 13.

85 O.H., 1915 Volume 2, 50.

86 *1st Corps Operation Order No. 83,* 14th May 1915. TNA:PRO, WO 95/591.

87 *1st Corps G.A.56.,* 16th May 1915. TNA:PRO, WO 95/591.

88 *1st Corps G.286.,* 18th May 1915. TNA:PRO, WO 95/591.

89 *Memorandum on Artillery Organization in Army Corps,* 18th January 1915. TNA: PRO, WO 95/707.

90 *Scheme of Attack For the 1st Division to Secure the Haisnes-Douvrin Ridge,* 1st June 1915. TNA:PRO, WO 95/591.

91 *1st Corps No. 356 (G).,* 1st June 1915. TNA:PRO, WO 95/591.

92 O.H., 1915 Volume 2, 73-4, fn. 3.

93 Farndale, *Artillery,* 343-5.

94 I Corps CRA Diary 1915-18. TNA:PRO, WO 95/619. For the composition of the corps artillery staff, see *No. 1/R.A.S./11,* 1st September 1915. See also *First Army No. G.S.135/13 (c).,* 31st August 1915. Re the lifts etc., see *I Corps No. 494 (G) 46.* 16th September, 1915. TNA:PRO, WO 158/345.

95 *1st Corps No. 494 (G).,* 10th September 1915. TNA:PRO, WO 158/345.

96 *Operation Order No. 35 by Lieut.-General Sir H.S. Rawlinson…, Commanding IVth Corps. 20th September 1915. Instructions Issued to IVth Corps Artillery by Brig.-Gen. C.E.D. Budworth…* (The latter was appointed IV Corps BGRA in October.) TNA:PRO, WO 95/711.

97 *Lecture Given at Head-Quarters, 3rd Army, on 14th December, 1915, on Action of IVth Corps at Loos, 25th September, 1915.,* 5. TNA:PRO, WO 95/711.

98 *Notes of Conference held at Headquarters 1st Corps 25th August, 1915.* TNA:PRO, WO 158/345.

99 See *FSR I*, chapter 2, and especially 27-32 (section 12, *Operation Orders*).

100 *No. 520 (G).*, 6th October 1915. TNA:PRO, WO 95/592.

101 Messenger, Charles, *Call to Arms. The British Army 1914-18* (Weidenfeld and Nicholson, 2005), 64-5.

102 Haig Diary for 3rd October 1915. TNA:PRO, WO 256/5.

103 Blake, Robert (ed.) *The Private Papers of Douglas Haig, 1914-1919* (Eyre & Spottiswoode, 1952), 100, 103.

104 Palazzo, *Seeking Victory...*, 76.

105 Richter, Donald, *Chemical Soldiers. British Gas Warfare in World War I* (Leo Cooper, 1994), 67.

106 Issued as *1st Army G.S. 164 (a)*, 6th September 1915. TNA:PRO, WO 158/345.

107 Prior and Wilson, *Command...*, 102-3.

108 See Rawlinson Diary for August 1915, passim. Field Marshal Lord Rawlinson Papers, National Army Museum.

109 *First Army No. G.S. 193.*, 18th October 1915. TNA:PRO, WO 95/159.

110 O.H., 1915 Volume 2, vii-viii.

111 *Report on a Conference of General Staff Officers at the Royal Military College, 13th to 16th January, 1913.* TNA:PRO, WO 279/48.

112 GHQ *OAM. 97*, 26th October 1915. TNA:PRO, WO 95/159.

113 *First Army – 1915. Instructions for Training*, 10th November 1915. TNA:PRO, WO 95/160.

114 O.H., 1915 Volume 2, 91.

115 *Note on the Next Offensive*, 14th December 1915. Piece no. 56. TNA:PRO, WO 158/18.

116 *Notes on Conference held at G.O.C.'s House 5:30p.m. 20:12:15.* TNA:PRO, WO 95/592.

CHAPTER 2

Corps Command and the Battle of the Somme

This chapter is intended to show how the role of corps in the BEF changed during the Battle of the Somme (1st July to 18th November 1916). It begins with a brief examination of the expansion of the BEF and the movement of divisions through corps. Then the administrative functions of corps from early 1915 to mid-1916 are discussed. Next, changes in the operational functions of corps between the end of the Battle of Loos in 1915 and the planning for the Somme offensive are examined. Lastly, the chapter shows, through the stages of the battle, how those functions altered. All of this is done with reference to corps' changing relationships with Army and division.

Before moving on to the planning of the Somme offensive, a note on the enlargement of the BEF before it is required. At the end of 1914, the BEF contained four infantry corps; a year later, this had risen to 11, and by the end of June 1916, 18.[1] This expansion was accompanied by an increase in the number of staff officers at corps HQ from 18 at mobilization to 24 by June 1916. Of the extra six officers, five came from the artillery – the CHA and his Brigade Major and Staff Captain, and the GOCRA's ADC and Staff Officer. And the greater responsibilities of corps were demonstrated by the rise in number of Corps Troops. From consisting of only a cable section in 1914, they now were composed of a corps cavalry regiment, a cyclist battalion, a motor machine-gun battery, the corps signal company and associated troops, the corps ammunition park, three supply columns, an ASC company, mobile ordnance workshops, several HAGs, and engineer and RFC detachments.[2] Given the complexity of functions now undertaken by corps and the increase in their number, it is not surprising that there was a shortage of experienced staff officers.[3] Hence, X Corps told its divisions in September 1915 to "ensure that staff officers know and can readily use the ciphers. [underlined in original]"[4] In addition, the corps stated that "our staffs and troops are not fully trained or accustomed to manoeuvre…"[5] A former staff officer wrote that his BGGS regularly drilled the corps staff in the issue of operation orders, since he realised that it was imperative that these reach units in plenty of time, and Sir Henry Rawlinson even found himself having to lend the 51st Division his BGGS not long after its arrival in France.[6]

The frequent moves of divisions in and out of corps is often cited as a problem for the BEF.[7] It has been argued that the excellence of the Australian and Canadian Corps was the result of their always containing the same divisions, so that corps and divisional staffs were able to develop a closer and more efficient working relationship than was the case in British corps.[8] The number of infantry divisions moving through the corps upon which this chapter focuses was as follows (the figures given are for divisions which were in the relevant corps in the period 1st July to 18th November 1916, whether they saw action or not):

V Corps – 18
VII Corps – 8
VIII Corps – 12
X Corps – 25
XIII Corps – 16
XIV Corps – 17[9]

These figures exclude divisional stays of two days or fewer and multiple stays by the same division (some were in the same corps on three separate occasions). If the moves are averaged over V, X, XIII and XIV Corps (since VII and VIII were only involved in the battle during July, whereas the shortest stay amongst the others was two and a half months), then 19 divisions passed through each. At the start of the battle the BEF comprised 58 divisions, so it can be seen that just under a third of the total passed through each corps.[10] This was undoubtedly a high turnover. In contrast, corps moves were far less frequent, and Griffith's assertion that "there was always a great movement of army corps from one army to another" seems rather dubious. Fourth Army began with VIII, X, III, XV and XIII; it lost VIII and X to Reserve Army on 4th July. In August, XIII was relieved by XIV, and at the end of October, I ANZAC relieved XV. By the end of the year, it consisted of III, I ANZAC, XIV and XV Corps – two of which it had under it at the start of the battle, and another which it had acquired in August.[11] Moves were somewhat more frequent in Reserve (later Fifth) Army, but much the same picture appears. Of the 15 British corps in the BEF at the time, nine were engaged on the Somme, which seems initially to indicate a high turnover. But only four of them (II, III, XIV and XV) took part in six or more of the 12 battles which comprise the campaign.[12] This implied that if Army or GHQ felt that a given corps constituted a safe pair of hands, it was left in place. Certainly Lt.-Gens. Jacob and Lord Cavan (of II and XIV Corps) enjoyed good reputations, and Horne (XV Corps) was given command of First Army on 30th September.[13] The reputation of the GOC III Corps, Lt.-Gen. W.P. Pulteney, was more mixed.[14] By contrast, VIII Corps, which suffered the worst casualties of any corps on 1st July (and gained no ground), had been sent to the relatively quiet sector of the Ypres Salient by the end of that month, notwithstanding its commander's protestations that he had not been 'Stellenbosched.'[15]

To what extent was corps' role defined by its relative immobility? In administration, it seems that it was most important; corps was responsible for the infrastructure under which its divisions functioned. It should be noted, however, that another reason why moving of divisions in and out of corps was not popular, was that in administrative matters, "not only had each [corps] its own system of 'returns' but their whole method of staff work was diversified..."[16] This was another illustration of the improvised nature of the BEF. To return to the question of immobility, it could be argued that in operations, it was necessary to have a body of men – even if it was only the corps staff – who knew the area to be fought over well, and these could not be from divisions, owing to their need to rest and recuperate after any period of offensive action. Exceptions to this seem to prove the rule; the OH cited dissatisfaction in brigades at being taken from their 'native' divisions and being used to reinforce those already engaged, but pointed out that this meant that a divisional commander and staff who knew the ground and situation could be left in situ.[17] In addition, if only divisions were moved, reliefs were easier, although no corps spirit could be built up.[18] As for the question of whose the responsibility was for the movement of divisions in and out of corps, it seems that "Corps and divisions were assigned to or removed from... [Army] by the commander-in-chief."[19] Nevertheless, Army seem to have had the right at times to move divisions around when under their command and certainly were prepared to take corps' views into consideration when discussing moves, though those of GHQ would always take precedence.[20] Since GHQ had overall control of manpower, which was always short, this is not surprising.[21]

Transportation, of men, animals and material was obviously a vital function within the BEF. It had always been seen that this would be split between rail transport and other forms of transport, and the former will be dealt with first. In pre-war planning rail transport was the responsibility of the Inspector-General of Communications, whose headquarters resided at a supply base, and not GHQ. However, it rapidly became clear in the fighting of 1914 that this official was not in a position to be sufficiently responsive to the needs of the BEF, and so by the end of the year his responsibilities were transferred to the QMG at GHQ.[22] Initially the QMG had highly centralised powers, not only selecting railheads, but also where supply columns would rendezvous, but it soon became apparent that this was unnecessary, and so control of supply columns passed to corps and the control of traffic within a corps area was given to its GOC. Although railway transport remained throughout the war very much the province of GHQ (with some delegation to Army), it is clear that even in 1914, corps had a role to play in the organisation of supplies in advance of the railhead.[23]

As stated above, corps came to control road traffic in their areas by late 1914. Although this took place during the phase of mobile warfare, it continued once the trenches had been established. Evidently their relative immobility left corps in a better position to undertake this kind of administrative role than divisions. Divisional military police had initially undertaken such duties, but frequent divisional moves made it easier to centralise the work under corps, which kept troops specifically for the task.[24] No decentralisation of road maintenance and construction was ever contemplated, corps proposing their requirements for construction and the employment of existing roads to Army. The latter were responsible for the overall transport system within their area, and were therefore in a position to co-ordinate the demands of the corps below them, and if offensive operations were looming, to tell them what roads to construct or improve.[25] The movement of supplies from the railhead or railheads allocated by the QMG, to the divisional filling points, was the responsibility of corps. It is worth noting that, whether as a matter of administrative convenience or simply because the division was the basic unit of the BEF, trains arriving at the railheads were made up into divisional units.[26] However, the same was not true for engineer, ammunition and other supplies. Indeed, the growth in requirements for these commodities led to such demands on the road transport system that as early as 1915, Corps Roads Officers were appointed to oversee their maintenance even in divisional areas (normally the territory of divisional engineers).[27] Furthermore, divisional supply columns were placed under corps, as were their ammunition parks.[28] As in operational matters, the pressure of events led to corps encroaching upon divisions' authority, which reflected their increased gunnery responsibilities. This would also seem to be borne out by a reorganisation (and decentralisation) of the RFC in January 1916, when 'Corps Wings' of one squadron apiece were formed.[29]

In other administrative duties, however, the split between corps and divisions was less biased towards the former. Divisions retained their ordnance responsibilities, though corps gained ordnance staffs of their own to deal with the demands of corps troops.[30] Canteens were organised at divisional level, as were chaplains (although corps, as more senior formations, were provided with deputy assistant chaplains-general).[31] Responsibilities for the care of the dead fell evenly; divisions provided burial parties, and corps, the burial grounds themselves.[32] Training was split between GHQ, Army, corps and division, and corps seem not to have been especially jealous of their position in this respect.[33] An imminent shortage of signallers in late 1915 led X Corps to order its divisions to train more, and VIII Corps' first conference on the Western Front (it had come from Gallipoli) firmly delegated the responsibility of training at all levels, from brigade staffs and battalion COs down to "young N.C.O.s and Privates likely to make N.C.O.s" onto division.[34] Most of the other new administrative functions, such as the post and printing, were exercised by Army or GHQ. This would again seem to indicate that the growth in corps' authority over subordinate formations was principally artillery-related (though the inexperience of divisional staffs may have led corps to be more prescriptive than they would otherwise have been), and did not constitute centralisation for its own sake.

Indeed, it can hardly be argued that corps greedily snatched control of new weaponry from divisions. Trench mortar batteries were allocated either to divisional artillery or to brigades, depending upon their calibre (while heavy mortars became a corps responsibility, few were available until the end of 1916), and machine-gun companies were established at brigade. Although anti-aircraft guns were provided at corps level, this only reflected their function of defending essentially static installations.[35] While they did not in themselves constitute a new weapon, the importance of engineers under the prevailing circumstances had increased consider-ably, and they were augmented by the addition of an extra field company per division and the appointment of three or four assistants to the CRE of a corps (there were also changes to Armies' engineer complement).[36] The RE 'Special Brigade' of gas troops was parcelled out to Armies, although operational command at times fell on both corps and divisions.[37]

The changes in corps' role with regard to artillery have been touched upon both above and in the previous chapter, in the latter case with par-ticular reference to the Battle of Loos. However, it will be discussed further below, since it was vital in defining the roles of corps and divisions during the fighting on the Somme.

A good example of the ability of the BEF to learn from experience was provided soon after Loos. The CGS stated that the recent fighting had demonstrated "once more" the need for a carefully worked-out artil-lery plan, which required effective artillery command for its execution.[38] Consequently, the status of the BGRA was raised, and he became the 'General Officer Commanding Royal Artillery' (GOCRA) of the corps. The memorandum went on to say that he "will be charged with the co-ordination of the action of the artillery of the Corps, and the executive command of such portions of it as the Corps Commander may direct..." Although this did not extend to the heavy artillery, divisional artillery could now be withdrawn from the command of the divisional GOC if the corps commander wished it, representing a significant increase in the power of corps.

At the same time, each Army was given one of the existing HAR Groups as its own Heavy Artillery Group (HAG). At this point, some confusion as to who commanded whom plainly arose, and Second Army (for example) felt obliged to issue a memorandum to clear the matter up: "when... a corps is employed as a whole in any operation the general officer commanding the artillery of the corps will... make out the artillery plan, and will co-ordinate the action of the whole of the artillery."[39] The GOCRA was to act as a link between the Army HAG and the field artillery, and ensure that administrative matters, such as the placement of gun positions and the inspection of billets and wagon lines, were attended to.

Unfortunately, GHQ badly muddied the waters when it decreed the appointment of a CHA to each corps in early March 1916.[40] Two HAGs were allotted to each corps under this officer, who, like the GOCRA, was a Brigadier-General. Furthermore, in the memorandum creating the position of CHA, the GOCRA was referred to as the "Brig-Gen. R.A. of the corps." Consequently, his position relative to the former was unclear. XIV Corps issued a memorandum to its divisions and CHA on 5th April, to the effect that it had consulted Second Army, and "the status of the G.O.C., R.A. of the Corps was not altered... except that he now has subordinate Heavy Artillery Commanders directly under him..."[41] Similarly, at a conference with his corps commanders the following day, Sir Henry Rawlinson, the GOC Fourth Army, stated that "the recent instructions from G.H.Q. must be taken to imply no change in the status of the B.G.R.A."[42]

Nevertheless, GHQ issued another definition in May, when the GOCRA was given "executive command of any concentration of the corps and divisional artillery." This meant that the CHA could claim a separate jurisdiction under other circumstances. However, the GOCRA continued to be referred to as such, in Fourth Army at least, and although the CHA certainly enjoyed some independence of action at the start of the campaign he was subordinated to the GOCRA as it went on.[43] It might be argued that a negative aspect to this centralisation of artillery control was that it slowed down planning of operations and hence reduced tempo. However, this is difficult to prove, since corps sometimes were more up to date with the situation in the front line than divisions, receiving information from the corps wing RFC.

The discussion above is intended to give some of the background to the way in which corps functioned in the planning and execution of the Somme campaign. Before going into the details of these processes, it seems appropriate to comment on the decision-making mechanism in the BEF. There are two diametrically opposed views on this matter. The first is that of the Official Historian, who asserted that "Before any offensive took place there were... not only conferences between the Commanders-in-Chief, but between the Commander-in-Chief and his Army Commanders, between the Army Commanders, their staff, and their corps commanders, etc., etc."[44] The second is typified by the work of Travers, who argues that discussion, especially of GHQ's plans, was by no means encouraged, and that a similar tendency applied at Army commanders' conferences, though not to the same degree. Indeed, he applies this argument to corps commanders too, though he only mentions them in the context of Army conferences.[45]

The planning of operations was one of the most important functions of corps. The optimistic Hunter-Weston wrote to his wife, the night before the Somme offensive began, that "I have, with my excellent staff, done all possible to ensure success... I have nothing more to do now but to rest till well after the attack has taken place."[46] Plainly he felt that he had no further part to play after zero hour, and that all depended on planning.[47]

The overall plan for the start of the Somme campaign has been dealt with in depth in numerous works, generally concentrating at GHQ and Army level.[48] Some of the more recent have commented on the absence of tactical direction from GHQ and Fourth Army, and that the latter's famous *Tactical Notes* of May 1916 were not as pernicious in their effects as had previously been thought, since corps and divisions were left to devise their own means for taking their objectives. None has commented on the surprising fact that this seems to have been the first time when definite daily objectives were set. In 1915, troops had been left to press on as fast as possible from objective to objective, all on one day, so success or failure was to a large extent left in the hands of the local commanders.[49] Consequently, during the planning for the Somme, Army and GHQ were unusually hands-on in setting objectives for the stages of the advance, but characteristically hands-off about how they should be attained.

Once the frontage of the attack had been defined, it was up to each corps to take the necessary steps to ensure it could do its job.[50] X Corps will here be used as an example. Firstly, from March 1916, artillery resources had to be gathered and positions prepared, although the arrival of guns from other sectors would be delayed until as late as possible in order to retain a degree of surprise.[51] At this point, though the frontage of the attack was settled, the depth was not. Dugouts for gunners, magazines, observation posts, telephone lines and exchanges, roads, light railways and tramways (these last three for the carriage of ammunition) all had to be constructed.[52] The 'A' Staff had to arrange traffic control and ammunition supply, and signalling arrangements were made.[53] As well as artillery, the corps was told how many divisions it had been allotted, what RFC support it could expect and what labour was available for its preparations.[54] Liaison with neighbouring corps was undertaken, owing to the necessity of siting some of X Corps' batteries in their areas.[55]

Once all these matters had been settled, the corps was "now able to begin to draw up the plan of attack definitely." The assaulting divisions were known – 32nd and 36th, with 49th in reserve. Although Army was not prescriptive in its attitude to tactics, it was necessary for it to co-ordinate all corps' artillery, so "the MGRA produced the first ever Army Artillery Operation Order." This was not unduly detailed, laying down "tasks for the guns... but not targets... But proportions of guns to tasks, the tasks themselves, fireplans, observation and deployment were... left to GOCRAs."[56] Nevertheless, crucially, the timetable was very much Army's, though corps could make their own arrangements within it.[57] No creeping barrage was to be employed to cover the infantry's advance, a lifting one being used instead. The question of artillery control was then considered. In 1915, the practice had been for corps to control divisional artillery until the assault began, when it was decentralised back to its original owners.[58] However, for the attack of July 1st, all remained in corps' hands through-out, unless corps chose to release it.[59] Consequently, GOCs of divisions and brigades were unable to change the fireplan if things did not go as expected. But since the corps squadron RFC and the FOOs of the heavy artillery liaised with corps rather than division, the former was more likely to know what was going on than the latter. This cannot be described as a flexible approach to the attack, though the suggestion was made that since brigade commanders would be more in touch with the situation at the front than anyone else, they should have some field artillery attached.

Thereafter, the paper went on to describe the bombardment and the attack itself, all of which makes most unedifying reading. No comment on the decision of the corps commander (Lt.-Gen. Sir T.L.N. Morland) to spend the day up "an observation tree" two miles away from his head-quarters (though linked to it by telephone) was made, nor any on his piecemeal misuse of the 49th Division, though putting in the reserve was the only way (impromptu barrages in an attempt to improve the situation were not helpful) in which he could exercise effective command after the initial assault had placed the 32nd and 36th Divisions beyond his reach.[60] The process of planning is most revealing regarding the latitude – within limits – allowed corps by Army, and not allowed division by corps.

Conferences were an essential part of the planning process. The rea-son why X Corps began this as early as 7th March is that the GOC was instructed to do so at an Army conference on that day.[61] Indeed, he held his own conference on the same day, inviting schemes for the attack from 32nd and 36th Divisions, and exhorting them to begin improving roads and the like.[62] That discussion was encouraged is apparent in a memoran-dum from 32nd Division, which the GOC began by saying "I agree with the notes forwarded with the letter quoted, but would observe that... conditions have considerably changed since the notes were written."[63] Likewise, the GOC 36th Division began his contribution by explicitly agreeing with corps, and then going on to make a number of suggestions regarding the attack.[64] The corps commander was rather acting as a post-box at the beginning of his next conference, relaying no fewer than eight points which had been raised at an Army conference.[65] The meeting then moved on to a discussion of the attack plans. Morland made some general statements, and then a wider discussion ensued, in which divisional dividing lines were agreed and the GOCs of the divisions and the "BGRA" outlined their plans.

At the Army conference of 16th April, the same pattern emerged.[66] Rawlinson raised those matters he felt should be passed on to divisions and the artillery and then went through changes to the overall plan. The corps commanders having outlined their plans, Rawlinson went on to comment on them, much as the former had with their divisional commanders. The general points on infantry and artillery were uncontentious, and Rawlinson's comment that "counter-battery work is becoming more and more important" showed greater prescience than was displayed by X Corps' gunners. Although the tenor of this conference tended less to debate than in X Corps, it is apparent that discussion did take place.

By late April, Army asked to see both corps and divisional plans.[67] However, detailed planning was devolved to corps and divisions, especially the former. X Corps' outlined the objectives, the possibilities of exploitation on taking the first one, the difficulties of wire-cutting without adequate artillery observation, the distribution of the artillery and trench mortars, the use and position of reserves, the options regarding a short versus a long bombardment and views on the use of gas and smoke.[68] The schemes of the two attacking divisions were attached, and though they were mutually inconsistent, Morland stated that he intended to await Rawlinson's approval of the overall plan before he co-ordinated them. Obviously divisions were in a position to say how they intended to get to their objectives, but the framework within which they worked was the creation of corps. In fact, given the amount of discussion going on, the plan was more corps' overall responsibility than its sole creation, since it relied, to a far greater extent than Travers' view would allow, on the views of division. He seems to base his argument too much on individuals' anecdotal evidence of events at GHQ, and to have extrapolated from that to lower formations, without examining documentary evidence at the corps or divisional levels.

The next question to be raised is to what extent X Corps' preparations differed or otherwise from those of other corps. The CHA of V Corps visited III Corps just before the offensive and made notes on their preparations.[69] These were, obviously, concerned with the action of the artillery, and went into more detail in some respects (such as the attachment of artillery officers to brigade and battalion commanders) than the X Corps equivalent. The timetable for bombardment and wire-cutting was raised, and a good instance of co-ordination afforded when it was stated that, to facilitate observation, divisions would be asked in which areas they proposed to do their wire cutting at any particular time. The heavies would then refrain from bombarding these locations at those times. Furthermore, the GOCRA was permitted to set objectives in addition to those defined by Army.

VIII Corps seems to have kept its divisions on a tighter leash than X Corps. Hunter-Weston held two conferences, on 21st and 23rd June, the specific object of which was "to give Brigadiers an opportunity of discussing their plans with each other."[70] However, there is no hint of discussion in the report of the conferences. Hunter-Weston's RE background was demonstrated by a rueful acknowledgement that the dead would be too numerous to allow of cremation, and so they should be buried in pits, in layers about a foot apart and with individual corpses separated by the same distance. It is fortunate that the section headed "All Units Must Push On Resolutely" preceded, rather than followed, this encouraging advice.

The corps orders, however, differed little from those of X or XIII Corps.[71] Divisions were permitted to use their initiative to some extent, such as moving a limited number of batteries into no man's land after zero, but unlike X Corps, VIII retained overall control. And, "the infantry attack will be carried out in accordance with the instructions laid down in VIII Corps scheme for Offensive…"

The sheer volume of that scheme – over 70 pages under 28 headings – may go some way to explaining Hunter-Weston's feeling that he could do nothing more once the attack had started. It went into great detail, such as the formations to be adopted by the infantry (down to company level) for the advance to the second and third objectives, and the need to halt in order to dress the ranks, after which the troops would "cross the trenches, keeping left shoulders well up…"[72] Details of strongpoints to be constructed were outlined, as were their map references. And the artillery and trench mortar dispositions were set out, as were those of the reserves, the barrage plan was detailed and administrative matters such as water supply and treatment of prisoners dealt with. The whole document seems to have been constructed on the basis that nothing could or would go wrong.[73] It is all the more ironic that of the three corps which tried to employ a creeping barrage on the day of attack, only VIII Corps was completely unsuccessful.[74] It must be noted also that the nature of *Fourth Army Tactical Notes* was such that the approaches of corps were easily able to vary in their specificity regarding subordinate formations.[75] Given the notes' orientation towards *FSR I*, this leaving of detail (while enunciating principles) to the man on the spot is quite understandable, though why Hunter-Weston left his subordinates so little scope for the exercise of their initiative is less so. His experiences at Gallipoli, where Sir Ian Hamilton's hands-off command style had proved ineffective, may have contributed to this attitude.[76] However, since Hamilton's style had prevented him from intervening in Hunter-Weston's mishandling of his forces on the day of the landings (25th April 1915) it may be overly charitable to think that the latter was capable of such a degree of self-criticism.

The X and XIII Corps plans contained much the same information as VIII Corps', but presented it in a far less detailed manner. For example, regarding infantry formations, XIII Corps went no lower than brigade.[77] This bears out Prior and Wilson's thesis that Fourth Army did not impose any significant degree of uniformity upon its corps and divisions before the attack of 1st July, though the similarities between the plans are likely to have been as a result of the principles expressed in *Fourth Army Tactical Notes*.[78]

So far, this chapter has dealt with Fourth Army's preparations for the Battle of the Somme. However, VII Corps, ordered to make a diversionary attack to the north of VIII corps, was in Third Army. The relationships between Army, corps and divisions did not differ greatly from those in Fourth Army. Corps provided support to division in order to ensure that it could do what was required of it, but reserved the right to criticise or amend divisional plans. It also made requests to Army on divisions' behalf, such as for 56th Division to have artillery assistance from its neighbour. Army's reply, telling corps that all had been arranged, also said that "Fourth Army have given VIII Corps instructions to co-operate in counter battery work where possible, and to make arrangements in direct communication with you."[79] As the corps on VII's right flank, VIII was in a position to help, but this quotation implies that if neighbouring corps were in different Armies, communication had initially to be made via the latter.

In planning the details of the offensive, VII Corps had a different task from the corps in Fourth Army. Since its role was diversionary, the attack had strictly limited objectives, and this was made clear to divisions when their plans were requested.[80] More importantly, the artillery plan was based on the infantry plan and not vice versa. However, like Fourth Army, Third was required by GHQ to outline its proposals and preparations for the offensive, and so in turn asked the same of VII Corps.[81] Its reply was under more or less standard headings: "Reconnaissance and digging of sections of enemy trenches to be attacked for practice…"; "Organization of trenches for attack"; "Signal Service"; "Artillery Preparations"; "R.E. arrangements" and "Administrative."[82] Unsurprisingly, corps exercised its co-ordinating function in all this. Snow, the corps commander, did not think Gommecourt a good place for a feint, and said so to Army, which passed on his views to GHQ.[83] However, GHQ wished especially to protect VIII Corps' attack from flanking artillery fire, and so insisted.[84] Since this was not unreasonable, it should not be seen as GHQ dictating to lower formations for the sake of it. And Third Army was obviously prepared to discuss the matter with VII Corps, as well as raising it with GHQ. In fact, the planning for the Gommecourt attack followed much the same pattern as for the main assault to the south.

The exercise of corps command on 1st July 1916 can be dealt with briefly. All the GOC could do once the attack had begun, was to distribute his reserves and to alter the artillery plans to take account of the situation as it appeared at corps HQ. This might not bear very much relation to what was actually happening, but owing to the difficulties of getting information back from the attacking troops, it was all that the corps commanders had to go on.[85] Interestingly, Hunter-Weston, notwithstanding his belief the night before that he would have nothing to do on the day, actively directed the operations of his divisions to prevent further losses and to make what gains they could (see Chapter 8).[86] In contrast, Congreve, of XIII Corps, actively directed his divisions only twice during the day.[87] The reason would seem to be that the more things went to plan, the less the corps commander had to do; under those circumstances, divisions could look after themselves. And once XIII Corps had taken its objectives, there was no more to be done on its front, since no reserves were available for quick exploitation.[88] The inflexibility of Fourth Army's plan robbed its subordinates of the chance to use their initiative unless it broke down. The question of tempo again arises. Bearing in mind that this is defined as "the rate or rhythm of activity relative to the enemy," it is hard to see how the Fourth Army was going to achieve higher tempo than the Germans. Had the plan worked and a breakthrough been achieved, with the Reserve Army ready to charge through the gap in the German line, they might have been caught off balance. Had XV and XIII Corps had the Reserve Army ready behind them, a similar effect might have been achieved. However, the weight of artillery and techniques available to it did not permit this. As in 1915, the means were lacking, and so was surprise, another important element in catching the enemy off-balance. Strategic surprise was not possible, given the need to register the artillery before the offensive began. Once it had begun, the British were not in a position (for want of resources and the need to register guns) suddenly to move their artillery elsewhere and start again, in order to throw the Germans off-balance. Tactical surprise was hardly more attainable, given the need for a prolonged bombardment to damage the German defences sufficiently to ensure that the infantry could enter them. The night attack of 14th July was made in the small hours not because of a desire to surprise the enemy but because no man's land was too wide to be crossed safely in daylight, so the attackers had to assemble part-way across it, under cover of darkness.[89]

After 1st July, a number of minor, poorly co-ordinated operations were undertaken by Fourth Army, in order to position itself for its next large-scale attack on 14th July, involving XIII and XV Corps.[90] Meanwhile, preparations for the latter went ahead. The attack was originally set for 10th July, and XIII Corps held a conference on the 7th.[91] The notes of this meeting are briefer than many of those before the attack of 1st July, but discussion and delegation still took place. After Congreve had regurgitated GHQ's over-optimistic assessment of the German strength facing the corps, he went on to the taking of the important flanking position of Trônes Wood.[92] Here, he gave orders, rather than discussing the matter, saying what 30th and 9th Divisions were expected to achieve. However, after 9th Division had passed through the northern part of the wood, someone had to be responsible for it, and this was left for the two divisions to sort out between themselves. And Congreve was happy to accept Maj.-Gen. Furse's (GOC 9th Division) suggestion that the attack be made at dawn. This idea has been ascribed to Congreve, and the OH states that Rawlinson arrived at the idea after discussion with his corps commanders.[93] Plainly their status had increased enormously since the post-box days of 1914, even though the dawn attack was Furse's idea. Notwithstanding Haig's opposition to the plan, which was only overcome by the intervention of his MGRA, preparations for it still went ahead.[94] It is unusual to find the C-in-C's view being disregarded in this way.

However, 9th and 30th Divisions failed to capture Trônes Wood, and 18th Division was given the task. The corps order for this one-division operation differed in two ways from those before 1st July. The division was to take over its jumping-off position from 9th Division, "at an hour to be arranged between the Divisional Commanders concerned."[95] And the GOC 18th Division (Maj.-Gen. F.I. Maxse) directly arranged artillery support with the GOCRA. If only one division was involved, corps had no need to exercise close, co-ordinating control. This provides another demonstration that centralisation of authority was a question of operational necessity, and not merely done for its own sake.

Trônes Wood having already proved to be a tough nut to crack, the corps was by no means certain that 18th Division would succeed. Consequently, it requested new plans of attack from its other divisions on 12th July.[96] As before, it laid down the objectives (which were dictated by Army) and left the details up to divisions.[97] The actual operation order was not especially prescriptive, and less confident than before 1st July; the failure of 7th and 3rd Divisions was contemplated and appropriate action ordered.[98] As before, the establishment of strongpoints and consolidation of the positions captured were also dealt with, and (a departure from the practice on 1st July) the need for a protective barrage during consolidation was stressed. 18th Division having failed to capture the whole of Trônes Wood before, it was to take it on 14th July. If it could then press on further to the west and take the village of Guillemont, so much the better, but "This operation will not be undertaken without reference to Corps Headquarters." It is likely that corps was exercising its co-ordinating role in restricting 18th Division's advance unless 9th Division, on its left, had made an appropriate amount of progress. A new idea, from the CRAs of

3rd and 9th Divisions, was the shortening of the period of intense fire just before the attack to five minutes. This was intended to avoid the problem that a longer phase of intense fire advertised to the Germans that the assault was imminent.[99] More flexibility was built into the plan this time as well. Hence, "The Divisional Artilleries will conform to the lifts of the Corps Artillery but may remain on a little longer if desired by Divisional Commanders."[100] And in addition to a greater emphasis on counter-battery work, the heavies were expected to respond to calls from aeroplanes, which were the least unreliable source of information as to the progress of the battle.

The attack on 14th July (the Battle of Bazentin) did manage to attain a degree of surprise (if unintentionally), but there was no question of effective exploitation of the success. After the initial thrust, the rate of activity of the attackers did not exceed that of the defenders and slow movement forward of British reserves was overtaken by more rapid movement of their German equivalents.[101] Fourth Army could not attain a tempo higher than its opponents', though at least the preparation time for this battle was considerably less than for its predecessor.

After the 14th July attack, Fourth Army lapsed again into poorly co-ordinated, smaller operations, suffering heavy casualties. Prior and Wilson blame this on Rawlinson, pointing out his tendency to order attacks which were deficient in manpower or artillery support or both.[102] In the meantime, Congreve went back to England, a sick man, on 10th August. By 16th August, his corps was replaced on the right of the BEF's line by XIV Corps, under Lord Cavan. This formation had arrived on the Somme front at the end of July, replacing VIII Corps in Reserve Army. The latter had taken over VIII and X Corps under Fourth Army on July 2nd, becoming an independent Army command on July 3rd. Although it had yet to establish the bad reputation it later bore, it was quick to order an attack by 14th and 75th Brigades, in 32nd Division, under X Corps, which was originally scheduled for 3.15am on July 3rd.[103] This time being found to be far too soon for 75th Brigade to be ready, the attack was postponed until 6.15am, when it proved to be a costly failure since the artillery, owing to communications difficulties, had fired off half the available ammunition before being notified of the postponement. Gough's biographer states that Gough personally telephoned III Corps, in conjunction with which the attack had been intended to take place, to notify it of the postponement.[104] However, Neill Malcolm, Gough's MGGS, asked for an explanation of "why the attack by the 32nd Division did not take place at 3.15am on July 2nd [sic] as ordered."[105] The picture becomes more confused, however, since the OH stated before its comment that half the bombardment was fired accidentally, that Gough had agreed with III Corps that it would be done deliberately.[106] This illustrates the controversy surrounding Hubert Gough and the problems of his apologists. And Malcolm's memorandum is a pointer to a more assertive style of army command than that practised in Fourth Army.

Cavan began his service on the Somme with a rather apologetic flexing of his muscles. On 3rd August he issued a document which clearly revealed in its first paragraph the command style favoured by the BEF, its attachment to established principles and its willingness to learn within their framework. Thus,

> Without wishing in any way to curb the initiative of Divisional Commanders, I should like to impress the following short memoranda on the minds of all, which are based on the experiences of this battle, backed by the teaching of our text books.[107]

The need to attack in depth was stressed, with the responsibilities of divisional, brigade and lower commanders briefly outlined. The use of heavy artillery for destructive fire was mentioned, as was the need for infantry to stick as close as possible to the barrage. Consolidation of captured positions was dealt with, as well as the leapfrogging of successive waves of attackers through the first, the experience of "many Brigadiers" being invoked to back this up, while also providing a good example of the upward dissemination of information in the BEF. In keeping with the tenor of his first paragraph, he did not order them, but made an "appeal to all divisional commanders" to ensure that they got troops across no man's land as soon as possible since the German counter-bombardment could render it almost impassable. Most important, however, was his stress on "Communications by runners, pigeons, visual and signal to the air."

Cavan's relationship with Reserve Army was less diffident than that with his subordinates. In correspondence with Army over a plan to capture Beaumont Hamel, he began by stating that "After further discussion with Divisional Commanders, I would prefer to adhere to the original plan submitted...," and went on to explain why.[108] He dissected Army's memorandum, paragraph by paragraph, reminding them that three of theirs were identical to his, and in the case of paragraph four, "The arguments put forward in para: 4 of this [i.e. his] letter bear even stronger weight." His parting shot was to observe that VIII Corps had made the same attack on July 1st with far more support from neighbouring corps. All this argues against the one way, top-down communication and climate of fear described by Travers, although Cavan was less likely to fear the termination of his military career than most, having retired from the army once (in 1913) already.[109]

That divisions were still permitted to use their initiative is underlined by a plan of attack devised jointly by the GOCs 6th and 49th Divisions (Maj.-Gens. C. Ross and E.M. Perceval, respectively), and submitted to XIV Corps on 8th August.[110] Although Cavan's response was not uncritical, he again began his response almost apologetically – "Without in any way wishing to interfere with your arrangements…"[111] Corps' role in the dissemination of information downwards was then exemplified by his reminder that there should be no change in the rate of heavy artillery fire before the attack, and that the 'creeper' should begin as close as possible to the time when the infantry would reach the German trenches. This last point was not entirely correct, and Ross responded by reminding Cavan that the barrage should start early enough to suppress machine-gun fire during the infantry advance.[112] He stayed in post until 20th August the following year, so no dire consequences for him appear to have followed this exchange of views. That 6th and 49th Divisions were liaising over the projected attack also affords an example of corps-corps co-operation, since the former was in XIV and the latter in II Corps. This is emphasised by a conference on 11th August between the two corps commanders, the divisional commanders and their staffs.[113] The heavy artillery of each corps would support the other, and 6th Division's artillery would provide a smoke barrage for 49th Division. This degree of liaison between neighbouring corps was only sensible; that it would have occurred under Fourth Army seems unlikely from the criticism of Rawlinson already cited. It is noteworthy that at no time was the CHA given any independence from the plans of the GOCRA in either corps, or in any other documents referred to thus far in this chapter, after 1st July.

Having arrived on the Fourth Army front, Cavan's task was to capture Guillemont and advance his line to the north and south of the village. A conference was held at Corps HQ, at which the corps warning order for the assault formed the basis of discussion.[114] This document contained a number of points of interest. Firstly, it was stated that "The attack throughout the front of the XIV Corps will be continuous [underlined in original]." This ties in with Prior and Wilson's argument that Haig was at the time pressuring Rawlinson to ensure that his next attack was not delivered with too few troops on too narrow a front.[115] In addition, it pointed out that "There is a tendency in some quarters to consider that supervision of higher commands borders on interference." However, Haig himself had ordered that staff officers from higher formations should henceforth closely inspect their subordinates' preparations.[116]

Plainly, Haig was keen to emphasise the role of higher commanders in the preparations for the battle.[117] However, that Cavan was aware of the tendency mentioned above indicates that divisional commanders were by no means supine, and resented encroachment on their perceived autonomy as the man on the spot. It is also interesting that while Haig felt that "close supervision" of subordinates before an attack was important, "In actual *execution* of plans, when control by higher Commanders is impossible, subordinates on the spot must act on their own initiative…"[118] Given that he wrote this as part of what Prior and Wilson drolly refer to as a "boys'-own-guide on how to command an Army," it is an unfortunate reflection on Sir Henry Rawlinson's command style at this time.

In any case, Cavan felt no inhibitions about keeping a close eye on his divisional commanders. They were exhorted to "consider what weapons can be employed," and since the Germans were using long-range machine-gun fire to disrupt the arrival of British reinforcements, similar, retaliatory action should be considered.[119] Importantly, the establishment of observation posts for both infantry and artillery was mentioned, with "telephonic, visual; and pigeon communications…" That there was no radical change in the role of division was stressed: "It is of the greatest importance that Divisional plans, both Infantry and Artillery, should be made immediately, so that they can be studied by subordinates [underlined in original] and checked by Corps Headquarters."[120]

The conference itself was as free a discussion as any other reviewed in this chapter. One of the most important points raised was that the GOCRA intended to consult divisional commanders over areas which required special artillery attention, and that although he would indicate the general lines of the barrages, divisions would work out the details.[121] This argues for, if not actual decentralisation of the handling of the artillery, a reasonably high degree of latitude for divisions within the constraints of the GOCRA's plan, which was confirmed in the artillery order for the attack.[122] As in some previous attacks, divisions regained control of their artillery at zero hour, apart from those 18-pounder guns taking part in the barrage and some of the 4.5-inch howitzers. Again corps was exercising a co-ordinating role, not centralising for its own sake.

Before addressing the Battle of Flers-Courcelette (15th-22nd September) the situation in Reserve Army must be reviewed. Hubert Gough's command style has been referred to earlier and he wasted little time before leaving corps commanders in no doubt of his views on how they should do their job. Thus, the whole of a memorandum of 16th July read: "The Army Commander considers that in any bombardment scheme the exact points to be attacked by Heavy Howitzers should be selected by the G. Branch of the Corps in conjunction with the Corps Artillery Commander."[123] Four days later, corps were informed that "Whenever bombardments are ordered by Army or subordinate units, the R.A. Staff will call for reports on the following points at least daily…" and "These reports should always be laid before the General Staff for the information of the G.O.C. concerned."[124] Plainly Gough and Malcolm had little faith in the common sense of their corps commanders.

It is strange that Gough felt the need to provide all of his subordinates with his own "boys'-own-guide" to drafting orders and commanding a corps. His biographer records that he "found Morland… slow and inclined to be over-cautious," but once again he was also addressing corps commanders whom he felt to be competent – his preference for Jacob over Morland was why he wanted II Corps to replace X.[125] It is difficult to assess how the recipients of this advice felt, though Hunter-Weston's comments to his wife provide a clue. Before coming under Gough's command, he wrote that "Hubert Gough is a first-rate man whom I like much."[126] After almost a month in reserve Army, VIII Corps moved to Ypres, and he appeared to have changed his mind:

> My staff are really glad to be here in 2nd Army rather than in the Reserve Army (Gough). Things from a staff point of view did not run smoothly in his Army. I like him and think he is a good soldier, but I fear he is hardly a big minded enough man to make a really good Army Commander...[127]

Whilst operating in conjunction with Fourth Army with its right flank, Reserve Army also had its eye on the strongpoint of Thiepval, to its centre and left. Planning for an attack had begun early in August, and on its arrival in Reserve Army on 16th August, taking over from XIV Corps, V Corps continued this. However, its approach was more in keeping with Gough's authoritarian ethos than XIV Corps'. A conference was held on 23rd August at which corps stated that the attack should take place in the afternoon. Presumably the GOC 6th Division was unable to make his objections to this known at the time (notes of the conference have not survived), and so wrote to the corps commander (Lt.-Gen. E.A.Fanshawe, who had the unique distinction of having taken the corps over from his own brother) to outline his reasons for preferring a dawn attack, as originally planned.[128] The BGGS' (Br.-Gen. G.F. Boyd, later GOC 46th Division at the end of the war) reply was dismissive and ignored division's comment that the proposed assembly trenches were not deep enough to be safe for use in daylight, and that there was not time to deepen them, airily stating that the time of attack was "definitely settled" and that Fanshawe "trusts you to carry on the work necessary in deepening and clearing trenches."[129]

Army issued its order for the attack the next day.[130] This went into far more detail than anything from Fourth Army; the objectives of the attacking divisions (one from each corps) were given – not as lines to be seized by corps, but explicitly by division. Each division was told what it should do in the way of flank protection, pushing forward patrols in the event of a success, and maintaining a reserve. Corps were scarcely mentioned at all and in effect, Army used them purely as post-boxes. Gough seems to have gone to the opposite extreme to Rawlinson, and was so hands-on as to render his immediate subordinates virtually irrelevant.

Nevertheless, the attack (on 3rd September) failed.[131] Fanshawe conducted a post-mortem on 39th Division's attack, sending his comments to the GOC (Maj.-Gen. G.J. Cuthbert), at the insistence of Army.[132] These were a blend of blame for the division's (or its GOC's) perceived and actual shortcomings and flat statements of things beyond 39th Division's control, such as a comment that zero was too early (a problem raised by division before the attack). However, since Cuthbert remained in command of 39th Division until August 1917, V Corps' criticisms should be interpreted more as an exercise in pinpointing what went wrong than one of simply apportioning blame.

However, when compared to X Corps' efforts in Fourth Army to learn lessons from the earlier fighting (which resulted in the issue of a 20-page summary of divisions' views on 16th August) it seems that in Reserve Army – in August and early September, at least – discussion was less open and decisions were handed down from on high to a greater extent.[133] In view of Rawlinson's poor performance in this period, the latter tendency may not have been as bad as it appears at first glance, and at least Gough expected his corps commanders to notify their subordinates when they found fault with them. The differing command styles of the two men underlines the scope they were given to impose their own preferences during the planning process.

The planning for Flers-Courcelette provides another illuminating example of the process of discussion at work in Fourth Army. At the first conference held to discuss the forthcoming offensive, Rawlinson, after outlining the strategic situation as it appeared at GHQ, as ever provided the corps commanders (Pulteney, Cavan and Horne being present) with his proposals for their objectives.[134] He then outlined the need for an all-out 'push' and for divisions to attack in depth and asked his corps commanders for their views, being apparently open to their queries and keen to do his best to help them with their concerns. For example, Horne stated that communications were vital, but roads were in a bad condition in his sector. Rawlinson promptly instructed his CRE to push the necessary labour forward and to extend the railway system to make good the deficiencies of the back area roads. Then the use of tanks was discussed; here Rawlinson did most of the talking. Although he favoured a night attack, in order to make them less vulnerable to German artillery fire, it quickly became obvious that this was impractical. The idea was dropped, and the question of artillery co-operation with tanks was raised by the GOCRA of XV Corps (Br.-Gen. E.W. Alexander). After explaining his own views, Rawlinson asked his subordinates to consider the positions of the tanks and the attacking infantry and to discuss the plan and use of tanks with their divisional commanders. Discussion, at least between Army, corps and divisional commanders, was alive and well in Fourth Army. However, it is puzzling that Rawlinson seems not to have solicited much in the way of ideas on tank-artillery co-operation. After all, one of his corps commanders (Horne) was a gunner by training. This tendency also manifested itself in the next conference, on 5th September.[135]

Before the third meeting (on 10th September), corps commanders were sent a memorandum, accompanied by a map showing corps boundaries and "the proposed objectives for the attack," so that they could consider them and settle them at the conference.[136] In addition, they were asked to "consider... the question of artillery barrages and artillery lifts," so that the co-ordinated artillery plan could be drawn up later. However, once again a different attitude manifested itself when it came to tanks – "The general lines on which the Army Commander wishes the 'tanks' to be worked has been explained to you..." – though the memo went on to say that "your final proposition for their employment should be thought out before the conference." This was not merely a gesture, since at the latter, each corps commander was called upon in turn to put forward his views on the matter.[137] It was at this point that Pulteney made the alarming remark that "The tanks will go quickly through High Wood because they will have cover all the way."[138] As Pidgeon remarks, what he meant by "cover" is debatable; but in any case, why they should have been supposed to move more quickly through a shell-smashed, cratered wood than across open ground is unfathomable, not least because a Mark I tank was incapable of moving quickly under any circumstances. Then Horne gave his views on how the tanks should be used (in threes rather than fours, as proposed by Rawlinson), and these were accepted.[139] He went on to give a clue as to why, perhaps, he had not been consulted about tank-artillery co-operation. The statement that "The only use of a creeping barrage is to clear out men who are lying about in shell holes. I could never follow what is the value of a creeping barrage," casts doubt on his grasp of the methods being used in his own corps at the time (though it was not strictly necessary to use a 'creeper' if the enemy were confined solely to trench lines).[140] It is tempting to ascribe his elevation to the command of First Army, soon afterwards, more to the fact that he "as a rule saw eye to eye with Sir Douglas Haig" than to his technical abilities. One author has described him as "highly professional, a zealot for detail" and that as GOC XV Corps he "gained some notable successes by the skilled handling of his artillery, in particular the development of the creeping barrage."[141] Such a view seems ill-founded. While XV Corps' 'creeper' was the most sophisticated of those employed on 1st July, it was the idea of the GOCRA.[142] However, the planning for the 15th September attack was taking place in the same atmosphere of open discussion as had prevailed before the success of 14th July, and at no time did any of the commanders express the luddite views often attributed to Great War generals when confronted with new technology.

Cavan held a conference of his own after Army's. It is apparent that by now the need to give junior commanders time for preparation and reconnaissance before a major attack had been recognised (it took a minimum of six hours for corps orders to reach company commanders), and so

Cavan said that "It is essential to get out a clear cut-and-dried scheme as soon as possible so that all ranks may know what they have to do."[143] The engineering side of the operation was not neglected either; divisions were to select routes by which guns could be brought forward, and improve them if necessary. The corps' CRE was to be notified of these in order to avoid "over-lapping of work". And the ruse of Chinese attacks was to be employed once again. When the thoroughness of these preparations and exchange of views and information is considered, it is all the more surprising that there was effectively no liaison between corps commanders and the Heavy Section, Machine Gun Corps (i.e. the tanks). Corps were allotted tanks by Army, which they passed on to division, and the latter organised matters with the commanders of the tank sections (or even the individual tank commanders).[144]

As preparations went ahead, the evolution of the final plan continued. 56th Division queried the necessity of taking certain trenches which Army felt would give it observation into the village of Combles.[145] Corps backed division, and Army agreed; communication regarding conventional problems was still working well. Corps and Army orders for the operation were issued on 11th September, both including instructions for the artillery and on the use of tanks.[146] XIV Corps' tank instructions put them firmly under the control of divisions, even though the Army instructions gave the impression that they were the responsibility of corps. However, it is not possible to ascertain whether this was because corps felt that divisions, as the people on the spot, would best be able to work out where and when the new vehicles should be used, or because they were unsure of how to use them in the first place and so simply delegated the problem downwards.

As regards communications, it became apparent at this time that, because they were well served by contact aeroplanes, corps could at times have more idea of the tactical situation than front-line divisions or brigades; forward as well as backward transmission of information became essential.[147] This is borne out by a letter from Cavan to Edmonds in which he stressed "the vital importance of sending information <u>forward</u> [underlined in original] – not back..."[148]

Unfortunately, XIV Corps had a difficult time on September 15th.[149] The principal cause of the troops' misfortunes was that lanes were left for the tanks in the barrage. These exposed the attackers to severe enfilade machine-gun fire, especially from a German strongpoint known as the Quadrilateral, and the situation was exacerbated by the failure of 13 out of the 15 tanks allotted to the lanes to appear. In any case, as before, the pace of operations was too slow to ensure higher tempo for the attackers; the battle took 26 days to prepare. Even had the plan gone according to Haig's wilder imaginings, and the tanks had permitted the infantry to get past the German second line, an artillery bombardment would have been required to get them through the third line. This was never going to be possible; the BEF did not have sufficient artillery both to follow the infantry (and keep up with them, advancing across extremely heavily shelled terrain) and to provide the barrage. Even had artillery successfully kept up with the infantry, the techniques were not yet available to permit ranging on targets without a good deal of time spent in registering the guns on fresh targets.[150]

Reserve Army had carried on with its own operations during September, including a substantial involvement in the Battle of Flers-Courcelette. Much of this fighting was carried on immediately to the left of Fourth Army, but the Battle of the Ancre Heights (1st October-11th November) was conducted further to the west. On 5th October, Fifth Army issued a memorandum on attacks, which "has been written by the Army Commander for the guidance of Divisional and Infantry Brigade Commanders."[151] Once again, Gough seemed happy to bypass his corps commanders. The document was a summary of lessons learned during the campaign to that date, dealing with the need to attack in depth if deep penetration of the German position was the aim. Owing to the difficulty of getting information back, if waves succeeding the first one or two were kept in hand by a brigade or battalion commander, they might suffer very heavy losses and even be driven back. Consequently, the conditions at the time required a new way of looking at reserves. They were not "a body of troops who have no definite objective previously assigned to them [and] who are kept to meet unforeseen circumstances..." Indeed, this idea was explicitly rejected, since "the reserve can never receive orders to act in time and it is always wasted." Therefore it was essential for a brigade commander to reorganise the troops holding each objective, since once the second was being assaulted, the troops who had taken the first would constitute his reserve. This necessitated his keeping in close touch with the situation, so "It is a very serious error, almost an unpardonable one, when Brigadiers do not go forward as their command advances." Obviously Gough's propensity for telling his subordinates their jobs extended further down than just corps. Detailed examples of how to apply these principles were also provided; although the Army commander was happy to reject the principles of *FSR I* regarding reserves, he was happy to stick to the concept of principles itself. Nor did divisional commanders escape his attention. They had to reorganise the attacking brigades in order to create their own reserve. And both divisional and brigade HQs had to be sited so that, if at all possible, the attack could be observed. In this way they could keep in touch with what was going on even if communications with the troops at the front broke down. An important point was that "Any increase of distance between Divisional Headquarters and brigades adds greatly to the difficulty of communication, whilst an increased distance between Divisional and Corps Headquarters presents little difficulty." Presumably this was because divisional and corps HQs would be connected by tele-phone, and once the attack had started and divisions had regained control of their artillery, contact with corps heavies was less important than in the preliminary bombardment. Furthermore, corps would have the benefit of the RFC to see what was going on, and any reserves they held would be too far back to be any use, while counter-battery work could be under-taken throughout, without reference to divisions. If anyone was in any doubt that they were being told how to do their job, Gough stated that

> The art and difficulty of command lies in maintaining communica-tions, knowing the position of your troops and their tactical situa-tion, and thus being in a position to control them and form a sound plan based on the actual facts.

He went on to say that communications still presented major problems, since telephone communications were out of the question and runners took too long to get back with their reports. Consequently, rather than surrender the initiative to the enemy through inaction, the only way of addressing this problem was "the immediate energetic employment of supporting bodies in large force [which] will clear up the situation and regain touch with the advanced troops." How communications were to be maintained with these supporting bodies was not mentioned. However, the answer seems to have lain in inflexibility. All troops were to be "<u>previously</u> and <u>definitely</u> detailed to their objectives." The impli-cation was that if enough men were put in place, they would succeed in taking their objectives (though in fairness to Gough, he was obviously trying to maintain a high tempo). This is very reminiscent of VIII Corps' view before 1st July, and in the October fighting Reserve Army fared lit-tle better than that corps had, though the weather and the mud made its task far more difficult. Nevertheless, given Gough's cavalry background, it is interesting that he felt able to be quite so prescriptive when dealing with his subordinates. This may, of course, have been a quite reasonable reaction to the completely different nature of warfare in late 1916 to anything contemplated earlier. In July, the CIGS (Sir William Robertson) had written to Haig, in a somewhat bewildered tone, that "no war was ever so peculiar as the present one, and Field Service Regulations will require a tremendous amount of revising when we have finished…"[152] This exemplifies the difficult and novel situation to which the High Command struggled to adapt in 1916. At this time solutions were tried which were later discarded in favour of more traditional approaches and Gough was doing this in his command style, which was a depar-ture from *FSR I*. The difference between him and Rawlinson is marked; while the latter delegated authority to his subordinates at corps, Gough employed them as postmen.

Operations continued into November, GHQ applying pressure on Gough to achieve something substantial before the campaign was closed down, in order that Haig might have the benefit of a success at a conference of allied commanders on 15th November.[153] The state of the ground was discussed and that "there was… some difference of opinion as to whether the ground would be sufficiently dry." In addition, Fanshawe was able to discuss the time of the attack with Army, and "The question was referred to G.O.C. II Corps and to the divisional commanders." Obviously Gough was sometimes prepared to permit some discussion.

It also seems that the desire to continue attacks was not just restricted to Haig and Gough. Although Travers writes that "various Corps and Divisional commanders and staff… protested at the continuation of operations," another *Memorandum on Future Operations*, dated 16th November had Fanshawe perceiving (on 14th November) "a serious break on his front" and therefore wanting to attack.[154] He put the scheme, which for his corps consisted of capturing Munich and Frankfurt trenches, to the Army commander, who agreed to it. The first attempt failed, and on the 16th Fanshawe held a conference of divisional commanders to discuss the next effort.[155] Discussion of the barrage took up the bulk of the meeting, or at least of the notes, but there was also an exchange with the GOC 37th Division regarding the number of troops involved and the final objective. It may be that the corps commander was being especially careful to leave nothing to chance, given the failure of 2nd and 51st Divisions on the 15th.

That action was the subject of a detailed post-mortem; the divisions were asked to provide details of how they had carried it out, and the response is interesting.[156] The GOC 51st Division (Maj.-Gen. G.M. Harper) was far from cowed. He blamed his division's failure on the men being caught in their own barrage, and asserted that this was due to their impetuosity and that they were used to a faster moving 'creeper' than that used on the day. He even issued a veiled rebuke to Fanshawe, saying that "the chances of success would have been greatly increased if the attack had been carried out by a formation under one command."[157] The GOC 2nd Division (Maj.-Gen. W.G. Walker) was more careful simply to cover himself. He stated that he had told the Corps Commander that the only troops he had available were not familiar with the ground and that "the previous attack carried out by the… 112th Brigade had been very hurried and had failed and I was afraid if this was carried out in a hurry it would fail too."[158] Fanshawe having told him that "there was no alternative," he asked that the operation be delayed to permit the brigade at least to see the ground in daylight; "This proposal was not accepted…" Wisely, therefore, the commander of the brigade asked that the attack be run by the commander of the 99th Brigade, which had previously held the sector in question. However, in his report to Army, Fanshawe made it plain that he did not accept all of these points, since the positions had been attacked before and should therefore have been familiar. He did, however, concede that "More time was wanted for preparation..."[159] This did not shield him from Gough's criticism, though he replied to counter some of the latter's views.[160] However, pencil annotations to the Army document, presumably made by Fanshawe, were revealing. Army asserted that the corps order "puts too much on to the divisional commanders and does not exercise sufficient control over the operation. The want of strict Corps control is evident in several respects, e.g. ... No mention made of the capture of MUNICH TRENCH." The marginal comment was that "They do not understand that I am at the end of a telephone in touch with both Divisions and [illegible] has arranged for the MUNICH TRENCH in concert with me, but my order went out before."[161] The unfortunate Fanshawe was popular with no-one over the decision to use two divisions. Army "realised that the whole operation could not well be put under one commander, as suggested by the G.O.C. 51st Division, but this very fact made Corps control of timing and alignment very necessary."[162] Gough then moved on to the question of why 112th Brigade was placed under the GOC 99th Brigade, of which he strongly disapproved.[163] However, although Fanshawe's marginal comment was that he agreed with the action taken, his memorandum made no mention of this. He was most eloquent, though, in his marginal comment next to Gough's that "Copies of these remarks have been sent direct to the G.O's.C. 2nd and 51st Divisions." This was a presumably heartfelt "I hope not all of them."

All of this reveals that the two divisional GOCs were more prepared to stand up for themselves to Fanshawe than he was to Gough. Indeed, rather than blame his brigade commanders, Harper was prepared to blame corps. The reverse was true of Fanshawe, who obviously agreed with Walker and Harper over the questions of the barrage and the placing of 112th Brigade under 99th Brigade's CO, but was not prepared to say so to Gough, and even tried to deflect the latter's wrath downwards. The relative vigour of the divisional commanders' response may be explained by their feeling that they were more likely to be relieved of command than Fanshawe was (and Walker lost command of 2nd Division on 27th December 1916). The whole affair undoubtedly reflected far less well on both Gough and Fanshawe than the other protagonists; the former for his poor reasoning and indifference to the views of the men on the spot, and the latter for his dishonest transfer of blame.

Nevertheless, it is also true that genuine efforts were made to learn from experience. A number of these have already been mentioned, and after the battle was closed (on 18th November) Fourth Army produced a document entitled *Artillery Lessons of the Battle of the Somme*.[164] Its reflections upon the respective roles of Army and corps, were interesting, especially because of the existence of three different versions of the relevant page. All began by stating that the basis of the artillery plan must be set down by Army, with special emphasis on co-operation between neighbouring Armies and corps. (with slight variations in punctuation). In all three versions, the terms of reference of the artillery boiled down to counter-battery work, the type and duration of the preliminary bombardment, the employment of artillery in assisting the attack, night firing, and the use of balloons, anti-aircraft guns, long range guns, and survey posts.

The onus of responsibility for the operation fell on corps – "It is for Corps to build up their plan of action on these foundations." Furthermore, the plan had to ensure co-operation between and the best use of heavy and field artillery. The implication was that Army's role was to ensure that corps did its job, but that the plan of attack and the artillery component thereof were very much the responsibility of corps. While bearing this out, the next two sentences varied the most. In the first version, it read:

> The plan must be a Corps plan and the will of the Corps must prevail. Subject to this the greatest possible latitude should be allowed to subordinate commanders...

In the second, it read:

> No change in the general Artillery policy and plan of action should be permitted, except for strong reasons.... It is most important that subordinate formations and units should be afforded ample time to study and digest their tasks.

And in the third: "The full destructive powers of the available Artillery must not be sacrificed to or impeded by the whims of subordinate Commanders." The second sentence was as in version two. Obviously the author was unsure as to precisely how corps should treat division, though versions two and three indicate that an authoritarian attitude was preferred. That only version one went anywhere at all towards *FSR I* in its view of the importance of the man on the spot is perhaps the principal indicator of the direction in which the wind was blowing by late 1916. The enormous changes in the style and techniques of warfare employed by the BEF, and the need to impose consistency on a number of corps and divisions undreamed of in 1914, had led to a more prescriptive style of command. This was made all the more necessary because the commanders and staffs of corps and divisions had not been trained at these levels of command and consequently lacked the trained judgement required to use *FSR I* effectively. At Army level the prescriptive style was reflected by the increasingly active role taken by the comparatively authoritarian Hubert Gough as the Battle of the Somme went on, and even, perhaps, by the active role he played in 1917's fighting, whereas Rawlinson did not stage another major battle until 1918. The potential benefit of this to divisions was that at least it was stated in black and white that they required a reasonable amount of time in which to prepare for an attack; but this principle was often disregarded, if the Germans were thought to be in difficulties, as the V Corps attacks in November 1916 discussed above illustrate. It is plain that the question of how Army and corps commanders should best exercise their functions was by no means settled by the end of 1916, but the experiment of the Somme was leading towards inflexibility on their part. Communications had become so difficult on a Western Front battlefield that the solution offered by late 1916 was to try to deal with all eventualities before an attack. Despite the enormous difficulties in so doing, it is easy to see why experience led to a reluctance to permit any variation from the plan, lest it throw the whole complex machine out of gear. The vital need for a comprehensive artillery programme to permit any infantry advance exacerbated this. Such a programme in its turn was dictated by the relatively unsophisticated technology available to artillerymen, so that they needed time to carry out their tasks before any advance could be begun.

The remainder of this chapter is devoted to a summary of the arguments put forward and the conclusions drawn. In logistic matters, it became apparent soon after the war began that divisions' relative mobility made them unsuitable for traffic control in a given area, while corps, which to a far greater extent held the same part of the line all the time, were much better suited to the role. As the rail and road systems developed, corps also acquired definite responsibilities in relation to Army and their divisions regarding road maintenance and the supply of food and munitions. However, this was not merely the result of some abstract desire within the BEF to centralise for the sake of it. The role of corps expanded principally in the field of artillery command and control, notwithstanding the confusion that reigned for a time over the precise role of the corps GOCRA (or BGRA). In consequence, corps also received their own RFC units, which placed them at a crucial point in the chain of communications. They were closer to the fighting than Army, and could receive information about events in the front line faster than divisions. That machine-guns and mortars (for example) were concentrated mainly at divisional level indicates that the division was still viewed as the basic tactical unit of the army, and there is no evidence that corps staffs saw any reason to differ with this.

As a result of their role being larger than had been envisaged in 1914, and to a greater extent, the expansion of the BEF, far more experienced staff officers were required for corps than were actually available. The same was true of divisions, but while more expertise was required in simply moving them around than at corps level, the corps staff had to cope with providing an administrative infrastructure for a variable number of divisions, and the command of a frequently changing group of them. The OH suggests that there was a deliberate policy of keeping corps relatively static simply because to relieve all of their divisions at once was both difficult and time-consuming. Furthermore, although the corps most heavily involved in the Battle of the Somme had almost a third of the BEF's divisions pass through each of them, at least the corps commanders and their staffs were able to provide continuity of command in their sectors of the front, to know the ground and to inform newly arrived divisions of the important points. In addition, corps command of heavy artillery also tended towards immobility, since those batteries were very time-consuming to move (for example, a 9.2-inch howitzer took 36 hours to prepare for transit). It might be thought that corps commanders were more assertive in handling divisions than in 1915 because two-thirds of the former were pscs. However, this does not hold water, since on the Somme, of 10 corps commanders, only three were pscs, and of those, two (Hunter-Weston and Snow) were involved only at the start of the battle.[165]

The most important feature of the role of corps was in operations, and in particular in their planning. It is over this point that issue must be taken with Travers' view that discussion was discouraged in the BEF. Comparison of the planning for the start of the Somme offensive by III, VIII, X and XIII Corps (in Fourth Army) and VII Corps (in Third) reveals a consistent pattern of consultation between the Army commanders and their subordinates at corps, and between the latter and their divisional commanders. Objectives would be agreed between Army and corps, resources allocated and divisions expected to come up with the actual plans of attack. These, however, had to fit in with the corps artillery plan, which in itself had to conform to the very broad guidelines issued by Army. But the corps provided the parameters within which divisions operated, rather than dictating every detail to them (VIII Corps, however, was something of an exception in this respect), and conferences took place at corps as well as Army, in which genuine discussion arose. The differences found between corps' approaches to the planning process can themselves be explained by the hands-off approach of Fourth Army (and there is no evidence that Third Army was any more prescriptive) permitting them this latitude.

It is unfortunate that, notwithstanding this, the main plan of attack for 1st July proved to be so inflexible. At least partly owing to the difficulties of communications once the assault had gone in, corps commanders were powerless to do very much on the day. If an attack went very well, as for XIII Corps, there was little scope for initiative, since Army had not allocated them sufficient reserves for successful exploitation. If it went disastrously, as for VIII Corps, all the corps commander could do was to feed in his reserve division as best he could, given the limited information available, and attempt to change, on an ad hoc basis, an artillery plan devised weeks before. This was one of a number of factors which denied both Fourth and Fifth Armies the chance to attain higher tempo than their opponents during the whole campaign. The others were lack of strategic surprise and the sheer slowness of the advances made, combined with the lack of enough artillery both to support them and simultaneously advance to assist the next attack. The Germans always had sufficient time to react and the BEF lacked the men and material to launch a major attack elsewhere in order to unbalance them.

The pattern of discussion at all levels within Fourth Army continued throughout the battle, and though Sir Douglas Haig spent time in August telling Rawlinson that it was vital for him to supervise his subordinates closely, this was only intended to apply to the planning and not the execution of the fighting. In any case, it seems to have made no difference to the way in which corps handled their divisions, with the GOCRA XIV Corps permitting divisional CRAs to organise the precise details of their own barrages. Even the introduction of tanks was thoroughly discussed, albeit in an at times rather confused way. Interestingly, corps were quite happy to pass the detailed handling of the new weapon down to division on the day. However, the most important change in corps' role in Fourth Army by the end of the battle was that it had been realised how important it was for them not only to pass information back to Army, but forwards to division, as a consequence of their access to contact aeroplanes. From being a post-box in 1914, the corps was becoming a vital clearing house for information by late 1916.

From the start of its active role in the Somme campaign, Fifth (initially Reserve) Army exhibited a different way of doing things to Fourth. As early as 3rd July, a more hands-on and assertive command style was evident. Admittedly this seems to have made no difference to the way in which the Earl of Cavan did things in XIV Corps, but Lt.-Gen. E.A. Fanshawe of V Corps did his best to conform. By the end of July, Hubert Gough was attempting to instruct all his corps commanders in how to do their jobs. By August, orders were issued which virtually ignored corps and simply told divisions what to do. This may have reflected Haig's concerns about Rawlinson's excessively hands-off style at this time, but in any case, Gough continued in the same vein to the end of the battle, even issuing a memorandum in early October, telling divisions and brigades how to conduct an attack. The methods he advocated were implicitly inflexible, and relied upon having enough troops attacking in depth to cater for any eventuality, since communications were bound to break down and so deprive anyone but the man on the spot (if he had enough troops to hand) of the ability to influence matters. By the end of the battle, Fourth Army seems to have been in accord about the need for a strictly structured attack, under the close control of corps.

Finally, two factors were crucial in defining the role of the corps in 1916, and especially during the Battle of the Somme. The first was its more or less static position in the line, and the second its control of its own and its divisions' artillery. From the former came – it was hoped – a close knowledge of the ground, at a time when even small features of the terrain became vital to the success of attacks. From the latter flowed enormous influence over the planning of operations, for artillery was the key to success on the Western Front, and almost as importantly, corps' close liaison with attached RFC formations gave it possession of better information about what was actually happening on the ground than either Army or division. From this knowledge, power did not necessarily flow, for it was still imperfect and subject to delay in its transfer from the pilot to the corps staff, and thence to division. The adoption of a more prescriptive style of command in Fifth Army, and its commander's advocacy of close control over planning of operations was one answer to this problem. How the BEF attempted to apply the lessons of the Somme as it moved towards a solution to the problems posed by the new warfare, in the Battle of Arras, and subsequently in the great siege operation of Messines, is the subject of the next chapter.

NOTES

1 These were the British I–XI, XIII–XV and XVII, and the Canadian and I and II ANZAC Corps.

2 O.H., 1916 Volume 1, 58.

3 See Bond, Brian and Robbins, Simon (eds.) *Staff Officer. The Diaries of Walter Guinness (First Lord Moyne) 1914-1918* (Leo Cooper, 1987), 11, for the shortage of staff officers by 1916.

4 *10th Corps – No. G.S. 77.* Undated, but seems to be 21st September 1915. TNA: PRO, WO 95/850.

5 *Notes on Role of 10th Corps*, 22nd September 1915. TNA:PRO, WO 95/850.

6 Letter dated April 23rd 1930, from Major Philip R. Currie to Sir James Edmonds. TNA:PRO CAB 45/132. Rawlinson Churchill College Cambridge (CCC) diary, 11th June 1915.

7 See, for example, Griffith, Paddy, *Battle Tactics of the Western Front*, (Yale University Press, 1994), 214.

8 O.H., 1918 Volume 5, 610-11.

9 James Papers, IWM. Ledger book for 1916. (Order of battle information in this collection is organised in yearly ledger books.)

10 O.H., 1916 Volume 1, 57.

11 James Papers, IWM.

12 James, Captain E.A., *A Record of the Battles and Engagements of the British Armies in France and Flanders, 1914-1918,* (London Stamp Exchange, 1990) 10-14.

13 For Jacob, see Terraine, John (ed.), *General Jack's Diary,* (Eyre and Spottiswoode, 1964) 225. and 266. For Cavan, see Nicholson, *Behind the Lines*, 163-5.

14 In O.H., 1916 Volume 1, 364, III Corps' decision to send tanks into High Wood

on 15th September 1916 was described as "a tactical blunder." These are strong words for the OH.

15 O.H., 1916 Volume 1, 450. Hunter-Weston letter to his wife, 27th July 1916. Hunter-Weston Papers, British Library, no. 48365. 'Stellenbosched' was the term used in the South African War for those removed from active command in disgrace.

16 Nicholson, *Behind the Lines*, 192-3.

17 O.H., 1916 Volume 2, 569.

18 O.H., 1916 Volume 1, 186, fn. 3. Carrington, *Soldier...*, 104. "Corps we did not know and... the Corps Commander was rarely popular." A contrary opinion is given by Anthony Eden – "we were for most of the next eight months in Tenth Corps, commanded by General Morland, himself an officer in the Sixtieth whom we respected and liked." Eden, Anthony, *Another World*, (Allen Lane, 1976) 124.

19 Prior and Wilson, *Command...*, 137.

20 O.H., 1916 Volume 2, 202, 345, 457. Volume 6 (*Conferences and Various Source Papers*) of the Rawlinson Papers, IWM. In the conference of 29th September 1916, XIV Corps asked for 4th Division, but was told that GHQ's permission was required.

21 See the chart in GHQ papers entitled *Statement Showing Number of Days each Division has been in Front Line in Somme Battle*. TNA:PRO, WO 158/19.

22 Letter from the C-in-C to the War Office, dated 20th November 1914. See Henniker, Col. A.M. *Transportation on the Western Front*, (HMSO, 1937) 80-1. Also see Brown, *British Logistics...*, 54.

23 Henniker, *Transportation...*, 88.

24 Henniker, *Transportation...*, 152.

25 Henniker, *Transportation...*, 151.

26 Henniker, *Transportation...*, 102-3.

27 Henniker, *Transportation...*, 326-7.

28 O.H., 1916 Volume 1, 90.

29 O.H., 1916 Volume 1, 85.

30 O.H., 1916 Volume 1, 117-8.

31 O.H., 1916 Volume 1, 134, 137.

32 Longworth, *The Unending Vigil*, 12 and 19.

33 O.H., 1915 Volume 1, 12, fn. 1.

34 *10th Corps No. G.211*, 15th December 1915. TNA:PRO, WO 95/850. *Notes on a Conference held at VIII Corps, Headquarters, on 1st April 1916*. TNA:PRO, WO 95/820.

35 O.H., 1916 Volume 1, 61-4.

36 O.H., 1916 Volume 1, 65-6.

37 O.H., 1916 Volume 1, 78. Richter, *Chemical Soldiers*, 127.

38 *O.B./446*, 23rd October 1915. TNA:PRO, WO 95/757.

39 *R.A. 2nd Army, No 763*, 30th November 1915. TNA:PRO, WO 95/757.

40 O.H., 1916 Volume 1, 60-1.

41 Untitled XIV Corps memorandum, *ref. G.10/1.*, 5th April 1916. TNA:PRO, WO 95/910.

42 Conference of 6th April 1916, in Volume 6 (*Conferences and Various Source Papers*) of the Rawlinson Papers, Imperial War Museum (IWM).

43 See, for example, *VIII Corps G.*, 10th July 1916, which is addressed (amongst others) to the "GOCRA" and the "BGRA, CHA", and *XIV Corps No. S76/55*, of 25th August, addressed to the "GOCRA" and "XIV Corps, HA" (again, amongst others). TNA:PRO, WO 95/820 and TNA:PRO, WO 95/910, respectively. Re the CHA see *VIII Corps Scheme for the Offensive*, where the CHA was intended to be in telephonic contact with divisional artilleries but not the GOCRA. TNA:PRO, WO 95/820.

44 O.H., 1916 Volume 1, 25, fn. 2.

45 Travers, *The Killing Ground*, 105-7.

46 Letter dated 30th June 1916. Hunter-Weston Papers, BL, no. 48365.

47 See also Chapter 8.

48 For example, O.H., 1916 Volume 1, passim, Travers, *The Killing Ground*, 127-151, Prior and Wilson, *Command...*, 137-170. The latter does pay some attention to corps and divisions. Prior and Wilson, *The Somme...*, 58-61.

49 O.H., 1915 Volume 2, 11.

50 These were laid down retrospectively in a document produced early in 1917 by the CHA of X Corps: *Part Played By Artillery. Illustrate* [sic] *From Somme Battle*, 2nd January 1917. TNA:PRO, WO 95/863. Hereafter '*Part Played by Artillery.*' Notwithstanding its date, this document does not give a view purely based on hindsight. It deals with the preparations for the offensive as made at the time and only at the end is any critique of X Corps' or Fourth Army's plan offered.

51 *Part Played by Artillery*, 5.

52 *Part Played by Artillery*, 4.

53 *Part Played by Artillery*, 11.

54 *Part Played by Artillery*, 7.

55 *Part Played by Artillery*, 12-16.

56 Farndale, *Artillery*, 142.

57 *Part Played by Artillery*, 17.

58 O.H., 1915 Volume 2, 176.

59 *Part Played by Artillery*, 21-2.

60 O.H., 1915 Volume 2, 416.

61 *Fourth Army G.X.3*, 7th March 1916. TNA:PRO, WO 95/850.

62 *10th Corps G.S. 187*, 8th March 1916. TNA:PRO, WO 95/850.

63 *32nd Division SG 14/23*, 26th March 1916. TNA:PRO, WO 95/850.

64 *36th Division No.G.S./22/439*, 25th March 1916. TNA:PRO, WO 95/850.

65 *Notes on the Conference held at Xth Corps, Headquarters, on 6th April, 1916*. TNA:PRO, WO 95/850.

66 *Notes on Conference held at Fourth Army Headquarters, 16th April, 1916*. TNA:PRO, WO 95/850.

67 *Fourth Army GX 3/1*, 21st April 1916. TNA:PRO, WO 95/850.

68 *Xth Corps No: G.S. 187/2/4*. Undated, but in reply to the previous memo. TNA:PRO, WO 95/850.

69 *Report on a Visit to III Corps by Brigadier-General R. Benson, Commanding Heavy Artillery, V Corps*. Undated, but a reference in it to the Reserve Corps implies a date before 1st July 1916. TNA:PRO, WO 95/757.

70 *Notes of two Conferences held at Corps Headquarters – 21 & 23-6-16*. TNA:PRO, WO 95/820.

71 *VIII Corps Operation Order No: 3.* 15th June, 1916. TNA:PRO, WO 95/820. For XIII Corps' orders, see O.H., 1916 Volume 1, Appendices, 182-3.

72 *VIII Corps Scheme for Offensive.* Undated. TNA:PRO, WO 95/820.

73 O.H., 1916 Volume 1, 308. This reveals that VIII Corps' inexperience was Sir Douglas Haig's "only doubt" on the night before the battle began.

74 O.H., 1916 Volume 1, 431. Prior and Wilson, *Command...,* 165.

75 O.H., 1916 Volume 1, Appendices, 131-47.

76 Till, Geoffrey, 'The Gallipoli Campaign: Command Performances' in Sheffield and Till, (eds.) *Challenges of High Command in the Twentieth Century,* 35-6.

77 O.H., 1916 Volume 1, Appendices, 154.

78 Prior and Wilson, *Command...,* 158-160, *The Somme...,* 58-61.

79 *Third Army No.S.G.R.33/10,* 26th May 1916. TNA:PRO, WO 95/804.

80 *VII Corps G.C.R.* 237/8, 16th May 1916. TNA:PRO, WO 95/804.

81 *Third Army S.G.R. 33/7,* 23rd May 1916. TNA:PRO, WO 95/804.

82 *VII Corps G.C.R. 237/19,* 24th May 1916. TNA:PRO, WO 95/804.

83 Letter from Maj.-Gen. Sir L.J. Bols to Sir James Edmonds, 31st May 1929. TNA:PRO CAB 45/132. In 1916, Bols was Third Army MGGS.

84 O.H., 1916 Volume 1, 454.

85 Prior and Wilson, *Command...,* 182-4.

86 *Narrative of Operations of 1st July 1916, Showing the Situation as it Appeared to General Staff, VIII Corps, From Information Received During The Day.* Undated. TNA:PRO, WO 95/820.

87 O.H., 1916 Volume 1, 337 and 340.

88 Prior and Wilson, *Command...,* 184.

89 Prior and Wilson, *Command...,* 190.

90 Prior and Wilson, *Command...,* 187-190.

91 *Conference at 13th Corps Headquarters 7.7.16.* TNA:PRO, WO 95/895.

92 O.H., 1916 Volume 2, 24.

93 "Congreve... appears to be the man principally responsible for this highly innovative tactic and operational plan that was to be employed" Moreman, T.R. 'The Dawn Assault – Friday 14th July 1916', *Journal of the Society for Army Historical Research,* LXXI (Autumn 1993), 182. Thanks to Dr. J. Bourne for this reference. O.H., 1916 Volume 2, 62.

94 O.H., 1916 Volume 2, 65-6, and Prior and Wilson, *Command...,* 194.

95 *XIII Corps Operation Order No. 24.* 12th July, 1916. TNA:PRO, WO 95/895.

96 *XIII Corps 132/68 (G).,* 12th July, 1916. TNA:PRO, WO 95/895.

97 *Fourth Army Operation Order No. 4,* 8th July 1916, in O.H., 1916 Volume 2, Appendices, 1. *XIII Corps 132/68 (G).,* 12th July, 1916. TNA:PRO, WO 95/895.

98 *XIII Corps Operation Order No: 25,* 13th July, 1916. TNA:PRO, WO 95/895.

99 O.H., 1916 Volume 2, 66.

100 *XIII Corps Artillery Operation Order No. 5.,* 11th July 1916. TNA:PRO, WO 95/901.

101 Prior and Wilson, *Command...,* 199-201.

102 Prior and Wilson, *Command...,* 203-226.

103 See Bond and Robbins, *Staff Officer,* 162-3. Guinness was by no means the only officer who was critical of Fifth Army's methods in 1917.

104 O.H., 1916 Volume 2, 11, 14. And see Farrar-Hockley, Anthony, *Goughie,* (Hart-Davis MacGibbon, 1975) 185-6.

105 *Reserve Army GS 406/49,* 3rd July 1916 (presumably Malcolm was confused over dates at this point). TNA:PRO, WO 95/851.

106 O.H., 1916 Volume 2, 11.

107 *XIV Corps S.72,* 3rd August, 1916. TNA:PRO, WO 95/910.

108 *XIV Corps S.72,* 4th August, 1916. TNA:PRO, WO 95/910.

109 Travers, *The Killing Ground,* 168-9.

110 *6th Division – Battle Scheme:- Plan of Operations worked out in conjunction with G.O.C. 49th Division.* 7th August, 1916. TNA:PRO, WO 95/910.

111 *XIV Corps S.72,* 8th August, 1916. TNA:PRO, WO 95/910.

112 *6th Div. No. G/85/4.,* 8th August, 1916. TNA:PRO, WO 95/910.

113 *Notes on Conference held at XIV Corps Headquarters.* Date of 11th August 1916 given in text. TNA:PRO, WO 95/910.

114 *XIV Corps No. S.76/55,* 25th August, 1916. TNA:PRO, WO 95/910. Henceforth known as *Warning Order.*

115 Prior and Wilson, *Command…,* 222.

116 *Warning Order,* 1.

117 Prior and Wilson, *Command…,* 223. O.H., 1916 Volume 2, 202.

118 Prior and Wilson, *Command…,* 222-3.

119 *Warning Order,* 2.

120 *Warning Order,* 3.

121 *Notes on Corps Commander's Conference with Divisional Commanders. 25th August, 1916.* TNA:PRO, WO 95/910.

122 *XIVth Corps Artillery Operation Order No.14.* August 27th 1916. TNA:PRO, WO 95/915.

123 *Reserve Army G.A. 3/1/1,* 16th July 1916. TNA:PRO, WO 95/518.

124 *Reserve Army S.G.3/1/3,* 20th July 1916. TNA:PRO, WO 95/518.

125 Farrar-Hockley, *Goughie,* 188, 190. Henry Wilson later reported that Morland told him "how impossible Goughie was [,] taking command of his Divs. and Bdes. and patrols!" Wilson diary for 21st October 1916. Wilson Diaries DS/MISC/80 Reel 6, IWM.

126 Letter dated 1st July 1916. Hunter-Weston Papers, BL, no. 48365.

127 Letter dated 3rd August 1916. Hunter-Weston Papers, BL, no. 48365.

128 *6th Division No. G/85/24/9.,* 23rd August 1916. TNA:PRO, WO 95/747.

129 *V Corps G.X. 7204,* 24th August, 1916. TNA:PRO, WO 95/747.

130 *Reserve Army Operation Order No. 22,* 24th August 1916. TNA:PRO, WO 95/518.

131 O.H., 1916 Volume 2, 279-82.

132 *V Corps G.X.7417,* 9th September, 1916. TNA:PRO, WO 95/747.

133 *X Corps G.12/1/1.,* 16/8/16. TNA:PRO, WO 95/851.

134 *A Conference was held at Army Headquarters at 9.30 A.M., 31st August, 1916, Attended by the G.O's.C. III, XIV and XV Corps.* TNA:PRO, WO 158/419.

135 Pidgeon, Trevor, *The Tanks at Flers,* (Cobham, Surrey: Fairmile Books, 1995) 53-4.

136 *Fourth Army 299/16(G),* 9th September, 1916. TNA:PRO, WO 158/419.

137 Pidgeon, *Tanks at Flers,* 54-5.

138 Conference of 10th September 1916 in Volume 6 (*Conferences and Various Source Papers*) of the Rawlinson Papers, IWM.

139 Pidgeon, *Tanks at Flers,* 55.

140 Conference of 10th September 1916, Rawlinson Papers, IWM.
141 Blaxland, Gregory, *Amiens: 1918,* (Frederick Muller, 1968), 14. Thanks to Dr. John Bourne for this reference.
142 O.H., 1916 Volume 1, 349, fn. 2.
143 *Notes For Conference. XIV Corps S78/22.* Undated, but from the context the meeting was on 10th or 11th September. TNA:PRO, WO 158/419. O.H., 1916 Volume 2, 292. See also *2nd Division No.-G.S.1001/1/52,* 16th August 1916, in which the GOC, Maj.-Gen. W.G. Walker, VC, outlined lessons from recent fighting, including the importance of issuing preliminary orders and also the stages in the organisation of an attack by a brigade. TNA:PRO, WO 95/851. *Notes For Conference. XIV Corps S78/22.,* 3.
144 Pidgeon, *Tanks at Flers,* 57.
145 *XIV Corps S.78/29,* 11th September, 1916. TNA:PRO, WO 158/419.
146 *XIV Corps Operation Order No.51,* 11th September 1916. TNA:PRO, WO 95/911. *Fourth Army 299/17(G).,* 11th September 1916. TNA:PRO, WO 95/431.
147 O.H., 1916 Volume 2, 292.
148 Letter from Cavan to Edmonds, 28th March 1935. TNA:PRO CAB 45/132.
149 See Prior and Wilson, *Command...,* 239.
150 Prior and Wilson, *Command...,* 231-2.
151 *Reserve Army S.G. 43/0/5.,* 5th October 1916. TNA:PRO, WO 95/518.
152 Woodward, D.R. (ed.), *The Military Correspondence of Field-Marshal Sir William Robertson, Chief of the Imperial General Staff, December 1915-February 1918* (Army Records Society, 1989), 73.
153 *Fifth Army S.G.72/81 Memorandum on Operations.* 13th November, 1916. TNA: PRO, WO 95/518. The Reserve Army was redesignated Fifth Army on 30th October.
154 Travers, *The Killing Ground,* 187. *Fifth Army S.G.72/90* TNA:PRO, WO 95/518.
155 *Notes on Conference Held at V Corps Headquarters on 16th. November, 1916.* TNA:PRO, WO 95/747.
156 *V Corps GX.8325,* 16th November 1916. TNA:PRO, WO 95/747.
157 *Report On Attack By 51st (Highland) Division On Munich And Frankfurt Trenches On November 15th, 1916.* 18th November, 1916. TNA:PRO, WO 95/747.
158 *2nd Division G.S.1017/1/176,* 17th November 1916. TNA:PRO, WO 95/747.
159 *V Corps GX.8325,* 21st November 1916. TNA:PRO, WO 95/747.
160 *Fifth Army S.G. 72/86,* 25th November, 1916. TNA:PRO, WO 95/747.
161 *V Corps GX. 2325/2,* 26th November 1916. TNA:PRO, WO 95/747.
162 *Fifth Army S.G. 72/86,* 2.
163 *Fifth Army S.G. 72/86,* 2.
164 Undated. TNA:PRO, WO 95/431.
165 The non-pscs were: Congreve (XIII Corps), Cavan (XIV Corps), Du Cane (XV Corps), Horne (XV Corps), Fanshawe (V Corps), Jacob (II Corps) and Pulteney (III Corps). The pscs were: Hunter-Weston (VIII Corps), Morland (X Corps) and Snow (VII Corps).

CHAPTER 3

Corps Command between the Somme and Third Ypres: April to June, 1917

The Battle of Arras (9th April to 15th May 1917) is usually taken as the demonstration of the BEF having learnt from the Battle of the Somme, and implicitly as part of the argument for the latter not having been entirely a bad thing.[1] This chapter describes how the exercise of corps command at Arras differed from that on the Somme. Given that the revisionist point of view argues that the British Army's art of attack evolved steadily during 1916-17, corps command in the Battle of Messines (7th-14th June 1917) is then discussed and compared to Arras.[2] The evidence leaves no doubt that Arras did encapsulate the lessons of the Somme and that Messines represented a further progression in tactical and operational thought.

The historiography of the Battle of Arras falls into two groups. The first is the body of work dealing with the Canadian Corps' attack on Vimy Ridge, at the start of the battle, or with Julian Byng, its commander at the time.[3] Given that this attack, though very successful (partly through its having limited objectives) was actually a subsidiary affair to protect the flank of the main attack, its extensive literature would be surprising, were it not for its being a clear-cut victory (rare on the Western Front) and its importance in Canadian national mythology.[4] The second group is that concerned with the career of Edmund Allenby, then GOC Third Army; the most recent of these should be approached with caution, since it is given to making curious assertions, such as that Sir Henry Rawlinson was "unstuck" since he "detected some of the inbuilt contradictions within Haig's thinking [in 1916]."[5] Each set of literature tends to treat the other as something of an afterthought, with the latter in any case reducing Allenby's somewhat inglorious tenure of command on the Western Front to the status of a prelude to the revelation of his true abilities in Palestine. The only modern work on the battle as a whole is a largely anecdotal account.[6] It must be said that Arras has been badly neglected compared to the other battles of 1917.

The formations considered for this chapter are GHQ, First, Third and Fifth Armies and I, VII, XVII and XVIII Corps. Although XVII Corps is not in the original sample for this book, its central role in the offensive made its inclusion necessary. This is all the more so since this chapter is written principally from the point of view of Third Army and its corps, which undertook the brunt of the fighting. Unlike the Battle of the Somme, the same Armies and corps were involved in the Arras offensive, or remained in the same area, almost throughout, though the rate of divisional turnover was higher at Arras. However, it is not really possible to make meaningful comparisons between the figures for the two battles, given their different durations and the nature of one as the BEF's main effort for the year, and the other, as a subsidiary attack to assist the French. For information, however, a total of 30 divisions (including the same divisions passing through several corps) went through the active corps involved in Arras and the associated actions (e.g. Bullecourt), out of a total of 62 British and Empire infantry divisions on the Western Front at the time.[7]

Further changes to the composition of corps HQs took place after the Battle of the Somme. The GS branch acquired an extra staff officer and of the three GSO2s, one was now designated 'GSO2 (Operations)' and another 'GSO2 (Intelligence).' That this last post had previously been held by a GSO3 indicates how much more seriously the Intelligence function was now being taken at corps. In addition, a Corps Machine Gun Officer was appointed. The GOCRA's staff was increased by the attachment of a Lt.-Col. in charge of counter-battery work (the CBSO) and a Staff Captain (as a result of changes in the organisation of field artillery), and his ADC became the Reconnaissance Officer.[8] Intelligence Corps officers had been appointed to Corps heavy artillery headquarters in May 1916, but had remained under the control of GHQ Intelligence. However, in February 1917 they became part of the CBSO's staff. These changes reflected especially the greater importance paid to counter-battery work as the Battle of the Somme went on and the employment of machine-gun barrages, which required an officer to co-ordinate them.[9]

The planning for the offensive, as might be expected, began with GHQ allotting tasks and the wherewithal to attempt them to Armies, late in 1916.[10] This included the allocation of corps and divisions.[11] A clear pointer to the importance of the corps as a level of the BEF's organisation by early 1917 was a note from Haig's chief of staff, Kiggell, to Allenby in January 1917.[12] Since the latter was to have five or six divisions in reserve by the time of the attack, he was requested "to consider the advisability" of forming these into two corps, on the grounds that Haig thought that were there to be a successful attack, "they may be able to pass through and operate as corps." Before the war, of course, Haig had been in favour of the corps organisation simply because six divisions would be too many for one commander to handle (see Chapter one). Now he viewed corps as an effective operational unit and not just an administrative convenience. No reserve corps had been employed during the Battle of the Somme, although Reserve Army was first formed under the title of 'Reserve Corps' in April 1916. How XVIII Corps, as the reserve, was to function in both theory and practice will be related below.

The Army staff put forward its initial proposals for the offensive on 28th December 1916, based on the guns, ammunition and men available and on the "lines indicated by GHQ."[13] That choice of phrase hardly indicates a very prescriptive approach on the part of GHQ, and as the men on the spot, the Army staff felt able to amend their remit somewhat by placing a corps to the north of the River Scarpe. However, this was not particularly novel as compared to the Somme planning at an early stage. In fact, the same process of consultation and negotiation as for the Somme seems to have characterised the preparations for the Battle of Arras. That said, Haig delved into the detail of corps, divisional, and even brigade plans, discussing them with the commander of the formation in question, and amending in each scheme what he considered to be its weak points. That he also interfered in Army's plan was nothing new.[14]

The most important change to the Army scheme was the amendment to Allenby's artillery plan. He wanted a bombardment of only two days, but his MGRA (Maj.-Gen. A.E.A. Holland), the originator of the plan (and Allenby's sole supporter) was spirited out of the way to a corps command. His replacement (Maj.-Gen. R.St.C. Lecky), like everyone else, favoured a longer bombardment; Allenby then gave in. The OH is careful to record the dispute and its outcome without comment, although Lawrence James stresses the plan's unorthodox nature and Holland's freedom "from attachment to old dogmas."[15] However, since the 'dogmas' here were the products of the experience of the Somme, and so only just past the stage of themselves being experimental, it is more than a little unfair to present Allenby and his MGRA as far-seeing progressives, surrounded by stick-in-the-mud traditionalists.

In any case, that dispute lay in the future. Third Army having put forward its initial plan, GHQ supplied more details of their requirements in January.[16] Nonetheless, the Army plan of December and the requests for men and artillery therein were apparently accepted by GHQ. Therefore it was forwarded to corps "with instructions to draft their proposals..." The Third Army plan also dealt with the Army's needs in tanks, gas and aircraft (both balloons and aeroplanes).[17] Their operational control was not mentioned, however.

By this time the lessons of the Somme had been encapsulated in perhaps the most important of GHQ's ever-increasing series of helpful pamphlets, *SS135* or *Instructions for the Training of Divisions for Offensive Action*, dated

December 1916.[18] This 89-page booklet contained, to use modern jargon, the 'methodology' to be used by the BEF in planning and executing future offensives. It should not be thought, however, that *SS135* was designed for all offensives. Its introduction made it clear that the new document was intended "to apply specially to training for methodical attacks on prepared positions" and *FSR I* still applied for open warfare. Nor did it simply deal with training drills and the like, but with how the division was to organise for and plan an operation, and what the respective responsibilities of corps and division were. Thus, in Section I ("Issue of Orders by Divisional and Brigade Commanders") it was laid down that corps would allot divisions their tasks, and that the divisional commander would then devise his infantry plan. Once this had been approved by corps it could be issued.[19] This was reiterated and expanded upon later: "The Corps allots the task to be executed by the Division. The Divisional Commander will be informed of the frontage, objectives and assembly area allotted to his Division, as well as the Artillery support he may expect and the action of the Divisions on his flank."[20] It was also made clear that the artillery plan was now (other than for minor operations) a corps affair, to be co-ordinated by the GOCRA after consultation with divisions, though divisional commanders were enjoined to suggest any modifications to the plan which might make success more likely.[21]

Section II ("Objectives") dealt with the criteria divisions were to employ in selecting objectives "for each body of Infantry within the Division in any one operation." and so corps were omitted.[22] But in the next section ("Co-Operation Between Artillery and Infantry") it became clear that artillery planning was very much the province of corps:

> The plan for this Preliminary Bombardment is made out by the G.O.C., R.A., Corps, under the orders of the Corps Commander, and provides for the employment of all the artillery resources of the Corps[,] the co-operation of the Artillery of Corps on either flank being co-ordinated by the G.O.C.,R.A., Army, under the orders of the Army Commander.[23]

Clearly, as a result of its operational control of virtually all the artillery involved, corps had become the highest operational unit involved. Army was only mentioned in so far as it retained "general control" and would attend to liaison between corps in consequence.

Nevertheless, given their good local knowledge, divisions were to check aerial photographs of the enemy positions and nominate to corps points to be given special treatment.[24] If they needed assistance in wire-cutting from neighbouring field artillery, they were to request it via the corps GOCRA. Similarly, the GOCRA would organise and co-ordinate counter-battery work and the howitzer bombardment at zero hour.[25]

However, the creeping barrage was less a purely corps responsibility, given the need for good infantry-artillery liaison and also for infantry training in the techniques required to follow and exploit it. Consequently, its timing was to be fixed by corps after consultation with divisions, and though corps retained control of the barrage during the attack, divisions were allotted a number of batteries to deal with unforeseen circumstances on their front and were permitted the latitude to delegate their control down to brigades.[26]

Most of the subsequent sections dealt in impressive depth with the infantry's tasks and their means of achieving them, and little further mention was made of corps. Some traditional features appeared, such as the section on "Action of Reserves," which was based on the prewar (but still relevant) concept that commanders at any level should always have a reserve in hand. It also stated that "The man on the spot is the best man to judge when the situation is favourable…"[27]

The corps was briefly mentioned in its RE role – "The general policy for the employment of R.E. and Pioneers will be laid down by the Corps…" – in signals (as a provider of wireless sets to divisions), and it was stated that medium trench mortars would be incorporated into the corps artillery plan.[28] No mention of either corps or division was made in the section on tanks, which perhaps reflected their novelty.[29] *SS135* was the distillation of the experience of the Somme, and provided a template for subsequent attacks on prepared German positions, as will be seen in the planning for Arras.

The XVII Corps (commanded by Lt.-Gen. Sir Charles Fergusson) plan may be taken as typical of those submitted by the corps in Third Army, which it is to be hoped reflected greater experience and homogeneity of outlook among corps staff officers by this stage of the war than a year earlier.[30] For example, VII Corps staff issued its divisions with a list of files related to the offensive which – implicitly – they should have studied.[31] The XVII Corps plan was a 56-page document, of which 11 were devoted to operations, 10 to administration, 13 to the artillery, two to communications and 19 to "Subsidiary Instructions and Alterations" (this was issued on 17th March) to the administrative section. Fergusson stated in his covering memo that he wished "to issue this plan as the 'Instructions' on which Divisional Commanders are to work out their own plans in detail…" The detail of the document plainly reflected the lessons of the Somme, such as the emphasis on counter-battery work, the leapfrogging of assaulting battalions and brigades, long pauses on the objectives, the use of a creeping barrage, and specific proposals for dealing with German counter-attacks. The plan seems at first sight to have left little for divisional commanders to decide. However, that is the point. Following *SS135*, corps was quite happy to prescribe what generally went on, but left it to divisions to come up with their own ideas as to what they should do when the situation did not fit the general run of things. So, the positions of the assaulting and supporting battalions within each brigade were explicitly laid down earlier – but these were principles to be followed by all brigades in all divisions within the corps. This split in the nature of the responsibilities of corps and division, between the general and the specific or local, is not quite so obvious in plans for attacks on the Somme, and plainly shows the influence of SS135.

Another lesson from the Somme was in the handling of machine-guns. During the days before the attack they were intended to "prevent the enemy from repairing his wire" and "by indirect fire to search communication trenches, lines of approach, road junctions etc." Divisional commanders were therefore enjoined to co-ordinate the machine-gun and artillery programmes. In addition the tasks of these weapons in the assault itself were outlined. Though they were to accompany their own brigades, some were beforehand "to cover the advance of the infantry" and others to employ indirect fire, linked to the artillery barrage.[32] In XVII Corps, the control of this again fell to division, since although machine-guns were organised at brigade level, the artillery was not.[33] One officer not mentioned here, and apparently always neglected, was the corps Machine-Gun Officer, who never attained the independence or prestige of his artillery counterpart, in British corps at least (the Canadian Corps scheme for the Vimy Ridge attack gave him overall control of "machine gun barrages and fire organization…").[34] Like the GOCRA in the first half of 1915, the CMGO was more an adviser than a commander, since "The arrangements for the barrage for the whole Corps front may be co-ordinated by the Corps Machine Gun Officer… but the control of the barrage on each Divisional front must be entirely in the hands of the Divisional Commander immediately the attack starts."[35] Since the machine-gun barrage was linked to that of the artillery, it is most likely that the CMGO (if his services were required at all) simply acted as a liaison officer between divisional MGOs and the GOCRA.

Gas was still very much a separate arm, and corps was quick to pass it on to division – "600 gas projectors are being allotted to this Corps… Targets will be selected by divisional commanders."[36] Of course, it also fell within their remit, as a weapon to be used for specific tasks in definite areas. To an extent the same was true of the corps trench mortars which were allotted by corps but handled by division, as in 1916.[37]

However, tanks were a different matter. For the Arras offensive they were allocated to corps by Army, since they "were to operate on a plan co-ordinated for the whole Army front against selected objectives…"[38]. Therefore "Tank detachments will be placed under the orders of Corps Commanders in whose areas they are working," who were directly to liaise with the tanks' brigade staff.[39] Whether they liked it or not, corps commanders had control of the tanks in their area. Indeed, the tank brigade commander was to "act as adviser to Corps Commanders, will communicate with them on all matters of detail, and will send them his operation orders," which implied that corps commanders were even expected to take an interest in such arcana. It is interesting to speculate whether this reflected a view of tanks as being more valuable than they had been perceived to be on the Somme, and so not to be squandered willy-nilly by divisional commanders, but to be carefully handled by corps. A memorandum from 56th Division staff to the local tank commander made it clear that the divisional commander would come up with the detailed plan for the tanks, but the fact that the document was copied to corps indicates that it was necessary for corps to see and approve division's actions.[40] This is borne out by a scheme for the employment of tanks issued by the Heavy Branch, MGC on 1st April. It stated that bad weather meant that some tanks should be held in reserve for the time being, but that "a definite decision as to whether it will be expedient to employ these tanks should, I suggest, be made by the Corps concerned… after consultation with the Officers on the spot."[41]

The administrative portion of the plan was somewhat different from its equivalent on the Somme. The reception of new divisions was specifically dealt with, a file for each "containing detailed medical, traffic and provost arrangements" being prepared.[42] The details of ammunition supply reflected the creation of the Directorate-General of Transportation on 10th October 1916, the latter being requested to construct and operate the railway line for the corps heavy artillery's supply.[43] Corps (and Armies) now also lost such control over road construction and maintenance as they had previously enjoyed, this passing on 1st December 1916 to the Directorate of Roads. However, roads close to the front remained the responsibility of CREs of divisions, the boundary (which was that between the shelled and unshelled areas) being known as "the D.G.T. line."[44] Another novelty was the establishment of divisional salvage companies, which were to work under the aegis of "an Officer appointed to co-ordinate and supervise" their work; corps salvage depots were also established.[45] Traffic control was placed in the hands of divisions according to this plan; this is in contradiction to the OH Transportation volume.[46] Details of railheads, ammunition dumps, the processing of casualties and prisoners and the like, however, were much as in 1916.

One striking innovation was regarding the burial of the dead. It had been found from experience that "this duty must be carried out by troops not engaged in fighting…" who would therefore be drawn from a labour company. A Corps Burial Officer (colloquially known as 'the cold meat specialist') was appointed, who would collaborate with his divisional equivalent. Corps allocated cemeteries in back areas and divisions were expected to establish them in or near no man's land.[47] An appendix of five pages laid out the arrangements, from how to find an appropriate site for a cemetery, to how to mark graves.[48] The use of wood for crosses or markers was discouraged, since "troops will use it for firewood," and a diagram of the sort of pegs and tags to be employed instead was attached.

The artillery scheme at this stage was based on Allenby's and Holland's 48-hour bombardment, but the principles behind it were still based on lessons learned from the Somme. It was systematic right from the beginning. The numbers of guns for the length of front had been worked out and also the length of wire to be cut, and the bombardment was to be carefully observed. Different calibres of guns and howitzers were allotted tasks according to their capabilities, and several different barrages were to be fired on 'Z' Day, giving great depth to the area swept by shellfire. Crucially, compared to 1st July 1916, or even 15th September, counter-battery work was heavily stressed.[49] This was reflected by the setting up of the counter-battery staff under the CBSO and sound-ranging (to locate German artillery batteries) was coming into its own at this point too.[50] Although the overall principles of the artillery plan were Army's, the choice of targets was corps', in accordance with SS135.[51]

Essential to a successful conclusion to all of the foregoing activities were communications, and a Corps Signals Officer was appointed early in the year "to co-ordinate artillery communications."[52] The pamphlet SS148, Forward Inter-Communication in Battle was prepared at this time too, in only eight days.[53] Though it was not issued until March, it was an elaboration of the principles laid down in SS135, and so it is reasonable to assume that staff officers were mindful of it when planning in January and February 1917. However, its influence was not especially obvious in the corps plan, since it mainly dealt with what was to be done by lower formations after the attack had started, while the plan covered the corps arrangements which were to apply beforehand. The two pages of the communications section of the plan were a careful explanation of what telephone lines were needed and why.[54] As well as vertical (i.e. battalion to brigade to division) communications being catered for, so were lateral (e.g. between a battalion and its neighbours) and, importantly, those between a battalion and its supporting artillery. It was up to divisions and their subordinates to organise 'Forward Inter-Communication' in accordance with the SS pamphlets and to inform corps of their proposals. Corps would then act in its usual fashion as co-ordinator and guardian of the current orthodoxy. Hence, VII Corps asked divisions what their arrangements were for locating the leading infantry.[55] The next day, it issued the corps instructions for signal communications (presumably an amalgam of the information received from divisions), which covered "Telegraphs and telephones," "visual," "pigeons," "power buzzers," "wireless," codes, and liaison with the RFC, all of which had sections in SS148.[56]

Another innovation which emerged from SS148 was the presence of intelligence officers on the battlefield. These officers, from division downwards, were expected to move forward with the HQ to which they were attached and report from there back to their parent HQs. Those with the Forward [communications] Station of the brigade would "get in touch with attacking companies and platoons and report the situation at fre-quent intervals by message from the Brigade Forward Station." Whether this was tied to the elevation of a GSO3's post to the GSO2 (I) on the corps staff as the corps Intelligence Officer at this time cannot be determined, but it is obvious that serious efforts were being made to try to get informa-tion back from the attacking troops. After all, without it, higher formations could not exercise command at all responsively, and therefore, effectively, once the attack had been launched.[57]

Third Army's response to XVII Corps' plan was brief. The corps was instructed to send in "Details of the preliminary artillery bombardment giving zones, tasks, and ammunition allotted, for every group of... artil-lery" and also "The lifts, barrages and bombardments on the day of attack."[58] Plainly the original had not been sufficiently detailed, though in Third Army Operations no criticism of it was made, unlike the VI and VII Corps plans.[59] Corps responded as requested, with the caveat that

> Owing to the shortness of time I have had no opportunity of con-sidering these proposals in detail, and, as you are aware, only one divisional commander [presumably Maj.-Gen. H.T. Lukin of 9th Division] is at present available to consult as to the requirements of the different units, I cannot therefore bind myself to the proposals as they stand.[60]

Fergusson was stating that he favoured a consultative management style, and was not prepared to dictate – at this stage of operations – to the man on the spot. This was not a prescriptive method of command, though he was also covering himself against possible criticism.

The same style was evident in corps conference minutes.[61] Discussion was evident – "The method of concentrating the three attacking divisions in their assembly positions was discussed..."; "The future employment of the 184th Tunnelling Company was discussed..." and, most importantly, "The Artillery Programme was discussed..." The control of machine-guns was left to divisions (with schemes to be co-ordinated by the CMGO), and they were referred to *SS135*, Section XVI ("Machine Guns"). Its influ-ence was also shown when 56th Division's instructions on dress and equipment explicitly stated that they would be "as laid down in the pam-phlet... S.S.135...."[62] Nevertheless, the GOC 34th Division (Maj.-Gen. C.L. Nicholson) was still prepared to suggest an attack plan for his division which differed from the corps scheme, though Fergusson rejected it.[63]

The only Third Army conference minutes found for the period leading up to the battle are mutually contradictory in style. The first were like XVII Corps' in that discussion was encouraged among the officers present, and it was noted that "Every encouragement is to be given to [subordinate] officers to send forward their ideas..."[64] The second offer something of a

contrast. Although brief in the extreme, and so relatively difficult to inter-
pret, there is no hint of discussion. Allenby seems only to have solicited
progress reports from his corps commanders and other subordinates, and
passed on extracts from GHQ documents.[65] Tight control of corps was
evident, with the dictation of counter-battery principles and alteration of
attack plans without explanation.[66] An exception to this was the Cavalry
Corps, which was left to liaise with other corps as it saw fit, and even
with Fifth Army, without the usual exchange of preliminary memoranda
between the Army staffs.[67] Notes from a conference in late May intimated
that "situations affecting future operations on the Army front were discussed," but no record of anyone's views but Allenby's was preserved.[68]
It is difficult to establish a definite view of how he commanded the corps
in his Army with so little evidence of this kind, but what there is suggests
a prescriptive style, which would accord with the general view of his
character.

In general, corps was at its most assertive regarding gunnery, as per
SS135. In the corps artillery plan, the movement forward of batteries
was also dealt with in some detail, even down to the construction of
gun pits and trenches to link them.[69] The allocation of only field guns
and howitzers to breaking up counter-attacks, another innovation, was
covered, as was the establishment of artillery liaison officers (contained
in both *SS135* and *SS148*). In the event, these officers had mixed for-
tunes, the field gunners' work with the infantry being fairly successful,
but the heavy artillery officers' less so.[70] In addition, corps set out the
policy that "The commander of all field artillery grouped to cover the
attack of any division must be the C.R.A. of the division carrying out
the attack..."[71] There was, perhaps something of a de-mystifying of
the gunner's art at this time – the artillery techniques employed by the
BEF had begun to become more routine than before (a VII Corps GS
document issued in March refers to "the usual barrages").[72] Indeed,
it was impossible for any senior officer in the BEF to avoid becoming
something of a technocrat, once sophisticated artillery techniques were
established. However, the GOCRA's dominance was confirmed in a
document issued by the War Office in January 1917, which stated that
"there can be but one commander of the artillery of the corps, both field
and heavy" and this was him. Perhaps the most important aspect of
all this was that "all the artillery, for the first time, worked to the same
master plan."[73]

The planning of the Battle of Arras was very much a reflection of the
lessons of the Somme, as expressed in the pamphlet *SS135*. Since staffs
were now more experienced, corps were less prescriptive in their dealings
with divisions too, and their respective responsibilities were now clearer.
Corps dealt with the general (or operational) and divisions with the local
(or tactical).

The role of corps in the actual attack was minimal. In his account of the first day's fighting, Captain Falls made only a few references to them, usually in the context of corps commanders agreeing to break off the action at nightfall and issuing orders to carry on the next day, or ordering reserve divisions forward. *Third Army Operations* dealt only with what they reported to Army.[74] As on the Somme, corps commanders could do little to influence events once the attack had started, at least until reports on the situation at the front of the attack began to come back. The situation of Sir Ivor Maxse was even worse. The XVIII Corps, as the Army reserve, had originally been envisaged as advancing as a complete corps to exploit the success and its constituent divisions were to be trained in that role.[75] However, at some point in mid-March Allenby's ideas seemed to change, perhaps in response to the German withdrawal to the Hindenburg Line, and XVIII Corps began to be seen just as a convenient administrative hole in which to put reserve divisions until they were needed by one of the active corps.[76]

It appears that the end of the First Battle of the Scarpe (up to 14th April) was marked by a failure in inter-corps co-ordination, notably between the left of VII Corps and the right of VI Corps.[77] *Third Army Operations* mentions that there was a discrepancy between the respective positions of the two corps, but does not apportion blame. However, from the point of view of the exercise of command, the most striking event in the Battle of Arras took place on 15th April. Allenby (having been told of Haig's decision that there should be a pause in operations) received via VI Corps a report of a 'resolution' by the commanders of 17th, 29th and 50th Divisions at a conference held on the 15th April and attended by VI Corps' BGGS (Br.-Gen. Lord Loch). This 'resolution,' it is alleged, took the form of a protest to Haig regarding Allenby's persistence in launching small, poorly co-ordinated attacks, with little hope of success and considerable casualties. Notwithstanding this unusual way of proceeding, the divisional commanders were informed that Allenby agreed with their proposals.[78] James makes the affair out to be rather sensational, but he relies on Edmonds' tittle-tattle as his source.[79] However, the matter was not even mentioned in Haig's diary and Haldane's simply recorded the conclusions of the meeting without mentioning any 'protest' at all. It is therefore difficult to be sure whether the meeting actually took the form Edmonds suggested. Surely Haig or Haldane would have noted a case of corps sending a round robin to the C-in-C, which was hardly the customary way of doing things in the BEF!

Nevertheless, a spirit of forthright expression was evident in Third Army at this time, since Maj.-Gen. Hull wrote to VII Corps on 17th April that he did not favour an operation proposed for the 20th. His battalions were under strength, and the weather was so vile that "if it keeps wet then this Division [56th] will be in no state to attack."[80] His views must have had some effect, since the division was moved to XVIII Corps on 20th April.[81]

Hull's case was doubtless assisted by the fact that the VI and VII Corps commanders and General Horne of First Army all wanted postponements of operations at this time, and, and Allenby himself told GHQ that "he considered it inadvisable to undertake any operations before the 22nd, as the troops would then be in better condition."[82] As a result, "Sir Douglas Haig, as almost always, deferred to the wishes of the commanders on the spot."[83] This he was not prepared to do in May, when Allenby himself objected quite persistently (by the standards of disagreements with Haig) to the continuance of attacks with tired troops in bad conditions.[84] But as Haig's immediate juniors, Army commanders probably had their ideas more often overridden by him than did anyone else.

From the point of view of the exercise of corps command in the field, the rest of the battle followed much the same pattern as has already been described. A good example of corps leaving matters to the man on the spot was VI Corps permitting divisions to arrange their own barrages on the afternoon of 23rd April, although the confusion existing at the time was such that it was probably the only viable option if another attack were to be launched that day.[85] However, some points of interest and changes to procedures followed earlier did arise. For example, barrage speed was varied to suit the state of the ground, and the SS series of pamphlets continued to be in evidence, *Third Army Artillery Instructions No.12* (of 18th April) referring specifically to *SS134, Instructions on the Use of Lethal and Lachrymatory Shell* and an Army memo regarding low flying German aeroplanes called attention to *SS142, Notes on Firing at Aircraft with Machine Guns and other small Arms.*[86] The tank arrangements for the fighting after the First Battle of the Scarpe were different from those for the latter, since though once again tanks which could not be used were to be kept in corps reserve and not used without Army's permission, active tanks "in Corps area [sic] may be placed under direct orders of Divisional Commanders if Corps Commanders wish to do so."[87] Army took the view that "It seems very doubtful whether, except in the case of limited objectives where strong hostile resistance is practically certain... it is sound tactics to detail Tanks to objectives in the original plan of attack." and that they should be placed "at the disposal of Divisional or even of Brigade Commanders, to be used as circumstances may decide, to overcome such local opposition as may hold up the advance of the infantry."[88] This also brought out the differentiation between the local or tactical, which fell into the province of division (or below), and the general, or operational (i.e. relating to the operation as a whole), which did not. The Heavy Branch MGC themselves preferred to be corps troops, being allotted objectives by corps and having reserves held at that level. The one person, it seems, whom they did not expect to control tanks during operations, was the senior tank commander at corps or Army, who was expected to act only as an adviser.[89]

In order to deal with German counter-attacks, Army told corps to consider the use of wireless to send warning to batteries set aside for this duty.[90] It is likely that other forms of signalling had been found wanting earlier; certainly the OH takes the view that communications and consequent poor preparations for attacks were generally a weak link in the British effort at Arras, doubtless reducing tempo too.[91] That the counter-attacks were taken very seriously is shown by the stress placed on registration of their probable forming-up areas and routes forward in *Third Army Artillery Instructions No.13*. This reflects their increasing effectiveness as the First Battle of the Scarpe went on and German tactics were improved.[92]

Third Army were quick to circulate "Notes on points of instructional value" after the First Battle, issuing them on 19th April.[93] Their ultimate destination was obvious, given that "Sufficient copies are forwarded to admit of issue to battalions." Another tactical lesson was expressed in Army's view that "The recent operations have brought out strongly the necessity of the appointment of a Divisional Machine Gun Officer if full value is to be obtained from the Machine Guns in the Division."[94] Indeed, since the matter had already been raised with GHQ in February, Army announced that it now was unilaterally going to permit divisions to appoint these officers if they wished. No mention was made of CMGOs, and the arrangement of barrages and the like was allocated to Divisional MGOs in any case.[95] Division was still the BEF's basic tactical unit, at least as far as Third Army was concerned. Fifth Army's approach differed, since an order in May said that "Corps machine gun officers will arrange to co-operate in a realistic manner in all artillery feints. Programmes to be drawn up by the Corps machine gun officers and G.O.C., R.A. for the approval of Corps Commanders."[96] However, this emphasis on the CMGO may only have arisen because in this specific case the operation in question was primarily one of artillery, and that, of course, was controlled at corps. No mention was made of command being exercised by the CMGO. This was surely very sensible, since machine-guns were capable of use at a far lower tactical level than artillery, and to concentrate their command at corps would have rendered them inappropriately inflexible at the tactical, divisional, level.

The emphasis on division was reinforced in a document issued by GHQ and passed on by Third Army to corps for their views.[97] It stated that "A large number of different forms of drill for rapid wiring are at present taught in divisions and schools" and that a standard to be applied across Armies was required, since "As divisions are continually changing, a general agreement on the subject is desirable." Presumably the 'changing' referred to was both in their internal composition, as replacements for casualties arrived, and as they were moved between corps. This also demonstrated that Third Army was prepared to canvass opinion from corps in administrative matters. This was confirmed later, when Army asked corps to consider the retention or otherwise of the Corps Depot Organisation, the final decision being left to the corps commander.[98]

First Army, under Sir Henry Horne, encouraged far more discussion than in Third Army. The GOC XI Corps (Lt.-Gen. R.C.B. Haking) wrote to Army on 18th March with a frank statement of his view of at least part of a corps commander's role. He protested at the assignment of only two divisions to hold a four-division frontage in his area, with deleterious effects on the troops involved, because of both the amount of work expected from them and anxiety at the width of their frontage. After all, "The Company and Battalion Commanders are... subject to the ordinary frailties of human nature, which in most cases have not been eliminated by many years of military training." (So much for the New Armies.) Consequently, though Haking did not wish to be presumptuous by actually suggesting any change in dispositions, he felt obliged to raise the issue. Finally,

> My Divisional Commanders bring their troubles to me, and I can encourage and cheer them and their troops to exceptional exertions, so long as I can tell them that we are helping in the great battle... If, however, I am unable to tell them this, or if I cannot produce sufficient arguments to carry much conviction the situation is not so satisfactory.

Interestingly, Horne himself spoke to Haking, in order to reassure him, and did not leave it to his MGGS to convey his reply, as was usually the case.[99]

Conference minutes bear out this consultative style. Thus, "The Army Commander asked for the opinion of corps commanders as to whether the enemy intends to withdraw," and the response of each was recorded. Horne explained the overall plan of operations for First Army to them, and "Discussion then took place as to the roads which could be allotted to Corps."[100] He then pointed out to the corps commanders that they, as well as Army, were entitled to give priorities to Corps Roads Officers in their work, and other administrative details were arranged. The most striking of these was that "Corps Commanders will go into the question of battalion arrangements for resting the men at every opportunity; and of feeding the men before the battle... Good results were obtained in XV Corps on the SOMME, by reports from divisions... that food had reached... troops in the line." Horne had had a more active tenure as a corps commander (in large-scale operations, anyway) than Allenby or Gough, and so could more reasonably refer to it. Furthermore, his experience put him in a better position to interfere with this sort of administrative detail in divisional arrangements. Thus, "The importance of the Infantry communicating with contact aeroplanes is to be emphasised. It is likely to be neglected by tired men under fire."[101] And "Anything that can be done...

to indicate to the artillery the position of the infantry well repays the trouble taken..." The consultative tone continued, since the next conference had as its object "to obtain the views of Corps Commanders as to the earliest date on which they could launch the attacks for which they were to be responsible..."[102]

The conclusions which may be drawn regarding the operations of corps at Arras are as follows. Firstly, the whole process of planning the attack was more routine and standardised than before, thanks to *SS135* and the experience of the previous year. The relationships between commanders' subordinate officers were also clearer, so that the MGRA exercised overall control of artillery techniques and made sure standard principles were followed, while the GOCRA actually planned the use of the guns on the ground; divisional CRAs were responsible more to the GOCRA than to their own GOCs. Indeed, standardisation of artillery techniques was such that non-specialists were familiar with at least the concepts. No such consensus yet existed with regard to the use of either tanks or machine-guns, but opinion may have been moving towards the corps planning the use of both, with the execution being the province of the specialists in liaison with divisions. The pattern of influence between corps and divisions seems to have been quite settled as a split between the operational and tactical, which, given the problems of communication that still existed, seems appropriate. Not everything could be foreseen in the corps plan, or even in the divisional plan, on the day, so it was necessary to delegate – as in *FSR I* – to the man on the spot. Despite the efforts made in improving communications, it was not possible for corps to be responsive enough to exercise battlefield control of infantry.

Notwithstanding the innovations of Arras, exemplified in *SS135*, the latter did not replace *FSR I*. Nor did it impose an especially prescriptive style of command on the BEF, even though works published since the 1960s provide a picture of senior officers down to GOCs brigade as obedient automata, terrified of being sent home. Discussion and the expression of dissent at the Army-corps (depending upon the Army) and corps-division levels were alive and well, and corps and divisional commanders were quite prepared to express strong opposition to Army and even, perhaps, to undermine their Army commander by appealing to GHQ if necessary. That the Army-corps relationship was more open to variation than corps-division, may be an indication of how much more headstrong and opinionated generals were inclined to be, the more senior they became. In addition, corps commanders were less likely to be sacked than their divisional counterparts, for it was harder to find even half-competent corps commanders than new divisional GOCs. Furthermore, the influence of a formation over how an attack actually went declined in inverse proportion to its distance from the front after the first, fully planned, set-piece attack, with reviews at all levels, had gone in. Therefore the high point of

Army control was actually before it began its offensive, and this was the Army commander's biggest chance to get the organisation right; it is not surprising that some incumbents tended to throw their weight around in consequence. Although this was partly true for corps, it did control the artillery and so retain more direct control after zero hour, and being more junior in any case, corps commanders presumably were more inclined to follow the rules regarding interference with subordinates.

Turning to the question of whether the BEF was able to achieve higher tempo than the Germans, it must be said that the situation was little better than in 1916. Staffs were now experienced and a formula for launching a successful limited attack had been devised, but artillery techniques were still at a stage of development where observed fire was essential to achieve accuracy, and such fire necessarily took time and advertised the location of the forthcoming attack to the defenders. Even when a success such as that of 9th April 1917 was achieved (errors on the part of the German commander leading to it being to some degree a strategic surprise), the tempo of the attack was not high enough for the advance to be exploited before the Germans brought up reserves. Had the BEF had the artillery, a feint bombardment could perhaps have been launched elsewhere on the front, but this was not possible in early 1917.[103] And communications were still not yet good enough to assist in raising the tempo of operations; once attacking troops left HQs with telephones behind, they were still effectively lost to view.

The plan for the attack at Messines started, as usual, with Army asking corps to propose plans for a scheme of attack, months before it actually took place. In January 1917 X Corps produced three documents relating to a draft plan, including a detailed artillery appreciation which contained numerous calculations of the frontage (considerably greater at this point than it was in June) and depth to be shelled and consequent requirements in guns and ammunition.[104] From March to May, the usual process of negotiation between Army and corps and corps and divisions took place so that a definite plan could be arrived at, though discussions between Haig, Rawlinson and Plumer led to a final choice of objectives being made later in the planning process than might otherwise have been expected.[105] On 18th March, Army issued a general plan of attack, including objectives.[106] Corps in its turn passed these on to its divisions and requested plans from them, with a statement of what they should contain.[107] It went on to send Army its plan at the end of the month.[108] However, the whole process was repeated after Haig rejected Plumer's March plan, so Army sent out a memo on 13th April which increased the depth of the attack, triggering another flurry of planning on the parts of corps and divisions.[109] The final version of the plans was indicated in *Second Army Operation Order No.1*, dated 10th May, followed down the line of command by *X Corps Operation Order No.83*.[110] This plan, brought on by a further increase in the depth of the advance ordered by GHQ, was attended by an increase in the artillery available to Second Army which it was hoped would make this possible.[111] By then, one important difference from earlier attacks which had arisen was that "The Army will shortly co-ordinate the objectives of the different Corps taking part in the offensive and the times at which they are to be reached and the Corps will then lay down the objectives and barrage times for the Corps front."[112] From this, it appears that Army was not so much prescriptively setting the exact action of the artillery, as its timetable, on the understanding that corps would follow whatever artillery principles had been laid down, while still adhering to schedule. Indeed, to ensure that all went according to plan, Army sent two staff officers round its corps, each day from 31st May, to glean information on the progress made in wire cutting, destruction and counter-battery work.[113] Although corps were permitted to put forward their own ideas for the timing of the operation, the final decision was Army's.[114] Corps then indicated to divisions the positions to be occupied, and how soon after zero hour this was to be done. Their artillery instructions described organisation and ammunition requirements and displayed a less prescriptive style, in that a memorandum had "been sent to Divisional Artilleries indicating on general lines the positions, and arrangement of arcs of fire of batteries... also suggestions as to the most convenient grouping with a view to economy in communication."[115] Evidently division arranged the details of their artillery and machine-gun barrages (within the limits of the time-table), and the GOCRA co-ordinated the final overall arrangements for the corps.[116]

All these plans were very much based on experience gained during the fighting of 1916, demonstrated especially in their emphasis on counter-battery work, the time-tabled barrage throughout the operation, and the application of machine-gun barrages. The ideas behind them were encapsulated in the pamphlets SS135, SS148, SS98 (*Artillery Notes*) and SS145 (*Notes on R.E. preparations for, and the employment of, the R.E. in offensive operations*, dated February 1917).[117] In addition, documents such as *Some lessons from the Operations of the Third Army in April and May 1917* (referred to above, with regard to the employment of tanks) and SS158 (*Notes on Recent Operations on the front of First, Third, Fourth and Fifth Armies*, dated May 1917) provided information on lessons from Arras.[118] Consequently, the artillery plan was closely modelled on First Army's at Arras[119] (which included the Vimy Ridge attack), and for X Corps machine-guns, "the organisation adopted was that used in the Canadian Corps," which seemed to give the CMGO rather more to do than usual.[120] Tanks were dealt with much as at Arras, though in the corps operation order for Messines their limitations were stressed more than before Arras.[121] This presumably reflected more realistic expectations of their performance now. Corps was slightly more concerned in the handling of gas than at Arras, since the use of gas shell meant its integration into the corps artillery plan.[122]

However, communications was the area in which methods differed most between Arras and Messines. As ever, observation of the area to be bombarded was vital to success, not least since part of the German position was on a reverse slope, so the role of balloons and aeroplanes was given more emphasis than before. This was all the more important since it was realised to what extent the German defensive system now relied on depth and the use of counter-attacks, for the defeat of which good observation and aerial photography were required.[123] Counter-battery work was also assisted by tying RFC Flights to counter-battery units.[124] Furthermore, once the attack had begun, contact aeroplanes, especially marked as such and sounding klaxons to summon forth the desired flares from the infantry, were vital in getting tactical information back to HQs.[125] Others were detailed to patrol in order to give warning of German counter-attacks. Reliance was also placed on getting telephones forward, though a report after the battle stated that "The system introduced by G.H.Q. SS.148 was to a great extent a failure, and its failure would have been more noticeable if... the weather had been less favourable for aeroplane work."[126] This view would seem to be borne out by the fact that many casualties on the overcrowded ridge on 7th June were caused by poor communication with the artillery.[127] The usefulness of divisional and brigade liaison officers as prescribed by *SS148* was mixed, but those with battalions were generally not much good, owing to their inability to communicate after the advance.[128]

Not mentioned in *SS148* were Army and corps liaison officers, though their employment was one of the most significant innovations of the battle. Plumer's most recent biographer wrote that "To each of his corps he attached a young liaison officer, his special task to know each of the thirty or so infantry battalions in the corps and to spend at least two nights a week in the front-line trenches with one of them."[129] This does not give a great amount of detail, and it is even possible that these officers and the corps liaison officers were the same men referred to in different ways. Powell makes no mention of there being a corps equivalent of his Army observers, though this may just reflect the tendency of Great War generals' biographers not to say much about their subordinates. The corps, however, did not detail officers to battalions only. Their primary role was to assist divisions or lower formations and to act as a go-between if they had lost touch and only secondarily were they "the eyes and ears of the Corps Commander" since divisions were necessarily going to be too busy to pass detailed information back.[130] Normally they would make a "tour" of unspecified length and then report back to corps HQ, but if necessary they could send an immediate report "by telephone, telegraph or despatch rider." The use of these forms of communication would seem to preclude the observers' being involved in action, but this was not the case and they were also supposed to report back during the attack. Attention was especially to be devoted to reporting whether or not neighbouring units were in touch. German artillery fire was to be assessed, presumably to assist the counter-battery staff at corps. On captured ground, the progress of consolidation and the presence of good or bad observation and of perceived weak spots in the new line were to be passed back, as was the state of communications. All this represents a substantial effort to alleviate the communications difficulties which characterised the battlefields of 1916 and 1917, and hence to raise tempo. As a means for corps and Army to find out what was happening in subordinate formations before an attack started it seems to have been useful. However, it is hard to see how these men could have got round the sheer physical difficulties of getting information back across the zone disrupted by the attack, especially if it had been successful and the attackers had got well forward across badly ploughed up ground, so tempo was not likely to be affected by their efforts.[131]

However, the use of liaison officers does provide a pointer to one crucial way in which Second Army's style differed from those of its peers. The plans and reports for the Battle of Messines all show the pattern of discussion and evolution of plans characteristic of the BEF (in varying degree according to Army) and seen earlier in this chapter. However, the differences in the way the artillery plan was organised have been pointed out already. In addition, it is reasonable to extrapolate from the brief of the corps liaison officers that their Army equivalents were to act as the 'eyes and ears' of Sir Herbert Plumer. In that role they not only could raise problems in the Army's provision of services but also deficiencies in the corps' or divisions' application of the principles laid down by Army. Thus, having laid such principles down (helped by reference to the appropriate SS pamphlets), Army could use the liaison officers (as well as more traditional sources of information) to ensure that their remit was followed, and so there was no need to interfere in the details of their subordinates' plans other than to exercise the necessary co-ordinating role. Furthermore, if anecdotal accounts are to be believed,[132] Army stressed to subordinates down to battalion level that its role was to help them do their job, rather than simply to press them into conformity with the Army plan. This was the carrot; since Plumer was also careful to ensure tight control of patronage in the Army, he also had a stick, lest any corps commander (for example) be tempted to deviate from what was a well thought out and complex scheme.[133] This relatively indirect style of organising the participants in the offensive was perhaps more 'managerial' than that of any other Army.[134] Plumer's MGGS, Maj.-Gen. C.H. Harington, said after the war that Plumer's method "was not to fix objective lines, but to suggest some – and then take every corps and divisional commander's opinion, adjusting to local [i.e. tactical] needs and opinions until all agreed with the final lines. [A] Policy of trust…" This successfully combined with the question of patronage and his "continually travelling about the 33-mile front and [having] staff officers [i.e. liaison officers] living in sectors in touch with troops."[135]

As has already been noted, however, a striking difference from the planning before Arras was that corps permitted divisions more latitude in the handling of their artillery, and in this way were acting much as did Second Army. Close liaison of heavy artillery with divisions was helped (in X Corps) by placing HAGs into Double Groups, the commanders of which liaised directly with divisional GOCs and CRAs and organised their daily programmes to conform to divisions' wishes as much as possible. At the same time they also had direct telephonic communication with the corps CHA, so that although it was "impossible for the B.G.C.H.A. and G.O.C.R.A. Corps to collaborate personally in detail with divisions… the Corps Commander was, through his G.O.C.R.A., assured of control of the bombardment programme, and each evening had the opportunity of examining the programme for the next day, and issuing instructions for its amendment where he considered necessary." So corps did not give up the responsibility of command just because it devolved control somewhat. Obviously the smooth flow of information was important for this, and the artillery report cited above also stated that the system of telegraphic and telephonic reports in the morning and evening "appeared to work satisfactorily, gave the maximum of information, with the minimum of reports, and attained its object in keeping the authorities in close touch with the situation…" Overall, no clearer example arose of corps leaving matters up to divisions if they could than in the matter of the batteries 'superimposed' on the barrage, "With regard to the four batteries which the Divisional Commander was at liberty to take out of the barrage for special tasks, each Division adopted a different method."[136] The timetable being the key to the whole thing, it is not surprising that the infantry plan was devised before the barrage which accompanied it. Indeed, it was stated that "The infantry scheme must be cut and dried, and co-ordinated by the corps before the barrage plan is made. Changes in the infantry attack after barrage arrangements are made lead only to confusion and waste of labour."

In tactical matters, the relatively small changes made at Messines from earlier practices indicated the desire to learn from them. The outstanding features of the battle, therefore, were the 'managerial' style of command favoured by Second Army, and the close supervision that was nevertheless attained through the use of liaison officers. The attention to detail – and to the timetable of the attack – that characterised the operation, reflected the rippling of this style of command down at least to division and the care Army took in organising the co-operation of its constituent units.

The tempo of operations in June was no better than in April, but in any case, Messines was a limited attack and not designed to break through the German position. Tactical surprise was most definitely achieved by the employment of the 19 mines which blew the German position apart, but they were very much a single-use weapon. Arguably, one of the great failures of Haig's command was not to exploit the Germans' being off-balance after Messines by launching the Ypres offensive quickly.[137] However, it has been pointed out by Ian M. Brown that the six-week delay between the two battles was essential for logistical reasons, and that no offensive could have been launched before late July because of the need to construct the necessary roads and railway systems into the territory captured at Messines in order to consolidate it.[138]

In conclusion, the assertion that the Battle of Arras saw the application of the lessons of the Somme is borne out by the evidence. The importance of the *SS* series of tactical pamphlets in the dissemination of this information seems to have been vital, and especially *SS135*, the influence of which on plans and operation orders was plainly considerable. After the Somme, as during it, Army commanders' command styles varied, with Plumer the most outstandingly 'managerial.' Below Army, *SS135* had clarified roles and left no-one in any doubt of corps' relationship with divisions (especially regarding command of artillery), as well as standardising the process of planning and conducting an attack – in its first phase at least. In this it was backed up by the other manuals and pamphlets, and after Arras, by the documents dealing with the lessons of that battle, all of which clearly demonstrate the adaptability of the BEF in 1917.

Notwithstanding the standardising effect of the GHQ pamphlets, the style of command was not, even under a notoriously ill-tempered and bullying commander like Allenby, wholly authoritarian. He could never be everywhere at once, so there was always room for discussion with and contributions from the man on the spot. Indeed, the Arras planning shows clearly that the split in responsibilities between corps and division lay in their respective needs to attend to general (operational) or local (tactical) problems. This applied even more during the planning for Messines, when the emphasis was not so much on the plan itself as the schedule of the attack, which left more freedom for corps and divisional commanders within the bounds of these parameters.

Tactically, the handling of gas, tanks and the like generally reflected the local/general split alluded to above, though there were variations, such as those in the handling of machine-guns. However, communications still presented a major problem which defied solution. Even though so much else was now soundly organised, the slowness of getting information back meant that control was out of higher commanders' hands once the attack began. As on the Somme, plans still went into great detail, in order to try to predict as much as possible what might occur, though the efforts now made to shift some gunnery control back to divisions obviously represented an attempt to reduce response times (as well as reflecting the greater firepower available and the consequent ability to spare the guns in question). At the end of the day though, telephones were still the best way (given the limitations of other methods) of quickly getting information from the front line back to division or higher formations, and it was simply impossible to get them reliably set up far enough forward to be of any use in an attack. Even the new liaison officers, who proved so helpful in Second Army before 7th June, were much less useful on the day.

Nevertheless, there is no doubt that by mid-1917 the BEF had the techniques and tools to break into a strong German position, even if defended in depth, given time and enough attention to detail in the planning. However, the techniques which had worked so well at the start of Arras and Messines were not reproducible over several days of continuous fighting, which precluded a break-out, and the next chapter will consider how the Second and Fifth Armies fared in the prolonged Third Battle of Ypres.

NOTES

1 See, for example, Peter Simkins' introduction in McCarthy, Chris, *The Somme: The Day-by-Day Account* (Arms and Armour Press, 1993), 13.

2 Griffith, *Battle Tactics…*, 84-6.

3 Examples are McKee, Alexander, *Vimy Ridge* (Souvenir Press, 1966) and Williams, *Byng of Vimy*.

4 See Berton, Pierre, *Vimy* (Toronto: Penguin Books Canada, 1987). This book is execrable.

5 James, Lawrence, *Imperial Warrior* (Weidenfeld and Nicholson, 1993), 90.

6 Nicholls, Jonathan, *Cheerful Sacrifice* (Leo Cooper, 1990). Jonathan Walker's excellent *The Blood Tub* (Staplehurst: Spellmount, 1998) deals only with the fighting at Bullecourt.

7 James Papers, IWM. Ledger book for 1917.

8 Farndale, *Artillery*, 344-5.

9 Regarding Intelligence officers, see Beach, James Michael, 'British Intelligence and the German Army, 1914-1918.' (Ph.D. thesis, University of London, 2005), 98, 102. Regarding the artillery, see Marble, William Sanders, 'The Infantry cannot do with a gun less: the place of artillery in the BEF, 1914-1918.' (Ph.D. thesis, University of London, 1998), 81.

10 *Third Army Operations 1917*, 1 of undated document in TNA:PRO, WO 95/363. It dates from late April or early May 1917, since on 52 the dates for the second phase of operations are given as "April 23rd to May 2nd", with the latter date in manuscript. The page numbers of that part of the document dealing with actions from May 3rd onwards are also in manuscript. This document will be referred to hereafter as *Third Army Operations*.

11 *O.A.D. 177 Note for C-in-C*, 10th October, 1916 informed Haig of the proposed moves. *O.A.D. 171*, 7th October 1916, contained a forecast of these moves for Army commanders. *Movements of Corps Headquarters*, undated but refers to the

redistribution of troops "by 7th November", so presumably it dates from early October. TNA:PRO, WO 158/19.

12 Letter from Kiggell to Allenby dated 8th January, 1917. TNA:PRO, WO 158/223.

13 *Third Army Operations*, 3.

14 O.H., 1917 Volume 1, 176-9. Haig diary entries for 5th-7th March 1917. TNA: PRO, WO 256/16.

15 James, *Imperial Warrior*, 95.

16 *Third Army Operations*, 3.

17 *Third Army Operations*, 10-11.

18 Note also the artillery notes issued under *SS139*. See *Extracts From Third Army Artillery Instructions No. 6*, 23rd March 1917. TNA:PRO, WO 95/805. This dealt with "General principles to be observed in the preparatory bombardment and on the day of attack."

19 Anon., *Instructions for the Training of Divisions for Offensive Action* (Military Press International, 1995), 4. Hereafter the pamphlet will be referred to as *SS135*.

20 *SS135*, Appendix A, 74.

21 *SS135*, 75.

22 *SS135*, 6.

23 *SS135*, 8-9.

24 *SS135*, 9.

25 *SS135*, 11.

26 *SS135*, 13-14.

27 *SS135*, 24.

28 *SS135*, 78, 41-2, 61.

29 *SS135*, 48-50.

30 *XVII Corps No. G.S. 32*, 20th January 1917. TNA:PRO, WO 95/935. Hereafter *XVII Corps No. G.S. 32*.

31 *VIIth Corps G.C.R.604/D*, 16th March 1917. TNA:PRO, WO 95/805.

32 *XVII Corps No. G.S. 32*, operations section 9. This accorded with *SS135* 52-4.

33 *XVII Corps Conference 22nd February, 1917*, 3. TNA:PRO, WO 95/935.

34 See Griffith, *Battle Tactics…*, 128. O.H., 1917 Appendices, 34.

35 O.H., 1917 Appendices, 52.

36 *XVII Corps No. G.S. 32*, operations section 9.

37 Griffith, *Battle Tactics…*, 115. *XVII Corps No. G.S. 32*, operations section 9.

38 *Third Army Operations*, 23.

39 *Third Army No. G.S.8/31.*, 3rd April, 1917. TNA:PRO, WO 95/361.

40 *56th Division GA67*, 25th March, 1917. See *VII Corps G.C.R. 604/313*, 6th April 1917, for confirmation of this. Both TNA:PRO, WO 95/805.

41 Heavy Branch, MGC, *S.G.62*, 1st April 1917. TNA:PRO, WO 95/91.

42 *XVII Corps No. G.S. 32*, administration section 1.

43 Henniker, *Transportation…*, 193. *XVII Corps No. G.S. 32*, administration section 2.

44 Henniker, *Transportation…*, 215-6.

45 *XVII Corps No. G.S. 32*, administration section 7-8.

46 *XVII Corps No. G.S. 32*, subsidiary instructions, para. 9. Henniker, *Transportation*, 150.

47 *XVII Corps No. G.S. 32*, subsidiary instructions para. 11.

48 *XVII Corps No. G.S. 32*, subsidiary instructions, Appendix B.

49 *XVII Corps No. G.S. 32*, artillery section, 1-4.

50 Farndale, *Artillery*, 158, 161.

51 O.H., 1917 Volume 1, 182.

52 Farndale, *Artillery*, 159.

53 Priestley, R.E., *The Signal Service in the European War of 1914 to 1918 (France)* (Chatham: W & J Mackay & Co., 1921), 181.

54 *XVII Corps No. G.S. 32*, communications section, 1.

55 *VII Corps G.C.R. 604/246*, 2nd April 1917. TNA:PRO, WO 95/805.

56 *VII Corps G.C.R.. 604/257*, 3rd April 1917. TNA:PRO, WO 95/805.

57 For more on the corps Intelligence function see Beach, 'British Intelligence...', Chapter 5.

58 *Third Army No. G.S. 1/13*, 3rd February 1917. TNA:PRO, WO 95/935.

59 *Third Army Operations*, 13-17.

60 *XVII Corps G.S. 32/1*, 5th February, 1917. TNA:PRO, WO 95/935.

61 *XVII Corps Conference 22nd February, 1917*. TNA:PRO, WO 95/935.

62 *56th Division G.A.117*, 1st April, 1917. TNA:PRO, WO 95/805.

63 *34th Division G.S. 217/2*, 25th February 1917. It seems from the plans that divisions permitted brigade commanders freedom of action only if communications between them broke down. *XVII Corps G.S. 32/22*, 27th February 1917. Both TNA:PRO, WO 95/935.

64 *Third Army No. G.S. 13/7. Army Commander's Conference. 26th Feb. 1917*. TNA: PRO, WO 95/168.

65 *Third Army No. G.S. 13/9. Army Commander's Conference. 13th March, 1917*. TNA: PRO, WO 95/935.

66 *Third Army No. G. 3/182.*, 2nd March 1917. *Third Army No. G.S. 4/14.*, 25th March 1917. Both TNA:PRO, WO 95/361.

67 *Third Army No. G.S.21/15.*, 6th April 1917. TNA:PRO, WO 95/361.

68 *Proceedings of Third Army Conference May 24th, 1917*. TNA:PRO, WO 95/363.

69 *XVII Corps No. G.620/1*, 13th February 1917, 2. TNA:PRO, WO 95/935.

70 O.H., 1917 Volume 1, 545.

71 *XVII Corps G620/2*, 18th February 1917. TNA:PRO, WO 95/935.

72 *VII Corps GA43 Appreciation and Instructions*, 19th March 1917. TNA:PRO, WO 95/805.

73 Farndale, *Artillery*, 172.

74 O.H., 1917 Volume 1, 213, 214, 221, 222. *Third Army Operations*, 31-5, passim.

75 *Third Army Operations*, 7, 11. and Third Army *Appreciation and Instructions*, 11th March 1917, 3. TNA:PRO, WO 158/223.

76 *Third Army Operations*, 19, 22, 26.

77 O.H., 1917 Volume 1, 289 and 551. On the latter page the placing of corps boundaries on rivers is blamed for the problem to some degree.

78 O.H., 1917 Volume 1, 378.

79 James, *Imperial Warrior*, 102-3. Letters from Edmonds to A.B. Acheson (of the Cabinet Office Historical Section) in 1946, TNA:PRO, CAB 103/115, nos. 101-2.

80 *56th Division No. G.A.296*, 17th April 1917. TNA:PRO, WO 95/805.

81 James Papers, IWM.

82 *Third Army Operations*, 48.

83 O.H., 1917 Volume 1, 379.

84 *OAD 291/26 Note of Proceedings at Army Commanders' Conference, held at DOULLENS on Monday, the 7th May, 1917, at 11 a.m.* TNA:PRO, WO 158/311.

85 O.H., 1917 Volume 1, 387.

86 *VII Corps Preliminary Order No.88*, 19th April 1917. TNA:PRO, WO 95/805. *Third Army Artillery Instructions No.12. Third Army No. G.1/158*, 19th April 1917. Both TNA:PRO, WO 95/362.

87 *Third Army No.G.S.37/7*, 19th April 1917. TNA:PRO, WO 95/362.

88 *Some lessons from the Operations of the Third Army in April and May 1917.* Undated, but presumably from soon after the battle. TNA:PRO, WO 95/363.

89 *SG 52/59 Summary of Tank Operations – 1st Brigade, Heavy Branch 9th April-3rd May 1917.* 17th May 1917. TNA:PRO, WO 95/91.

90 *Third Army Artillery Instructions No.13*, 19th April 1917, 4. TNA:PRO, WO 95/362.

91 O.H., 1917 Volume 1, 552.

92 Wynne, Captain G.C., *If Germany Attacks: The Battle in Depth in the West*, (Faber and Faber, 1940) 213.

93 *Third Army No. G.14/66.*, 19th April 1917. TNA:PRO, WO 95/362.

94 *Third Army G26/110*, 21st April 1917. TNA:PRO, WO 95/362.

95 *Third Army G26/112*, 26th April 1917. TNA:PRO, WO 95/362.

96 *Fifth Army Order No 62.*, 5th May, 1917. TNA:PRO, WO 95/363.

97 *Third Army No. G.9/36.*, 21st April, 1917. TNA:PRO, WO 95/362.

98 *Third Army No. G.29/70.*, 24th May 1917. TNA:PRO, WO 95/363. See also *Third Army No. G. 38/17.*, 24th May, 1917. TNA:PRO, WO 95/363.

99 *XI Corps SS.1226/16.*, 18th March 1917. TNA:PRO, WO 95/168.

100 *Minutes of Conference of Corps Commanders Held by G.O.C., First Army, at Chateau Philomel, 29th March, 1917.* TNA:PRO, WO 95/168.

101 *Minutes of Conference of Corps Commanders Held by G.O.C., First Army, at Chateau Philomel, 29th March, 1917.*, 3.

102 *Minutes of Conference of Corps Commanders Held at Headquarters, Canadian Corps, Camblain L'Abbé, 5p.m., 15/4/17.* TNA:PRO, WO 95/169.

103 O.H., 1917 Volume 1, 542.

104 *X Corps G.86/7/1*, 8th January 1917; *X Corps G.86/7/2*, 17th January 1917; *X Corps G.86/7/3*, 17th January 1917 (this contained the artillery details) and *X Corps G.86/8/2*, 29th January 1917. TNA:PRO, WO 95/852.

105 Prior, Robin and Wilson, Trevor, *Passchendaele: The Untold Story* (New Haven and London: Yale University Press, 1996), 46-8.

106 *Second Army G.288.*, 18th March 1917. TNA:PRO, WO 95/852.

107 *X Corps G.88/8/4*, 19th March 1917. TNA:PRO, WO 95/852.

108 *X Corps G.88/8/7*, 31st March 1917. TNA:PRO, WO 95/852.

109 Prior and Wilson, *Passchendaele...*, 57. *Second Army G.200.*, 13th April 1917. *X Corps G.88/8/22* [with appendices], *X Corps G.88/8/23*, and *General Advance Scheme*, all 25th April 1917. TNA:PRO, WO 95/852.

110 *Second Army Operation Order No.1.* TNA:PRO, WO 158/215. *X Corps Operation Order No.83.* 11th May 1917. TNA:PRO, WO 95/852.

111 Prior and Wilson, *Passchendaele...*, 58.

112 *X Corps G.88/8/5*, 11th April 1917. TNA:PRO, WO 95/852.

113 *Second Army G.393*, 31st May 1917. TNA:PRO, WO 158/291.

114 *X Corps G.88/8/7*, 31st March 1917, 1. TNA:PRO, WO 95/852.

115 *General Advance Scheme*, 25th April 1917, 2. TNA:PRO, WO 95/852.

116 O.H., 1917 Volume 2, 48, fn. 1.

117 O.H., 1917 Volume 2, 35.

118 *Some Lessons…*Undated, TNA:PRO, WO 95/363.

119 O.H., 1917 Volume 2, 43.

120 The corps directly involved were IX, X and II ANZAC. X Corps papers are here used to demonstrate the planning process. *Report on Xth Corps Machine Gun Barrage, 7th June 1917*. Undated, but probably compiled soon after the attack. TNA:PRO, WO 95/852.

121 *Second Army Offensive. Xth Corps Instructions. Appendix VIII*, 27th May 1917, 1. TNA:PRO, WO 95/852.

122 *Second Army Offensive. Xth Corps Instructions. Appendix IX*, 24th May 1917, p.1. TNA:PRO, WO 95/852.

123 *X Corps G.88/8/7*, and (attached) *R.A. X Corps 9/6/101 Xth Corps Artillery. Outline of Principles of Employment*, both 31st March 1917. TNA:PRO, WO 95/852.

124 *R.A. X Corps No.9/6/492*, 5th July 1917, 6. TNA:PRO, WO 95/852.

125 *Xth Corps G.88/8/22. Appendix 'B'. Aeroplane Co-Operation*. TNA:PRO, WO 95/852.

126 *R.A. X Corps No.9/6/492*, 5th July 1917, 4. TNA:PRO, WO 95/852.

127 Prior and Wilson, *Passchendaele*, 62.

128 *Notes on Recent Operations Carried out by X Corps*, undated but post-Messines, 3. TNA:PRO, WO 95/852.

129 Powell, *Plumer*, 157.

130 *Notes on Liaison Work*, 26th May 1917. TNA:PRO, WO 95/852.

131 Powell, *Plumer*, 157.

132 Powell, *Plumer*, 156, and see Eden, *Another World*, 136-7.

133 A suggestion from VIII Corps' Sir Aylmer Hunter-Weston for a feint on his corps front, five minutes before the main attack to the south went in, was firmly quashed by Army. *VIII Corps G. 8670*, 2nd June 1917, and *Second Army G.597*, 3rd June 1917. TNA:PRO, WO 158/291.

134 See, for example, a letter from X Corps to Harington (MGGS Second Army), dated 14th April 1917. TNA:PRO, WO 95/852.

135 Quoted in Liddell Hart diary for 31st March 1927, Liddell Hart Papers 11/1927/1, Liddell Hart Centre for Military Archives, King's College London (hereafter LHCMA). Given the frequency with which this source is quoted with no other corroboration, it is noteworthy that Powell (*Plumer*, 156) gives the same information but cites Harington's biography of Plumer.

136 *R.A. X Corps No.9/6/492*, 5th July 1917, 5-6. TNA:PRO, WO 95/852.

137 Prior and Wilson, *Passchendaele…*, 49-51.

138 Brown, *British Logistics…*, 164.

CHAPTER 4

Corps Command During Third Ypres: May to November, 1917

The Third Battle of Ypres, commonly referred to as Passchendaele, was the most controversial fought by the British Army in the Great War. Although the Somme has in the last 25 years come to occupy as large a place in the popular imagination, Third Ypres generated debate from the start.[1] The battles of the memoirs during the 1920s and 30s ensured the continuance of what was all too often for the participants a tendentious, self-serving debate. Over the years it has frequently been used as a stick with which to beat the reputations of Haig, his staff and British generals as a whole, without in any way furthering the analysis of the war. The whole emphasis on the role of Sir Douglas Haig has distorted the pattern of research and the question of how the BEF did its job under appalling circumstances has to a great extent been neglected.

Robin Prior and Trevor Wilson's *Passchendaele: the Untold Story* is the most important book on the campaign to be published for many years (not least for its use of sources unavailable to historians before the 1970s and largely neglected until recently). However, it concentrates heavily on the artillery battle while tending somewhat to neglect infantry tactics. Nevertheless, corps command is treated with greater prominence than in earlier work. This chapter demonstrates how corps command operated during the campaign. It argues that, firstly, the offensive was still very much based on *SS135* and other manuals; secondly, the process of learning from earlier offensives continued; and thirdly, that staff work and techniques of conducting operations became to some extent routine within the BEF as the battle went on – in effect, a system for making attacks was developed. Consequently corps required less and less information from Army in order to plan operations. Nevertheless, it is interesting that corps seems to have been more of a conduit for information from Army and GHQ than earlier in the year. This may have reflected the increasingly standardised nature of the attack based on *SS135* etc., and that any additions to, or variations from, its precepts stemmed from the experience of earlier fighting. Finally and most importantly, it establishes that corps was from the start the level of command principally responsible for the organisation of the battle.

Third Ypres consisted of eight battles.[2] Which corps were involved in which of them is shown in the table below:

Battle	Dates	Corps Involved – Second Army	Corps Involved – Fifth Army
Pilckem Ridge	31/7-2/8	X	II, XIV, XVIII, XIX
Langemarck	16-18/8	X	II, XIV, XVIII, XIX
Menin Road	20-25/9	IX, X, I ANZAC	V, XIV, XVIII
Polygon Wood	26/9-3/10	IX, X, I and II ANZAC	V, XIV, XVIII
Broodseinde	4/10	IX, X, I and II ANZAC	XIV, XVIII
Poelcappelle	9/10	IX, X, I and II ANZAC	XIV, XVIII
First Passchendaele	12/10	IX, X, I and II ANZAC	XIV, XVIII
Second Passchendaele	26/10-10/11	II, IX, X, I ANZAC, CAN	XIV, XVIII, XIX

Although only one fewer corps was employed than on the Somme, the most actions any one undertook in the earlier battle was eight (out of 12), while at Third Ypres, three corps took part in all eight. The pattern that emerges is that for Fifth Army, XIV and XVIII Corps did most of the fighting (backed up by II, V and XIX) and for Second Army, IX, X and I ANZAC (the first two of which had just fought under it at Messines) did most, backed up by II ANZAC (also at Messines) and the Canadian Corps, with II Corps for one battle only. On this basis, and that of the original sample, the formations considered in this chapter (as well as GHQ) are Second, Third and Fifth Armies and V, X, XIV and XVIII Corps.

Fifth Army was entrusted with the main attack at the beginning of Third Ypres, and Second Army was relegated to a supporting role, advancing to cover its neighbour's flank. The saga of the discussions between Gough, Haig, Plumer and others has been exhaustively discussed in the works cited above (and many others), as has the evolution of the Fifth Army plan.

From the point of view of the relationship between corps and Army, it began conventionally enough, with Gough holding what seems to have been his first conference on the matter on 24th May, before he had even moved his HQ to the Ypres sector. The composition of the Army for the offensive was already known (down to the divisions), even though it only comprised II and VIII Corps at this point.[3] The corps taking part in the initial attack were to be II, XIV, XVIII and XIX (Second Army was to use IX, X and II ANZAC) and which divisions they were to have under them were also listed.[4] It is not clear how these corps were selected, though some conjecture is possible. That they were definitely chosen for the job and it was not just left to the corps in the line is obvious, not least because it is unlikely that any Army commander would place his hopes of victory in the hands of Sir Aylmer Hunter-Weston of VIII Corps. In any case, the Army boundary was moved before the attack, in order to help Fifth Army's plans.

However, the provisional nature of the arrangements until Fifth Army and its corps took up their positions was stressed in the conference notes, and so only general points were raised. Amongst these were that machine-guns should be used "on a Corps scheme – under the Corps Machine Gun Officer" and that the pamphlets *Preparatory measures to be taken by Armies and Corps before undertaking operations on a large scale* (this was issued in February 1916, but was the only document dealing with command above the divisional level) and *SS135* were to be used in planning the operation.[5] A number of suggestions were made regarding the care of divisions, which were "to be informed whenever possible what their particular task will be; i.e. the original attack, and if so [sic] the exact frontage and objective…" From this first conference, Gough's approach seems to have been more hands-off and consultative than in 1916. Hence "it is proposed that each corps should have two divisions in front and two in reserve" and "it is suggested that part of the staff of relieving divisions and brigades should be at the headquarters of the divisions and brigades which are to be relieved, from the beginning of the battle." Perhaps he felt less need to act in an authoritarian manner because the whole system of command and of planning and executing battles was far more developed by now than in 1916, and since the corps-Army relationship was better-defined, there was a reduction in tension.

He was certainly in close contact with at least one of his corps commanders regarding the philosophy behind the plan. Maxse of XVIII Corps wrote to him on 31st May (cordially addressing him as "My dear Sir Hubert") and was, as ever, forthright in his views, telling Gough that "I have had a good look over the ground and have satisfied myself that, if you order me to capture my final objective at one hour before sunset, I can do it."[6] He attached a paper giving his reasons for objecting to dawn attacks and why he preferred to schedule an attack backwards from one hour before sunset. The main points were that forming up in daylight gave the troops more rest the day and night before the assault, so that they were fresher on gaining their objectives and readier to press on during the next day. Furthermore, taking the objectives so close to nightfall gave the Germans too little time to work out where the British troops were and so rendered them unable effectively to counter-attack before the latter had consolidated their positions.[7] Plainly the rough objectives had already been decided, since in the covering letter Maxse also pressed to be permitted to advance "further than the Black Line: namely to the River STEENBECK," since "the present Black Line is on the wrong slope of the hill for infantry though suitable for artillery observation." He concluded – after expressing his urgent desire to move his HQ to the convent then occupied by VIII Corps HQ – by saying that "The G.O.C., 39th Division [then in the line under VIII Corps], is acquainted with my views and is working on them."

Gough's response was equally cordial, beginning by saying that "I am very much in agreement in all you say. I would like very much not to attack before midday," – though he went on to avoid committing himself – "when one has to co-ordinate a fairly long front, along which circumstances vary, we may be forced to depart from even our dearest wishes!" Gough went on to ask "what other steps and arrangements do you think should be carried out to enable troops to form up? Please let me know, as it will be useful for everyone…" Moreover,

> I also agree very much with your idea of gaining as much ground as we possibly can, particularly the Steenbeck, and not letting the Bosch get settled down again close in front before one moves again. This seems to me to have been one of the great errors committed in the III Army [at Arras], but I may be wrong. I would very much like to discuss a lot of these points with you, [such as] lessons from III Army, and our new policy for the future.[8]

Plainly the pair regarded Third Army's failure to capitalise on its success on 9th April as a cardinal error, and were keen not to repeat it.

The next Army conference with corps took place on 6th June. Again, the tone was far less prescriptive than in Fifth Army in 1916, with free discussion taking place. The style of the meeting seems to have been that Army laid down its approximate plans and the corps commanders, acting as the level of command which would actually carry the job out, then gave their views for and against the tasks and attack frontages allotted to them. None seems to have been reluctant to dissent.

Thus, Gough laid out the first day's tasks, and expressed the hope that "Should the enemy be thoroughly demoralised during the initial attack, it might be possible to gain portions of the red line [i.e. the next day's objective] during the first 24 hours…"[9] Jacob's views are not recorded, but both Maxse and Cavan expressed the view that the range of their artillery would limit their advance on the first day, and time would be required to bring it up. Gough then went on to outline the principles which he hoped would guide the assault.

> He wished a line drawn between bold action against disorganized enemy forces and an organized attack against... organized resistance. Boldness and speed must be the key-note of action in the first case; careful plans and preparations, especially of artillery... must be allowed for the second. Organized attacks will require from 3 to 7 days, though speed in preparation is again all important. Subordinate commanders must try to realise the difference and ascertain the situation. Pressing on with small bodies of troops against organized resistance merely leads to heavy casualties and subsequent loss of moral. The A.C. [i.e. Gough] asked Corps Commanders to try to instil these ideas into Division and Brigade commanders.[10]

Both these ideas and the proposed advance to the Red Line were in no way contradictory to *SS135*.[11] Nevertheless, they would require careful interpretation on the ground. Going on to the Red Line could in itself convert a well-organised and well-supported assault into an affair of small bodies of troops coming up against the next line of organised defence. Meeting that without adequate artillery support (which, on the first day – in places at least – would only extend to the Green Line) meant that a repulse was almost inevitable. This need not be a problem if the Green Line could still be held, but troops who had just been forced back might not be in very good shape to resist further German counter-attacks.

Discussion of the hour of attack then followed, with everyone apart from Lt.-Gen. H.E. Watts of XIX Corps favouring Maxse's idea, put forward by Gough. "Corps commanders' wishes were noted" in the matter of corps schools, and miscellaneous items were raised. The DD Signals asked that all telephones in front of battalion HQs be removed at least a month before the offensive – an idea he had obviously borrowed from Canadian Corps notes on the Vimy attack (which were also discussed).

The first fruit of this conference was an exposition of the principles by which Army expected the offensive to be governed.[12] It reiterated the arguments Gough had given in the conference, about exploiting the "demoralisation and confusion" of the enemy, and citing the examples of 1st July 1916 (presumably referring, optimistically, to the southern flank of the attack), 13th November 1916 (the beginning of the Battle of the Ancre) and, of course, 9th April 1917. Consequently, "platoon, company and battalion commanders" were to occupy ground abandoned or lightly held by the enemy and "These officers must be taught and encouraged to act upon their own initiative and responsibility. There is no time for reports to go back or orders from Corps or Divisional Commanders to come forward." This was the most important of his points, in which he was pressing the need to make the junior officers, accustomed to trench warfare, independent of the need for guidance via the normal communications system for as long as possible, since it would inevitably cease to function reliably or sufficiently responsively for a while once the attack had begun. This adds emphasis to the point made in the last chapter that Army commanders had their best opportunity to win a victory before the fighting began. Gough did not recognise that simply advancing would lead his men on to stronger German defences (though he apparently was aware of the deep and complex German defensive systems on his front), instead attributing the inevitable pause in the forward movement to his own men. "Unfortunately, there comes a time when troops are exhausted and must be rested or relieved.[13] This gives the enemy his opportunity to bring up fresh troops and reorganize." This was now the time to break off the small attacks and return to a careful approach, as stated earlier. However, "The real difficulty is to discover the right moment at which to change from one method to the other, and in forming a decision [note that this was not left to the formation on the spot] the higher command is very dependent upon the judgement of subordinate leaders and upon their reports." Gough concluded by saying that it was important "that there should be mutual understanding and confidence between the command and the regimental officers on these points, and that Corps Commanders will take the necessary steps to make his [Gough's] views known to all ranks..." This memorandum does not seem to have been written in a spirit of dictation from the top; Gough wanted his plans not merely to be carried out, but understood.

On 12th June, XIV Corps issued *Instruction No. 2* to divisions, which reflected the Army conferences and also indicated that no time was lost in applying the lessons of Messines as well as those of Vimy. It contained the exhortation that "once the main objective is reached battle patrols will be pushed forward to secure all ground further to the front that can be obtained." (The idea of these patrols was to seize any ground to their front which the Germans might have vacated) and also stated that "incessant raiding is necessary."[14] This was not simply for reasons of morale, but so that troops might gain experience for the actual attack; this had apparently been invaluable for the Canadians. As ever, counter-battery work with regular aerial photography was stressed and one lesson from Messines was that a corps model of the area of operations was to be constructed. Furthermore, divisions were, "it is hoped," to have a training ground each, upon which brigade attacks could be practised. Once again, they were required to submit their plans to corps, in rough form only at this stage. Corps indicated their own areas of concern in the list of points which the divisional plans should show. This included rough details of the infantry plan, "the position and action of machine guns," "the number of heavy and 2" mortars required," the position of trench mortar batteries, "a trench tramway system," the positions of dumps and headquarters, "signal communications, including wireless and power buzzers," "medical arrangements" and "a scheme of camouflage." It is noticeable that the CMGO still was not expected to run the corps machine guns at all closely and that corps was otherwise, as it had been since early 1916, largely concerned with heavier weaponry (such as heavy mortars) and matters of infrastructure. Communications were, unsurprisingly, still an important issue, for "If we are to obtain the best results in battle, the intercommunications between infantry and aircraft must be further improved." Therefore, divisions were to arrange direct with the 9th Squadron RFC, which had been allotted to the corps, "for the necessary instruction…" Who was to instruct whom was not explained; nor were any suggestions made as to the system to be employed. The same could not be said of infantry training, where "Frequent tactical schemes for C.O's and junior officers will be carried out by Divisional and Brigade Staffs. By this means only is it possible to ensure that subordinates will rapidly appreciate and meet changing situations." Here corps was echoing Army's need for officers on the ground to overcome their training in and experience of trench warfare, in order to adapt to the semi-open variety. In addition, "Experience of recent engagements has shown the enormous importance of visual signalling, which must be constantly practised." After all, the value of regimental officers pressing ahead with their men, no matter how skilfully, was considerably reduced if they could not get information of their whereabouts back to brigade.

To continue to use XIV Corps as an example, it is evident that Fifth Army's corps followed its lead. At a conference with his divisional commanders on 14th June, Cavan regurgitated the sentiments of his superiors; this need not indicate anything more sinister than his agreement with them. The commander-in-chief had recently visited the corps, and Cavan began by referring to points raised by him, the second of which was that "It is absolutely essential to adhere to the text books on the training of Platoons and Divisions, S.S.143 and S.S.135."[15] Cavan then explicitly referred "to Fifth Army G.671/1, in which are outlined the principles which the Army Commander proposes to carry out in the forthcoming operations" and to the Canadians' views on raids. Then followed a description of the corps' task and his suggestions to the GOCs of the Guards and 38th Divisions as to how they might carry it out, with due note being taken of Gough's forward patrols. Discussion followed, and all parties seemed to feel confident in expressing their views, as ever in Cavan's conferences. The local/general split in responsibilities between division and corps already noted at Messines and Arras was obviously continuing. Notes from the next Army conference were sent by XIV Corps to its divisions, dealing mainly with the Army artillery plan; to a certain extent, corps was acting as a post-box.[16]

However, this was not invariably the case. The next significant event in the planning process was the production in late June by the BG(O) at GHQ,

John ('Tavish') Davidson, of a memorandum which put forward his views on how to conduct the new offensive. It should be a series of careful, step by step, limited attacks, with plenty of time between each in order to bring artillery forward, restore communications and minimise casualties. Because of the limited objectives – the memo states "not less than 1,500 yards and not more than 3,000 yards"[17] (which Prior and Wilson give as 1,750 yards)[18] – and because long periods of intense barrage fire would not be needed, artillery fire could remain at a steady level, while some guns would always be moving forward in order to support the next stage of the advance (Prior and Wilson appear to ignore this when they take the view, based on their 1,750-yard steps, that there would be twice the density of shellfire over the area to be attacked if Davidson's approach were adopted in preference to Gough's). None of this really differed too much from Gough's own views, as expressed in *Fifth Army S.G. 671/1* and his reply to Davidson, that he fully acknowledged the need for a careful, step-by-step approach.[19] The real difference lay in the fact that Davidson would limit the advance no matter what the state of the defenders on its front, whereas Gough's view was that – as expressed earlier – if they were in poor condition and ground was there for the taking, it should be taken. This discussion would not really require so much space in this chapter except that Gough's views were again identical to those of Maxse, and as is well known, Maxse's copy of Davidson's memorandum is littered with pungent remarks about its content, and he referred again to the example of Arras more than once.[20] On his copy of Gough's reply, he specifically blamed the failures after 11th April on attacks being launched without adequate preparation or artillery support, and then went on to comment that "can anyone say that we should have won the battle of the 9th April by advancing only 3000 yards?"[21] But at no time in these documents did either Gough or Maxse advocate a "hurrooch" as has been said elsewhere.[22] That Sir Henry Rawlinson believed that this was Gough's plan may reflect his opinion of the Fifth Army commander's temperament given that he was not included in these discussions.

It may be that Maxse appears more influential in comparison to the other corps commanders than he actually was, since his correspondence with Gough has survived, and theirs (if there was any) has not. However, Cavan had done all his fighting on the Somme under Fourth Army, not Fifth and Watts of XIX Corps had not seen action as a corps commander before July 1917. Claud Jacob of II Corps had gone through the 1916 fighting under Gough, but his BGGS (until his death in September 1916), Philip Howell, had been critical of Gough's Army and Neill Malcolm in particular, which does not argue for a particularly cosy relationship.[23] Maxse had been an aggressive and successful divisional commander under Gough in 1916, so it is reasonable to surmise that his views carried more weight than those of the others, on the grounds both of his temperament and past experience. This is not to say that such highly regarded generals as Cavan and Jacob were disregarded, but merely that perhaps their opinions (and it is obviously difficult to be certain in a matter of this kind) were less eagerly sought than those of Maxse. The unfortunate Watts had no solid reputation or previous experience with Fifth Army to help him and appears to have had a less comfortable time there as a result.[24]

Gough's next conferences with his corps commanders took place on 26th June, and the results of the discussions were published as orders.[25] The philosophy behind these was much as before, though infiltration beyond the Green, not the Black Line, was now envisaged. Resumption of control by both corps and Army, upon the attacking troops reaching the Black Line (now the main objective) was stressed, and forward patrols were to be sent out once the protective barrage had lifted. However, corps were to bear in mind that a clearly defined line was necessary as the jumping-off point for the next stage of operations. Gough was still keen to emphasise that this was the first stage in "a series of organised battles" and that re-organisation after each had to be planned carefully in consequence. Army again had control over the artillery, in the sense that the MGRA organised the overall plan under which it operated. However, once the protective barrage on the Green Line had been lifted, "All barrage arrangements will be placed under Corps control." Though the previous barrage timetable had been laid down by Army (a slightly more hands-on approach than at Messines), it was obviously felt that devolution to corps after the main objective had been taken was necessary.

Attached to these notes were the timetable for the battle – based on barrage lifts – and Gough's comments on each corps commander's scheme. Although he went into more detail on Watts' and Jacob's than on Cavan's and Maxse's (the latter only received one generalised paragraph, compared to over a page on Jacob's plan), the style was not unduly prescriptive. Army was co-ordinating its corps with a view to leaving as little to chance on the day as possible, since then it would be relatively powerless to affect events.

On 30th June, another memorandum was issued by Fifth Army which largely restated the ideas put forward already. It also raised the possibility of, after 36 hours' fighting, the Holy Grail of open warfare being attained, which would bear out Gough's critics regarding his alleged expectation of a breakthrough. However, it also stated that "This is a result which we can hardly hope to attain until the enemy has been beaten in two or three heavy battles."[26] In addition, this memorandum is notable for Douglas Haig's pencilled comments upon it, to the effect that the Passchendaele-Staden Ridge must be the object of the offensive, not simply the defeat of the German forces in front of Fifth Army.

In the meantime, corps carried on with their preparations for the attack. Because of the rolling offensive envisaged by Army, XVIII Corps instructed its divisions to work in pairs on a two-division front, so that the rear divisions could support those in front and leapfrog through them for further attacks. As prescribed by Army, definite units were detailed for offensive patrolling once the Green Line had been taken, a cavalry squadron being available to assist if required. Divisions were to construct defensive strongpoints (presumably to guard against counter-attacks) and inform corps of their proposals in this regard. Liaison with neighbouring units was stressed, and divisions were not only to organise liaison at their HQ level but to ensure that their brigades liaised with those of the divisions on their flanks. The parties detailed for this, like those to be sent on patrol, were to be especially trained over model trenches. Another important aspect of liaison was that divisions were to send officers to be attached to corps HQ from 10 days before zero.

Control of machine-guns was split between corps and divisions. The first barrage was to cover the initial advance up to the Black Line, and was under corps control. The second was to prevent German "artillery retiring from the STEENBECK valley"[27] – which lay in front of the Black Line – to protect the Line itself and to support the further advances to the Green and dotted Green Lines (an intermediate line), respectively, of the 51st and 39th Divisions. This was under divisional control.

Tanks were again allocated by corps to divisions, and the former left all further details to the latter. In practice, divisions devolved their control to brigades.[28] However, divisions must have allocated the tanks to their brigades, hence their split between those supporting the assault on the Black Line and those supporting that on the Green Line. An innovation for the new attack was the use of signal (i.e. wireless-carrying) tanks, in XIX Corps, which proved to be only of limited use on 31st July.[29]

Gas now definitely came under corps control, in so far as the policy regarding its use was that "Divisions will notify Corps Headquarters their requirements, if any."[30] These were in addition to the harassing activities of the relevant Special Company RE (as gas units were known) under corps orders. Furthermore, GHQ decreed in late October that Divisional Gas Schools be abolished and replaced by corps schools instead.[31]

It is apparent that the issue of familiarity with the ground was now taken far more seriously than at Arras. As before Messines, a corps model of the area under attack was constructed and all ranks encouraged to inspect it. The trenches dug for training have already been mentioned, and in addition, corps supplemented Fifth Army's issue of maps with its own, to be issued "to Divisions at the rate of 2 per platoon."[32] All these ideas can be found in *Notes Collected by 24th Division, as a result of their attack on June 7th, 1917*, which Maxse certainly possessed.[33] He also owned a copy of 16th Division's administrative report on Messines, which he circulated around his senior staff officers.[34] This was sent to him by the divisional commander (Maj.-Gen. W.B. Hickie), which implied that the routes for dissemination of information within the BEF were neither entirely formal nor all top-down.

Of course, it was necessary not only for the attacking troops to know where they were, but also for corps to know. Arrangements for contact planes were rather more detailed than in X Corps' plans for Messines.[35] The recognition markings on the aeroplanes were given and the system of flares to be used by the infantry in response to aeroplane signals (by klaxon and flare) was specified, and also the marking of brigade and battalion HQs. Once an aeroplane had gleaned all the information, it was to drop it at specified corps and divisional Dropping Stations. On the more general subject of signal communications – by telephone, pigeon and the other means described for Arras and Messines – no change of system was made for the new offensive, and *SS148* provided the scheme for the laying of cable as the attack progressed.[36]

Other appendices dealt with RE arrangements (roads, rail- and tramways and water supply), Intelligence arrangements and, unusually, the German dispositions opposite the XVIII Corps front.[37] The intelligence arrangements – given in more detail than for previous battles – listed the sources of information as being balloon and aeroplane observation (both Army and corps squadrons), FOOs, German prisoners, British wounded, flanking formations, wireless interception and Corps Observers. The latter were to be "attached as required to advancing Brigades," though their role was otherwise left undefined.[38] However, given the desire of higher commands to know what was going on once an attack had started, they presumably were expected somehow to get information back from their brigades to corps. An idea taken almost word for word from 24th Division's notes on Messines was for patrols to follow the attacking divisions and once the Black Line had been taken by the latter, to "find some place to observe as far as the GREEN LINE."[39] From there they were to obtain information regarding the morale of the enemy and whether they were massing to counter-attack, retiring or pulling guns back. Obstacles, landmarks and the presence of machine-guns were also to be reported, as well as "any points other than these useful to the infantry advancing."[40] The reports were to be delivered to divisional Advanced Report Centres, and presumably from these to corps. Divisions themselves were also expected to pass on anything they gleaned to corps, and were instructed that "The number of the regiment to which prisoners belong and the time and place of capture will be reported by wire." Naturally enough, in view of what went before, changes in German dispositions were of considerable interest.

What is perhaps most striking about *XVIII Corps Instructions No: 1* is that the document was only 23 pages long, including appendices. Instead of the corps producing a large and detailed plan for the attack, the principles under which the offensive was to be organised and conducted by it and its divisions were elaborated. This was entirely consonant with *FSR I*, which stated that "Operation orders, especially in the case of large forces, should not enter into details except when details are absolutely necessary.

It is usually dangerous to prescribe to a subordinate at a distance anything that he should be better able to decide on the spot, with a fuller knowledge of local conditions."[41] Presumably staff were by mid-1917 sufficiently experienced for this reversion to *FSR I*. Many of the details were by now more or less routine, so the emphasis of the instructions was on what was new. This was especially reflected in the increasingly elaborate efforts to get information of all kinds back to corps and Army, and to make the advancing troops self-sufficient within the framework of the plan, so that in the absence of communication from above they would still do what it envisaged. If the tempo of attacks were to be increased, the attackers could not always be tied to orders from behind. The locus of control remained firmly at the corps-Army level – so long as control was possible. It seems that divisions now had greater access to artillery than before, with the guns at their disposal being overlaid on the barrage so that they might be diverted without significantly thinning it. But this was simply a question of the division taking care of local matters with field artillery. They were only permitted these guns because enough were available; the heavies and the execution of the artillery plan as a whole remained in the hands of corps.[42]

XIV Corps approached things in Lord Cavan's usual consultative style, which seemed even milder in tone than in 1916. In a conference on 5th July, Cavan invited the views of the GOC Guards Division on the question of whether the German front line should be occupied before zero or not, adding that "The Corps Commander does not wish to bias him in any way, and any proposals made will be put up to the Army."[43] But as in XVIII Corps, training, the use of the corps model, liaison with flanking units and lessons from Vimy were all raised, as well as the need to tell all ranks of the phased and carefully prepared operations ahead. XIV Corps' *Instruction No. 4* can be taken as its equivalent of XVIII Corps No. 1, and was of a similar length – 27 pages, including appendices.[44] Neither the layout nor the contents were precisely the same, XIV Corps dilating more on the action of the artillery, for example, and not at all on enemy dispositions.[45] Interestingly, the CREs of the 20th and 29th Divisions were placed under the command of XIV Corps CRE, as a means for him to delegate the supervision of road maintenance in order to facilitate the move forward, and to make good the damage occurring presumably as a result of the crowding in the Salient and the easy targets thus presented to the German artillery.

Notwithstanding these minor differences, the same impression emerges from the XIV Corps Instructions as from those of XVIII Corps. This was of corps as the level of command which actually organised the attack, within the guidelines set by Army.[46] This was further borne out by two memoranda issued by XVIII Corps in late July. The first, to Army, reiterated Maxse's "intentions" (as he put it) for consolidation of the Black and Green Lines and capture of the crossings over the Steenbeck, together with the co-ordination of their machine-gun defence with the adjoining corps.[47] The second was lengthier, and addressed to divisions.[48] Its intention was that they should be aware that a staff officer from corps would shortly be visiting them in order to ensure that "each Divisional Commander is personally satisfied that all the following points have been attended to..." The first was that all ranks should understand what the plan of operations was and their own role therein. The remaining twenty-five points formed a checklist of things the divisional commander should either have told his men or organised himself, from briefing them on how to follow the barrage to making sure that trench traffic rules were adhered to. In effect, Army devolved the organisation of the offensive down to corps but retained overall control, especially over the artillery. However, if conference minutes are to be believed, Fifth Army permitted more discussion – at this planning stage, at least – than it has been given credit for. It might be argued that such minutes indicate this more consultative style of command because they were official and so censored. That, though, is to assume that any interested party or censor would view consultation to be as desirable as later historians have done; Gough himself seems only to have perceived that he was being criticised in late 1917.[49] Furthermore, like is here being compared with like – official documents from the Somme with those from Third Ypres – and the above is undoubtedly the picture that emerges.

Second Army's preparations were no different in style from those for Messines. Since its corps had only a secondary role at this stage, they were not involved in the controversies raging around Gough's head, though Plumer himself was consulted by Haig et al. So, in mid-June, Army asked corps to submit their plans for the forthcoming operations, and that they should indicate their requirements of guns and men.[50] Unfortunately for IX Corps, three of the four divisions which it had at Messines were taken away, since, as the CGS explained in a letter to Plumer, "the Field-Marshal [i.e. Haig] is anxious to place the best divisions available into our main operations."[51]

Once II Corps had taken over the 23rd Division's line (on 4th July[52]) and also responsibility for all of the attack in the Tower Hamlets sector, Second Army's attack was reduced to a feint.[53] The Army *ARTILLERY INSTRUCTIONS No. 1* therefore began "In order that there may be no apparent line of demarcation between the Second and Fifth Armies, Corps will conform generally to the principles laid down in Fifth Army Artillery Instructions so far as they are applicable."[54] In particular, the cadences of heavy artillery fire and of barrages were to be uniform between the Armies.

Because it was attacking only on a frontage of one division (the 41st), X Corps placed the field artillery (drawn from several divisions) under the command of the GOC of that division.[55] Although corps retained command of heavies (for long-range bombardment and for counter-battery work), a senior liaison officer from Corps HA was to be at 41st Divisional HQ. Again, corps was primarily concerned with co-ordinating the actions of its divisions, so if only one were to conduct an attack it would be left to organise its own field artillery support. That said, the CMGO, as well as the DMGO, was required to organise the machine-gun barrage, but what his actual function was is not clear. In his report on machine-gun operations on 31st July, the CMGO (Lt.-Col. H.F. Bidder) made no mention of his own activities, giving the impression that everything had been organised by the DMGO.[56]

As in Fifth Army, special attention was paid to liaison with flanking units. The X Corps instructions, unusually, named the officers who were to attend to this, the forward liaison officer being Captain R.D. Ross, who was to attend to the junction of the X and II Corps, and the other being Major R.K. Grant, who would "keep in touch with II Corps… and make a personal reconnaissance of ground captured by II Corps."[57] In the event, Ross was unable to establish contact with the 24th Division's troops, describing the confusion he found on going forward: "I wandered about in the neighbourhood of the Red Line but was unable to find either of the Battalion Headquarters [he was trying to find the 10th West Kents and 20th DLI] There were parties of both battalions in shell holes but none were able to give me any clear information."[58] In addition, he gave details of the effects of the bombardment and barrage and commented on the timetable, the early start having led to the moppers-up missing German troops, some with machine-guns, in shell holes, which had led to "troublesome" firing later. Gough might have done better to have heeded Maxse, but he cannot be blamed for the morning having been unusually dark owing to the thick, low cloud which presaged the torrential rain of later in the day.

The causes for the limited nature of the debatable success (the ground gained meant that Ypres was virtually no longer overlooked, but no breakthrough was possible) in the Battle of Pilckem Ridge, as the attack on 31st July was called, were varied.[59] II Corps' counter battery work had not been anything like good enough. Counter-battery work is not dealt with in any detail in this chapter since it operated in much the same way as at Messines, though it was hampered much more than in June by the weather and the lie of the land. As a result, German artillery was able to put down a curtain of fire between the attacking troops and the divisional HQs, which completely disrupted communications. Consequently, neither corps nor divisions had any accurate information about the progress of the battle until after 10am.[60] In addition, some troops had become lost in the dark and missed their objectives, while others had encountered uncut wire and German strongpoints which had survived the preliminary bombardment. XVIII and XIX Corps initially were very successful, moving to the Green Line and in places beyond, before they were halted, and in some cases driven back to the Black Line by counter-attacks. Had divisional commanders been aware of this, they could no doubt have sent reinforcements up, but again communications had broken down, the bad light and state of the ground rendering even visual signals and runners (respectively) useless. XIV Corps had also taken its objectives up to and beyond the Black Line, but the troops had lost the barrage and been halted by stiffening German resistance.[61] Second Army's attack was a not especially successful feint, drawing little German attention away from Fifth Army.[62] (See map, page 249 for Fifth Army operations, 31st July.)

Pilckem Ridge was followed by discussions about what should be done next. GHQ issued a new set of tactical notes, based around the stiffening of German resistance, the further an attack was pressed, which Fifth Army passed on to its corps for comment on 7th August.[63] Maxse's response was emphatic and opinionated, but with reason, to judge from the tactical performance of his infantry on 31st July. Their capture of a number of German strongpoints through the use of fire and movement were testimony to his skills as a trainer.[64] In addition, planning for the continuation of the offensive went on in much the same way as before, with the colours of lines to be gained steadily increasing in range (though all falling between the original Red Line and the start point of 31st July). After more or less unsuccessful operations on 10th and 16th August, Gough held a conference on the 17th at which he solicited corps commanders' proposals for the next phase of operations, and was informed that "II Corps wished to capture the BROWN line before attacking the dotted YELLOW line," while "XIX Corps wished to attack the PURPLE line."[65] However, "XVIII Corps proposed to attack the dotted PURPLE line" and it would then be "prepared to take the YELLOW line in conjunction with the XIX Corps." In the end, he decided upon a more or less staggered approach, first one corps attacking and then another, which invited the sort of treatment the Germans had meted out to Fourth Army's piecemeal attacks the previous year. Throughout, though admittedly crippled by the weather, he failed to stick to the principles of careful preparation he had defined at the start of the planning for the offensive. While corps orders were as careful as before, the operations they defined were doomed to fail if their artillery could not suppress the defence and the ground was impassable.[66]

That said, XVIII Corps carried out an ingenious small-scale operation on 19th August, for the devising of which Maxse claimed partial credit.[67] The objective was the capture of four strongpoints and a gun-pit (this last found to be unoccupied in the event) which had held up the large-scale attack on 16th. The artillery blinded potential observers on local high ground with smoke shell and with smoke, H.E. and shrapnel fire prevented any reinforcements from coming forward. Then only 240 infantry and a dozen tanks captured all the objectives. Vital to the success of the operation was that the tanks were able to make their advance up the St. Julien-Poelcappelle road; the terrain elsewhere was far too boggy for them and any which left the road became ditched.[68] Plainly, though ingenious, this was not the way to Berlin. However, further large-scale attacks launched on 22nd and 27th August were no more successful than those before. Gough had by now realised that the German defensive tactics were less passive than had been thought previously, and had issued a paper entitled *"Modifications Required in Our Attack Formations to Meet The Enemy's Present System of Defence"* on 24th August.[69] But he failed to identify that artillery superiority was essential for the infantry to deploy into these new formations ('waves' followed by 'worms') without prohibitive losses. (Incidentally, these new tactics were demonstrated at Third Army Infantry School to corps commanders in that Army on 14th September, which demonstrates the efficient dissemination of tactical information by this time.[70]) According to Prior and Wilson, the scale of losses to the divisions in Fifth Army was what prevented Gough from undertaking further substantial operations immediately after the failure of 27th August. By the time he might have launched another ill-prepared assault, control of the offensive had passed to Second Army and he had to wait until they were ready (though XIX Corps suffered heavily in small attacks in the meantime).[71] It is interesting to wonder how pointed was a comment made by Lord Cavan, on the covering note to the 38th Division's report for Pilckem Ridge. He observed that "The most interesting part of this account... shows very clearly the necessity of outflanking concrete m.[achine] g.[un] emplacements thus entailing attack on a broad front. Small attacks on strongpoints are not likely to be successful."[72]

This brings up the question of what Fifth Army's – or more specifically, Gough and Malcolm's – relationships with subordinate commanders were. As has already been stated, conference minutes reveal more discussion than these officers are often credited with permitting, but tradition insists upon there being a climate of fear in Fifth Army.[73] It may well be that the truth lies somewhere in the middle, and some officers had a harder time than others; mention has already been made of Gough's obvious regard for Maxse.[74] Fifth Army requested that Maxse furnish information on "Fitness to command a division during active operations" and "Capacity for training a division." of all divisional GOCs in XVIII Corps between 31st July and 22nd September.[75] Maxse was dismissive of Maj.-Gen. H.D.Fanshawe of 58th Division (former GOC V Corps). "In the planning stage he plays a minor part and appears to have little influence over his subordinate commanders... I see no signs of grip or drive..."[76] Nor was he favourable to Maj.-Gen. Cuthbert of 39th Division – "He appears to have few ideas regarding the tactical employment of a division in the battle, beyond rigidly adhering to certain paragraphs in a text book. I do not consider him a good trainer nor is he ready to learn." Cuthbert had already been sent home, giving up his command on 20th August. H.D.Fanshawe relinquished his on 6th October. Both protested that Maxse was being unfair, but to no avail, since Gough backed him up.[77] But of the other two commanders whose reports remain, Maxse was glowing in his views on Sir George Harper of 51st Division (soon to get a corps) and not unfavourable to Sir Robert Fanshawe (the third of the brothers) of 48th Division. So this limited sample does offer some insight into how different officers might have formed different views of Fifth Army.

The circumstances of Sir Herbert Plumer's taking over the main command of the offensive are one of the more controversial aspects of Third Ypres, but are beyond the scope of this book.[78] He asked for, and was granted, a three-week pause (a figure suggested by the GOCs of X and I ANZAC Corps) in operations to prepare for Second Army's attack.[79] The minutes of the 27th August conference indicate that Plumer was proceeding very much in his usual style – thorough and consultative. The only differences of note from earlier attacks were that more emphasis was placed on training and on resting the artillery than before. But essentially, corps again developed their plans in line with a rough framework provided by Army. To assist in this, Second Army also issued a document entitled *General Principles on Which the Artillery Plan Will be Drawn*.[80] This was noteworthy both for the depth and number of barrages it proposed (five, extending in a belt 2,000 yards from front to back) and for its insistence that cratering be minimised in order not to generate fresh obstacles to the advance while destroying those placed in the way by the Germans (the proportion of shell to be fired with Fuze 106, which detonated the shell on graze, was specified later).[81] In addition, less formal discussions were taking place, leading Harington to write a note to Davidson to accompany the Second Army proposal, asking for II Corps to be pulled out of the line and replaced by I ANZAC and X Corps.[82]

More consultation took place over the timing of practice barrages, including that of the machine-gun barrage, the duration of which was left entirely to corps commanders.[83] A striking example of learning from earlier mistakes arose regarding the timing of zero, with both corps and Army carrying out visibility tests in order to determine when it should be set.[84] Also raised at the Army conference of 15th September was the availability of both wireless- and gun-carrying tanks, with I ANZAC and X Corps being authorised to call upon their services. However, the preparations outlined in the conferences may have been becoming rather routine, which may be why Plumer raised a number of points on 4th September which he felt required attention. Thus, "the preparation of barrage plans by higher authority does not absolve divisional commanders from full responsibility to obtain a barrage meeting all their requirements. The division is bound to see that preliminary bombardment and projected barrages deal with all 'sore places' on their front; of these places they have more definite knowledge than any higher authority."[85] He was also careful to stress that leapfrogging units should not become embroiled in the gaining of objectives which their predecessors had failed to secure, not least because in such an event, the barrage would have moved on and so rendered the fresh troops as unlikely to take the position as the first wave. This was, of course, a restatement of the old military dictum that failure should not be reinforced. It also implied that the failure of recent attacks was the result of poor local control.

In parallel with the Army's activity, corps were, as before, making the preparations on the ground. X Corps' first instruction for the attack was much as usual for a preliminary instruction, giving very approximate times, and boundary lines so that divisions could begin their preparations. In addition, "Details as regards dispositions of enemy and nature of country to be crossed will be issued by Xth Corps Intelligence at an early date."[86] Doubtless this indicated the experience of German defensive tactics thus far in the battle. The next instruction specified divisional HQs and ordered divisional commanders to take over their sectors well before the attack (the line still being held by troops from other divisions) in order to establish their communications and for them to supervise the preliminary bombardment. This signified a definite emphasis on divisional responsibility for the attack.[87]

Furthermore, brigades of the attacking divisions were to take over their HQs several days before the attack "and place a detachment of the brigade Signal Co. in them in order to ensure the working of the communications." Corps were moving the locus of control forward, whether divisions liked it or not. Perhaps this was an acknowledgement of their inability to do very much once the attack had started, making the need for other formations to handle local difficulties all the more pressing. Perhaps also, divisions needed to be reminded that they were still (comparatively) the man on the spot, notwithstanding the need to conform to the Army artillery plan.

On 7th September a more definite set of instructions was issued, giving a more detailed overall plan, and in tune with the phased approach of Second Army to the attack, pointing out that the Green Line was the objective of the coming assault and the Black Line was that of the next. The depth of the barrage had now shrunk to 1,000 yards, but as a matter of course it was to be supplemented by a machine-gun barrage. The CMGO was to co-ordinate the divisional schemes and liaise with the GOCRA to ensure that they corresponded to the artillery plan.[88] No fewer than eight appendices went on to give the details of the plan. That for signalling was seven pages long; divisions were to organise communications on the basis of SS148, and brigades to set up "one Brigade Forward Station between the enemy's front line and the final objective."[89] Not mentioned in previous attacks was the presence of a Corps Intelligence balloon, which was in place to receive visual signals, day and night.[90] The same was true of corps observers receiving an allocation of pigeons. Captain Ross was again the forward liaison officer, though HQ liaison was now carried out by Major

A.G.F. Isaac. Corps observation stations, manned by troops from the corps cyclist battalion, were to report to the Corps Advanced Intelligence Report Centre, on which notable emphasis was placed. Its object was "to receive special Intelligence from various sources and to disseminate this Intelligence to all concerned with the least possible delay. This scheme contemplates the co-ordinating of all the special means of obtaining information of both the enemy and our own troops from sources other than the front line itself..."[91] Presumably what was meant by 'special intelligence' was information gathered by aeroplane reconnaissance, from observers on the ground and from POWs.

The trend towards passing more responsibility back to division continued with the next set of instructions, which laid out the timetable and boundaries of the creeping barrage nearest the attacking troops, and stated that "Within these limits Divisions will arrange their own barrages and submit [them] early to Corps Headquarters."[92] In addition, divisions were responsible for harassing fire in the German forward area.[93] All the field artillery involved in supporting a division's attack was placed under the command of its CRA, whose staff would be "reinforced as necessary." Each CRA was to superimpose a brigade of artillery on the barrage and "The batteries of this Brigade may be withdrawn by the Divisional Commander from barrage tasks during the assault to deal with any emergency that may arise without reference to Corps HQ... liaison between these batteries and subordinate infantry commanders will be arranged as the Divisional Commander may deem necessary." Bombardment double groups were affiliated to each divisional HQ, linking them closely to the heavy artillery – "Programmes for Heavy Artillery barrages will... be drawn up by Bombardment Double Group Commanders in consultation with B.G.R.A. of Division and Divisional Commander..." These double groups, used by X Corps at Messines, were the result of placing pairs of HAGs under one commander. Perhaps the most clearly defined piece of decentralisation was in the handling of machine-guns, a report on the fighting stating that "No Corps scheme was attempted in this or the subsequent operations. Divisions worked out their own schemes under the general supervision of the Corps Machine Gun Officers. This plan worked very well."[94]

X Corps' attack on 20th September (the Battle of the Menin Road Ridge) clearly demonstrated the time lapse between events happening in the front line and their being reported at corps. For example, "The advance from the BLUE line to the GREEN line was timed to take place at 9.40 a.m..... At 11.42 a.m. 41st Division reported that their right Brigade... had not made progress towards the GREEN line..."[95] Nevertheless, the day was considered a great success, which X Corps ascribed to the barrages and neutralising artillery fire, the machine-gun barrages, the ease of assembling troops beforehand, owing to well-prepared tracks and roads and the "very satisfactory" co-operation of the infantry and artillery with the RFC.[96]

Fifth Army prepared for its subsidiary role in the attack in much the same way as before. Though it had now to conform to the Second Army barrage plan, Gough insisted on substituting a hurricane bombardment for 24 hours before the attack in place of the more methodical week of firing preferred by Second Army.[97] New infantry tactics were also adopted (in both Armies) in order to deal with pillboxes. Since advancing in a wave formation was inappropriate when trying to cope with defences organised in a chequered layout, units (each specifically allotted to a given target) advanced in small columns, preceded by a thin line of skirmishers.[98] These tactics were one of the four "distinguishing features" of the attack, according to Maxse. The others were the use of the rifle (in preference to hand grenades, upon which it was felt the troops had placed too much reliance since the Somme) to repel counter-attacks, the use of 3-inch Stokes mortars to supplement the creeping barrage, and the 'draw-net' barrage. This rather fiendish invention was a field-gun barrage which started 1,500 yards behind the German front line and moved slowly back to it. Having been repeated several times before the attack, it was (unsurprisingly) very demoralising to the unfortunate recipients. Maxse also felt, ironically in view of his role in advising Gough in June, that limiting the objectives to about 1,000 yards had been very valuable. In fairness to him it must be said that he was not aware of the new defensive system used by the Germans until the fighting of August had revealed it. This failure of intelligence was understandable, given how difficult pillboxes were to spot, and how the Germans only revealed their tactics of giving ground and then counter-attacking by applying them.

With the Battle of the Menin Road Ridge, the pattern for subsequent attacks was established and Second Army orders and artillery instructions became increasingly formulaic. Orders almost invariably began with the words "Ref. 'Attack Map'" and objectives were marked on this map, as well as the stages of the attack being described in relation to it. Other than that, the orders were terse statements of the timetable, which corps were involved, any corps movements and when the attack should actually take place. *Second Army Operation Order No. 12* exemplified this, beginning (after the reference to the map) "The Canadian Corps having captured PASSCHENDAELE the operations (<u>Ninth Phase</u>) [my underlining] will be resumed on November 10th."[99] Another seven paragraphs followed, following the form described above, and the whole thing was less than a page long. Artillery instructions tended to be slightly longer but no less routine. *Second Army Artillery Instructions No. 11* began by saying that "the attack will be supported by barrages in depth as in the case of attacks (1), (2), and (3)" [attack (1) was that of 20th September].[100] Then the timetable, spacing and rate of movement for the barrages were laid out. This particular set of instructions was unusual in that it had an appendix attached, laying out the responsibilities for the co-ordination of the 'A' barrage (the one closest to the troops) for the attack. Army were to specify the rate of advance of the barrage and the time of its lifting off the protective barrage line (placed on intermediate objectives). Corps were to establish their boundaries with their neighbours and the map co-ordinates of the jumping-off line, the intermediate and final objectives, the start line for the barrage and its lifts. This appendix was referred to in later instructions.[101] From late September onwards, only if normal practice were to be departed from did Second Army's orders and instructions go into any detail.

X Corps also adopted a more or less standard form for its orders, again based on those issued for the Battle of the Menin Road Ridge.[102] These were longer than Second Army's (not surprisingly, since corps were actually organising the attack's details) and continued to insist that divisions be active in their planning. The first set asked the GOCs of the assaulting divisions to "forward their opinion as to the hour they consider best on K day for the attack to take place, and whether they recommend the employment of tanks." In preparing for the Battle of Broodseinde (4th October), Morland submitted his outline plan to Army in the form of a short memorandum, with a map showing objectives attached.[103] After the battle, as after that of 20th September, a set of preliminary comments was drawn up, noting the effectiveness of communications, equipment and tactical points.[104] This was repeated for subsequent actions too. One notable feature of the attack on 26th October (the Second Battle of Passchendaele) was that the attacks of the two divisions of X Corps involved, 5th and 7th, were "to a certain extent independent of one another and they were able to adjust the pace of their respective barrages and pauses independently."[105] Since the attack failed completely, this devolution of responsibility did them little good; the state of the ground was so appalling by this stage of the battle that the barrages were hardly relevant.[106]

Fifth Army did much the same as Second after 20th September, its increasingly brief orders also being supplemented by maps.[107] In conference notes, corps again gave very much the impression of being the formations organising things, and making suggestions and pointing out difficulties in Army plans accordingly; indeed, they were even setting their own objectives at times, and by late October were quite bluntly saying that no further attacks were practical.[108] Not surprisingly, they also standardised their orders and attached maps to them.[109] As ever, minor changes were made to the formula.

XVIII Corps was up against relatively weak German defences for the Battle of Broodseinde, and so Maxse opted for a hurricane bombardment beginning at zero, rather than a preliminary bombardment which would advertise that an attack was imminent. He also employed a dozen tanks, which, like the infantry, were given definite objectives.[110] The latter were, however, warned not to wait for the tanks but to get on to their own objectives; obviously the risks of mechanical problems or ditching were high.

The attack was a notable success, not least because of the effect of the tanks on German morale.[111] And because the attacks were becoming more standardised does not mean that training was being neglected; a document referring to company officers' training for Broodseinde has annotations by Maxse: "Nurse Reserves. Tanks. Mop Up. Command Posts."[112] In addition, a *Report on Work Carried Out at the XVIII Corps School During the Summer Campaign – 1917* made it clear that battle courses for company commanders and other officers of divisions about to make an attack, courses for platoon commanders and their sergeants, a Lewis Gun course, and a signalling course were all run. All told, 3,142 soldiers of all ranks attended the school over four months from early July to early November, when XVIII Corps came out of the line.[113] The campaign concluded officially on 10th November 1917.

On an administrative point, the formalisation of systems in the BEF can also be seen in the summer of 1917, in the institution of reports to be completed by corps when a division left them, which were forwarded by the Army the division was going to, on to its corps. These reports were variable in length and detail, but generally covered the state of the divisional artillery (and sometimes the Field Companies, RE), the length of time the division had been in the line, what action it had seen and casualties suffered, sometimes together with reinforcements received. Comments were also made on the state of training of the troops and points which the commander of the corps being left felt needed attention. One which exemplifies the criticism made of the British corps system – that divisions went through them too fast to benefit from any continuity of command – was that of II Corps on 56th Division. It stated that "This Division was only with the II Corps for about a week. It fought on the 16th August but was unsuccessful in the attack it made on POLYGON WOOD and suffered heavy casualties.... I know very little about the Division."[114]

In conclusion, corps command at Third Ypres was not substantially different from corps command at the Battle of Messines; both were based on the application of experience to the SS series of instructional pamphlets. However, a number of changes of emphasis took place. In relationships with Army, it is noticeable that Fifth Army was much less assertive and prescriptive than in 1916; Second Army continued to be the paragon already observed at Messines. This, it is safe to assume, reflected the growing experience of staff officers at all levels of command, so that Army and corps could devolve responsibility more to divisions, as prescribed by *FSR I.* Army again set rough objectives, based as much on a schedule as on points of geography, and the MGRA devised artillery policy around these. Corps had the task of implementing these plans and principles (a concept to which senior officers were firmly wedded, perhaps in reaction to the chaos which awaited their troops after zero hour) on the ground, and as such the corps was the level in the BEF which organised the details of operations at Third Ypres; this was a tendency which increased as the battle went on, rather than diminishing, since the style of offensive became so stereotyped. This standardised approach permitted operations to increase in tempo as the battle went on, with shorter and shorter pauses between attacks. Though this was not enough to ensure a breakthrough (tempo after all being relative, and the Germans were well aware in which sector they were going to be attacked), it did give the Germans cause for concern. XVIII Corps' assault in the Battle of Broodseinde, where the preliminary bombardment was dispensed with, was a foretaste of operations in late 1918. Division continued to act as the man on the spot, and even regained some of the independence they had lost in 1915 and 1916. However, they seem to have been reluctant to assert this, judging from Second Army and X Corps' prodding regarding the need for their feedback into the artillery plan. Nevertheless, Corps did devolve control of some of the field artillery and of machine-guns to division, and the latter passed control of tanks to brigade, all of which argues for the locus of control moving forwards. The tactical flexibility of the infantry improved considerably during Third Ypres but it could not compensate for the need to overcome poor battlefield communications by trying to make sure all eventualities were met in a comprehensive artillery plan, and this was executed by corps. And as long as five different barrages were necessary to secure the (relatively) safe passage of the attacking troops into the German positions, corps would still dominate the planning and organisation of offensives.

NOTES

1 Bond, Brian, 'Passchendaele: Verdicts, Past and Present' in Liddle, Peter H. (ed.) *Passchendaele in Perspective* (Leo Cooper, 1997). See also letter to his wife from Sir Aylmer Hunter-Weston, dated 18th December 1917. Hunter-Weston Papers, BL, no. 48366.

2 James, *A Record of the Battles and Engagements of the British Armies...*, 21-24.

3 *Notes For Conference – 24/5/1917.* Maxse Papers, IWM, 69/53/10, 35/1.

4 The commanders were Lt.-Gens. Claud Jacob (II Corps), the Earl of Cavan (XIV Corps), Ivor Maxse (XVIII Corps), H.E.Watts (XIX Corps), A. Hamilton Gordon (IX Corps), T.L.N.Morland (X Corps) and A.J.Godley (II ANZAC Corps.)

5 The *Preparatory Measures...* pamphlet is reproduced in the OH, 1916 Vol. 1, Appendix 16. Thanks to Mr. Peter T. Scott for this reference.

6 Letter from Maxse to Gough, 31st May, 1917. Maxse Papers, IWM, 69/53/10, 35/1.

7 *The Hour of Assault.* Undated memorandum (though the context suggests that it was drawn up before Arras) in Maxse Papers, IWM, 69/53/10, 35/1.

8 Letter from Gough to Maxse, 1st June 1917. Maxse Papers, IWM, 69/53/10, 35/1.

9 *Notes on Conference Held at Lovie Chateau, June 6th.* TNA:PRO, WO 95/519.

10 *Notes on Conference June 6th*, 2.

11 *SS135*, 8.

12 *Fifth Army S.G. 671/1*, 7th June 1917. TNA:PRO, WO 158/249.

13 Prior and Wilson, *Passchendaele*, 75.

14 *XIV Corps Operations. Instructions No. 2*, 12th June 1917. TNA:PRO, WO 95/912.

15 *XIV Corps No. G. 53/2. Corps Commander's Conference With Divisional Commanders 14/6/17*, 15th June 1917. TNA:PRO, WO 95/912.

16 *Notes on Conference Held at Lovie Chateau*, 19th June 1917. TNA:PRO, WO 95/912.

17 Like Prior and Wilson, I have referred to Maxse's copy of this memo, 25/6/17. Maxse Papers, IWM. 69/53/10, 35/2.

18 Prior and Wilson, *Passchendaele*, 76.

19 Memo by Gough, 26/6/17. Maxse Papers, IWM. 69/53/10, 35/2.

20 Prior and Wilson, *Passchendaele*, 76.

21 Memo by Gough, 26th June 1917. Maxse's marginalia (including the word "BALLS!" several times), 4. Maxse Papers, IWM. 69/53/10, 35/2.

22 See Travers, *How the War Was Won*, 14-15.

23 See Howell diary entries for 23rd and 31st July, 3rd, 8th, 15th, 18th August, 1916. Br.-Gen. Philip Howell Papers, LHCMA. IV/D/13.

24 Personal communication from Professor Ian Beckett, based on his chapter in Liddle, *Passchendaele in Perspective.*

25 *Fifth Army S.G.657/44*, 27th June 1917. TNA:PRO, WO 95/519.

26 *Fifth Army S.G. 657/49*, 30th June 1917. TNA:PRO, WO 158/249.

27 *XVIII Corps Instructions No: 1*, 30th June 1917. Maxse Papers, IWM. 69/53/8, 32, 6.

28 *Tank Operations 31st July 1917* Undated but apparently contemporary report in TNA:PRO, WO95/92.

29 *Report on the Use of Signal Tanks Since the Beginning of the Present Offensive – 31st July, 1917*. TNA:PRO, WO 95/92.

30 *XVIII Corps Instructions No: 1*, 6-7.

31 *Third Army No. G.63/25*, transcript of GHQ memorandum, 23rd October 1917. TNA:PRO, WO 95/366.

32 *XVIII Corps Instructions NO: 1*, 7.

33 For the model etc., see 24th Division document with the title given. Maxse Papers, IWM. 69/53/10, 35/1.

34 *16th. Divn. No.M.O./5/Q*, 16th June 1917, with covering notes from Hickie to Maxse and Maxse to his staff. Maxse Papers, IWM. 69/53/10, 35/1.

35 *XVIII Corps Instructions No: 1. Appendix "B". Arrangements For Aeroplane Contact Patrols.* 11-12.

36 *Appendix "C". Signal Arrangements.* 13-15.

37 *Appendix "D"* 16-18. *Appendix "E"* 19-21. *Appendix "F"* 22-23. XVIII Corps also issued *Administrative Instructions No. 1*, 5th July 1917. Maxse Papers, IWM, 69/53/9, 32.

38 *Appendix "E"*. 20.

39 Compare *Notes Collected by 24th Division* para. 9 to *XVIII Corps Instructions No: 1. Appendix "E". Intelligence Arrangements*, 20-21.

40 *XVIII Corps Instructions No: 1. Appendix "E"* 21.

41 *FSR I*, 27.

42 For the GOCRA keeping overall control, see, for example, *XIV Corps Operation Order No. 136*, 23rd July 1917. TNA:PRO, WO 95/912.

43 *XIV Corps No. G.52/3, Corps Commander's Conference With Divisional Commanders.* 5th July 1917, 1. TNA:PRO, WO 95/912.

44 *XIV Corps Operations. Instruction No. 4. Revised 11th July, 1917.* TNA:PRO, WO 95/912.

45 *XIV Corps Operations. Instruction No. 4...,* 5-6. Note that divisions were allocated 6-inch and 4.5-inch howitzer batteries as well as the 18-pounders 'superimposed' on the barrage.

46 See *XVIII Corps No. G.S. 47/268*, 18th July 1917. Maxse Papers, IWM, 69/53/8, 33. This adverts to the GOCRA reporting to the MGRA regarding practice barrages.

47 *XVIII Corps No. G.S. 47/299*, 25th July, 1917. Maxse Papers, IWM, 69/53/10, 34.

48 *XVIII Corps No. G.S. 47/338*, 25th July, 1917. Maxse Papers, IWM, 69/53/10, 35/1.

49 Farrar-Hockley, *Goughie*, 239-40.

50 See *Second Army G. 377*, 18th June 1917. TNA:PRO, WO 158/207.

51 Letter from Kiggell to Plumer, 13th June 1917. TNA:PRO, WO 158/207. The divisions were the 11th, 16th and 36th.

52 James Papers, 1917. IWM.

53 Prior and Wilson, *Passchendaele...*, 73-4.

54 *Second Army Artillery Instructions No. 1*, 4th July 1917. TNA:PRO, WO 158/207.

55 *R.A. X Corps No.9/10/10. Xth Corps Artillery Instruction No. 24.*, 3rd July 1917. TNA:PRO, WO 95/865.

56 *Report on Machine Gun Operations in Attack by Xth Corps On July 31st, 1917.*, 17th August 1917. TNA:PRO, WO 95/853.

57 *Xth Corps Instructions. Appendix No. 8. Liaison.*, 18th July 1917. TNA:PRO, WO 95/853.

58 *Operations. 31st July, 1917.* 1st August 1917. TNA:PRO, WO 95/853.

59 Farrar-Hockley, *Goughie*, 221.

60 O.H., 1917 Volume 2, 154-5.

61 Prior and Wilson, *Passchendaele...*, 89-94.

62 O.H., 1917 Volume 2, 149-50. Powell, *Plumer*, 208.

63 *Fifth Army S.G. 671/9.*, 7th August 1917, and Maxse's response, 12th August 1917. Maxse Papers, IWM, 69/53/10, 35/2.

64 See, passim, 51st (Highland) Division Report on the fighting of 31st July-1st August 1917. Maxse Papers, IWM, 69/53/10, 36.

65 Prior and Wilson, *Passchendaele...*, 100-105. *Notes on Army Commander's Conference Held at Lovie Chateau on 17th August, 1917.* TNA:PRO, WO 95/520.

66 See, for example, *XVIII Corps Order No: 56* and *XIV Corps Instruction No. 14*, both 7th August. TNA:PRO, WO 95/951 and TNA:PRO, WO 95/913, PRO, respectively.

67 Baynes, *Far From a Donkey*, 175-6.

68 *Preliminary Report on Operations on 19th Aug. 1917* and *Report on Operations, August 19th, 1917, as the Result of Evidence Obtained From Officers Concerned.*

TNA:PRO, WO 95/951.

69 *Fifth Army S.G.840/7*. TNA:PRO, WO 95/520.

70 See *Third Army No. G.66/18*, 8th September 1917, and subsequent documents on the demonstration. TNA:PRO, WO 95/366. Third Army also disseminated GHQ's notes on artillery action as a result of experience in the offensive – *Third Army No. G.3/637*, also in TNA:PRO, WO 95/366.

71 Prior and Wilson, *Passchendaele…*, 108-110.

72 Manuscript comment by Cavan on *38th Division No. G.S. 7301*, 14th September 1917. TNA:PRO, WO 95/913.

73 Farrar-Hockley, *Goughie*, 231-2, 237, 239-40.

74 See also above personal communication from Professor Ian Beckett.

75 *Fifth Army G.A. 720/39*, 22nd September 1917. Maxse Papers, IWM. 69/53/11, 41.

76 *XVIII Corps No. G.S. 82*, 27th September 1917. Maxse Papers, IWM. 69/53/11, 41.

77 *AMS/5/4409/2*, 16th October 1917. Maxse Papers, IWM. 69/53/11, 41.

78 Powell, *Plumer*, 209-10.

79 *Proceedings of Corps Commanders Conference. 27th August, 1917*. TNA:PRO, WO 95/275.

80 *Second Army G.140*. Undated, but according to the O.H., issued on 29th August 1917. TNA:PRO, WO 95/275.

81 *Second Army Artillery Instruction No. 2*, 2nd September 1917. TNA:PRO, WO 158/208.

82 Manuscript note from Harington to Davidson, accompanying *Second Army G. 237*, both 31st August 1917. TNA:PRO, WO 158/208.

83 *Second Army G. 697* and *Second Army G. 721*, 7th and 8th September 1917. TNA:PRO, WO 158/208.

84 *Proceedings of Corps Commanders Conference. 15th September, 1917*. TNA:PRO, WO 95/275.

85 *Second Army G. 503*, 4th September 1917. TNA:PRO, WO 95/275.

86 *Xth Corps Instructions G.X. 1*, 1st September 1917. TNA:PRO, WO 95/853.

87 *Xth Corps Instructions G.X. 2 (Amended)*, 5th September 1917. TNA:PRO, WO 95/853.

88 *Xth Corps Instructions G.X. 6*, 7th September 1917. TNA:PRO, WO 95/853.

89 *Xth Corps Instructions G.X. 6, Appendix IV*, II.

90 However, the O.H. says that arrangements were the same as for Messines, including the use of balloons. See 1917 Volume 2, 248.

91 *Xth Corps Instructions G.X. 6, Appendix IV*, II.

92 *Xth Corps Instructions G.X. 7*, 10th September 1917. TNA:PRO, WO 95/853.

93 *Xth Corps Artillery Instruction No. 39.*, 3rd September 1917, 3. TNA:PRO, WO 95/865.

94 *Report of M.G. Work During Operations of X Corps 20th & 26th September, 1917.*, 24th October 1917. TNA:PRO, WO 95/853.

95 *X Corps Narrative. Zero hour 20th September to 6 a.m. 21st September*. Undated. TNA:PRO, WO 95/853.

96 *X Corps, G.101/31/26*. Undated. TNA:PRO, WO 95/853.

97 *Notes on Conference Held At Lovie Chateau 10th September, 1917*. TNA:PRO, WO 158/250.

98 *Third Battle Of Ypres. Second phase continued, 20th Sept. 1917.* Undated report in Maxse Papers, IWM. 69/53/10, 35/3.

99 7th November 1917. TNA:PRO, WO 158/209. It may profitably be compared with Order No. 5, of 23rd September. TNA:PRO, WO 158/208.

100 5th October, 1917. TNA:PRO, WO 158/208.

101 See *Second Army Artillery Instructions No.13*, 10th October 1917. TNA:PRO, WO 158/208.

102 See *X Corps Instructions G.W.1* and its eight appendices, 22nd September 1917. TNA:PRO, WO 95/853.

103 *X Corps, G.101/1/79.*, 28th September 1917. TNA:PRO, WO 95/853.

104 *Preliminary Comments on the Operations of 4th October, 1917.* Undated. TNA: PRO, WO 95/853.

105 *Plan Of Operations, 26th October, 1917.* Undated. TNA:PRO, WO 95/853.

106 See *X Corps Narrative Of Operations, 26th October, 1917.* Undated. TNA:PRO, WO 95/853.

107 See *Fifth Army Order No. 22.*, 23rd September 1917. TNA:PRO, WO 95/520. See also Nos. 23-30 in TNA:PRO, WO 158/250.

108 See, for example, *Notes on a Conference Held at La Lovie Chateau 22nd October 1917* and *Conference Held at Army H.Q., 26th Oct.,1917.* TNA:PRO, WO 95/520.

109 See *V Corps Operation Order No. 177*, 23rd September 1917. TNA:PRO, WO 95/148. Also see *XIV Corps Operations. Instruction No. 20*, 27th September 1917. TNA:PRO, WO 95/913.

110 The 11th Division's *Report On Operations – 24th September to 11th October 1917. 22*, pronounced this to be "most useful." Maxse Papers, IWM. 69/53/11, 39.

111 See undated report entitled *Third Battle of Ypres. Third Phase. 4th Oct. 1917.* TNA:PRO, WO 95/952.

112 *The Task of 11th and 48th Divisions.* Undated sheet in Maxse Papers, IWM. 69/53/13/ 53/2.

113 The report is dated 1st November 1917. Maxse Papers, IWM. 69/53/11, 42.

114 Report given under covering note *Third Army No. G. 13/1406*, 9th September 1917. TNA:PRO, WO 95/366.

CHAPTER 5

Corps Command in the Battle of Cambrai

The Battle of Cambrai (20th November to 7th December 1917), though a much smaller affair than the battles discussed in the preceding three chapters, was of great enough significance to warrant examination for several reasons. The view of it which grew up in the post-war period, not least through the writings of Liddell Hart and Fuller, was as the genesis of all later tank offensives (including those of 1939 and after). In addition, the school of thought which argued that there must have been an alternative to the artillery and manpower-based offensives of 1915-17 has seized upon it as the exemplar of a 'correct' offensive. This is strikingly illustrated by the use of a quotation from Sir Winston Churchill in Viscount Montgomery's *A History of Warfare*. Montgomery concluded his account of the battle as follows:

"On my birthday in 1953 Sir Winston Churchill gave me a copy of his *World Crisis 1911-1918*…. I found he had written the following about the Cambrai battle:

Accusing as I do without exception all the great ally offensives of 1915, 1916, and 1917, as needless and wrongly conceived operations of infinite cost, I am bound to reply to the question, What else could be done? And I answer it, pointing to the Battle of Cambrai, '*This* [italics in original] could have been done'. This in many variants, this in larger and better forms ought to have been done, and would have been done if only the Generals had not been content to fight machine-gun bullets with the breasts of gallant men, and think that was waging war.

It seems unnecessary to say anything more on the subject."[1]

Notwithstanding the anachronistic thinking inherent in a statement ascribing to the tank any possible role in 1915, Cambrai was actually significant as the first British offensive of the war where the artillery dispensed with a preliminary bombardment. It was not a 'tank battle' as such, if the term is taken to imply that tanks undertook the main role in the operation. The function of the Tank Corps was to ensure that gaps were made in the German wire so that the infantry could get through, and then to support the infantry attack. First World War tanks were not capable of acting like those of 20 years later, and, notwithstanding Churchill's impassioned (or rhetorical) view, the tactics to carry out even an operation like Cambrai had not been devised until late 1917. From the point of view of this study, it is of interest to see how corps functioned in planning an operation which relied on a very different artillery plan from its predecessors and comprised the BEF's first experiences of open warfare since 1914 (other than the advance to the Hindenburg Line in early 1917, which was not a planned offensive).

The traditional view of the offensive as having originated in the mind of Lt.-Col. J.F.C. Fuller (then GSO1 at Tank Corps HQ), or if not precisely there, at least somewhere at Tank Corps HQ has in recent years been cast into doubt.[2] It may actually first have seen light as a suggestion submitted by the BGGS of IV Corps (Br.-Gen. H.D. De Pree) to Third Army on 23rd August 1917, for "a surprise attack with the aid of tanks on the FLESQUIERES – HAVRINCOURT Ridge, to take advantage of the apparent weakness of the enemy on this front in guns."[3] As well as this last precondition for success, it was also important that "The ground is little cut up by shell fire," or the tanks would be useless. Though the original idea was considerably expanded by Third Army, the initiation of the project by Corps (in consultation with Br.-Gen. H.H. Tudor, the CRA, 9th Division) argues against the idea that plans were invariably imposed from above in the BEF.

In fact, the planning of the attack was, once Third Army had taken over, much like that of other offensives in 1917. Army issued its draft scheme in three parts, and "subject to such alterations as have already been approved by the Army Commander, the Draft Scheme will form the basis on which Corps [III and IV Corps were to undertake the initial attack] will formulate their Schemes and make preparations for carrying out the operation."[4] Objectives were shown on attached maps and the principles of the operation – especially the need for surprise and the consequent unusual lack of a preliminary bombardment – were stressed.[5] However, although the progression to the first and second objectives (the Blue and Brown Lines, respectively) was to be accomplished by divisions leapfrogging forward, the rest of the plan was less conventional. Once the Hindenburg Line had been breached, the second stage – exploitation by the cavalry up to the Red Line and beyond – was to begin. Notwithstanding the comparative lack of experience of the Cavalry Corps in major operations, it was treated in the same way in the plans as any other (although III and IV Corps had no involvement in heavy fighting since the Somme), with its tasks and approximate schedule being indicated by Army, but the precise details being left to the Corps GOC. However, although the scheme stated that tanks would be allotted to the cavalry and would accompany and support the advance, no mention was made of training in cavalry-tank co-operation at this or any other point.[6] Although some such training had been undertaken in September 1917, in preparation for the then expected breakthrough at Passchendaele, Cambrai was marked by poor tank-cavalry co-operation.[7] In the third phase of the operation, the cavalry were to press on and seize Cambrai, after which the infantry advance would continue, initially just by III Corps, but then successively by IV Corps and the two corps on the left flank of the front of attack, VI and XVII.[8] At this stage, objectives were described by approximate lines on the map and no operational details were suggested except for the all-important clearing of roads for the advance; it would not have been reasonable to adopt a prescriptive approach to operations so far ahead, both physically and temporally. However, for the cavalry to have swept round to the north of Cambrai it would have needed to advance about 10 miles, which was not a great deal more radical than the eight-mile advance proposed for the Arras offensive.[9]

The agenda for one Army conference confirms the impression given by the evidence cited above, of what was a largely routine planning process by this time, with discussion of objectives followed by corps commanders outlining their plans.[10] Army also dropped a number of hints to corps regarding their operations in subsequent memoranda. Indeed, the OH refers to Army's memorandum of 13th November to the Cavalry Corps as "special instructions,"[11] which reminded its GOC (Lt.-Gen. Sir C.T.McM. Kavanagh) of Byng's intentions and went on to stress his main tasks and how Byng expected him to achieve them, in which context liaison with both tanks and infantry were raised.[12] Similarly, III Corps, which was to use its reserve division (29th) to take the crossings of the St. Quentin Canal at Masnières and Marcoing (these were essential for the cavalry advance), was given clear advice on when to move that division forward.[13] This assertiveness on the part of the Army commander may have reflected the comments he received on the draft plan from Sir Douglas Haig, who informed him that "Tasks by Corps require to be more clearly defined…"[14] Haig also sought to clarify the organisation of the attacking force, defining four "commands," which were "III Corps, with a mounted detachment to secure and extend the right flank;" "IV Corps (with a mounted force)… [on] the left flank…," "The Cavalry Corps (less detachments as above) to be passed forward as soon as possible to seize Cambrai and cover the advance... of the V Corps..." and V Corps, which was to exploit the success.[15] Haig, of course, never felt any compunction about being prescriptive towards his subordinates if it suited him, whether they were the man on the spot or not.

The process of planning at the corps level was also largely conventional. For example, in response to the Army draft scheme, IV Corps issued its own on October 31st, which "laid down the object of the operation, its three stages, and the allotment of the troops. It gave an outline of the measures required for the preparation of the area and the assembly of the troops. On this Administrative, Intelligence and Signalling instructions were issued by the branches of the Staff concerned."[16] As the details of the attack and the distribution of forces were refined, so was the corps scheme, IV Corps' later instructions "defining more closely the role of the...Divisions of the Corps after the capture of the Hindenburg Support system." In view of later criticisms of the planning as leaving no reserves of tanks, it is noteworthy that corps appear to have been responsible: "It was decided that every Tank of the 1st Tank Brigade [assigned to IV Corps] should be used to its utmost capacity on "Z" day, so as to be able to gain as much ground as possible on the first day." However, as usual, other decisions relating to divisions were left to their commanders.

The same was true of training. One departure from previous practice was that, as far as possible, the divisions to be employed in the attack were not moved up until immediately before the assault, rather than having a few days to acclimatise to their part of the line but also to become tired. This had two merits. Firstly, the Germans would not be able to secure identifications of new divisions coming into the line before the attack, if they took prisoners, which helped towards achieving surprise (and so increased tempo). And secondly, time was available for the training which was plainly necessary, in view of the inexperience of tank crews and infantry in working together. It was the organisation of this training which IV Corps firmly delegated to divisional commanders, who were to "get in touch with O.C. 1st Tank Brigade... to draw up a training programme."[17] Although Tank Corps HQ drew up a number of training schemes, which were passed to corps by Army HQ, the OH nevertheless insisted that each division (and even brigade) followed its own ideas on joint training, and this ultimately reduced the effectiveness of the assault.[18] Certainly the 'lessons' section of the IV Corps report on these operations said that such training was very important, and "A universal system of combined attack by Tanks and Infantry should be laid down, and all Divisions should practise it..."[19] A Tank Corps report on the Cambrai operations stated that the organisation of "trench cleaning" platoons of infantry (designated to follow the tanks) was "as in S.S. 143" (*Instructions for the training of platoons for offensive action, 1917*).[20] Obviously the pamphlets issued earlier in the year were not viewed as having been superseded.

As regards the command and distribution of the tanks, little differed from earlier attacks. Tank Corps HQ passed to Army its recommendations for the distribution of its units amongst corps in late October, but Army had the final say.[21] However, as has been noted above, corps appear to have made the final decision as regards the allocation of their tanks. Travers is critical of Third Army for permitting such a degree of latitude, but apart from this contradicting his view that the command of the BEF was over-centralised, it also reflected the contemporary view of command coming from Tank Corps HQ (notwithstanding Fuller's comments to the Official Historian in 1945, cited by Travers).[22] This was that:

> The duty of the Tank is very similar to that of the Gun, consequently the command of Tank units can be made to approximate very closely to that of Artillery units.
> The senior tank commander and the senior subordinate Commanders under him should act in the dual capacity of Adviser to the Commander of the formation with which they are operating and as Commander of their own units, their action being based on what the Infantry Commander considers his men can do. The one object of the Tank or the Gun is to reduce resistance to the Infantry advance.
> The allotment of Tanks to Divisions and the routes and objectives will be made by the Corps.[23]

Much has been made of the decision by the GOC Tank Corps, Br.-Gen. H.J. Elles, to take his place in a tank in the centre of the attack, thus neutralising himself as an active commander. However, his action has not been considered from the viewpoint that once the tanks were allocated to corps and divisions, they did not act under his command, but that of the formations to which they were attached. One novel aspect of the control of tanks was the secondment of a GSO2 from each corps staff to its tank brigade HQ. These officers were "during the entire operations in intimate touch with the fighting troops and the tactical situation. They reported nightly to [tank brigade?] H.Q. Their information was invaluable."[24]

By far the most important innovation of the battle was in the use of artillery. The crux of this was that, as a result of technical developments in positioning guns relative to each other and their targets, using sound-ranging to locate the latter, calibrating both the artillery pieces and their ammunition, and taking meteorological factors into account, it was now possible to 'shoot off the map' (the maps themselves being by now much more accurate than earlier in the war). This meant that no preliminary bombardment was required to range the artillery on its targets. Consequently, surprise in the offensive was possible. Since preliminary wire-cutting could not take place if surprise were to be attained, the principal role of the tanks was, as stated earlier, to act as adjuncts to the infantry-artillery attack, designed to force gaps in the wire for the troops to get through. Travers overrates the tanks' capabilities and assumes that Byng mislead-ingly portrayed them in a subordinate role in the plan in order to make it more palatable to the 'reactionaries' at GHQ. However, it is apparent that they were only a subsidiary element – albeit a very important one – in the scheme.[25] Given that General Byng personally sponsored the scheme, overruling the more cautious of his gunners who wanted at least some ranging fire beforehand, it is not surprising that the artillery plan for the first phases of the attack was closely laid down by Army.[26] The first set of instructions concerned itself mainly with the principles underlying the attack and the measures to implement them, and corps were given little room for manoeuvre, being told, for example, not to let their boundaries affect their dispositions, and that in the transfer of batteries from the less active corps to III and IV Corps, "In certain cases there is no latitude for selection by Corps…"[27] In the second set, the details of the advance were given. A field artillery liaison officer was attached to each infantry brigade HQ and a senior heavy artillery officer to each divisional HQ, much as in Third Ypres. In addition, "Corps will detail such other Artillery officers as are deemed necessary for the special mission of watching the progress of the Infantry and keeping Artillery Commanders informed of the tactical situation." Corps balloons were also to be used again, in direct commu-nication with Heavy Artillery Groups. That the artillery plan, however radical, also drew heavily on past experience was strongly brought out by a reminder that corps should note "lessons drawn from the advance in the BAPAUME area [i.e. to the Hindenburg Line] during March 1917." These lessons especially covered the use of roads by heavy artillery (only a few guns should be brought forward until a proper road system had been established) and that battery commanders should use initiative and bat-teries work faster than in trench warfare. And, in a similar way to the Fifth Army plan for 31st July 1917, "As soon as a check occurs and an organized Artillery action becomes necessary it is essential for the Corps to resume close tactical control without delay."[28]

The third of Army's artillery instructions dealt with the bombardment and barrage (lifting, not creeping) on the day of attack, including counter-battery work. It was prescriptive where features of the plan were new, but if corps were best placed to decide on local artillery action, they were given a free hand to do so. Hence, the rate of barrage fire during the advance was as laid down by Army, but during periods of consolidation corps could vary it according to the tactical information they possessed.[29] The same applied to the proportion of smoke shell to be employed, and corps were even empowered to delegate this decision to divisions if they desired.[30]

Nevertheless, since Army planned the initial bombardment, the GOCRAs and divisional CRAs were left with the task of devising how best to support the later stages of the advance.[31] Consequently, for example, IV Corps' instructions of 13th November consisted half of an almost verbatim regurgitation of the salient points of Army's No.19 and half of instructions to divisional CRAs to forward as soon as possible Tables of Moves for use once the Brown Line (the second objective) had been taken (and the Hindenburg Line therefore breached).[32] But since the moving was corps RA's main organisational job, the next set of instructions, reflecting *Third Army Artillery Instructions No. 20*, saw them acting very much as a post-box and repeating the latter down to divisional CRAs.[33]

It should be noted that the guiding principle of the artillery fire at Cambrai was, for the first time, neutralisation rather than the destruction of the German troops, artillery and defences; even the usual destructive counter-battery shoots were not to be attempted. Since the programme was necessarily unrehearsed, corps RFC squadrons were given the task of spotting for this fire on the day, with the subsidiary role of reporting active German batteries and potentially dangerous concentrations of their infantry.[34] For the first time, a Tank Liaison officer was attached to each squadron too.[35] In addition, the duties of Branch Intelligence Officers attached to army wings and corps squadrons, were stressed. These officers were apparently established by a GHQ letter in late 1916 (strangely, the OH claims that they were created in late 1917) though no mention of them before Cambrai has been encountered in the course of this work.[36] The Branch Intelligence Sections run by these officers were to be "an integral portion of the Army or Corps Intelligence," and they were created with the idea of facilitating the "rapid dissemination of information of immediate tactical importance direct to the troops concerned." Therefore they were empowered – under the orders of the OC wing or squadron – to pass such information on without it going through corps or Army Intelligence first (though they would be simultaneously informed of what was being sent out). In addition, corps squadrons undertook their usual infantry contact patrols (with Army aeroplanes taking on a much expanded ground attack role) and as the tanks moved up immediately before the attack, low flying aeroplanes were used to drown the noise.

A novel function for the RFC stemmed from the extreme need for secrecy before the attack. No. 15 Squadron, for example, had the role of overflying IV Corps' back areas behind the British front line and reporting back on the visibility or otherwise of accommodation, vehicles (including the volume of traffic) or dumps.[37] For obvious reasons, Corps Camouflage Officers were appointed before the offensive in order to advise units (and especially the artillery) on how best to conceal their men and equipment. Lieutenant Cole, RE, of the Southern Special Works Park RE reported to III Corps HQ on 31st October in order to act in this role "for the present contemplated operations." As part of this, he was to liaise with the Special Works Park for the corps' material requirements.[38]

Like the artillery, the RE branch had to prepare for the advance. Roads across no man's land and beyond were to be repaired by the corps, the idea being that in the first 48 hours of the attack, corps (with supplementary labour from army) would take responsibility not only for their pre-advance complement of roads but also those taken by the advancing troops. After that, Army would also move the DGT Line (approximately, the demarcation between its and corps' responsibilities) forward to catch up, on a daily basis, corps then losing its extra labour.[39] However, in practice the system rapidly became overstretched, owing to the poor state of captured roads and the loss of the extra manpower to the Corps Roads Officer just when he needed it most.[40] Nor should the work of the Corps Water Supply Officer be forgotten, this individual being responsible not only for the supply of water for both horses and men before the attack (and its camouflage), but also for reconnaissance of new watering sites once the troops had advanced. Although lack of co-operation from divisions was complained of, the CRE's report concluded that water supply had nevertheless been completely satisfactory.

The CRE himself appears to have acted as a clearing house for information from divisional CREs, divisional 'Q' Branches, other corps' CREs and any other officer who felt he could contribute relevant information regarding the state of roads, bridges, water supply and even captured dugouts. He then passed it on to the divisional CREs and 'G' branches , corps 'G' and 'Q' and other concerned parties. These did not include Army 'G', though the CRE was informed.[41]

It is apparent that the scale of the advance at Cambrai placed unusual burdens on the Royal Engineers concerned. The problems with road construction have already been mentioned; roads which were kept open became and remained seriously congested. This contributed to severe communications problems. Telephone lines were not only cut by German shellfire but also by the men, tanks, horses, artillery and wagons moving forward. Buried cables were more or less absent, secrecy before the attack dictating that the necessary trenches could not be dug, and even if the cable could have been kept intact, its supply to divisions over the distance advanced proved very difficult during operations. Moreover, when it could be supplied, the great length of the cable meant that it had a high electrical capacitance, which reduced the power available to carry the telephone signal itself. Consequently, it was necessary to fall back on visual signalling, power buzzers, wireless and all the other alternatives mentioned earlier in this book. Most were of limited use, but visual signalling and mounted despatch riders were most effective, presumably because of the open ground over which the advance took place.[42]

Before considering other aspects of how corps operated during the operations themselves, it is worth noting that the command of machine-guns appears to have differed little, if at all, from that in Third Ypres. They were used in a corps barrage and then reverted to divisional control.[43]

It is not intended to give anything more than the broadest outline of the Cambrai fighting. Although the first day was a great success by Western Front standards, achieving a high degree of surprise, not all the objectives were reached. The inability of the 51st Division to capture the Brown Line at Flesquières appears to have caused loss of impetus to the whole IV Corps attack, so exploitation on to Bourlon Ridge and Wood, as had been hoped, was not possible. Failure of communication, or of the cavalry to use their initiative (or both) led to their never moving forward far or fast enough to assist 51st Division by outflanking the village. Nor did they, on the III Corps front, exploit opportunities to cross the St. Quentin Canal at Marcoing and sweep into the German rear areas (as planned) before the Germans could bring up their reserves. This study will not go into the detail of why they and 51st Division failed; the controversies are in any case not yet settled.[44]

However, it is noteworthy that control over the attack was even more difficult for corps than was usual in an offensive on the Western Front. Normally, they could exercise some control over matters by virtue of their command over divisional artillery, even if uncertainty as to the whereabouts of the infantry often made such intervention too late or simply pointless. However, after the initial advance on the first day of the battle there was no structured artillery plan to fall back upon, and divisions were hard in any case to contact; as stated above, communications were a considerable problem throughout. Indeed, at the close of 20th November even divisions were themselves unsure as to the location and condition of their forward troops.[45] Apart from that, the conduct of corps during the Cambrai operations was, despite the novel nature of the offensive, much according to form, and the usual stages of activity were followed. First, the launching of a carefully prepared and partially successful attack. Second, the slow and approximate appreciation of the actual position after early optimistic reports had been received. Third, the issuing of orders for the next day, which was less successful than the first (but still held out hopes of victory, or at least the winning of all the first day's objectives).[46] And fourthly, the persistent launching of further attacks with diminishing success and rising casualties as the scope for confusion rose with the deterioration of ad hoc communications, and as the standard of preparation fell far short of that for the first day, and a wasting fight took the place of a breakthrough.[47]

One factor in this was that corps-corps liaison seems to have been less satisfactory than usual. The normally discreet OH characterised the attacks of both corps on 21st November as "feeble and ill-co-ordinated" and said that on that day, IV Corps passed orders to 51st Division which were based on the mistaken impression that III Corps had arranged for 6th Division (to the right of 51st) to attack on its flank.[48] Captain Miles' (the compiler of this volume of the OH) target was perhaps IV Corps rather than III, since he also mentioned orders from the former to 40th Division for an attack to be made on 25th November with the support of 12 tanks, which was an obvious error, since Army had pulled all tanks into reserve.[49] Haig was unhappy with the performance of Lt.-Gen. Sir C.L. Woollcombe of IV Corps (and that of his GOCRA), so on 25th November he told Byng to "go personally into the situation."[50] It is not clear whether this was the cause of Byng's obduracy in insisting on the foolish and unsuccessful attack by the Guards Division on Fontaine on 27th November, against the protests of an experienced divisional commander. However, the latter, Maj.-Gen. G.P.T. Feilding, had asked for a conference with corps in which he put forward his objections, only to be told by Woollcombe that "he [Woollcombe] could give no decision, that the matter must be referred to the Third Army Commander."[51] Indeed, "the corps commander was unprovided with any plan, or artillery programme, or objectives, or divisional boundaries," so it would seem that Woollcombe was either not capable of or not permitted the exercise of any initiative. He lost command of IV Corps (to Harper of 51st Division) in early March 1918; Cambrai was the only major action IV Corps undertook while commanded by him, and it would seem that he was found wanting. Security would presumably have precluded the moving of a more able and experienced corps commander and his HQ into the area before the battle.

Once the attack had been abandoned by Third Army's order on 27th November, what was the role of corps? IV Corps' immediate tasks were to consolidate the ground won, while also constructing a number of defensive lines behind the front, maintaining a counter-attack reserve and disposing their artillery in the most efficient way possible to cover their front.[52] III Corps had assumed a defensive posture earlier, on 22nd November, but their position was inherently weaker.[53] Because their defensive frontage was at right-angles to their original line of advance (and so their lines of communication ran close and parallel to their front), their position was too shallow to permit the construction of any sort of defence in depth, and on their right flank, and particularly where their right division, the 12th, joined VII Corps' left division, the 55th, observation was very poor owing to the convexity of the slope. This made it easy for the Germans to assemble an attacking force in this sector, and it is not surprising that when they launched their counter-attack on 30th November, it was at this point that the blow fell hardest. The lack of observation was compounded by the fact that VII Corps were short of artillery on the 55th Division front. They later claimed that they had arranged with III Corps for the latter's artillery to provide the necessary support early in the morning of 30th November, but III Corps' version of events was that they were awaiting an SOS call from 55th Division or a phone call from VII Corps at the required time, and so did not open up.[54] The reports on this after the battle give the impression that III Corps were more sanguine about their position than VII Corps, since they were under the impression that all the bridges on their front across which the attack might come had been destroyed. Indeed, Maj.-Gen. H.S. Jeudwine, the GOC 55th Division, said that he had been informed by VII Corps some days earlier that he might draw upon the assistance of a brigade of 12th Division (although it was in III Corps). Upon the GOC 12th Division (Maj.-Gen. A.B. Scott) denying all knowledge of this, the two men arranged for 55th Division to take some heavy artillery support from 12th, but this idea was quashed by III Corps.[55] Travers ascribes all this to 'paralysis of command' and castigates III Corps for not taking the German threat seriously.[56] However, their misapprehension of the situation (though hardly creditable) explains their relaxed attitude, and the whole thing might as well be described as a series of misunderstandings as some form of institutional 'paralysis'; the commanders at fault were not immobile but mistaken.

During the German attack itself, if VII Corps is used as an example, it appears to have received situation reports from its divisions and parcelled out reinforcements and artillery support as best it could.[57] On 55th Division's front Jeudwine then actually told the reinforcing formations (such as the 4th and 5th Cavalry Divisions) where and how he wanted them disposed.[58] III Corps, with more resources, was able to organise counter-attacks, but rather ineptly. The 60th and the 16th Brigades were ordered by corps to make another counter-attack during the night of 30th November, but it seems that neither brigade knew what the other was doing, and nor did their divisional HQs.[59] Some degree of autonomy being accorded the man on the spot was inevitable under the circumstances, where communication delays were bound to occur (the 6th Division HQ "was out of touch with the III Corps by telephone from about 9.30am until 12.30pm" on 30th November) but corps still (within the bounds permitted by Army) controlled the allocation of reserves and artillery.[60]

Lastly, it is necessary to touch on the Court of Enquiry (conducted in January 1918) into the success of the German counter-attack on the III and VII Corps fronts. This has often been criticised as presenting a view of the fighting which avoided the issue of blame for the higher command and instead commented adversely on the readiness and training of the troops on the ground or blandly stated the need for a defensive doctrine.[61] However, this is unnecessarily harsh. Firstly, higher formations were criticised in about half of the report (admittedly in general terms only) for the poor siting of the boundary between III and VII Corps, the lack of artillery in the area, the lack of defence in depth and – by implication going all the way to GHQ – the lack of a proper defensive doctrine.[62] While all this may have avoided the issue of personal blame, it was still valid criticism. Secondly, the fact that the troops on the ground endured more fatigue, danger, discomfort and general suffering than their superiors (bearing in mind that Br.-Gen. R.B. Bradford, GOC of the 186th Brigade, was killed on 30th November) does not mean that they were faultless. They were inexperienced in defensive actions, which apparently require more military art than attacks, and especially more than attacks following a barrage.[63] One of the members of the Court was Sir Ivor Maxse, and he, as well as censuring both the divisional and corps commands (and even Army) in notes he made to add to the main findings, made the observation that the main thing hampering the proper training of troops and dissemination of doctrine in the BEF was the high turnover of divisions through corps, so that the "expert supervision" of their training that could be provided by corps commanders was largely lacking.[64]

In conclusion, notwithstanding the radical reputation of the plan for the Battle of Cambrai, it was largely based on previous experience within the BEF and was the product of continuity as much as – if not more than – change. Though its novel features, which as far as corps were concerned lay principally in the use of artillery, led to small differences in the planning style from that done for (say) Third Ypres, the process of preparation contained little that was radically new, apart from the training of infantry with tanks and the keeping of the assault divisions out of the front line until just before the attack. Indeed, previous experience, such as the logistical problems of getting heavy artillery forward after the German retreat in March 1917, was explicitly drawn upon. Tanks, by this time, were not a complete novelty to the higher staffs and notwithstanding numerous claims to the contrary, they were the means by which neutralising artillery fire could be made to work and not the *sine qua non* of the whole plan. Perhaps more novel for staffs than co-operation with tanks were the methods used to ensure that the artillery plan remained a surprise to the Germans (corps had not had their own camouflage officer before, for example) and the problems faced by the Royal Engineers in supporting so deep an advance. Given that these last manifested themselves on the day in the form of poor communications and problems in getting troops forward to the right places fast enough, they were hardly different in their effects from the shell craters and swamps of Ypres, and the battle itself acquired an increasingly conventional character as it went on. The potential to attain a higher tempo than the Germans slipped away after the initial assault. Had the resources been available to launch another attack – not necessarily with a large tank element – soon after, the Germans might have been caught off-balance and more achieved. As it was, the inept handling of the cavalry and some infantry divisions, combined with the stubborn German resistance, meant that the opportunity was lost, and the Germans themselves achieved higher tempo than Third Army in their counter-attack on 30th November. In fact, the Cambrai offensive, rather than being a revolutionary idea almost strangled at birth by red-tabbed reactionaries, was an excellent example of the BEF's ability to learn from its experiences and to bring old and new ideas to work successfully together within the existing command structure. That mistakes were made which prevented a greater success at the start and assisted the Germans in their counter-attack at the end of the battle do not alter this. The Battle of Cambrai was thoroughly conventional in its execution at the corps level, but its significance as the first time since Neuve Chapelle that strategic surprise was attained by the BEF should not be underestimated, particularly in view of the way in which the offensives of August 1918 onwards were conducted. How the lessons of Cambrai were applied will be considered in the next two chapters.

NOTES

1 Montgomery of Alamein, Field-Marshal Viscount, *A History of Warfare* (Collins, 1968), 479-80.

2 See Harris, J.P., *Men, ideas and tanks* (Manchester and New York: MUP, 1995). pp.110-112.

3 *IV Corps No. H.R.S. 1-A*, 23rd August 1917. TNA:PRO, WO 158/396.

4 *Third Army No. G.S. 56/6*, 1st November 1917. TNA:PRO, WO 95/367.

5 *3rd Army No.GY.1/1. Draft scheme for operation GY.*, 25th October 1917. TNA: PRO, WO 95/366.

6 *Third Army No. G.S. 56/6*, 1st November 1917. TNA:PRO, WO 95/367.

7 Badsey, Stephen, 'Cavalry and the Development of Breakthrough Doctrine' in Griffith, Paddy (ed.) *British Fighting Methods in the Great War* (London and Portland, Oregon: Frank Cass, 1996), 159-60.

8 *Draft scheme for operation GY. Third Stage.*

9 Badsey, 'Cavalry...' 160.

10 *Third Army No. G.S. 56/36*, undated but presumably early to mid-November. TNA:PRO, WO 95/367.

11 O.H., 1917 Volume 3, 20.

12 *Third Army No. G.S. 56/96*, 13th November 1917. TNA:PRO, WO 95/367.

13 *Third Army No. G.S. 56/102*, 14th November 1917. TNA:PRO, WO 95/367.

14 *O.A.D. 690*, 3rd November 1917. TNA:PRO, WO 95/367.

15 *O.A.D. 700*, 11th November 1917. TNA:PRO, WO 95/367.

16 *IV Corps, Havrincourt-Bourlon Operations November 20th to December 1st...*, undated but obviously retrospective. 6. TNA:PRO, WO 158/318.

17 *IV Corps No. H.R.S. 17/4*, 31st October 1917. TNA:PRO, WO 158/376.

18 For the training notes see *Third Army No. G.S. 56/14*, 30th October 1917, and the attached notes. TNA:PRO, WO 95/368. Also see O.H., 1917 Volume 3, 33-5.

19 *IV Corps, Havrincourt-Bourlon Operations...Part III. Lessons*, 6. TNA:PRO, WO 158/318.

20 *Preliminary Report on Tank Corps Operations With the Third Army 20th Nov. – 1st Decr. 1917*, 14th December 1917. 3. TNA:PRO, WO 95/92.

21 *Tank Corps S.G.502*, 28th October 1917. TNA:PRO, WO 158/351.

22 Travers, *How the War Was Won*, 22. Travers' view is challenged in Childs, 'British Tanks...', 154-5.

23 *Notes on Tank Operations April-October 1917*. Undated, but presumably just predating the Cambrai attack. TNA:PRO, WO 95/92. The quotation also explains why tanks were viewed as an 'adjunct' to the attack.

24 *Preliminary Report on Tank Corps Operations With the Third Army 20th Nov. – 1st Decr. 1917*. 5.

25 Travers, *How the War Was Won*, 20, 22.

26 Farndale, *Artillery*, 217.

27 *Third Army Artillery Instructions No. 18*, 29th October 1917, 3 & 5. TNA:PRO, WO 95/368.

28 *Third Army Artillery Instructions No. 19*, 10th November 1917, 2. TNA:PRO, WO 95/368.

29 *Third Army Artillery Instructions No. 20*, 14th November 1917, 4. TNA:PRO, WO 95/368.

30 *Third Army No.G.S.56/97B. Amendment No.2 to Third Army Artillery Instructions No.20.*, 18th November 1917. TNA:PRO, WO 95/368.

31 O.H., 1917 Volume 3, 29.

32 *IV Corps Artillery Instructions No. 76.*, 13th November 1917. TNA:PRO, WO 95/729.

33 *IV Corps Artillery Instructions No. 77.*, 16th November 1917. TNA:PRO, WO 95/729.

34 *Third Army Artillery Instructions No. 18*, 6.

35 *Notes on Tank Operations April-October 1917*. 16.

36 *O.B./1850*, 20th December 1916. TNA:PRO, WO 95/368. O.H., 1917 Volume 3, 30.

37 See untitled report dated 13th November 1917 from the CO of 15 Squadron to IV Corps RE. TNA:PRO, WO 95/368.

38 Untitled memoranda, both 28th October 1917, from the Major Commanding the Southern Special Works Park to III and VII Corps. TNA:PRO, WO 95/368.

39 Untitled memorandum, 8th November 1917, from the MGGS, Third Army to all corps. TNA:PRO, WO 95/368.

40 *IV Corps, Havrincourt-Bourlon Operations...Appendix C.2* [Notes by Chief Engineer]. TNA:PRO, WO 158/384.

41 IV Corps RE Notes for Cambrai. TNA:PRO, WO 158/378.

42 *Lessons From Recent Operations. Communications*. Undated. TNA:PRO, WO 158/316.

43 See III and IV Corps Operation Orders 224 and 320, respectively, reprinted in OH., 1917 Volume 3, 311-321.

44 Harris, *Men, ideas and tanks*, 125.

45 O.H., 1917 Volume 3, 94.

46 III Corps orders for 21st November O.H., 1917 Volume 3, 92.

47 O.H., 1917 Volume 3, 139.

48 O.H., 1917 Volume 3, 116 and 83.

49 O.H., 1917 Volume 3, 139, fn. 2.

50 O.H., 1917 Volume 3, 148. Haig diary for 25th November 1917. TNA:PRO, WO 256/24.

51 Headlam, Lt.-Col. C., *History of the Guards Division in the Great War, 1915-1918* (John Murray, 1924). Vol. I, 306-7.

52 *Third Army G.S.56/234*, 27th November 1917. TNA:PRO, WO 95/368.

53 OH., 1917 Volume 3, 108 and 165.

54 O.H., 1917 Volume 3, 172 and see *Report on Operations of the Third Corps on the 30th November, 1917*, 4th January 1918, and the associated artillery report. TNA:PRO, WO 158/52.

55 Document signed by Jeudwine and dated 4th January 1918. TNA:PRO, WO 158/52.

56 Travers, *How the War Was Won*, 28-30.

57 OH., 1917 Volume 3, 182-4.

58 55th Division's narrative of events for 30th November. TNA:PRO, WO 158/54.

59 OH., 1917 Volume 3, 195.

60 O.H., 1917 Volume 3, fn. 1.

61 Travers, *How the War Was Won*, 30.

62 Report of the Court in the Maxse Papers, IWM, 69/53/11, 40.

63 Sixsmith, Maj.-Gen. E.K.G., *British Generalship in the Twentieth Century* (Arms and Armour Press, 1970), 124-5.

64 *Note by a member of the Court of Enquiry*, Maxse Papers, IWM. 69/53/11, 40.

Barbed wire in front of the Hindenburg line. This indicates the need for tanks to crush the wire, or artillery fire to cut it. (IWM CO 3392)

Large reinforced concrete machine-gun post – another example of the obstacles faced by the BEF in 1918. (IWM CO 3481)

Corps 9.45-inch trench mortar on a pony cart for transportation. The cheerful gentleman is a Canadian officer. (IWM CO 3810)

Training: King George V (centre) watching a practice trench attack by Australian troops at the 5th Australian School near Sailly, March 14, 1916. (IWM Q 962)

Visitors: The King, accompanied by Sir Henry Rawlinson (on the right) and Walter Congreve (fourth from right), visiting the Somme battlefield. The Prince of Wales (later Edward VIII) is second from the left. (IWM Q 1012)

Visitors: The King of the Belgians (second left) being introduced to Lt.-Gen. Sir W.P. Pulteney by Rawlinson (first left), May 1917. (IWM Q 2192)

Visitors: As the visit of the King of the Belgians continues, his ADC finds a suspiciously well-preserved souvenir. (IWM Q 2199)

Corps heavies: manhandling a 9.2-inch howitzer near Ypres, September 1917. (IWM Q 3252)

Inspection of a machine-gun battery. (IWM Q 3272)

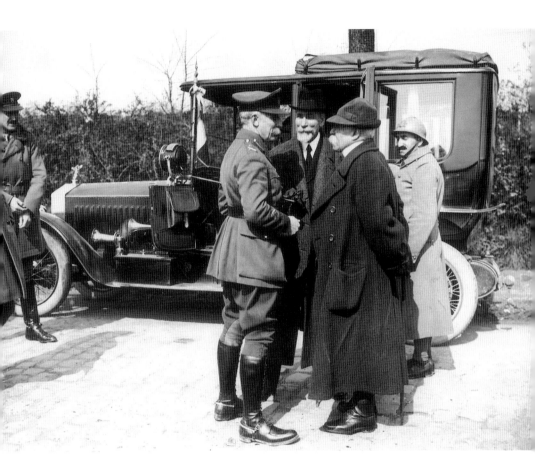

Opposite page:
Above: Corps heavies: 9.2-inch howitzer firing, September 1917. (IWM Q 3943)

Below: Training: A practice attack at a training school, August 1916. (IWM Q 4157)

This page:
Visitors: Sir Aylmer Hunter-Weston (left) talking to M. Clemenceau, the French Premier (opposite him, with the battered hat), April 1918.(IWM Q 6547)

Overleaf:
Medal parade: Sir Ivor Maxse presenting medals to men of the 152nd Brigade, August 1917. (IWM Q 6165)

LIEUT.-GEN. SIR F. IVOR MAXSE

Lt.-Gen. Sir Ivor Maxse, GOC XVIII Corps, sketched by Francis Dodd (who hoped to clear 12s 6d on each of the pictures in this series of senior officers) in 1917. Note the absence of a Sam Browne cross-belt; Maxse was officially rebuked in 1918 for turning up at the War Office thus improperly dressed. He was the foremost trainer of his generation.

LIEUT.-GEN. SIR CHARLES FERGUSSON

Lt.-Gen. Sir Charles Fergusson (Bt.), GOC XVII Corps from May 1916 to the end of the war. An unspectacular but thoroughly capable commander, who assisted in the rescue of a wounded man from no man's land when visiting the front line in 1916.

LIEUT.-GEN. SIR T. L. N. MORLAND

Lt.-Gen. Sir Thomas Morland, GOC X and XIII Corps. Despite forsaking his HQ for an observation tree on the first day of the Somme, Morland was seen as a safe pair of hands and his corps were involved in a number of successful actions from Messines onwards.

General Lord Cavan (left) when C-in-C of the British Force in Italy, 1918.
(IWM Q 26847a)

Communications: View of part of I Corps HQ in 1916. Note the despatch riders in the foreground and the large number of telephone lines and poles in the background. (IWM Q 27083)

Communications: VI Corps pigeon loft, August 1917. (IWM Q 27093)

Communications: Interior of XI Corps Signal Station. (IWM Q 27137)

Communications: Men of RE Signals, I Corps, burying telephone cable in a wooden case at the bottom of a trench. (IWM Q 27151)

CHAPTER 6

Corps in Defence: January to July 1918

The German offensives of March and April 1918, like the Third Battle of Ypres, have generated debate ever since they took place. That British forces could be forced back up to 40 miles in a matter of days, after struggling for years to advance fewer than 10, provoked an immediate search for scapegoats, but the swift sacking of Sir Hubert Gough (the Fifth Army commander) did not satisfy everyone. For example, the generals' apologists pointed accusingly (and have done so ever since) at Lloyd George for withholding badly needed manpower from the BEF at the start of 1918. Indeed, the Prime Minister faced a grave challenge in the House of Commons in May 1918 over accusations that he had lied to the House over the issue.[1] He defended himself successfully then and was later vehement in apportioning blame for the 'disaster' (in his memoirs) to Sir Douglas Haig and his supporters.[2] In contrast to this view, the most recent interpretation of the fighting in early 1918 argues that the command structure of the British Armies in France was so flawed that the question of numbers was irrelevant.[3]

How corps coped with the novel situation of being on the defensive in March and after has some bearing on these controversies, and is the main burden of this chapter. In addition, reference will be made to the role played in the defence of the Chemin des Dames in May by IX Corps, while it was in the still more unusual position of being under French command, and the BEF's continued ability to learn from experience in the first half of 1918 will be examined.

Analysis of the role of corps command in this period is fraught with difficulties. As discussed in the Introduction, operation orders are the main source for this research. However, for the March Retreat in particular, there are few formal orders. In XVIII Corps, for example, Corps Order No. 139 was issued on 15th March and No. 140 on 26th March.[4] Scraps written on army order forms are all that survives between those dates.

Even when corps wrote accounts of their doings, these are not documents which can be relied upon to give a completely unvarnished account of the retreat, since they are not likely to record events which would bring discredit on the corps concerned. Nor are divisional histories much better, for though men from other formations may have fallen back precipitately, it was never true of the division whose history one may be reading. Thus, 17th and 51st Divisions accused each other of retiring first; 63rd Division blamed 47th for retiring first, though the latter's history insists that they withdrew together under a corps plan.[5] However, as will be seen below, 47th Division in its turn felt that 9th Division, on its other flank, was too quick to withdraw. And 18th Division stated that it was ready to launch a counterattack on 21st March, but both its flanks were exposed by the withdrawal of its neighbours.[6]

Traditionally the manpower shortage has been seen as the root of the British problems (in the OH, for example), exacerbated by the reorganisation of divisions and on the day by fog, the power of the German artillery and the number of their infantry. However, Travers asserts that the source of the BEF's troubles was that the three-zone defence system was neither understood nor properly applied. From this stemmed the collapse of Fifth Army and the consequent retreat, which was attended by a collapse of the British command structure. As a result, Fifth and Third Armies separated and dangerous gaps opened in the line; the Germans were stopped only by their own exhaustion and a reversion to traditional mass tactics which caused them heavy losses.[7] He is supported in his view of the BEF's misunderstanding and misapplication of German defensive tactics by Martin Samuels.[8] Both also assert (though on different grounds) that there was no labour shortage for the construction of defences before March, and that in any case the British had enough troops to cover the front according to the German system.[9]

If the view that the German defensive system was misapplied by the BEF is accepted, this in no way means that it must be true that the British had adequate manpower for the tasks of preparing the defensive system and manning it when attacked. Indeed, the contrary appears to have been the case; as Samuels argues, the British viewed the battle and rear zone defences as requiring "a labyrinth of trenches and switches, tiers of wire, and hundreds of 'pill-boxes'..." and the construction of these was undoubtedly beyond their capacity.[10] However, such extravagant defences, though desirable, were not even approached in some areas; in the 36th Division's forward zone (partly for want of numbers in the garrison) "There was no touch between the battalion headquarters forts in the Line of Redoubts; they were in no sense mutually supporting."[11] Samuels' contention that, had the system been applied properly, the British would have been able to man it to the standard preferred by its inventors is based on his view that the number of combat troops in the 60 divisions of the BEF was the same as in the 84 German divisions which would have been required to hold a front as long as the British one.[12] However, this is arrived at by a comparison simply of numerical strength, and takes no account of the extreme undesirability of reorganising the British divisions any more than had already been necessitated by the reduction to nine battalions. Nor does Samuels' argument address the difficulty of overcoming the inevitable objections of Dominion governments to such a radical change to their forces, had it been proposed. Furthermore, it does not take into account the reality of the attack. Maxse's XVIII Corps, for example, had three divisions in line and one in GHQ reserve (i.e. actually held by GHQ but at XVIII Corps' disposal) on 21st March; against these were ranged eight German divisions with another six in immediate support, a far less favourable ratio than the "two to one" Samuels claims for the front of attack as a whole (an examination of the sketches in the OH, the source for his assertion, would actually seem to put this at three to one).[13] He also challenges the traditional view that the German artillery was overwhelmingly strong, since the average distribution of heavy guns was only 1.5 times that employed by the British on 1st July 1916. The totals he gives are 6,473 cannon and 3,532 mortars; the guns alone were to fire 1,160,000 shells in the five hour and forty minute preliminary bombardment.[14] The use of heavy gun density here seems misleading, since the accuracy of artillery was much greater in 1918 than 1916. In addition, the defensive systems under attack were not comparable and that the British artillery fired 1,500,000 shells in the seven days preceding 1st July 1916 argues for a far weaker artillery than one capable of firing over a million shells, not including those fired by the mortars, in less than six hours.[15] Admittedly, the British artillery was spread over a 14-mile front compared to the 50 attacked by the Germans in 1918, but up to a third of the shells fired in the June 1916 bombardment may have been duds.

Therefore, the view that the misapplication of the German system was the fundamental flaw in the British position simply does not take account of the tremendous German numerical and artillery superiority on the part of the front which gave way – the Fifth Army sector. Even if the German infantry's infiltration tactics, as used at Cambrai, had been better understood, the annihilating bombardment produced by the German artillery was entirely new to the British. Furthermore, Samuels' view carries with it the assumption that the then 'state of the art' version of the German doctrine was the only workable option and that this was why the British had such problems. However, on 28th March the German attack in front of Arras failed against well-prepared linear defences, where the front line was lightly held, in order to minimise casualties from the preliminary bombardment.[16] As will be shown below, regional variations did exist in the British defences, because they were modified according to local conditions, and not the least of these were the strength and position of existing defences. Travers' view that GHQ failed to impose uniformity of approach is entirely correct, but he fails to perceive that GHQ did not expect complete uniformity.[17] The man on the spot still knew best, as *FSR I* prescribed.

In the discussion of the organisation of the BEF's defences which follows, the plans of V, IX and XVIII Corps are specifically mentioned, each being used as an example for the Army to which it belonged (Second, Third and Fifth, respectively).

Because the lessons of Cambrai which were dwelt upon most were those from the first, offensive, part of the battle, captured German pamphlets were the main source for British thinking in late 1917, when the defensive policy for the beginning of the coming year was decided upon.[18] That is not to say that the German counter-attack was ignored, but it seems to have been taken for granted that the proper application of their own defensive principles would suffice to defeat any future German assaults; after all, as the Official Historian observed, "the enemy's experiences after nearly three years' defensive warfare on the Western Front.... [were] evidently well worth consideration..."[19] Haig outlined the necessity for a defensive posture to Army commanders on 3rd December, 1917 and asked them for their views on the policy to be adopted, in the light of the preliminary instructions he was issuing.[20] As a consequence of this consultation exercise, GHQ's Memorandum on Defensive Measures was sent out as the basis for all the BEF's defences, on 14th December. This outlined the probable method of attack to be adopted by the Germans – "we must expect an attack by masses of infantry, offering a very vulnerable target," to be preceded by a bombardment whose duration would vary depending upon whether the Germans intended to achieve surprise or not.[21] While this was, in the event, largely true, it appears that GHQ had failed to appreciate the significance (or presence) of the stormtroops preceding the masses of infantry at Cambrai; Travers' view that GHQ expected the Germans to attack in the same away as the BEF had appears to be partly confirmed by this, though infantry tactics in the BEF did not involve massed formations by 1918.[22] The memorandum went on to describe the three-zone defensive system to be adopted by the BEF. Defence in depth was the guiding principle. In order to absorb the enemy's assault and render him vulnerable to well-organised counter-attacks, the defences would consist of an outpost (or forward) zone, a battle zone and a rearward zone. Each of these would be organised in depth itself. The outpost zone (relying principally on machine-guns) would break up the enemy attack and compel considerable expenditure of his resources. A mile or two behind came the battle zone, 2-3,000 yards deep, which would be the main line of resistance, consisting of "strong successive systems of defence" (including artillery echeloned in depth) with switch lines dug to prevent any break-in permitting the attackers to roll the line up. Permanent garrisons were allotted to the most important features of this zone and "Plans and preparations for the employment of troops both in the defensive battle and in counter-attack" were to be carefully worked out."[23] Any penetration of this zone was to be dealt with by counter-attacks carried out by local reserves. If these failed, Army or corps reserves would be employed.[24] Lastly, the rearward zone was to be sited four to eight miles behind the battle zone and was a fall-back position in case of difficulty. However, it had the lowest priority for construction, and was in many places only marked out and not dug by the time the attack came in March.

The role of corps in all this was quite closely circumscribed. GHQ having outlined the principles it expected the defence to take, Armies were expected to disseminate these downward and to ensure that corps schemes adhered to them. They were also specifically told to ensure that corps' administrative arrangements were satisfactory, not least because corps had to be well enough organised to deal with substantial reinforce-ments (of both infantry and artillery) in the event of their particular sector being the focus of the German attack. In their turn, they were to permit lit-tle latitude to divisions, since "In order to ensure continuity amongst suc-ceeding Divisions" corps commanders were to state the policy of work in their sectors in considerable detail.[25] Thus, for example, the Fourth Army (which at the time was holding the Ypres sector) *Policy on the Army Front for 1918* directly quoted GHQ's memorandum on a number of points, such as the German method of attack and in the description of the policy for the three zones of defence.[26] Having also gone on to repeat the policy regarding corps and divisions, corps were also told to "detail a General Staff Officer, representatives of R.A., R.E., Machine Gun Corps, and Signal Service to draw up and supervise the details of the defence of that part of the Battle Zone lying within their Corps Area." And that "In order further to ensure continuity of work, officers should be placed permanently in charge of the defences of sectors of the Battle Zone."[27] Plainly the turnover of divisions through a corps was not going to be allowed to hamper the defence scheme, every effort being made to limit their freedom to depart from the prescribed plan. Nevertheless, the details on the ground were left to corps, which, just as for attacks, were expected to put into practice the principles enunciated by Army. This is not to say that the Army plans were sketchy; the Fourth Army document referred to above went into considerable detail as to what corps should consider for the artillery, RE and administrative aspects of the plan.

That said, it is plain that some grounds for discussion still existed. At a Fifth Army conference of corps commanders on 3rd February, once Gough had warned his subordinates that General von Hutier (who took Riga in September 1917 by using stormtroops and a hurricane bombardment) was now based opposite the Fifth Army front, corps commanders obviously were free to express their opinions and ask for resources. In the event that the attack was not a surprise, Gough expected corps to strengthen their two-division fronts by bringing forward a third. Both the III Corps and XVIII Corps commanders (Lt.-Gens. Butler and Maxse) asked that the reserves be brought forward in good time and Butler asked for a further division with which to reinforce his line. This was the longest corps front-age in the BEF, at 31,000 yards, and though part of it was marshy, Gough noted that von Hutier had crossed the River Dvina before his attack the previous September. Both requests, Gough said, would be referred to GHQ.[28] The corps commanders then went on to tell him that there was too much of a tendency to lay out the Battle Zone in their sectors in lines; both favoured strongpoints between the lines. That said, Gough was care-ful to exercise his co-ordinating function and reminded Butler and Maxse of their training responsibilities for the divisions under their command, pointing out that they should be mindful of the different dispositions required now that divisions were reduced from 12 to nine battalions (this change took place between 29th January and 4th March because of the shortage of manpower).[29]

The scope for divergence of ideas may have been greater than GHQ intended; at an Army commanders' conference on 16th February, in addi-tion to airing the latest intelligence regarding the likely time and place of the attack (and stating that the Germans would follow "sound principles and endeavour to wear us out and use up our reserves... with a view to throwing in his main weight at a later period...") Haig raised a number of issues. He stressed that troops should not be trained either for the defensive or the open warfare to follow it (he was obviously thinking of advancing once the German attacks had been repelled) at the expense of work on defences, but nor should the converse be true. Army command-ers were expected to take each case and portion of the front "on its merits." He emphasised the concept of defence in depth, asserting that the troops did not understand it but must be taught it through familiarity with the plan and their role within it, and went on to say that:

> A considerable diversity of principle appears to exist in the manner in which Armies and Corps intend to move their reserves should an attack be imminent. Some intend to interpolate divisions [in the line] before the battle begins, others intend to bring up reserve divisions to occupy the Battle Zone, while others intend to move forward reserve divisions into advanced positions preparatory to a counter-attack.[30]

However, owing to the variable circumstances on the ground, he felt that no definite rules could be laid down. But, in general, interpolation of reserves should only be resorted to if the frontage held was exces-sive, and reserves should be kept back as whole formations for as long as possible.[31] In the event, of course, the strength of the German attack and the over-extended nature of the Fifth Army position in particular meant that it was not possible to do this. Oddly, at a conference the next day, Sir Henry Rawlinson told his corps commanders very little of what the C-in-C had said, instead pressing them – reasonably enough – to press on more quickly with constructing their defences and to bear in mind his views on the possible use of tanks by the Germans, the siting of machine-guns and other matters. He also stressed the importance of ground-attack aeroplanes, both British and German, the result of both sides' effective use of aeroplanes in this role at Cambrai. Almost as an afterthought, Rawlinson raised Haig's concern: "Another point that the Army Commander wished to impress on Corps Commanders was the handling of their reserves. Reinforcements must not be put in too quickly."[32] In contrast, the minutes of the equivalent Third Army conference almost quoted GHQ's points verbatim and specified that of its corps, only VI required the interpolation of a division.[33]

In the meantime, corps were going about their tasks. The XVIII Corps *Instructions For Defence* briefly stated the principles of defence in depth and described the three-zone system and its layout. Unlike the Army instructions, it gave details of the zones' locations and also described the system of defence. The forward zone was to have permanently garrisoned outposts in a chequered pattern, backed up by a mobile reserve and supported by a line of strongpoints, which would constitute the main line of resistance in this zone; withdrawal from it was not to be contemplated. The mobile reserves, it should be noted, were complete units, "acting on the initiative of their own commanders" and poised to deliver counter-attacks where necessary.[34] The battle zone was to be organised on the same principles, though at the time of issue, little work had been done on its construction; it would constitute the main line of resistance if the forward zone was overrun. Immediate counter-attacks were not to be made from one zone to another, owing to the distance between them, but were to be deliberately organised under the aegis of divisional commanders. The defence of the rear zone was to be based on the same principles as for the battle zone, but it had no permanent garrison. However, the corps' counter-attack divisions would assemble in this zone. As in Army instructions, the corps stressed that all commanders of counter-attack units, from division downwards, must have a clear plan of action should the enemy come from either flank or the front, and the necessary troop movements were to be practised. In addition, divisional commanders were enjoined to ensure that liaison and mutual support arrangements with flanking units at all levels were agreed.[35] They were also informed that theirs was the responsibility for the construction of the forward zone, corps preparing the battle zone and Army the rear zone. The instructions then went on to lay down the policies regarding machine-guns, observation posts and communications, stressing that the use of wireless, pigeons, power buzzers and visual signals should be practised daily. Unit commanders were expected to explain to their men why they were digging whatever they were digging and its place in the general scheme. In view of the poor state of the XVIII Corps line, recently taken over from the French and in no way organised in depth, construction had to take priority over training.[36] However, at a conference on 1st March, Maxse stated that he expected the battle zone more or less to be complete by 7th March, after which "intensive training" would begin.[37]

Plainly the new defensive techniques needed to be explained, and in XVIII Corps Maxse organised a training course at the Corps School (from 17th-20th February) for senior officers to learn about them. The commandant of the School, Lt.-Col. the Hon. William Fraser, noted in his diary that "The object of the Course is to get – if not exactly uniformity of training – at any rate all training done on a really sensible and thorough system."[38] Maxse having given these officers (brigade and battalion commanders) an introductory talk, the discussion which followed appears to have been quite lively, notwithstanding the presence and participation of the Army commander.[39] More lectures, demonstrations and discussions made up the rest of the course, with lessons from Cambrai a prominent theme. That part of the front which succumbed to the German counter-attack had been organised in very little depth, which led Maxse and his staff to use it as justification for the new system. Furthermore, they felt that the linear defensive system lent itself to a shallow front, since it encouraged commanders to put all their men into the front line. In comparison, if 'blobs' – mutually supporting strongpoints – and 'keeps' were used, together with sensibly placed wire obstacles to funnel the attackers into positions where the defenders could most easily deal with them, depth was easier to attain and the relatively large frontage of XVIII Corps easier to defend.[40] A conference for company commanders followed in late February, and more still for platoon commanders were scheduled (the first began on 18th March); all these groups of officers, having been taught how to teach their subordinates, were expected to take the ideas back to their units and disseminate them (though it is likely that the course lessons were overtaken by events).[41]

An appendix to the XVIII Corps plan, dealing with artillery arrangements, was also issued. Decentralisation was the main feature of these, with divisions being in command of the field artillery, and from the start of an enemy attack, the CHA devolved command of the heavies to them also. In addition, there were two levels of counter-preparation. The first would be ordered by infantry brigade commanders or artillery group commanders if any intense bombardment of their front took place; it consisted of relatively irregular bursts of fire. The second counter-preparation was ordered by corps if the order to man battle stations was received or if a widespread intense enemy bombardment began. It was more regular and heavier than the first counter-preparation and its details were specified in divisional and heavy artillery defence schemes.[42]

The corps scheme also detailed the counter-attack schemes, intelligence and communications arrangements, those for the demolition of bridges (most of which were a corps responsibility) and the role of contact aeroplanes.[43] Administrative aspects of the scheme were described in less (though still substantial) detail under 11 separate headings.[44] Maxse also issued his staff officers, from the BGGS downwards, with a 'catechism' of questions to ask divisional and brigade staffs and battalion officers when they were touring the defences, in order to check their preparedness and stimulate activity in the right direction.[45]

In Third Army, V Corps' defence scheme differed in relatively few respects from that of XVIII Corps to the south, though the document was laid out quite differently. This probably reflected the unfamiliarity of the defensive to British forces, since attack orders were more or less standardised by this point. Stress was laid on the presence of low flying German aeroplanes being a possible indicator that an attack was imminent, and also that "Valleys leading into our positions must be especially guarded..."[46] Both of these were based on experience gained at Cambrai. Although XVIII Corps did not make the same point regarding valleys, its orders all dealt with artillery harassment of such features.[47] The main difference between V Corps' and XVIII Corps' schemes was that the former held the Flesquières Salient (the remnant of the ground won in the Battle of Cambrai) and needed to make special arrangements to pull its garrison out if the Salient were in danger of being pinched off by an attack on the base of each flank. Not mentioned in XVIII Corps' scheme was the use of Corps Guides, officers and men detailed to take reinforcements or relieving troops through the defences from the back area to a defined line, after which guides provided by the divisions in situ would take over.[48] In addition, the artillery arrangements of V Corps were considerably more detailed, as well as differing slightly in that corps retained one heavy artillery brigade while devolving the other four to its divisions. The avoidance of possible German counter-battery fire was heavily stressed, and only one form of counter-preparation was envisaged. This was that if a group's commander suspected from the intensity of enemy fire that an attack was imminent, he was to fire on his SOS lines and report it to his CRA and the CHA.[49] There were also sections dealing with low-flying aeroplanes, with tanks (the Germans were expected to use them), offensive counter-battery work, liaison (field artillery group commanders were expected to "live in close proximity to each Infantry Brigadier in the line" and to act as their advisors, not just carrying out their wishes) and communications (especially alternatives to the telephone system).[50]

Like Gough, Sir Julian Byng at Third Army kept watch on what his corps were doing (though little evidence exists for a comparison of their command styles at this time). Third Army sent out a memorandum in January, telling IV and VI Corps that the junction of their battles zones was not "entirely satisfactory," that of IV Corps being in front of its neighbour's, and requiring them to consult on the matter and report back.[51] Byng subsequently criticised IV Corps' machine-gun defences as lacking depth and failing to maximise the possibilities available for enfilade fire.[52] He also wrote to all his corps commanders on 27th January to explain that the divisions in the line were expected to hold the forward zone and the front line of the battle zone (Third Army's ideas seem to have been less 'blob'-orientated than Fifth Army's), with brigade and divisional reserves being used for counter-attacks in this area. Corps was responsible for the battle zone and its reserve division or divisions were to be used for counter-attacks here.[53] This was not surprising, given that GHQ had written to Byng the previous day and expressed a concern that "There appears sometimes to be a lack of co-ordination in the arrangements of defences, especially between Corps. It is desirable to avoid over-centralization, but… adjoining Corps should not be permitted to site defences on different principles."[54] This level of co-ordination appears directly to contradict the view taken by Travers that Army and corps were too hands-off in their approach when developing their defences.[55] He backs his case up by citing the example of a staff officer in 36th Division in XVIII Corps who perceived that 14th Division, in III Corps (to its right) intended to man its forward zone in strength, contrary to XVIII Corps' practice; however, the OH maps and the 18th Division's history both indicate a similar arrangement of battalions, and Maxse had written in February to Maj.-Gen. Nugent (GOC 36th Division) to make this point.[56]

Third Army also laid down that tanks were to be held in Army reserve and doled out to corps on application. Given the damage they caused to communications during the Cambrai operations, it is not surprising that places on the routes to their assembly areas where telephone lines might be damaged were to be marked and protective measures taken. Their use was restricted to counter-attacks to secure the battle and rear zones; the method for this was laid down in the new edition of SS135.[57]

On the Fourth Army front (held by Second Army until 20th December 1917) IX Corps issued its instructions for the defensive as early as 14th December 1917. Here the battle zone was referred to as a 'line' (though it was to be organised in depth), to consist of mutually supporting posts and keeps and to be constructed on the most appropriate ground for receiving an attack, "irrespective of the defences which we at present occupy."[58] This was another case of tailoring the defensive plan to the circumstances of the area in question; the Ypres Salient as a whole was hardly ideal defensive ground, simply by virtue of being a salient, in addition to the poor state of the ground and communications across it after the fighting between July and November. In fact, the position was sufficiently exposed for the existing front line to be viewed as an outpost line only, and in February Rawlinson wrote to his corps commanders to tell them that in certain circumstances it might be necessary to pull back to the battle zone in order to shorten the front and economise on manpower. They were to prepare schemes for a phased withdrawal, to be carried out in great secrecy over four days, the heavy artillery going back first and then the field artillery.[59] Within this blighted area, the Passchendaele Salient (only recently captured) was even more exposed than anywhere else, and being in VIII Corps area was the subject of much heartache for Sir Aylmer Hunter-Weston. Indeed, in early December, his worry that another offensive might be undertaken was so great that he told his wife that he was prepared to resign if Haig would not see his point of view – "my duty to the Empire was to make the C-in-C see reason".[60] Fortunately for the Empire, Haig did. As in the Flesquières Salient, the battle zone was dug as a chord across the base of the arc formed by the Passchendaele Salient. But apart from local issues referred to above and differences in the layout of the document, the IX Corps defence scheme was in principle no different from those already discussed.[61]

It can be seen that unusually strict control concerning the principles to be followed in constructing and fighting in the BEF's defences in early 1918 was exercised by GHQ over the Armies, and by them over corps and so on down the chain of command. This is hardly surprising; no matter how well corps staffs understood the mechanics of launching a set piece attack, they were not well-versed in constructing three-zone defensive systems, and so it was necessary for Army to ensure that they knew what they were supposed to be doing. As before Cambrai, a new approach led each level of command to be more prescriptive than usual towards its subordinates. Nevertheless, corps were still the level of command which was expected to organise the production of the schemes and the execution of the construction work, co-ordinating divisions' efforts to an unusually high degree. But despite that, the BEF was flexible enough for the three-zone system to be tailored to local circumstances in terms of the availability of both existing defences and fighting troops, and for resources – especially artillery – to be decentralised, in the plans at least.

The course of events in March, April and May is described comprehensively in the OH, and it is not the aim of this book to repeat their details. However, this part of the chapter highlights the way in which corps functioned during the fighting in March and April and demonstrates that, contrary to Travers' view, the command structure of Third and Fifth Armies did not collapse, despite the considerable strain to which it was subjected.

The first German offensive was launched on 21st March 1918, and though Third and Fifth Armies held their ground initially (though losing most of the forward zone) they were soon pressed to retreat. The process began on March 22nd with III Corps and XVIII Corps in the south and the rest of the line was forced to conform, swinging back from a point roughly five miles east of Arras, though maintaining the line in front of that town. As the prepared defences were abandoned and the line became increasingly attenuated, the problem of resisting the powerful German attacks became more difficult until, with French help, and at least in part owing to exhaustion on the part of the Germans, a new line was stabilised in front of Amiens by 5th April. On 9th April the Germans attacked again, hitting the First and Second Armies to the north and gaining over 10 miles on an eight-mile front before the offensive was abandoned on 30th April. Their last major attack on the British came on 27th May, when IX Corps was attacked on the Aisne, when acting as part of the French Sixth Army.

The situation on the British (and particularly the Fifth Army) front on 21st March and thereafter was that it was too lightly held and that it was therefore especially vulnerable to the type of assault launched against it. Samuels has described the problems the fog gave the attackers and thinks that its effect was more to their disadvantage than to the defenders'.[62] This is interesting, given how often smoke was used to blind defenders later in the war when fog was unavailable, which would imply that British attacking troops found it useful. He also stressed the effect on British morale of being in isolated positions when attacked, and the fog would have added to this, as well as making it easier to surrender discreetly. The effect on morale of the divisional reorganisation should not be discounted at this period too – another consequence of the manpower shortage – and the effect of the fog in blinding the British artillery was considerable. Between the German artillery and their infantry (and the fog), most of the garrisons of the forward zone were accounted for. Of the eight battalions XVIII Corps had disposed in the forward zone, only 50 men got back to the battle zone, and a similar situation pertained elsewhere across the fronts of Fifth and Third Armies.[63] The troops lost accounted for one-third of the defending divisions, which also suffered (in some cases, heavy) casualties in the troops manning the battle zone. This scale of losses clearly could not be maintained for long, and Fifth Army's decision to retreat seems to make sense if compared to its other option – to stand fast and be wiped out.[64]

For reasons described earlier, it is difficult to ascertain how corps coped on 21st March. As well as causing numerous casualties, the German bombardment seriously damaged the British communications by cutting the wires upon which the telephone network depended, despite their being deeply buried, an arrangement which had proved to be satisfactory in the war up to that date.[65] Of the other means available, only wireless was really any use in the fog, given the effect of the shellfire on pigeons and runners, and assuming that for any given set the aerial (or the set itself) had not been blown up. Consequently, the state of affairs in the forward zone was not apparent to corps for some time. Nor was it to the troops in the battle zone, who were, however, able to remain in touch by telephone with division and through them with corps. The only means of influencing the battle available to corps commanders was by their control of the reserves (their normal artillery control was delegated to divisions and in any case relatively ineffective owing to ignorance of the whereabouts of the Germans). In the case of XVIII Corps, this entailed waiting until late afternoon for 20th Division to move up to its assigned positions, but in any case, the likelihood of it actually being of any use in a counter-attack was slight.[66] Under the circumstances, a serious counter-attack was not really an option; even if the corps had restored its forward zone by using 20th Division (and had possessed the men to garrison it again), it would have been promptly outflanked by the Germans who had occupied III Corps' forward zone, to XVIII Corps' right, and there were not enough counter-attack divisions in Fifth Army for every corps to have one. Samuels concedes that there were not enough reserve divisions in Fifth Army to make the concept of the *Eingreif* division work, even if the defences had been laid out 'correctly,' and in Third Army there were too few for it to conform to the latest practice of the Germans, which is the standard to which he generally feels the British should have aspired.[67] In other words, once again there were too few troops to make the German system – or any other – work properly. Travers cites an aggrieved staff officer who felt that the placing of the 20th Division in the rear zone as a back stop for the formations in front was a waste, but quite apart from the fact that this was what had originally been planned for its assembly, there was little else that Maxse could do.[68]

The problem that confronted the BEF at this stage (and in the week that followed) was that it had lost the initiative to the attackers. The Germans had achieved higher tempo by misleading GHQ into thinking that the offensive would fall nearer the Ypres sector, so that Third and Fifth Armies were left undermanned. The tempo was further heightened by infantry tactics which were extremely effective against a thinly stretched front, and a bombardment of unprecedented intensity (the surprise not being that it would happen, which was known to the British, but its sheer power), so that the defending forces were quickly off-balance. Consequently, Fifth Army and much of Third Army had been forced out of their defensive positions, rendering previous plans irrelevant, and they lacked the manpower to do more than react to the German attacks. VII Corps retained a file note, showing that at 10.30pm on 21st March the GOCs of 21st and 16th Divisions came to see the corps commander (Lt.-Gen. Sir W.N. Congreve) and the line to be held on the next day was agreed. This was to be its line at the time of the meeting, with the left flank bent back to ensure that it joined V Corps (its neighbour, in Third Army); a Fifth Army order confirmed this discussion.[69] However, events overtook this plan and VII Corps (with others) was forced back to the Green

Line (i.e. the rear zone). This was not conducive to counter-attacking with a view to restoring the situation.[70] Maxse has been accused in a number of quarters of prematurely withdrawing XVIII Corps behind the line of the Somme on the 22nd, leading to the opening of a gap between his corps and Watts' XIX Corps, and between them and VII Corps. His biographer dismisses the wildest of the allegations, such as Edmonds' gossip to Liddell Hart that Maxse had been absent from his HQ for 48 hours after a shell burst nearby.[71] Maxse himself said in a letter to Edmonds that he objected to being made a scapegoat and claimed that he had planned his withdrawals carefully.[72] And an examination of the expanding frontage of XVIII Corps (from 16,000 yards on 21st to 22,000 on 22nd March) makes it seem possible that the opening of gaps was due to lack of troops as much as carelessness on Maxse's part. In any case, the role of corps commanders from now on was to retreat as ordered and to feed into the line whatever reserves they were given.

Travers makes much of the 'collapse of command' in Fifth and Third Armies as they withdrew, but this is harder to prove than it seems. Although he produces a number of anecdotes from which he generalises that corps and divisional staffs lost touch altogether and sat in their HQs, other sources contradict this. A note in the VII Corps files, which apparently was the result of the GSO2(I) bringing news from 9th Division, gave news of the situation on the Green Line in the late morning of 23rd March.[73] The commander of V Corps, Lt.-Gen. E.A. Fanshawe, wrote that because "it was difficult to grasp the situation, unless one went to see," his BGGS went up to the front on 24th March and Fanshawe himself on the 25th (as far as he was concerned, these were the worst two days for his corps), and they drove round his divisions on 26th March.[74] This is not to say that communication problems did not arise; they were bound to, under the circumstances. Lt.-Gen. J.A.L. Haldane, GOC VI Corps, noted in his diary that Maj.-Gen. Feilding, the GOC of the Guards Division, complained of being out of touch with corps for six hours on 26th March, but on checking, Haldane discovered that telephone messages were exchanged between his and the division's HQ five times during these six hours, and a liaison officer had been sent by corps to division. He felt that Feilding nevertheless expected too much of the limited communications available in open warfare.[75]

However, what the last two paragraphs demonstrate once again is the difficulty in establishing precisely what went on; anecdotal evidence, though attractive, is no more clear-cut than more official documents, and in the case of the latter it may be easier to see what axe the author had to grind. For example, the OH and the 9th Division history refer to a 'contretemps' between 9th and 47th Divisions in the afternoon of 22nd March. According to the 9th Division, its temporary GOC, Br.-Gen. Tudor, "had been most punctilious in his reports to the Forty-Seventh Division in order to avoid any misunderstanding about his [Tudor's] left flank, and to give that division timely warning of the measures to be adopted to maintain liaison." However, when the 9th Division was forced to withdraw to the Green Line, 47th told the staff officer sent by 9th Division to warn them of this event, that it was "not prepared to accept responsibility for connecting up its right on the Brown Line with our [9th Division's] left on the Green Line."[76] According to the OH, Gough went to see Byng, and they arranged that a brigade be made available by V Corps (to which 47th Division belonged) to cover any gap which might arise. This, the 99th Brigade, was initially put under 47th Division but later (at 9.10pm) handed over by V Corps to VII Corps (to its right in Fifth Army), which put it under the command of 9th Division.[77] According to the 9th Division's history, the matter was solved by the corps concerned.[78] However, the 47th Division's history took the view that the 9th Division was the villain of the piece "As early as 7.30am the Divisional Commander realised the danger on our right flank, caused by the withdrawal of the 9th Division.... By midday the 9th Division was already back on its second system... and an extension of our right was necessary.... At 4.10pm a Staff officer from the 9th Division reported that they were leaving their second system at 4.30pm." The 47th Division was therefore left to form a long defensive flank to save the situation and keep touch with VII Corps, a desperate situation made harder by 9th Division's announcement that it would have to make its final withdrawal of the day before nightfall and by the failure of the 99th Brigade, apparently placed under the command of 47th Division at 10.30pm, to get in touch.[79] However, the 47th Division's report, compiled soon after the battle, stated that it was aware of 9th Division's withdrawals and warned V Corps of the problems these would cause. Consequently, corps placed 99th Brigade under 47th Division at 2pm, but cancelled this at 2.35. Once the 9th Division sent its staff officer over in the early afternoon V Corps was informed and apparently said that it would attempt to delay the withdrawal. Obviously it failed and the narrative recorded that "4th R.W.F. [Royal Welch Fusiliers] would take up positions... to cover the right flank of the corps as far as possible...as this responsibility was placed by V Corps on G.O.C. 47th. Division."[80]

Needless to say, neither of the 47th Division sources quoted makes any reference to the later disintegration of the division to which Travers refers.[81] Be that as it may, the evidence he presents for the collapse of the command structure of the BEF does not hold water. The system may have been creaking at the joints – even anaemic for want of manpower, to labour the medical analogy – but it was not in a state of collapse. This is not to say that problems with communication, especially laterally, did not occur; Maxse blamed the tendency of units to retreat excessively readily on ignorance of what was happening on their flanks, but this can as easily be blamed on thinly spread divisions and tired staffs forgetting to tell higher formations where they had moved to for a few hours as on deep-seated structural problems at the corps and divisional level.[82]

As regards the Lys offensive of April, the same arguments apply. The divisions attacked (initially in IX, XI and XV Corps) were mainly the remnants of ones which had already been through the mill on the Somme (11 of the 13 divisions in line on 9th April had seen action on the Somme), their numbers topped up with young recruits. On the first day, the attack fell on the 55th, 2nd Portuguese and 40th Divisions. Of these, the 55th was fresh and well established in old fortifications, the Portuguese were unreliable and the 40th was weak, having been severely mauled while in VII and then XIX Corps to the south. Upon the rout of the Portuguese, the 55th was able to form a defensive flank which held for the rest of the battle, whereas the unfortunate 40th, holding a longer frontage as well as being weaker, was forced back. A peculiarity of this sector was that the defences appear to have been far more variable than was the case on the Somme. The GOC 55th Division (Maj.-Gen. Sir H.S. Jeudwine) professed ignorance of the three-zone system, claiming that "I do not recollect... hearing any talk of a Battle Zone." His superior, Sir R.C.B. Haking, the XI Corps commander, was less forthright and merely pointed out to Edmonds that "We would have no truck with the 'defence in depth' idea at Givenchy and should have lost the battle if we did."[83] (Travers takes the view that Haking was as ignorant as Jeudwine of the three-zone system, but Haking's letter merely indicates that he did not believe in it.[84]) Judging from the impressive performance of 55th Division, Haking may well have been right, which underlines the point made earlier that defence in depth on the German pattern was not the only correct solution in 1918. On IX Corps' front, "In theory the defences had been reorganized on the zone system" but in fact consisted of a forward area made up of a trench line in front of which were two lines of posts; behind this was a 'Corps Line' and behind that the 'Green Line.'[85] According to the 25th Division history the Corps Line was poor in its sector; according to the 9th Division, the defences in front of the Corps Line consisted of three lines of posts only.[86] Why these defences were so inconsistent is uncertain, but their poor quality may explain the tendency for the forward zone to be relatively heavily manned despite the lessons of March, to which Travers refers.[87]

The role of corps differed from March in one important respect, which was that there was no policy of trading space for time, so though they were constantly feeding in whatever dribs and drabs of reserves they could muster or were allocated, they were retreating only when forced to, and far more slowly than in March.[88] Consequently, they tended more to fall back along their lines of communication (and not, of course, across the devastated areas from 1916 as on the Somme) and so, according to a IX Corps artillery report, communications were less of a problem than in the earlier fighting.[89] That said, the CRA of 33rd Division wrote to Edmonds that shortage of cable was at times a source of difficulties, and IX Corps' report on communications conceded that problems with telephone lines were inevitable, though wireless was becoming more and more useful.[90]

It can be seen from the foregoing that the problems of the BEF in March and April 1918 stemmed from lack of manpower, and, especially in March, were exacerbated by severe casualties and the elongation of the front as it fell back. Given the limitations of the sources, it is difficult to establish precisely what occurred at times; accounts even in reputable works are contradictory. However it is apparent that command and control did not collapse, notwithstanding severe problems at times. Nevertheless, the loss of initiative at the start of each attack was difficult to recover from, given the lack of reserves on these fronts. Had the manpower been available, perhaps the BEF would have been better advised to attempt its defence on the model used in front of Arras, rather than in a pale imitation of the German system. In fact, the German attack in March was notable for its initial high tempo – much higher than the BEF's – which was another reason for the loss of initiative. As well as having stronger forces, the Germans were acting faster, and once the defenders were off-balance it was easier, given the problems which led them to retreat from their defences, for the Germans to keep them in that state. However, fatigue and logistic incompetence led to the slowing down of the attack – a reduction in its tempo – and the restoration of equal tempo by the time the Michael offensive ended.[91] In April the disparity in tempo was far less, and the advance consequently smaller.

After the German offensives in March and April were over, attempts were made to learn lessons from them. These reflected the perception that operations needed to be conducted with a view to increasing the speed of communications (and hence the operations), and also that surprise was vital. Both these tended towards an increase in tempo. Third Army issued a memorandum criticising the liaison between the RA and RAF (formed on 1st April), blaming it on the lack of telephone communications and ineptitude in wireless communications, either in the positioning of sets or of aerials. In addition too many artillery batteries were sometimes employed by divisions for them to be able to respond to aeroplane calls. More wireless sets were to be provided to heavy artillery brigades and field artillery brigades were to allot theirs to a particular battery if communications were difficult, so that aeroplane calls did not need to pass through brigade.[92] These solutions were, of course, much better suited to open warfare than the use of the telephone. As a consequence of this increase in the use of wireless, from July, weekly reports were issued by Army to corps, giving summaries of wireless traffic in the Army area and how it might appear to the Germans. For example, it seems that divisional boundaries, divisional reliefs and current or forthcoming operations could be detected by this means if discretion was not used, and this would militate against achieving surprise.[93]

XVIII Corps issued two papers on lessons. The first stressed that defences should not be held too thinly and pointed out the inevitability of formations diverging if they were called upon to retire on a wide front and for a substantial distance and that local reserves would not be enough to fill the gaps under these circumstances.[94] Most of the notes in the second document dealt with open warfare, communications figuring prominently, especially the need to break free from the telephone and employ other methods, including despatch riders. Improved lateral communications were also mentioned. Artillery-infantry liaison was to be improved by field artillery group HQs being established next to those of the infantry brigade they were to support.[95] All of these would increase tempo.

VII Corps took a more mixed approach. The first conclusion it came to was that because there were too few men to hold the front in depth, they should have been concentrated in the front line and the idea of posts abandoned, since "There is no evidence that the enemy's bombardments demolished our defences..." Like everyone else, the author bemoaned the low standard of training the infantry had in open warfare and also decried excessive reliance on the telephone in preference to other means of communication (Third Army later announced days when telephones were not to be used – other than in special circumstances – at all, so that staff officers could become used to operating without them).[96] Like XVIII Corps, VII Corps advocated the provision of more vehicles for the use of despatch riders, especially for the artillery. Ammunition supply was a problem because troops – especially artillery – were not accustomed to the limitations on expenditure open warfare necessitated, and were too inclined to fire barrages they could not afford. In addition, SOS barrages were viewed as a waste of time and ammunition, since the infantry too often called on them as a precaution instead of sending out patrols to see what was occurring on their front, thus preventing the artillery from getting on with its own offensive role.[97] And to increase mobility, heavy siege artillery brigades, medium siege artillery brigades and mobile brigades should be formed, so that the former could be separated on the commencement of open warfare, since they were so slow-moving.[98]

New defence schemes were issued as a result of this activity. The general tenor of these was to follow the latest ideas as enunciated by General Foch and Haig, that the forward zone had to be thinly held to a depth of 1,000 to 1,500 yards in order that the intense enemy artillery fire be avoided. Counter-attack divisions should not be held too far back (a complaint in March) and once they moved into action all should be as in open warfare, even to the extent of the divisional commanders being on horseback (a sensible idea for getting across country).[99] In May, the pamphlet *SS210, The Division in Defence*, was issued. This was a systematic statement of the principles of defence, based on recent experience. It prescribed little which has not been mentioned above, though it did favour linking strongpoints with trenches, partly to maintain the defenders' morale and partly to mislead the enemy as to the precise organisation of the defensive system.[100] The presence of trenches was, of course, one of the more significant differences between Fifth Army's position on 21st March and Third Army's in front of Arras in the failed German attack of 28th March. As before, Army would lay down the overall plan, corps would organise its sector and division would operate within the parameters set by corps, though with local variations if necessary.[101] The pamphlet referred frequently to others for specific points regarding, for example, artillery. But no document was mentioned more frequently than *FSR I*, the principles of which were obviously viewed as holding good even in 1918.[102]

In addition, the fighting in March and April had demonstrated that the BEF lacked training in open warfare, and the need for co-ordinated policy between schools in France and Britain was also recognised. Consequently, Sir Ivor Maxse was appointed Inspector-General of Training (IGT) on 20th June 1918.[103] Griffith alleges that this was a sideways move for him and that he was lucky not to have been sent home after March. While this is somewhat plausible, the present study has found no evidence to back it up, and Baynes cites a letter from Maxse which he claims amounts to a refutation of the idea.[104] In any case, the role was an advisory one only, though the IGT was empowered to descend upon commands in France and Britain at any time to suggest improvements to training and disseminate tactical doctrine. It should be noted that his duties included helping "to ensure that... training is carried out in accordance with Field Service Regulations, the official manuals and General Staff publications."[105] Nothing revolutionary was intended since, as the MGGS (Staff Duties) at GHQ put it, the main lesson of the German successes was "the necessity for thorough training on the recognised tactical principles... no essential modification of the tactical principles laid down for the training of the British Armies has been indicated... during recent operations."[106]

The first opportunity the British had for the application of the lessons of March and April came in May, when IX Corps, moved to the Chemin des Dames in the French Sixth Army's sector in late April, was attacked again. Three of its four divisions had been through the fighting in both March and April, the fourth having only been involved in March; all needed a rest. Unfortunately the Aisne proved to be a livelier sector than had been supposed, and on 27th May IX Corps (and French forces alongside it) were subjected to the most intense German bombardment yet. Since the French Sixth Army's GOC wished to hold the front line in strength (notwithstanding the protests of Lt.-Gen. A. Hamilton Gordon, the GOC IX Corps) the result was catastrophic. British reserves were not to hand, and as casualties mounted, all that could be done was to form composite units of survivors and fall back until 19th Division (also severely handled in March and April) arrived on 30th May.[107] This also fell back until 4th June, when it was withdrawn.[108] After this the lesson of holding the front lightly was definitely learned, as demonstrated by V Corps above.

In conclusion, the principal problem the BEF had in early 1918 was not that the command structure was unsound (though it did not always work well) or over-centralised – local conditions were considered whenever possible – but that it was short of troops. Even if the German defensive system had been applied properly, the weight of numbers of the attackers and their artillery power would have overcome so weak a force, and once the attack was launched, the BEF lost the initiative. Third and Fifth Armies (and later, First and Second on the Lys) had to fall back since they were so short of manpower and in the absence of prepared fortifications as they did so, this weakness became all the more apparent. Gaps opened up between formations as much because they were thinly spread as because of a 'collapse' of command structure, though communications undoubtedly presented substantial difficulties compared to what formations at all levels were accustomed to. Before the battles, corps had to execute the GHQ and Army plans for the defensive (just as they had executed plans for attacks the previous year); during them the role of corps was simply to fall back as much in accordance with Army orders as possible, until the situation could be stabilised by putting in reserves when they came up, and the initiative wrested from the Germans. But until enough troops could be brought up and the persistent infiltration through weak points stopped, this could not happen; corps commanders executed the retreat for Army, and in that sense the 1918 Battle of the Somme and the Battle of the Lys were Corps commanders' battles. However, assiduous efforts were made to learn from the experiences of the March and April fighting and the disaster which befell IX Corps in May was the result of these being disregarded by the French General Duchêne, the local Army commander. Consequently, new defensive plans were devised, techniques of open warfare were disseminated (especially regarding communications) and artillery was reorganised in order to make it more mobile. In addition, the need to train troops in open fighting techniques was recognised and efforts made to improve training in general. That training and doctrine still emphasised *FSR I*, even at this late stage in the War, indicates the continuing validity of its principles if properly applied.

NOTES

1 Turner, John, *British Politics and the Great War* (New Haven and London: Yale University Press, 1992), 298-9. The important political results of this debate fall outside the scope of this book.

2 Lloyd George, David, *War Memoirs* (Odhams, 1938), Volume 2, 1666-7, 1754 and passim.

3 Travers, *How the War Was Won*.

4 TNA:PRO, WO 95/953.

5 Atteridge, A. Hilliard, *History of the 17th (Northern) Division* (Glasgow: Robert Maclehose & Co., 1929), 293. Bewsher, Major F.W., *The History of the 51st (Highland) Division 1914-1918* (Edinburgh and London: William Blackwood and Sons, 1921), 281. Jerrold, Douglas, *The Royal Naval Division* (Hutchinson, 1923), 279. Maude, A.H. (ed.) *The 47th (London) Division 1914-1919* (Amalgamated Press, 1922), 152.

6 Nichols, Captain G.H.F., *The 18th Division in the Great War* (Edinburgh and London: William Blackwood and Sons, 1922), 272-4.

7 Travers, *How the War Was Won*, 50.

8 Samuels, *Command or Control...*, 203-210.

9 Samuels, *Command or Control ...*, 221-4.

10 Samuels, *Command or Control...*, 221-4, and see O.H., 1918 Volume. 1, 256.

11 Falls, Cyril, *The History of the 36th (Ulster) Division* (Belfast and London: McCaw, Stevenson & Orr, 1922), 192.

12 Samuels, *Command or Control...*, 222.

13 Samuels, *Command or Control...*, 246, and see O.H., 1918 Volume. 1, Sketches 12 and 14.

14 Samuels, *Command or Control...*, 249-251.

15 O.H., 1916 Volume 1, 302.

16 O.H., 1918 Volume. 1, 62-3.

17 Travers, *How the War Was Won*, 60-5.

18 For example, *IV Corps, Havrincourt-Bourlon Operations November 20th to December 1st...Part III Lessons*. TNA:PRO, WO 158/318.

19 O.H., 1918 Volume 1, 41 fn. 4.

20 O.H., 1918 Volume 1, 37.

21 O.H., 1918 Appendix 6, 23.

22 Travers, *How the War Was Won*, 53-4.

23 O.H., 1918 Appendix 6, 23-4.

24 O.H., 1918 Volume 1, 42.

25 O.H., 1918 Appendix 6, 25.

26 *Policy on the Army Front for 1918, 20th January 1918, Section II – Defensive Measures*, paras 4 and 5. TNA:PRO, WO 95/434.

27 *Policy on the Army Front...* , para. 13.

28 *Proceedings of a Conference held by the Fifth Army Commander... February 3rd, 1918*. TNA:PRO, WO 95/521.

29 See O.H., 1918 Volume 1, 51-5.

30 *O.A.D. 291/31. Record of a Conference of Army Commanders... 16th February 1918*. TNA:PRO, WO 95/521.

31 *O.A.D. 291/31.*, 2-3.

32 *Proceedings of a Conference held at Fourth Army Headquarters... 17th February, 1918*. TNA:PRO, WO 95/434.

33 *Minutes of a Conference held at Third Army H.Q. 21st February, 1918*. TNA:PRO, WO 95/369.

34 *XVIII Corps Instructions for Defence*, 10th January 1918, 1-4. TNA:PRO, WO 95/953.

35 *XVIII Corps Instructions...* 5-8.

36 *XVIII Corps Instructions...* 8-12.

37 *Proceedings of a Conference Held at XVIII Corps Headquarters on 1st March 1918...*Maxse Papers, IWM, 69/53/11, 43.

38 Fraser, David (ed.) *In Good Company: The First World War letters and diaries of the Hon. William Fraser* (Salisbury, Wilts.: Michael Russell, 1990), 214.

39 *XVIII Corps. Programme of Senior Officers' Training Conference.* Maxse Papers, IWM, 69/53/12/, 44.

40 *Lecture by Major L. Carr... February 18th 1918* and *Corps Commander's Lecture on 19th Feb. 1918. Lessons From Cambrai.* Maxse Papers, IWM, 69/53/12, 44 and 69/53/11, 40, respectively.

41 Fraser, *In Good Company*, 221-2. *XVIII Corps No. G.S. 41*, 10th March 1918. Maxse Papers, IWM, 69/53/11, 43.

42 *XVIII Corps Defence Scheme, Appendix "C". Artillery Arrangements*, 28th February 1918. TNA:PRO, WO 95/953.

43 *XVIII Corps Defence Scheme*, passim.

44 *XVIII Corps No. AC/544/351. XVIII Corps Defence Scheme.* Undated overall, though the last section is dated 1st March 1918. Maxse Papers, IWM, 69/53/11, 43.

45 *Catechism*, 18th March 1918. Maxse Papers, IWM. 69/53/11, 41.

46 *V Corps Defence Scheme*, 9th January 1918, 1. TNA:PRO, WO 95/749.

47 *XVIII Corps Order No. 137*, 13th March 1918, *No. 138*, 14th March and *No. 139*, 15th March. TNA:PRO, WO 95/953.

48 *V Corps Defence Scheme*, 5.

49 *V Corps Defence Scheme, Appendix 2. Artillery Arrangements*, undated, 4. TNA: PRO, WO 95/749.

50 *V Corps Defence Scheme... Artillery Arrangements.*, 5-9.

51 *Third Army No. G.9/309*, 6th January 1918. TNA:PRO, WO 95/369.

52 *Third Army G9/351*, 18th January 1918. TNA:PRO, WO 95/369.

53 *Third Army No. G.9/386* to *389*, all 27th January 1918 and sent to V, IV, XVII and VI Corps respectively. TNA:PRO, WO 95/369.

54 *O.A.D.291/29*, 26th January 1918. TNA:PRO, WO 95/369.

55 Travers, *How the War Was Won*, pp 64-5.

56 Nichols, *18th Division...*, 257. Maxse to Nugent, 10th February 1918. Maxse Papers, IWM, 69/53/11, 41.

57 *Third Army No.G.18/90.*, 17th February 1918. TNA:PRO, WO 95/369.

58 *IXth Corps Instructions for the Defensive*, 14th December 1918. TNA:PRO, WO 95/836.

59 *Fourth Army 161/9(G)*, 20th February 1918. TNA:PRO, WO 95/434.

60 Letter dated 7th December 1917. Hunter-Weston Papers, BL, no. 48366.

61 See *IXth Corps Instructions for the Defensive* and an untitled document which is obviously the corps scheme. TNA:PRO, WO 95/836.

62 Samuels, *Command or Control...*, 249, 255-266.

63 O.H., 1918 Volume. 1, 176, 216, 221.

64 Farrar-Hockley, *Goughie*, 277.

65 O.H., 1918 Volume. 1, 162.

66 *The German Attack on the XVIII Corps Front, from 21st March – 27th March, 1918.* Undated, but appendices are from late April. TNA:PRO, WO 95/953.

67 Samuels, *Command or Control…*, 218.

68 Travers, *How the War Was Won*, 58-9. *XVIII Corps Defence Scheme*, 2.

69 Undated file note, which from its content must relate to 21st March, and *Fifth Army Order No. 44*, 21st March 1918. TNA:PRO, WO 95/807.

70 O.H., 1918 Volume. 1, 265.

71 Baynes, *Far From a Donkey…* 195-8. See also meeting between Edmonds and Liddell Hart, 11th November 1937. Liddell Hart Papers, KCL. 11/1937/88.

72 Maxse to Edmonds, 7th October 1934. TNA:PRO, CAB 45/193.

73 Appendix. 87. TNA:PRO, WO 95/807.

74 Undated letter from Sir E.A. Fanshawe to Edmonds. TNA:PRO, CAB 45/185.

75 Extracts from Haldane's Diary. TNA:PRO, CAB 45/185.

76 Ewing, John, *The History of the 9th (Scottish) Division 1914-1919* (John Murray, 1921), 270-1.

77 O.H., 1918 Volume. 1, 299.

78 Ewing, *9th Division*, 271.

79 Maude, *47th Division…*, 152-4.

80 *47th (London) Division Narrative of Operations – March 21st to March 26th, 1918*. Undated, 5-7. TNA:PRO, WO 95/749.

81 Travers, *How the War Was Won*, 74-6.

82 *The German Attack on the XVIII Corps Front…* 4. TNA:PRO, WO 95/953.

83 Haking to Edmonds (including letter from Jeudwine), 25th August 1931. TNA:PRO, CAB 45/123.

84 Travers, *How the War Was Won*, 93.

85 O.H., 1918 Volume. 2, 205.

86 Kincaid-Smith, M., *The 25th Division in France and Flanders* (Harrison and Sons, undated), 193; Ewing, *9th Division*, 174-5.

87 Travers, *How the War Was Won*, 94.

88 *Report on Operations Undertaken by IX Corps Between 9th and 21st April 1918, 20th May 1918*. TNA:PRO, WO 95/836.

89 *Report on Operations… by IX Corps…, Appendix 'A'*.

90 *Report on Operations… by IX Corps…, Appendix 'B'*.

91 Brown, *British Logistics…*, 183-4.

92 *Third Army No.G.3/62*, 15th April 1918. TNA:PRO, WO 95/369.

93 *Third Army No.G.34/784*, 20th July 1918. TNA:PRO, WO 95/371.

94 *Lessons From the Recent Operations of the XVIII Corps. No. 1*. 28th April 1918. Maxse Papers, IWM, 69/53/11, 41.

95 *Lessons… No. 2*. 16th May 1918. Maxse Papers, IWM, 69/53/11, 41.

96 *Third Army No. G.34/675*, 5th June 1918. TNA:PRO, WO 95/371.

97 *Lessons From VII Corps Operations 21st March to April 6th 1918*. Undated. TNA: PRO, WO 95/808.

98 *R.A. VII Corps No.C/2251.*, 25th April 1918. TNA:PRO, WO 95/808.

99 *Notes on [V] Corps Commander's Conference with Divisional Commanders… 27th June*. TNA:PRO, WO 95/750. See also *XVIII Corps Instructions for Defence, 18th May, 1918*, 1. TNA:PRO, WO 95/953, *V Corps Instructions for Defence. No. 1, 26th April, 1918*, 1. TNA:PRO, WO 95/749.

100 Anon, *The Division in Defence*, May 1918, 10.

101 *Division in Defence*, 4.

102 *Division in Defence*, 7.

103 *O.B./2255*, 20th June 1918. Maxse Papers, IWM, 69/53/13, 54.

104 Griffith, *Battle Tactics...*, 184. Baynes, *Far From a Donkey...* 210.

105 *O.B./2255, Appendix A.*

106 *O.B./2266*, 8th July 1918. From Maj.-Gen. G.S. Dawnay to the DSD. Maxse Papers, IWM, 69/53/13, 54.

107 For the scale of initial casualties see *IXth Corps No. G.364/206.*, 29th May 1918. TNA:PRO, WO 95/837.

108 *IX Corps G.364/281. Report on the Operations of the IX Corps when in the French Army Area between the 23rd April and 4th July, 1918.*, 19th August 1918. TNA: PRO, WO 95/836.

CHAPTER 7

Corps in the Hundred Days: August to November, 1918

The victorious campaigns of the latter part of 1918 are the least contentious of those undertaken by the BEF. In general, the High Command's detractors choose largely to ignore them, leaving those who take a more positive view of the BEF's activities to argue amongst themselves in more measured tones than has often been the case in Great War debates. This side of the literature can conveniently be divided into the 'old' and the 'new.' The former works are characterised by a certain amount of rehashing of the OH, mixed with information gleaned from memoirs and unit and formation histories.[1] The latter, produced in the last 10-15 years, are based to a much greater extent upon fresh archival research.

Professor Travers is prominent in the 'new' group, arguing that although the BEF (and particularly the Canadians) had evolved a war-winning 'modern' tactical formula of tanks, infantry and artillery working in co-operation by August 1918, traditional thought still prevailed and the 'traditional' infantry-artillery offensive model, despite higher manpower costs, was the one mainly used in the Hundred Days. Consequently, victory was more the result of the Germans having defeated themselves through squandering their reserves earlier in the year, than of the Allied attacks in the autumn.[2] Brown's and Schreiber's work on the Canadian Corps, mentioned in the introduction to this book, both pointed out the technological nature of warfare as practised by the Canadians.[3] Prior and Wilson take the view that the firepower-based system of attack employed by the BEF was irresistible, and contrast it favourably with the manpower-based German tactics of the Spring, both in terms of effectiveness and the prevention of excessive casualties. They make the valuable point that casualty figures in the second half of 1918 are distorted upwards by the influenza pandemic, and that battle casualties were actually lower than has often been alleged.[4] Dr. Harris argues that during the Hundred Days, the BEF was operationally very sophisticated in its use of surprise and all arms in co-operation, and that tanks were used to the full after August, given the finite resources of the Tank Corps and the limitations of the technology. He differs from Travers especially on this point, arguing that the artillery techniques and infantry tactics employed were far in advance of anything envisaged in 1914, so the BEF was not waging traditional warfare, with or without tanks. However, he also feels that Prior and Wilson overstate the degree to which the BEF had a formula for success in this period, though the defeat of the Germans by Allied attacks rather than their own efforts is unquestionable.[5] Palazzo's work is unusual in its emphasis on chemical warfare as a vital part of the offensive effort (principally by suppressing German artillery fire in the short term and German morale over longer periods). It also stresses the continuing applicability of *FSR I*, even in 1918, and the flexibility of the ethos of the BEF, which made it able easily to adapt to new ideas without having to make wholesale changes to a doctrine it in any case did not possess as such.[6]

This chapter demonstrates the sophistication and flexibility of the BEF's offensive methods, as well as the ability of corps commanders to learn as the campaign went on, so that they drew upon very recent as well as more distant experience. In addition, evidence is produced to show the continuing importance of discussion in the decision-making process and the delegation of responsibility to the man on the spot whenever possible. And – confirming Palazzo's view – the use of *FSR I* even in this period is apparent. Lastly, the improvements made to the tempo of operations by the BEF in late 1918 are discussed.

Second, Third and Fourth Armies and V (in Third Army), IX and XIII (in Fourth Army) and X (in Second Army) Corps have been examined for this chapter. As well as being approximately consistent with the original selection of corps for this book, this gives a broad spread of formations across the attacking forces, with appropriate emphasis being laid upon Third and Fourth Armies, given the relatively secondary role of Second Army and still more so of Fifth Army, and the reliance of First Army on the Canadian Corps. Given that the latter and the Australian Corps fall outside the scope of this book, the Battle of Amiens is not considered here, III Corps' part in that action being in any case subsidiary.

Before proceeding to examine the fighting of the Hundred Days, it is important to clarify the ideas behind the conduct of these operations. From the point of view of corps, the most important statement of these was, as in 1917, the pamphlet *SS135*. When reissued in January 1918, its name had changed from *Instructions for the Training of Divisions for Offensive Action* to *The Training and Employment of Divisions, 1918*. This differed from its predecessors of December 1916 and August 1917 in a number of ways. Though Br.-Gen. Edmonds asserted that the new *SS135* contained 'nothing whatever' about defence, apart from instructions regarding the consolidation of a captured position, he was mistaken.[7] The Introduction, though generally dealing with the attack, also prescribed principles for troops acting on the defensive (mainly regarding counter-attacks) as might have been expected in a document produced before March 21st 1918. For both attack and defence,

> operations… may normally be expected to take the form of a methodical and progressive battle, beginning with limited objectives and leading up by gradual stages to an attack on deep objectives in chosen portions of the front. In the earlier stages…, the preparation and organization, both of the attack and of the defence, must be as thorough and methodical as for trench warfare. In the later stages the conditions will gradually approximate to those of open warfare.[8]

Furthermore, it asserted, "The general principles laid down in Field Service Regulations, Part I., Chapter VII., as to attack and defence in battle hold good today provided due allowance is made for the time and space conditions of the present war." This statement was not made in either earlier version; indeed, the original pointed out that though the pamphlet dealt with trench warfare, 'normal' fighting would be covered by *FSR I* (see Chapter 3). Nor were the steps of a successful offensive outlined. In 1918 these were the establishment and maintenance of mastery over the enemy's artillery and aircraft; the need for artillery and machine-gun barrages to protect the infantry advance; careful selection of intermediate and final objectives in order to facilitate the reorganisation of the infantry at each stage, and to permit the resumption of the offensive easily while still retaining artillery support. Since the objectives, when gained, needed to be put into a state of effective defence, the attack must be made with sufficient men to permit this, and the defences should be sited in depth, with counter-attack plans ready in the event of an enemy break-in. Lastly, preparations had to be in hand to make the next advance; indeed, plans should be in place for the next two attacks before the first of these was made, and then for the next one and so on.[9] This plainly indicates that the need to maintain a high tempo in attacks was appreciated. All this revealed the assimilation of the lessons of Third Ypres and Cambrai, both positive and negative. It also reflected the point that one important feature of fighting on the Western Front from the Battle of the Somme onwards was the gradual move away from fixed trench lines. Even the fighting at Third Ypres was classed as 'semi-open warfare' and Cambrai was obviously open warfare. *SS135, 1918* was written with a move to open warfare in mind. That the corps staff had acquired since 1917 the Deputy Assistant Director of Roads, the Labour Commandant and his assistant and the Assistant Director of Veterinary Services, indicates that mobility was now a major concern.

The relationship between corps and division, where corps allotted tasks for division to execute within the overall plan, was largely unchanged, though the sentence which originally read "The Artillery preparation now lies to a certain extent outside the province of the Divisional Commander, as the Artillery plan, except for minor operations, will be co-ordinated by the Corps Artillery Commander…"[10] now read "The plan for the Artillery preparation will ordinarily be drawn up by the Corps Artillery Commander…"[11] Nevertheless, as before, it was incumbent upon divisions to make their particular requirements known so that, where possible, the plan could be amended; the man on the spot was still important. This point was made explicit in *SS135, 1918*, although it was now stated more clearly than before that Army was responsible for the overall artillery plan. However, the corps GOCRA was to plan the preliminary bombardment and distribute the artillery resources of the corps, which for large operations might be placed under his direct command. However he was enjoined to solicit divisional commanders' views in drawing up the plan, since "it is they who have to carry out the infantry attack, and their estimate of the difficulties to be overcome will probably be the best guide…"[12]

Another new feature was that in the phase of the destruction of the enemy's position (which, it was pointed out, should be done with caution, since an excess of destructive fire could generate more obstacles than it cleared) heavy artillery brigades or groups were to be allotted to each divisional frontage. Each was to have a liaison officer resident at DHQ, who would be responsible for conveying the desires of divisional commanders to the corps CHA. This was a lesson from Cambrai. A IV Corps document written after that battle observed that it was most unsatisfactory to have definite heavy artillery formations allotted to divisions, since "the effective control of the Heavy Artillery was rendered much more difficult," but close liaison between the heavies and divisions was necessary.[13] That said, defence schemes issued before 21st March tended to devolve command of heavies to divisions in apparent breach of this. Nevertheless, the Fourth Army's MGRA (Maj.-Gen. C.E.D. Budworth) commented in April that in the March fighting it was erroneously understood that the artillery in mobile operations should remain under the command of the GOCRA. This was not the case, and in future mobile operations "The command of [mobile] H.A. Brigades… should be decentralised on Divisions. This is assisted materially by … the general custom of affiliating H.A. Brigades to Divisions in normal warfare."[14] Hence, orders issued by XIII Corps in May and XVII Corps in August stated that on the commencement of mobile warfare, the RGA Brigades affiliated to divisions would come under their tactical command, though the CHA would retain administrative responsibility for them.[15]

An important tactical aspect of the new *SS135* was its insistence on the deep barrage, in order to prevent effective enemy fire from as far in front of the assaulting infantry as 2,500 yards; the shape and pace of barrages received detailed consideration, the section in question concluding with a comment that the barrages it described were those which experience had demonstrated to be effective, but that methods should be reviewed and modified whenever necessary.[16] In addition, the barrage timetable was now to be agreed between corps and divisional commanders, the latter (again as the man on the spot) raising at conferences any points of particular significance. Unlike in 1916-17, it was specifically stated that "Divisional Artillery barrages are worked out by C.R.A.s of divisions in accordance with the directions of their Divisional Commanders; the divisional and heavy artillery barrages are then co-ordinated by the G.O.C., R.A., Corps under the orders of the Corps Commander." So, to some extent, divisions were gaining more influence in the planning of the attack and artillery resources were decentralised from corps to division, which would conduce to increased tempo. During the attack, as in 1916-17, corps retained control over the barrage, but divisions could call upon 'superimposed' batteries as necessary and delegate them to brigades if they so wished.[17]

The next section, 'Frontages for the Attack,' began with a clear statement of policy: "The allotment of frontages for the attack will be governed by the considerations enumerated in Field Service Regulations, which have been fully borne out by the experience of the present war." This was followed by a substantial quotation from *FSR I Part I*, a reference to section 104, paragraph 3, and the statement that "These principles still hold good, and Commanders must use their discretion in applying them to the different sectors of a large front."[18] The earlier editions had not been so definite as regards the applicability of *FSR I*; it is tempting to speculate that the war seemed too novel and confusing until the operational procedures used during the Second Army attacks in Third Ypres had clarified matters. This should not be taken as meaning that the attack was completely stereotyped, however. In 1917, *SS135* had prescribed the speed of advance and assumed that a linear formation would be adopted; by 1918 the view was taken that "It is not desirable to lay down hard and fast rules as to the formations to be adopted in an attack." And only the functions of the waves (a term not here implying a linear formation) were described; it was up to divisional commanders to decide how to get their men forward on the day.[19]

Subsequent sections dealt, as before, with the infantry's tasks, and little mention was made of corps. However, in the section on Engineers, the 1916 edition's injunction that "The general policy for the employment of R.E. and Pioneers will be laid down by the Corps" (see Chapter 3) had been replaced by a statement that the divisional commander would deal with them.[20] The CMGO was now not mentioned at all, and barrage fire was placed under the "Divisional Machine-Gun Commander."[21] Not everything was devolved to divisions, though; as in 1916-17, medium trench mortars were to be included in the corps artillery plan.

Lastly, it should be stressed that, like its predecessors, *SS135, 1918* was not intended to be used in isolation. Reference was made within it to no fewer than nine other pamphlets in the *SS* series (from *SS123 – Notes on the Use of Carrier Pigeons* – to *SS192 – The Employment of Machine Guns*) some of which had also been revised since their first issue. And in addition to the occasions already mentioned, *FSR I Part I* was again invoked at the beginning of the section in *SS135, 1918* on Situation Reports.[22] The overall philosophy behind *SS135, 1918*, seems to have been one of decentralising control of operations from corps back to divisions where it was feasible, in readiness for open warfare: plainly it was felt at the start of 1918 that experience had demonstrated the need to shift control forward if possible, presumably to raise the tempo of operations. How this was achieved in practice will be addressed in the remainder of this chapter.

The foregoing should not be taken as meaning that the BEF was poised to launch its attacks as soon as the crises of the first half of 1918 were past. Sir Douglas Haig's diaries contain repeated references to an expected German offensive on the Third Army front from early May to mid-July.[23] Also in July, Fifth Army issued a new defensive scheme for its sector and V Corps notified its divisions that a precautionary period before the German attack would begin on 9th July.[24] However, on 5th July, Haig nevertheless told Horne and Byng to prepare a small offensive on their fronts. On 11th July he and Sir Henry Wilson (the CIGS) agreed that the BEF was now in a better situation than before 21st March, and on 26th July, Haig ordered Horne and Byng to prepare for the offensives they were eventually to launch in August, in support of Fourth Army.[25] An important ingredient of the forthcoming offensives was camouflage. This had apparently been organised on a relatively ad hoc basis before, but was now formalised as surprise played a greater part in operations than earlier in the war, thus raising tempo. Hence, Third Army informed its corps that dummy tanks were now available for deception purposes and in a similar vein, GHQ reorganised the supply and staffing arrangements for camouflage.[26] Camouflage factories were to be established at Army level and a camouflage officer was to be appointed who would work under the CRE. On application from Army, Corps Camouflage Officers (one or two per corps) would be provided. The Camouflage Officer at each level was to act as technical adviser on all camouflage questions. In addition, the Army would supervise the corps officers and deal with the factories which produced the camouflage materials. The corps officers would deal with the issue of camouflage material from corps dumps and supervise "the erection and upkeep of camouflage objects."[27] Other routine measures, such as the weekly reports on monitoring of friendly wireless transmissions (mentioned in the last chapter), were continued throughout 1918.[28]

In the Hundred Days, Third Army and its corps operated as decentralised a style of command as was consonant with operational good sense. They largely did this by following the principles laid down in *FSR I* and *SS135, 1918*, though also learning from experience; tactics evolved to cope with the new situations which arose. Because some operations were necessarily set-piece, corps at those times exerted closer control over divisions than during phases of pursuit. However, this approach was entirely flexible and corps varied its style of command as the situation demanded.[29] Travers argues that the essence of the last part of the war was the struggle to adapt to the combination of set-piece and mobile fighting. This, he says, "had nothing to do with the prewar principles preached by the top brass at GHQ, but resulted from developments at army, corps and divisional level."[30] He is mistaken, and the successful application (at a high tempo) of doctrine culled partly from *FSR I* and partly from *SS135, 1918* was the key to success.

Hence, for the Battle of Albert (21st-23rd August) Army was relatively prescriptive in its handling of corps, since this was a set-piece (though they were more hands-off than in previous years). The Army instructions dealing with this attack followed the trend set at Third Ypres and were reasonably brief statements of objectives and the stages of the operations.[31] They also displayed an unusual degree of delegation of responsibility to corps, especially VI Corps.[32] The artillery plan was somewhat more centralised, as in *SS135, 1918*, being drawn up by Army and passed down. Indeed, it was explicitly stated that "Barrages will be as laid down in S.S.135, 'Training of Divisions' [sic]", though Harris states that corps organised their own barrages within these parameters.[33]

Army stressed that the whole affair was to be a surprise to the Germans, and considerable efforts were made to achieve this. In addition to devious use of the telephone silence drills established after March (see Chapter 6), to impose a security blackout on telephone calls before the attack, all troop and artillery moves other than those considered normal were to be made at night; artillery, wireless, aerial and road-building activity was to be kept to a normal level and new artillery in particular was not to register. Ammunition and RE dumps would be camouflaged and no new hospital signs were to be put up. All this seems to be much as was done before Cambrai, though no mention was made in these orders of British aeroplanes overflying friendly positions to ensure the efficacy of the preparations, as had been done before the earlier operation.[34]

An interesting note regarding hands-on command was issued by Army on 20th August. Corps commanders were enjoined to "emphasize to Divisional and Brigade Commanders of the 'break through' Divisions, the importance of being actually on the ground with their formations during the operations. The delay caused by the Commander not being on the spot to handle the reserves, may possibly annul initial success and prevent surprise being exploited to the utmost."[35] So if authority and control were passed down to the man on the spot, it was essential that he actually be on that spot! It is unsurprising that Byng still viewed the function of commanders in battle as the handling of the reserves, given that the limited means of communication and control over attacking troops once the battle had begun had not really changed since 1916.

V Corps therefore followed the pattern mentioned. As much freedom as possible was left to divisional commanders regarding operational decisions on the ground, and whereas in 1917 V Corps would have discussed with IV Corps any matter where a division from one corps was expected to act in conjunction with a division from the other, now this was left to the divisions concerned.[36] Should success lead to the Germans falling back, exploitation was to be carried out as specified in *SS135, 1918*, by battle patrols.[37] Consequently, only approximate objectives were set. As regards secrecy, V Corps only passed on the reminder to divisions that it was an "absolute necessity" for the operation; they were viewed as sufficiently competent to put what were largely administrative procedures into practice to achieve this, without further prodding. It should not, however, be assumed that divisions were given a completely free hand to do as they liked; V Corps sent the GOC 21st Division a detailed, 15-point critique of his orders for the operation, the day before it took place.[38]

As was appropriate for a set-piece attack, the GOCRA co-ordinated the corps artillery plan, allocating the field artillery to cover the divisions and the bulk of the heavies to counter-battery work; divisions were to notify corps of any special targets they wished to be engaged by the latter (as in *SS135, 1918*).[39] And it was entirely consistent with *SS135, 1918* that the organisation and camouflage of crossings and crossing materials over the River Ancre was a divisional responsibility. The CMGO was to "arrange for the co-ordination of the machine-gun barrage of the 21st Division with the 42nd Division, and as regards co-ordination of barrages to the South and East of the ANCRE..." Evidently – given this officer's absence from *SS135, 1918* – the CMGO was to co-ordinate machine-gun operations if they extended beyond one division, but, unlike the GOCRA in artillery matters, he did not actually command all the machine-guns of the corps under these circumstances. In a departure from earlier practice, the instructions, as well as giving the times at which the corps squadron, RAF, would arrange for contact aeroplanes to fly over the battlefield, also gave divisions the right to arrange for additional planes if required. However, no mention was made of the allocation of a squadron of ground attack planes to the corps, referred to in the secondary sources.[40]

After the limited success of 21st August, plans were immediately made for the resumption of the attack on the 23rd, though initially Third Army erred on the side of caution.[41] One of the outstanding features of the fighting in the Hundred Days compared to that in previous years was the increased tempo of operations; major offensives which had taken months to prepare (for example, from April to June 1916 before the Somme) now took only days or less. In the case of IV Corps, a conference of divisional commanders was held by the corps commander (Lt.-Gen. Sir G.M. Harper) at 4pm on 22nd August; "Then and there the starting line was fixed, opening line of the Corps barrage, pace of advance, bounds and final objective."[42] The artillery maps were printed by 2am and then sent to divisions, and the attack took place at 11am on the 23rd; the total time from the start of the conference to zero was 19 hours. This shows the high level of efficiency attained in some staffs by 1918. In addition, harassing fire and the use of gas in particular were designed to reduce German tempo by disrupting their communications, and tiring their troops and causing casualties, especially to their gunners.[43] However, because of fears that it might cause casualties to British troops as they advanced, the use of gas overall declined except in set-piece operations.

After 21st August, GHQ felt that the time for bold strokes was at hand, and on the 23rd, Third Army passed to its corps "for your information and guidance" the C-in-C's appreciation of how offensive action should be pursued.[44] This document began by Haig directing "the attention of all Commanders to F.S.R., Pt.I, Chapter VII, and in particular Sections 103, 104 and 105." These were the first three sections of "The Attack", and were entitled 'General Principles,' 'Preliminary Measures' and 'The General Conduct of the Attack,' respectively. Amongst the more important principles enunciated here were that the decisive attack should be the culmination of a process of mounting pressure on many points; reconnaissance before attacking must be thorough; the attacking forces should be set definite objectives or tasks on a properly defined frontage; and "The choice of the manner in which the task assigned to each body of troops is to be performed should be left to its commander."[45] Haig pointed out that, given the depth of the German defences, a swift breakthrough was unlikely. Therefore the use of advanced guards (also recommended in *FSR I*) was vital, not least because of their usefulness in locating the exact locations of the enemy defences, before the discovery of which a deliberate assault would be unwise. However, once the Germans had been evicted from their prepared positions, it was vital to press on rapidly: "units and formations should be directed on *points* [emphasis in original] of strategical and tactical importance some distance ahead… and they should not be ordered to move on objective lines. It is essential that subordinate commanders should use their initiative and the power of manoeuvre and not be cramped by the habit of moving in continuous lines." In addition, "reserves must be pushed in where success has been gained…"[46]

Under these circumstances, it is not surprising that V Corps' next operation order set only rough objective points. Divisions were told to advance regardless of the progress on their flanks and to direct reinforcements where progress was being made and not the reverse, and the artillery was decentralised to a greater degree, as the heavies allotted to divisions were to move forward under their orders. The artillery orders had the GOCRA doling out 60-pounder guns and 6-inch howitzers to divisional CRAs, with liaison officers being sent by the heavy artillery to the artillery HQ of each division, so though divisions moved the artillery (presumably to conform to the infantry advance and hence, their tactical requirements), control was still as in *SS135, 1918*.[47]

However, as the advance slowly accelerated over succeeding days, Army orders became increasingly sketchy, on occasion not even setting a time for zero hour, it being assumed that corps would begin their attacks early.[48] As Dr. Harris notes, both Army and corps were somewhat redundant at this period, just pressing their divisions on but otherwise leaving the detail of operations much to them, though corps did still allot objectives; control was less centralised.[49] As the advance increased its pace, divisions were required by Army to form up in depth with advanced guards, complete with cavalry for exploitation (one cavalry regiment was allotted to each corps in Third Army on 24th August, a squadron was to be allotted to advancing divisions) and cyclists to help with communications.[50]

However, once the V Corps attack on 27th August failed in the face of stiff resistance, more centralised control was reasserted. Corps staffs had failed properly to co-ordinate their divisions, owing to fatigue.[51] The GOC V Corps, Lt.-Gen. C.D. Shute, sent divisions a note, soliciting the commanders' views on how best to take the next objectives, very much as per *FSR I* and Haig's memorandum.[52] In addition, he canvassed divisions' views as to whether a co-ordinated attack should be made, even though "such co-ordination has not been previously considered in the present circumstances in view of the C-in-C's letter…" The result, after a conference on 28th August, was a more structured attack: "Artillery barrages will be co-ordinated by the G.O.C., R.A. Barrages by Machine-Guns will be generally co-ordinated by the C.M.G.O…" In addition, contact planes were arranged.[53] Partly because the Germans were falling back in any case, the attack proved a success, and corps orders for 29th August loosened control again, though if stiff resistance was encountered, "it may be necessary for the G.O's.C. of these divisions to arrange mutually to ensure concerted action. It may also be necessary for the action of all artillery to be co-ordinated by the G.O.C., R.A."[54]

As has already been noted, divisions reorganised in depth (from 3rd September) and with advanced guards, as the pace of the German retreat increased. The policy for the days after was for corps to put as many divisions into reserve as possible (providing rest and training for the troops, both artillery and infantry) and to press the Germans only with the advanced guards. These would drive in the enemy's outposts and ascertain his dispositions. No major actions were to be undertaken until

Army decided that a deliberate action was required, which would be when the next major line of resistance was reached.[55] Corps largely acted as a conduit for Army policy at this time and left divisions to their own devices within the parameters set; the pre-war idea of the division as the basic tactical unit of the army was more relevant in open warfare than in set-piece operations, where corps took a far more active role.[56]

The style of command appropriate for this period was exemplified in a conference held by Shute with his divisional commanders in early September.[57] He offered them a great deal of advice on how to conduct their operations, without prescribing a particular approach. However, having asked whether corps could assist them in the co-ordination of attacks, he remarked that "As regards the latter, circumstances alter so quickly that it is difficult for the Corps to co-ordinate attacks. This however will be done when the circumstances arise, and when Divisions require it." Logistics being a crucial concern at this stage in the war, Shute went on to canvass opinion as to whether his subordinates wished to organise their own road repairs, or whether they wanted them done under corps arrangements; they preferred the former suggestion. The meeting concluded with a contribution from the OC No. 15 Squadron, RAF, who "pointed out that communication with Divisions by telegraph is not good." He proposed to set up an advanced landing ground from which information could be telephoned directly to divisions; in addition, it was stated that "All messages dropped at the Corps dropping ground will be telephoned by Corps to Division immediately such messages are received." It appears that, by virtue of its location in the communications network, corps might still in 1918 enjoy better information about events in the front line than divisions. This conference demonstrated how, in open warfare corps adopted a hands-off policy towards divisions, but this did not absolve them from the duty of pointing out what they thought might be the best approach. Shute was able and willing to interfere if correction was needed, but generally willing to let divisions do things (including logistical arrangements) their way so long as operations were not compromised. At the same time, he clearly gave notice that once the front had stabilised to a greater degree again, operational arrangements would to some extent revert to the corps level.

Unsurprisingly, therefore, corps resumed closer control of operations while the attack on the outposts of the Hindenburg Position, on 18th September (the Battle of Epéhy) was planned.[58] The attack order itself made it plain that corps was back in control, allotting the objectives as coloured lines, just as in any set-piece of 1917. Divisions were expected to co-ordinate their efforts, a level of control not permitted to them in 1917, but the GOCRA and CMGO organised the artillery and machine-gun barrages, "in consultation with G.Os.C. Divisions and Headquarters Flank Corps." Though no preliminary bombardment was undertaken before the attack (corps again only saying that "Attention is drawn to the absolute necessity of preserving secrecy..."[59]), divisions were requested to advise corps of locations they wished to be gassed or bombarded by heavy artillery before the attack. Not everything fell under corps, however; as prescribed by *SS135, 1918*, RE tasks were organised by divisions, the GOCRA notifying them of his requirements for getting heavy artillery over existing trench lines. As ever, signals were to be maintained by non-telephonic means, and contact planes would be used to try to locate the attacking troops. The RAF was to undertake ground attack missions in support of the infantry and, as promised in the conference on 6th September, an advanced landing ground had been set up with three aeroplanes.[60] This was a notable decentralisation of RAF resources. Within this framework, V Corps quite properly still left the details of the attack to division; the 17th Division's historian comments upon the considerable detail into which the divisional orders for this set-piece went, as compared to the operations preceding it.[61]

The planning for the main attack on the Hindenburg Line was done in much the same way, V Corps' instructions followed the pattern set for the preceding attack, with more delegation to divisions than in set-piece attacks earlier in the war, but less than during open warfare. Suggested attack schemes were included, but divisions were given leave to devise their own if they wished (and could justify their ideas).[62] A conference three days later saw the corps commander very much exercising his role as overseer and co-ordinator, without being in any way prescriptive about the details of divisional plans. He gave commanders details of the Army's plan, from the attack on 28th September until the Hindenburg Line had been breached, and discussed inter-divisional liaison. The GOCRA and local tank commander "said that all instructions were clear and arrangements complete."[63] The use of trench mortars was stressed by Shute, who "urged the G.O.C. 33rd Division to use as many mortars as he possibly could as the amount of artillery available to support the attack was not great. All the lessons we have learnt during recent operations point to the enormous value of trench mortars." He went on to remind all present of the need to be careful not to incur unnecessary losses, since the troops would be needed for further operations. The same applied to tanks, though GOCs of divisions were to use them as they thought best, in liaison with "their own tank officers." Plainly Shute did not intend to be unnecessarily dogmatic as to how even a set-piece attack might be carried out, and encouraged discussion of his and his subordinates' plans, though he was also mindful of the ideas set out in Haig's memorandum of August 22nd.

In the event, V Corps' attack met with little success and they were not able to advance until Fourth Army, to the south, had induced the Germans to withdraw. Having crossed the St Quentin Canal and the main Hindenburg Position by 5th October, the corps approached the Beaurevoir

Line, the last portion of the Hindenburg system left to the Germans, which it attacked on 8th October.[64] Army still set the first objectives as points to be gained, rather than lines, with the ultimate objectives (also points), some 20 miles way.[65] Otherwise corps appear to have organised the attack, as before; it seems that Third Army were operating a hands-off style of command whether operations were set-piece or not. By contrast, V Corps did allot quite detailed objectives (as coloured lines) to its divisions.[66] However, though overall details were laid down, each division was allowed to decide the speed of its barrage, though corps reminded them to ensure that they co-ordinated this with units on their flanks. This may partly reflect the haste with which the operation was planned; it seems that in the 38th Division at least, the attack orders could not be given to brigade commanders before 3pm on 7th October, the attack being scheduled to start at 1am the following day.[67] However, notwithstanding the very scrappy nature of the fighting, the artillery fire not being as useful as normal, V Corps took its objectives on 8th October.

The successes all along the line on 8th October compelled the German retirement to the River Selle, so operations from 9th to 13th October took the form of a pursuit and Third Army again displayed a light touch in its control of corps. Once more, points only were set for the advance and corps were left otherwise rather to their own devices.[68] Another feature of the advance on 9th October was that the use of artillery varied widely between corps. The Canadians kept theirs centralised and put down a barrage if they encountered relatively slight resistance; XVII Corps put a brigade of field artillery with the advanced guard of each division and had its remaining brigades of both field and heavy artillery leapfrogging behind, ready to provide a barrage when necessary; V Corps, however, dispensed with barrage fire altogether, though artillery advanced closely behind the infantry to give support when required.[69] The 33rd and 17th Divisions (in V Corps) went forward with advanced guards, but Shute was critical of their handling, issuing a memorandum on the 9th in which he reminded the GOCs of the two divisions of Haig's memorandum, and especially the need to press forward rapidly and to outflank opposition when it was encountered. He felt that "The well known principles of the action of advanced guards are being completely neglected" and whole divisions being held up by "a few machine-guns." He stressed the need to follow *FSR I Part I*, Sections 68 and 112 ('Advanced Guards' and 'The Pursuit,' respectively), that advanced guard commanders should be in the vanguard in order personally to ensure that delays would not occur, and that divisional commanders were responsible for ensuring that all this happened.[70]

While the pursuit to the Selle was taking place, plans were in preparation for the next operation. Third Army told corps to halt at the river and to prepare to capture the east, (i.e. German-held) bank in due course, making arrangements between themselves as necessary.[71] More time was available for planning than had recently been the case, since logistical considerations dictated that a pause was required in order to bring up ammunition for the assault, and though V Corps was intended originally to attack on 17th October, this was postponed to the 20th.[72] Presumably because the operation was part of a joint effort by First and Third Armies, the latter's orders were slightly more detailed than of late, setting zero hour and the objectives and insisting that there be no preliminary bombardment. The co-operation expected between Third Army's corps and between them and those in other Armies was outlined, but the details of the operation were left to corps.[73] As was now becoming almost routine, V Corps ordered divisions to prepare their attacks, and since this was a fully co-ordinated assault, it reserved the artillery plan to the GOCRA. The attack was expected to turn swiftly into a pursuit, so divisions were enjoined to keep their cyclists handy and to get them well forward in the event of the Germans falling back. Although there was a machine-gun barrage, for some reason the CMGO was not involved in its planning or execution, both tasks being delegated to divisions.[74] They also undertook liaison with the limited number of tanks available.[75] It should be noted at this point that Travers' insistence that there was a 'modern' alternative to warfare as practised on the Western Front at this time, i.e. the use of massed tanks, is incorrect simply because of the substantial logistical demands of the tanks.[76]

Subsequent attacks during the Battle of the Selle were a success for V Corps; it then undertook only minor operations until the Battle of the Sambre on 4th November, resting to allow transport facilities to catch up with the advance, and for materiel to be accumulated for the attack.[77] By now, logistical considerations were the main constraint on tempo. Third Army orders for the Sambre fighting followed the same pattern as for the previous two attacks, Army leaving the detail to corps.[78] Shute had asked his divisional commanders to suggest plans of attack two days previously, since the country across which they were expecting to advance was initially very enclosed with hedges, after which the attackers would be confronted by the Forest of Mormal, a very large wooded obstacle.[79] V Corps orders were more comprehensive than for any of October's attacks, an initial scheme being followed by the full Operation Order with several appendices. These related to the artillery plan – very much a corps barrage, which (once in the trees) troops would follow less closely than usual, lest tree tops cause premature shellbursts – and the Engineers' Instructions, whereby each division was to employ a Field Company, RE, and a company of pioneers to move up as advanced guard troops and clear obstacles to the advance, as well as erecting bridges whenever necessary. Such work had regularly been undertaken throughout the advance since August, but this was the first time it was specifically included in corps orders.[80] In addition, there were addenda relating to the employment of the few tanks available and to signal communications, again a departure from usual practice, and here designed to ensure that the corps main air line route could be pushed forward as soon as possible as divisions advanced.[81] This was presumably to improve communications in the pursuit; it should be noted that in October, Third Army had sent a memorandum to corps, instructing them to organise a communications patrol by the corps RAF squadron every morning, in order to locate the heavy and siege artillery batteries, which indicates the ease with which touch could be lost.[82] Notwithstanding these deviations from its normal practice, V Corps seems still to have permitted divisions as much latitude as possible within the constraints outlined above.

The operations on 4th November were successful and also the last substantial engagement in which V Corps took part. The next few days consisted of pursuing the Germans as their retreat accelerated.[83] Difficulties in keeping up were compounded by the poor state of the roads, and Third Army ordered that only one brigade of heavy artillery per division should advance, both to reduce the amount of road taken up and to ease supply.[84] In addition, they announced on 9th November the formation of an Army Advanced Guard under the GOC VI Corps (Lt.-Gen. J.A.L. Haldane), which, as prescribed by *FSR I*, was a force of all arms.[85] Indeed, the operations of the corps in Third Army in this period were characterised by the use of *FSR I, SS135, 1918* and the maintenance (on the whole) of a high tempo. The command structure was flexible and delegation of decisions by Army to corps and corps to division was practised whenever possible.

During the Hundred Days, Fourth Army also operated a flexible style of command. Most of its operations were set-piece attacks, so it perforce displayed less frequently than Third Army the ability to change from a structured to a relatively decentralised system of command, but even in set-piece attacks corps were increasingly left to organise the detail of operations (as had happened in September-November 1917 in Second Army) which took on an increasingly stereotyped form. And like Third Army, Fourth Army and its corps operated in an effective manner, with increasing tempo, within the conceptual framework provided by *FSR I* and the *SS* pamphlets of the time.

Fourth Army was quite happy to give its corps a free hand in the operations of late August and early September; as Harris puts it, "The pursuit and harassment of a retreating enemy could not be controlled in detail by Army commanders and their staffs. All they could do was to set general objectives, leaving the detail to be filled in by subordinate formations and units."[86] In any case, as has been demonstrated in relation to Third Army, authority was devolved if operations were not set-piece.

At about the same time, Haig confided to his diary that he was appointing Lt.-Gen. Sir W.P. Braithwaite, the successful GOC 62nd Division to replace Sir Alexander Hamilton Gordon as GOC IX Corps.[87] The latter was felt in some quarters to have been incompetent, but he may have retired simply as a result of ill-health.[88] In any case, IX Corps moved into the Fourth Army area on 11th September and Braithwaite took up his new post on the 13th, immediately holding a conference with his divisional commanders in order to discuss the forthcoming Battle of Epéhy. It is apparent that Fourth Army closely laid down the principles for the artillery plan, though its execution was organised by the GOCRA in consultation with divisions, as in V Corps. The latter of course, was the only Third Army corps attacking on 18th September, so its artillery plan was not an Army one. In addition, Fourth Army rather than corps laid down the objectives for the attack and corps simply passed them on to divisions. Strangely, Braithwaite did not raise at the conference that surprise was to be attained by the absence of any preliminary bombardment.[89] As was appropriate for a set-piece attack, the GOCRA took overall command of the corps artillery for the operation, and in general IX Corps seems to have been more prescriptive in its approach than V Corps was. Its instructions were comprehensive, even specifying that each division would attack on a frontage of two brigades, as well as covering artillery, RE, RAF and signals aspects of the attack in some detail.[90] This may reflect Braithwaite's experience as Sir Ian Hamilton's CGS at Gallipoli, where the latter's hands-off style of command (on Braithwaite's advice!) was a significant cause of the failure.[91] In addition, as a new corps commander, he might have felt the need to control his first battle closely. Prior and Wilson argue that Rawlinson was too hands-off at this point, failing to ensure that IX Corps employed a machine-gun barrage, as did his more experienced corps (the Australian and III Corps) and notwithstanding that he saw Braithwaite at conferences on 13th and 14th September and visited his HQ on the 15th.[92] This seems to have been a rather marked tendency of his at the time, since he was dissatisfied with the performance of Lt.-Gen. R.H.K. Butler, GOC III Corps, but nevertheless did nothing about it until after the Battle of Epéhy, as a result of which Haig replaced III Corps with XIII Corps (under Lt.Gen. Sir T.L.N. Morland, former GOC X Corps) on 1st October.[93]

IX Corps performed creditably on 18th September, but was required to make a further attack the next day in order to optimise its position for the attack on the main Hindenburg position. However, this was made piecemeal and failed; the corps showed little inclination to launch a properly organised, co-ordinated attack.[94] Braithwaite seems to have learned his lesson, however, and his next effort, on 24th September, was more carefully organised.[95] At a conference on the 20th he stressed the need for thorough preparation (though only about three days were available) and for divisions to notify him of any special needs they might have, such as for gas or tanks. In addition, the operation after next was discussed in a similar vein, following the precepts of *SS135, 1918* regarding the need to plan two attacks ahead. Despite the employment of a preliminary bombardment for 29th September, Braithwaite stressed the need for secrecy regarding both operations, noting that "it was also desirable that the French should not know of them for the present."[96] The attack of 24th September having been successful, planning continued for the main operation. The staff of the Australian Corps was responsible for producing the first draft, but it should not be thought that Rawlinson was only a bystander. The IX Corps plan was supplied by that corps itself, and Rawlinson had to over-rule the Australian Corps commander, Monash, who strongly resisted its inclusion in the main scheme of operations.[97] That said, both Army and corps issued prescriptive and detailed orders, as was appropriate for so structured an attack against so formidable a defensive system.[98] IX Corps' orders included detailed RE preparations, which was entirely reasonable, given that they intended to cross the St. Quentin Canal, instructions for tanks, and (invoking *SS191*) signal preparations for the exploitation phase of the operations. Mounted despatch riders were to be employed until then. However, liaison between the two attacking divisions (32nd and 46th) on the day of attack was left up to them, as the men on the spot. In addition, IX Corps made detailed machine-gun arrangements, with corps closely co-ordinating the barrage. No mention, however, was made of the CMGO.[99] Perhaps because it was making the principal assault on the day, and co-ordinating several corps, Fourth Army was undoubtedly more hands-on than Third (with only one corps involved), and IX Corps more so than V Corps, which had a more subsidiary role than the former, though the Australian Corps was making the main attack in Fourth Army.

In fact, IX Corps was more successful than the Australians, who were hampered to some extent by problems with the American II Corps, attached to them for the operation. Fourth Army maintained the pressure on the Germans in succeeding days, but not in large set-piece operations until it became clear that one was required to evict the Germans from the Beaurevoir Line. IX Corps' orders on 29th September for the following day were rather vague and expressed as Braithwaite's 'intentions,' which were "naturally liable to be modified according to the progress of events."[100] Once Rawlinson had decided that a more deliberate assault was required, however, things became more definite. That said, Army gave its orders by the issuing of maps with objectives marked on them and a single-sheet, six point plan, rather like Second Army in the later phases of Third Ypres.[101] IX Corps' orders were similarly brief, delegating the setting of zero hour, rate of the barrage and artillery command to the GOC 46th Division and his CRA.[102] Given that there were only two days between Rawlinson deciding that the attack had to be organised and its execution, perhaps this brevity was in part the result of haste; it certainly reflects a high operational tempo.[103] Again, the attack was successful but not entirely so, and another big assault was required, on 8th October, to breach the Beaurevoir Line completely. Since this was also arranged quickly, the orders were again brief, though on this occasion, as well as issuing its map, Fourth Army set out the speed and composition of the barrage (while explicitly leaving heavy artillery work up to corps).[104] IX Corps also again issued a map and delegated the field artillery command and organisation to 6th Division, which was carrying out the attack. In this case, the OC 9th Squadron, RAF, was told to report personally to the GOC 6th Division to organise contact patrols.[105] XIII Corps, though also distributing an objective map, gave more details of the barrage and the objectives themselves in its orders. However, since it had both 25th and 66th Divisions taking part, it may be assumed that it was acting as co-ordinator of these formations.[106] A GSO2 in 66th Division recorded in his diary that he and other staff officers were up drafting orders until 4am on 6th October, only to have to amend them after consultation with brigades, so that the final divisional orders were not completed until 4am on the 7th.[107] This seems to imply a degree of haste in preparing for the attack at higher levels too. However, these efforts were rewarded and Fourth Army for the next few days pursued the Germans to the Selle.

IX Corps did not set up advanced guards until 10th October, though on the 8th, orders were issued for a further advance and for a redistribution of heavy artillery, such that the more mobile pieces might move forward and the largest and least mobile be withdrawn into corps reserve.[108] The whole was screened by substantial cavalry forces.[109] However, XIII Corps seems not to have used advanced guards, perhaps because it was expected that stiff resistance would be encountered, as indeed it was.[110] But from 11th to 17th October, preparations were made for the Battle of the Selle and open warfare was not an option in any case. Problems in the Third Army sector with roads have already been mentioned, and the same obtained for Fourth Army, where road construction took over from bridge construction as the main RE activity, in order to ensure the build-up of ammunition and other materiel for the attack.[111] Here, as in Third Army, logistical problems reduced tempo more than any other factor.

Both Army and corps orders for the Battle of the Selle were brief and again relied on maps to describe objectives. This being a set-piece attack with a preliminary bombardment, the artillery plan was Army's, though it was obviously up to corps to release the heavy artillery placed in corps reserve some days earlier. In IX Corps the orders were rather more detailed than in XIII Corps; and stated amongst other things that on this occasion the machine-gun barrage was to be co-ordinated by the CMGO.[112] Artillery command in IX Corps was somewhat devolved, with the CRA of whichever division might be in the front line of the advance at a given time commanding the artillery covering it.[113] In general, all this was consistent with both Third and Fourth Army's practice for such an operation. Subsequent operations during the Battle of the Selle were organised in much the same way for Fourth Army and IX Corps, the orders of both becoming briefer (the plan in any case being agreed beforehand at a conference between Rawlinson, Braithwaite and Morland[114]) and corps expecting the attacking division to provide the plan for taking the objectives set by Army.[115] However, the advance required of IX Corps was relatively small and it was then to form a defensive flank for XIII Corps, to which were allotted five objectives. Unsurprisingly then, XIII Corps' orders for the attack of 23rd October were as lengthy and comprehensive as for any major set-piece attack.[116] After this, apart from minor operations, Fourth Army was not required to advance until the Battle of the Sambre. The orders for the assault followed the stereotype by now established for a set-piece attack, those of IX and XIII Corps being in a very similar format, with minor variations to cover the circumstances of crossing water obstacles, which entailed (in corps orders) more emphasis on the RE aspects than would otherwise have been the case. In addition, corps were responsible for the pace and composition of their own barrages, presumably because IX Corps attacked 30 minutes before XIII Corps.[117] It is noteworthy that by this time, corps were so far ahead of Army that control of bridging and the necessary materials, normally exercised by the latter, was devolved to the former, under the supervision of the Corps Bridging Officer, an appointment only made permanent in Autumn 1918.[118]

After the victory on 4th November in the Battle of the Sambre, the German retreat, as in front of Third Army, became increasingly rapid, and on 9th November Fourth Army, like Third Army struggling against dismal road and rail conditions, announced the formation of an Army Advanced Guard.[119] This was under XIII Corps for reporting purposes but was commanded by Maj.-Gen. H.K. Bethell of 66th Division, from which its two infantry brigades were drawn. Like its Third Army counterpart, it was composed of all arms.[120] Both the role and the resources of Second Army in the Hundred Days were less substantial than those of Third and Fourth Armies. However, its operations demonstrated the same flexibility and devolution of command, when required.

Second Army operations began on 28th September, with the Fourth Battle of Ypres. Since priority in resources had been given to Third and Fourth Armies, Second Army's offensive was a sideshow. The Army plan for the initial attack was brief and to the point, giving an objective line which was to be used as the basis for further advance without delay.[121] The Army artillery plan was lengthier than the general plan, and somewhat prescriptive, as was appropriate for a set-piece attack.[122] The initial advance was to be made by II and XIX Corps, and if their efforts paid off, X and XV Corps would also advance. Consequently, the X Corps plan was simply to provide heavy artillery to supplement the main attack and to send fighting patrols forward under a field artillery barrage arranged by divisions if the situation warranted such an advance.[123] X Corps were obviously concerned about communications, and issued a note suggesting the employment of mounted despatch riders (proven in March and at Cambrai to be the best means of passing messages in open warfare) in any advance.[124] In addition, arrangements for the attack included a specific document according to which contact aeroplanes would drop messages at both divisional and corps dropping stations and an aeroplane with wireless would patrol the corps front, sending messages back to a receiving station whence they would be forwarded to divisional or heavy artillery HQs or, if non-artillery, to corps HQ.[125]

Principally because of delays occasioned by the weather, the next substantial operation for Second Army was the Battle of Courtrai, which began on 14th October. Army orders were again very brief, with objectives and the barrage timing specified, but all else, including the organisation, left to corps.[126] X Corps set specific initial objectives for its divisions, but they were to push on further if possible, and the CHA was ordered to detail mobile brigades of heavy artillery for affiliation with divisions, presumably also with a view to further advances, as was the practice in other Armies (and as was prescribed by SS135, 1918).[127] In addition, the GOCRA was to co-ordinate the artillery schemes, but was not in command of the corps artillery for the operation; this was not as formal an affair as the attack on the Hindenburg Line and required less formal control by either Army or corps.

After crossing the Lys, the Second Army advanced towards the River Schelde, with divisions following forming advanced guards if the opposition was slight enough to permit it, or sending forward patrols if not.[128] However, large-scale set-piece operations were not possible, since delays in getting heavy artillery across the Lys (for want of bridges) meant that Second Army had to do without it until 24th October.[129] On the 25th an action – designated The Action of Ooteghem – took place, where II and XIX Corps and 34th Division (from X Corps) attempted to reach the line of the Schelde. X Corps' orders for this, as was appropriate for a one-division attack, displayed a light hand, merely telling 34th Division its objectives; the GOCRA was to arrange with the GOCRA of the neighbouring XIX Corps to give heavy artillery support to the attack as a whole.[130] Although this operation was not wholly successful, The Action of Tieghem on 31st October ensured that all of Second Army was close up to the Schelde, and preparations were made for a set-piece attack to get Second Army across the river.[131] However, this attack never took place owing to the German withdrawal on the Second Army front, followed by the Armistice.

None of the corps studied here, in any Army, seemed to show very much interest in the preservation of surprise. Army would issue orders regarding it (such as Third Army's quoted above), but corps simply told divisions to maintain secrecy and said nothing else on the matter. Even the Corps Camouflage Officer was not mentioned after the post was created in July. This may be because the vast majority of the documents which have survived relate to the 'G' (operations) branch of the staff, while the bulk of the methods to preserve secrecy would be implemented by the Administrative staff. The lack of a preliminary bombardment was the main 'G' function related to secrecy and this was referred to in corps orders. However, wireless security was undoubtedly tight in the Hundred Days, and on occasion wireless deception was employed (most notably before the Battle of Amiens).[132]

This chapter has demonstrated that in the final campaign of the Great War, the BEF was able successfully to marry its prewar ideas, as expressed in *FSR I*, with the experience gained on the Western Front, as expressed in *SS135, 1918* and other pamphlets. The main difference between *SS135, 1918* and its earlier versions was that in 1918 the intention was plainly to decentralise control of operations if possible and if the situation – open warfare – required it.

The operations of the Hundred Days were conducted in that manner, so during set-piece operations corps took greater control of operations than during open warfare, when as much as possible was delegated to divisions. This demonstrated the flexibility of the BEF's command structure, as well as the continuing importance of discussion of plans and consultation with the man on the spot whenever possible. And in the process, a high tempo of operations was achieved, which was a significant factor in the breakdown of the German forces.

Even though the set-piece operations, such as the attacks on the Hindenburg Line, look ponderous, they were launched at a far greater speed than their equivalents in 1917, indicating how efficient the staff work of the BEF had become by 1918 and how strong its logistical base was. It also demonstrates the ability of the BEF to adapt to the changing circumstances of the advance to victory.

NOTES

1 Examples of the 'old' literature are Blaxland, Gregory, *Amiens: 1918* (Frederick Muller, 1968), Essame, H., *The Battle for Europe 1918* (Batsford, 1972), Terraine, John, *To Win a War: 1918, The Year of Victory* (Sidgwick and Jackson, 1978) and Pitt, Barrie, *1918 The Last Act* (Reprint Society, 1964). The last of these is the only book of the 'Lions Led by Donkeys' school to be devoted to 1918, and as such is more characterised by passion than regard for historical accuracy.

2 Travers, *How the War Was Won*, 175-182.

3 Schreiber, *Shock Army of the British Empire*. Brown, 'Not Glamorous, But Effective: The Canadian Corps and the Set-Piece Attack, 1917-1918.'

4 Prior and Wilson, *Command...*, 289-391.

5 Harris, *Amiens...* 294-300.

6 Palazzo, *Seeking Victory on the Western Front*.

7 O.H., 1918 Volume 3, viii.

8 *The Training and Employment of Divisions, 1918* (hereafter SS135, 1918), 1.

9 *SS135, 1918*, 4.

10 *SS135* (1917) chapter 4, p.6.

11 *SS135, 1918*, 60.

12 *SS135, 1918*, 9.

13 *Notes on the Action of the Artillery IV Corps in the Operations about Havrincourt October 30th to December 1st 1917.*, 9. Dated 29th December 1917. TNA:PRO, WO 158/379.

14 *Artillery in the Recent Fighting*, 26th April 1918. Rawlinson Papers, NAM, 5201-33-78.

15 *XIII Corps Artillery Instructions No. 92*, 27th May 1918. TNA:PRO, WO 95/902. *XVII Corps Artillery Instructions No. 2*, 25th August 1918. TNA:PRO, WO 95/943.

16 *SS135, 1918*, 12-13.

17 *SS135, 1918*, 15.

18 *SS135, 1918*, 17.

19 *SS135, 1918*, 20.

20 *SS135, 1918*, 29.

21 *SS135, 1918*, 44.

22 *SS135, 1918*, 34.

23 Haig Diary entries for 8th, 12th, 18th and 27th May, 6th and 12th June and 4th July. TNA:PRO, WO 256/31-3.

24 See various documents issued by Fifth Army in mid-July 1918. TNA:PRO, WO 95/522. For V Corps see *V Corps IG.404*, 5th July 1918. TNA:PRO, WO 95/750.

25 Haig diary for 26th July 1918. TNA:PRO, WO 256/33.

26 *Third Army No. G.5/124*, 14th July 1918. TNA:PRO, WO 95/371.

27 *O.B./894*, 2nd July 1918. TNA:PRO, WO 95/371.

28 See for example, *Third Army G.34/833*, the weekly summary up to 28th July, and *Third Army G.34/842*, the same for the following week. TNA:PRO, WO 95/372.

29 Schreiber, *Shock Army of the British Empire*, 141, appears to believe – erroneously – that only the Canadian Corps did this.

30 Travers, *How the War Was Won*, 145.

31 *Third Army No.G.S.71/1*, 14th August 1918. TNA:PRO, WO 95/372.

32 *Summary of Operations of Third Army From 21st August, 1918, to 30th September 1918.*, 2. TNA:PRO, WO 95/372. Henceforth *Third Army Summary 21/8-30/9*.

33 *Third Army Artillery Instructions No.39*, 1. 14th August 1918. TNA:PRO, WO 95/372, and see Harris, *Amiens...*, 125.

34 *Third Army No.G.S.71/4, Notes for Operation GZ*, 14th August 1918. TNA:PRO, WO 95/372.

35 *Third Army No.G.S.73/24*, 20th August 1918. TNA:PRO, WO 95/372.

36 *V Corps Order No. 230*, 19th August 1918. TNA:PRO, WO 95/750.

37 *SS135, 1918*, 28-9.

38 *V Corps G.S.490/18*, 20th August 1918. TNA:PRO, WO 95/750.

39 *Vth Corps Artillery Instructions No.193*, 20th August 1918. TNA:PRO, WO 95/756.

40 O.H., 1918 Volume 4, 181. See also Jones, H.A., *The War in the Air, Vol. VI* (Clarendon, 1937), 470.

41 Harris, *Amiens…*, 132-5.

42 Letter from Brigadier F. FitzGibbon to the Official Historian, 16th October 1938. TNA:PRO, CAB 45/185.

43 Palazzo, *Seeking Victory on the Western Front.*, 174-6, 182-3.

44 *Third Army No. G.S.73/56*, 23rd August 1918. Haig's appreciation was *O.A.D. 912*, 22nd August 1918, TNA:PRO, WO 95/372. Dr. Harris quotes *O.A.D. 911*, but it would seem that the second document is more appropriate for putting Haig's views into their proper context, i.e. his (and others') continuing belief in the validity of *FSR I*.

45 *FSR I*, Part I, 137.

46 *O.A.D. 912*, 2.

47 *V Corps Artillery Instructions No.195*, 23rd August 1918. TNA:PRO, WO 95/756.

48 *Third Army No. G.S.73/73*, 25th August 1918. TNA:PRO, WO 95/372. O.H., 1918 Volume 4, 299.

49 *Third Army Summary 21/8-30/9*, 11, 13, 15, 17. TNA:PRO, WO 95/372.

50 *Third Army Summary 21/8-30/9*, 11 and 13. TNA:PRO, WO 95/372. Atteridge, *History of the 17th… Division*, 388-9.

51 O.H., 1918 Volume 4, 323.

52 *V Corps G.S.490/80* [?]. TNA:PRO, WO 95/750.

53 *V Corps Order No. 234*, 28th August 1918. TNA:PRO, WO 95/750.

54 *V Corps G.S.490/93*, 29th August 1918. TNA:PRO, WO 95/750.

55 *Third Army No. G.S.73/123*, 3rd September 1918 and *Third Army No. G.S.73/127*, 4th September 1918. TNA:PRO, WO 95/372. TNA:PRO, WO 95/372.

56 See *V Corps G.165* and *G.191* of 2nd and 3rd September, respectively. TNA:PRO, WO 95/751.

57 *Minutes of Corps Commander's Conference, held at 17th Division H.Q., 6th September.* TNA:PRO, WO 95/751.

58 See Harris, *Amiens…*, 175-180.

59 *V Corps Order No. 236*, 16th September 1918. TNA:PRO, WO 95/751.

60 *V Corps Order No. 236* and *Addendum to V Corps Order No. 236*, 16th September 1918. TNA:PRO, WO 95/751.

61 Atteridge, *17th Division*, 410-11.

62 *V Corps G.S.496/2*, 23rd September 1918. TNA:PRO, WO 95/751.

63 *Minutes of Corps Commander's Conference held at V Corps H.Q.*, 26th September 1918. TNA:PRO, WO 95/751.

64 O.H., 1918 Volume 5, 156-7.

65 O.H., 1918 Volume 5, 199.

66 *V Corps G. 375*, 6th October 1918. TNA:PRO, WO 95/751.

67 Munby, Lt.-Col. J.E. (ed.), *A History of the 38th (Welsh) Division* (Hugh Rees Ltd., 1920), 66-7.

68 *Third Army No.G.S.76/190.*, 8th October 1918. TNA:PRO, WO 95/374. O.H., 1918 Volume 5, p.219.

69 Farndale, *Artillery*, 304. O.H., 1918 Volume 5, p.219. *XVII Corps No. G.(O)263*, 9th October 1918. TNA:PRO, WO 95/943.

70 *V Corps G.X.4477*, 9th October 1918. TNA:PRO, WO 95/751.

71 *Third Army No.G.S.76/206.*, and *G.S.76/215.*, 10th and 12th October 1918, respectively. TNA:PRO, WO 95/374.

72 O.H., 1918 Volume 5, 245.

73 *Third Army No.G.S.76/250.*, and *G.S.76/285.*, 17th and 19th October 1918, respectively. TNA:PRO, WO 95/374.

74 *V Corps Operation Order No. 237*, 13th October 1918. TNA:PRO, WO 95/751.

75 *V Corps Operation Order No. 238*, 17th October 1918. TNA:PRO, WO 95/751.

76 Childs, 'British Tanks…', 177-190, 199.

77 O.H., 1918 Volume 5, 362-4, 375-7.

78 O.H., 1918 Volume 5, 477-8.

79 *V Corps G.S.518*, 28th October 1918. TNA:PRO, WO 95/751.

80 *V Corps G.S.518/6*, 31st October 1918 (Scheme of Attack). *V Corps Operation Order No. 239*, 1st November 1918. TNA:PRO, WO 95/752.

81 *V Corps G.S.518/34* and *V Corps G.S.518/43*, 2nd November 1918. TNA:PRO, WO 95/752.

82 *Third Army Artillery Instructions No.44*, 2nd October 1918. TNA:PRO, WO 95/374.

83 Harris, *Amiens…* 283-4.

84 O.H., 1918 Volume 5, 496.

85 *Third Army No.G.S.78/75.*, 9th November 1918. TNA:PRO, WO 95/375.

86 Harris, *Amiens…*, 148.

87 Entry for 27th August. TNA:PRO, WO 256/35.

88 Thanks to Dr. John Bourne and Mr. Tony Cowan for this information. See also Bond and Robbins, *Staff Officer*, 134.

89 *Notes on Corps Commander's Conference…13th Sept: 1918*, TNA:PRO, WO 95/837. *Fourth Army No. 20/18(G)*, 13th September 1918. TNA:PRO, WO 95/438.

90 *IX Corps Instructions – Series "A" Nos. 1-5*, 15-16th September 1918. TNA:PRO, WO 95/837.

91 Travers, 'Command and Leadership Styles in the British Army; The 1915 Gallipoli Model.'

92 Prior and Wilson, *Command…*, 353. Rawlinson Diary, September 13th-15th 1918, National Army Museum, (henceforth Rawlinson NAM Diary) 5201-33-29.

93 Prior and Wilson, *Command…*, 353-4, 359. Haig diary entry for 22nd September. TNA:PRO, WO 256/36.

94 *IX Corps Order No. 134*, 18th September 1918. TNA:PRO, WO 95/837.

95 Harris, *Amiens…*, 205.

96 *Proceedings of Corps Commander's Conference*, 20th September 1918. TNA:PRO, WO 95/837.

97 Harris, *Amiens…*, 206, 210-12.

98 *Fourth Army No. 273(G)*, 23rd September 1918. TNA:PRO, WO 95/438. *IX Corps Instructions – Series "B" Nos. 1-8*, 26-27th September 1918. TNA:PRO, WO 95/837.

99 *IXth Corps No. G.364/305/109*, 23rd September 1918. TNA:PRO, WO 95/837.

100 *IX Corps No. G.364/305/241*, 29th September 1918. TNA:PRO, WO 95/837.

101 *Fourth Army No. 20/28(G)*, 2nd October 1918. TNA:PRO, WO 95/439.

102 *IX Corps Order No. 140*, 2nd October 1918. TNA:PRO, WO 95/837.

103 Montgomery, Maj.-Gen. Sir Archibald, *The Story of the Fourth Army in the Battles of the Hundred Days, August 8th to November 11th, 1918* (Hodder and Stoughton, 1919), 177.

104 *Fourth Army No. 20/31(G)*, 5th October 1918. TNA:PRO, WO 95/439.

105 *IX Corps Order No. 143*, 5th October 1918. TNA:PRO, WO 95/837.

106 *XIII Corps Order No. 159*, 6th October 1918. TNA:PRO, WO 95/897.

107 Bond and Robbins, *Staff Officer*, 230.

108 *IX Corps Order No. 144* and *IXth Corps Artillery Order No. 32*, 5th October 1918. TNA:PRO, WO 95/837.

109 Montgomery, op. cit., 197-201. Marden, Maj.-Gen. T.O., *A Short History of the 6th Division, Aug. 1914-March 1919* (Hugh Rees Ltd., 1920), 68.

110 Montgomery, op. cit., 201. O.H., 1918 Volume 5, 237.

111 *Report on RE Operations, IX Corps, 1918*, 25th January 1919. TNA:PRO, WO 95/844.

112 *IX Corps Order No. 145*, 15th October, 1918. TNA:PRO, WO 95/837. For XIII Corps, *Preliminary Instructions No. 1. Series "B"*. 13th October 1918. TNA:PRO, WO 95/897.

113 *IXth Corps Artillery Order No. 37*, 15th October 1918. TNA:PRO, WO 95/837.

114 Entry for 21st October 1918, Rawlinson NAM Diary.

115 *Fourth Army No. 20/44(G)*, 20th October 1918. TNA:PRO, WO 95/439. *IX Corps Order No. 147*, 19th October, 1918. TNA:PRO, WO 95/837.

116 *XIII Corps Instructions Nos.1-7, Series "C"*, 19th-22nd October 1918. TNA:PRO, WO 95/897.

117 *Fourth Army No. 20/48(G)* and *20/49(G)*, 25th and 29th October 1918. TNA:PRO, WO 95/439. *IX Corps Instructions Nos.1-4, Series "C"*, 31st October-2nd November 1918. TNA:PRO, WO 95/837. *XIII Corps Instructions Nos.1-9, Series "D"*, 30th October-1st November 1918. TNA:PRO, WO 95/897.

118 Anon, *The Work of the Royal Engineers in the European War, 1914-19: Bridging* (Chatham: W & J Mackay & Co., 1921), 24, 44.

119 *Fourth Army No. 20/54(G)*, 9th November 1918. TNA:PRO, WO 95/439.

120 *XIII Corps Order No. 166*, 10th November 1918. TNA:PRO, WO 95/897.

121 *Second Army Order No. 35*, 19th September 1918. TNA:PRO, WO 95/277.

122 *Second Army Artillery Instructions No. 1*, 20th September 1918. TNA:PRO, WO 95/277.

123 *Xth Corps No: G.32/2/1.*, 21st September 1918. TNA:PRO, WO 95/854.

124 *Xth Corps No: G.32/2/3.*, 24th September 1918. TNA:PRO, WO 95/854.

125 *Xth Corps No: G.32/2/23.*, 25th September 1918. TNA:PRO, WO 95/854.

126 *Second Army Order No. 42*, 4th October 1918. TNA:PRO, WO 95/277.

127 *Xth Corps Order No: 201*, 5th October 1918. *Xth Corps Artillery Instruction No.3*, 7th October 1918 TNA:PRO, WO 95/854.

128 O.H., 1918 Volume 5, 283-90, 427.

129 Harris, *Amiens...*, 259.
130 *Xth Corps Order No: 208*, 23rd October 1918. TNA:PRO, WO 95/854. O.H.,
    1918 Volume 5, 283-90, 427.
131 Harris, *Amiens...*, 260.
132 Harris, *Amiens...*, 71-2, 123, 171.

CHAPTER 8

In Command of a Corps – The Daily Life and Work of British Corps Commanders

Studies of generals and generalship in the Great War have almost invariably concentrated their attention on operations and operational planning. As a result, the day-to-day activities of generals have been neglected. Terraine and de Groot deal only with the fighting or politics, when writing about Haig in 1914.[1] Farrar-Hockley's biography of Hubert Gough does touch on his subject's desire to visit and inspect the troops in his corps, but without offering any analysis of this aspect of the job.[2] Baynes' biography of Ivor Maxse also neglects all non-operational aspects of his job, apart from training. Even the seminal *Command on the Western Front* deals only with Rawlinson's operational role, and Plumer's most recent biographer reduces him when a corps commander to a "shadowy figure."[3]. Unsurprisingly, the opposite point of view, the 'lions led by donkeys' school, fails entirely to engage with Great War generalship in any sensible way. Therefore the question of what corps (or other) commanders actually did with the substantial portion of their time when they were not engaged in operations has never been asked before.

This gap in the literature has contributed to a false and detrimental picture of generalship on the Western Front. The more measured works cited above at least only neglect the daily grind of the general's job. However, Alan Clark's *The Donkeys* and Leon Wolff's *In Flanders Fields*, to name but two, peddle an unrealistic and misleading impression. They depict château generals living in splendour, unaware of or indifferent to the sufferings of the men under their command, interested only in intrigue and horses, and never going anywhere near the front line. Fortunately, the 'lions...' school of thought has now been discredited. In reality, although corps commanders lived in some comfort, and often in châteaux, they had little option in this, since a large building was required for their headquarters and staff. Hospitality was part of their job, so formal dinners were held. Coming from the class they did, that they rode frequently is unsurprising, and given that small four-by-four vehicles like the jeep had yet to be invented, it was also essential for them to get across country. And all six corps commanders studied for this chapter went into the front line from time to time, as circumstances dictated. As will be seen, several came under fire more than once and one sustained serious injury.

The aim of this chapter is to fill the gap in the literature referred to above by examination of the diaries of Walter Congreve[4], Douglas Haig[5], Aylmer Haldane[6], Aylmer Hunter-Weston[7], Henry Rawlinson[8] and Henry Wilson[9]. These have been studied for the periods from when the six generals became corps commanders on the Western Front to the end of their tenure or of the war, whichever was sooner. Other corps commanders, such as Smith-Dorrien or Snow, also left papers or diaries, but the generals examined here provide a full spread of experience of the corps commander's role on the Western Front for the whole of the war. Of the six in the sample, Haldane and Hunter-Weston are referred to most frequently because their diaries contain more detail than others in the group and cover a longer period, from mid-1916 to the end of 1918. This coincides with the portion of the war in which corps assumed their greatest importance, so a tendency to emphasise the 1916-18 period at the expense of 1914-15 does not detract from the arguments in this chapter. Between them, these six generals played a part as corps commanders in all the BEF's major operations apart from the later part of the Somme and the fighting in Flanders in 1917. That they at times held quiet sectors adds to the value of the discussion in this chapter, which attempts to look at the job of command as a whole, not just when battles were being fought. Indeed, the time spent fighting battles was surprisingly small; Congreve spent 14.38% of his time as corps commander doing so, Haig 63.16%, Haldane 18.77%, Hunter-Weston 4.85%, Rawlinson 9.03% and Wilson 0.29%. Haig's abnormally high percentage reflects that his 84 days as a corps commander saw the hectic operations of 1914 rather than the slower pace of trench warfare, as reflected by the figure for Rawlinson.[10]

These diaries were of considerable importance to their authors, though of the generals under consideration, only Haldane and Wilson kept diaries before the war. However, it appears that they were all sufficiently aware of the importance of their role in the history of the Great War (which began to be turned into history almost from its beginning[11]) to write diaries from the outbreak of hostilities.[12] Most of these diaries were definitely meant to be read by someone other than the writer at some point and certainly Haig's, Hunter-Weston's and Haldane's were revisited by their authors after the events recorded in them. Haig's original was typed up after 1918, with extra material added.[13] Hunter-Weston's was transcribed, with extracts from his letters, newspaper cuttings and photographs, into a series of imposing volumes which were deposited after his death in the British Library. Annotations to the typescript of Haldane's diary show that he typed it up much later, though given that he also wrote both published and unpublished memoirs, it is not clear whether he intended the diary to be read or just quarried it himself for material to be included in his memoirs.[14] Nor is it possible to tell definitely what Wilson's, Congreve's and Rawlinson's intentions were. The latter's diaries are in two parts, one a manuscript which records his views on events and strategy and often omits meetings and the like, and another in typescript, which recorded little of what he thought but is a better (if still fallible) record of what meetings he had.[15] There seems to have been little point in his having this diary typed up unless he intended it to be preserved, and the same applies for Congreve. Only Wilson's remains entirely in the original manuscript.

Nevertheless, these retrospective alterations do not diminish the diaries' value to historians. Bourne and Sheffield have dispelled doubts as to the reliability of the Haig diaries.[16] Haldane's changes appear largely to take the form of corrections to errors in the original. Furthermore, for a source to be doctored in order to suit how the writer wishes to be viewed by posterity, they must have made assumptions about how posterity will do it. These may well not match the reality. Hence, Aylmer Hunter-Weston comes across as an extremely pompous and self-important man; if he sought to portray himself more favourably than was the true picture, he conspicuously failed. A recent author, seeking to prove that the Haig and Wilson diaries are unreliable, has used as evidence Bernard Ash's generalisation that "People of Wilson's generation confided in their diaries, sometimes let their imaginations run riot in them, certainly recorded in them their fantasies of wishful thinking…"[17] However, Ash entirely fails to substantiate this statement. Memory is notoriously fallible, and human nature leads diarists to emphasise themselves rather than others. In addition, they include what they perceived as significant events and ignore others. These factors are as likely to make these diaries not entirely accurate as any desire to falsify the record. Nevertheless, their having been written at the time of the events they describe (even if added to later) makes them more likely to reflect what the diarist thought or did than an anecdote recounted years after the event, distorted by the passage of time and coloured by the knowledge of subsequent controversies.

Unsurprisingly, the information held in these accounts can be rather patchy. However, the principal activities of these generals are clear. Diarists tend to record what was interesting about the day, not what was routine, so on superficial inspection, these generals seem virtually never to have talked to their staffs, for example. In addition, where letters exist as well as the diaries, as in Hunter-Weston's case, it is apparent that sometimes he went to meetings or inspections which are mentioned in the former but omitted from the latter.[18] Rawlinson states, as if it were an exception to the rule, "No letters or papers tonight.", but he never mentions working on either as an evening activity.[19] Similarly, he once and only once mentions "my hour at the office before breakfast when I usually do most of the administrative work of the Corps..."[20] Examples like these do not, however, indicate that these diaries are unreliable. They merely serve to point out that they do not lend themselves to a precise statistical analysis of how these generals spent their time, along the lines of 'Wilson spent 32.5% of his time riding to inspections of the corps cyclists.' Furthermore, the rather haphazard recording of events indicates that there was no consistent effort by the diarists to portray themselves in any particular way. In an atypical entry of Rawlinson's, he describes what he actually did in full (the erratic punctuation is as in the original):

> My day is as follows – Called at 6.30 out for a ride at 7.15 – in the office at 8. – visit the hospital at 9 – Breakfast at 9.30[,] office from 10 to 1 then lunch – After lunch motor out to the... [divisions] send my two horses to meet me at one or the other of their Head Qtrs [sic] then ride around some of the Art[iller]y positions and visit the Brigade H-Qtrs [sic] of some of the units. Sometimes if it is fine I go to an observing place to have a look at the enemys [sic] positions after which I return to the office at 7 for half an hour before dinner which we usually have at 8pm. After dinner I devote myself to the Times and to writing private letters on a variety of subjects and my one for Merrie [his wife] every night with what news I can collect. I keep up a pretty regular correspondence with Clive Wigram [Assistant Private Secretary to the King] and with Lord K[itchener] so as to keep HM [the King] and K informed of what is going on in the units of my Corps. At present I have plenty of time for letter writing but when we have offensive operations in prospect there is little time to spare.[21]

Judging from the evidence in these six diaries, this can be taken as approximating to a typical day for any active corps commander. It is, therefore, unsurprising to see that the noteworthy activities these corps commanders recorded fell into six main categories (here given in no particular order): (1) attending inspections, parades, demonstrations or less formal visits; (2) meetings (with subordinates, superiors, other corps commanders or allies), including operational planning; (3) fighting battles, for which inspections etc., meetings and planning were all essential both beforehand and during; (4) meals with other people (a form of meeting which could overlap with those above) and entertaining; (5) exercise, which often overlapped with inspections etc.; and (6) being on leave, sick leave and under-employed.

Though it is difficult to establish quite how these generals learnt to do their job, the basis for their activities appears to have been *Field Service Regulations (1909) Part 2 (Organization and Administration)*, which will henceforth be referred to as *FSR II*. No formal training in generalship was given in the British Army, but most would have acquired experience of staff work and command in the course of their rise to the level of corps commander.[22] The theory of command in the BEF was laid down in *FSR II*, which stated that the system of organisation must be appropriate for the operations undertaken and sufficiently elastic to meet any conditions which might arise.[23] Therefore, rather as in *FSR I*, only general principles were stated, which boiled down to the need for "sub-division of labour and decentralization of responsibility among subordinates... At the same time central control and co-ordination of subordinate parts for the attainment of the common objective must be assured."[24]

Consequently, command was exercised by the C-in-C (assisted by his staff) exercising authority over his subordinates, who exercised theirs over their subordinates (in accordance with the C-in-C's plans) and so on down the chain of command.[25] The subordinate commander was expected to be "responsible for the efficiency of his command, and for the control and direction of the duties allotted to him."[26] How this was to be done was not, however, laid down.

Nevertheless, it is unsurprising that in his first conference of Army commanders after becoming C-in-C, Douglas Haig stressed the importance of staff work and "the need for adhering to the principles of FSR Part II."[27] Information in *FSR II* on the role of the branches of the staff was expanded and amplified with helpful diagrams in a later publication, the *Staff Manual (War) Provisional 1912* (henceforth *Staff Manual*). Significantly, it pointed out that "the efficient performance of staff duties is far more difficult in a new organization than in one which has existed for some time, and in which commanders and Staff know each other well and are accustomed to work together." This point was particularly pertinent for corps in 1915-18, when they might have 30 divisions pass through them in a year.

The only definite information that *FSR II* was used came at the end of 1918. Immediately after the war, Sir Walter Braithwaite, who had commanded IX Corps in late 1918 and been Sir Ian Hamilton's CGS at Gallipoli, was ordered to report on how the staff system had performed over the course of the conflict.[28] He and the other members of his committee consulted numerous officers, including all the theatre commanders, three of the BEF's Army commanders and 13 Lt.-Gens. (seven of whom were corps commanders). The Braithwaite report was broadly in favour of the retention of the existing organisation, pointing out the value of the tenets of *FSR II* "We have been much impressed by the fact, established by the evidence given, that in the Formations where these principles have been adhered to, the Staff work has had the happiest results...″[29] Later came the only concrete hint in any of the three documents discussed above on how to command:

> ...for a Commander to attempt to co-ordinate the work of the Staff himself, imposes an undue strain on him during prolonged operations and is likely either to overburden him, or to leave him insufficient time *to visit the troops* and perform the other functions of a Commander. In the opinion of many... *the best method of testing the efficacy of the work of a Commander's Staff is by paying constant visits to the lower formations*, where the results of the Staff work of the higher formations are most readily apparent.[30] (present author's italics)

While there is plentiful evidence that *FSR I* was applied by corps commanders (it was cited in orders and operational plans, for example), the Braithwaite Report is the only explicit indication that the same was true of *FSR II*. Since it did not mention the visits which apparently were so important to ensure the efficiency of the staff (and hence the corps), what led commanders to adopt this approach to command is not apparent. As has been remarked above, training in generalship was not given in the British Army, but there were opportunities for officers to gain staff and command experience. Walter Congreve, the only one of the corps commanders considered here who was not a psc (Staff College graduate), had been a brigade major and a DAAG in the course of the South African War and before taking over XIII Corps had (in late 1915) also commanded both a brigade and a division.

Experience cannot have been the only factor in determining how corps commanders did their job, however; simple common sense may also have played a part.[31] Henry Wilson was notorious for having never commanded any unit larger than a company, despite extensive staff experience at the War Office, so his knowledge of how to command his corps was more theoretical than most.

Nevertheless, his activities as a commander were not markedly different from those of other corps commanders. The advice of his BGGS could have pointed him towards inspections and visits as a primary part of his role; both of Wilson's BGGSes were experienced staff officers, if not necessarily as BGGSes.[32] But in any case, like all the officers studied in this chapter, Wilson was capable of using his common sense and realising that apart from visiting the troops he would need to have meetings with other commanders, above, below and at the same level as himself in order to ensure that he understood and could implement what was asked of him and that his subordinates understood what he wanted from them. In the days before conference calls, meetings were the best way of imparting information to a group of people and then discussing it.

The six categories of corps commanders' activities will now be examined in the order in which they are listed above.

Attending inspections, parades, demonstrations or less formal visits

"Yesterday, I spent the morning in going round the Heavy Artillery with a retinue of Generals, Colonels etc. and to them I gave addresses on various essentials of their job. They were very interested and thanked me for what I had taught them… It is curious to find that in almost all the different Arms, which vary so much in their material and training, I know a good deal more of… [these officers'] job than they do… However, I suppose that is what ought to be the case with a General!" (Letter from Sir Aylmer Hunter-Weston to his wife, Lady Grace, 8th September 1918.)

Visits, inspections and the like took up a great deal of the corps commanders' time, and were essential to maintain the efficiency of the corps. All regimental officers were required to inspect their troops to ensure that standing orders were followed, so corps commanders had been accustomed to doing this from the start of their careers.[33] Furthermore, Haig noted that, having been round the billets of various battalions and a Field Company RE, he "got home… having learnt much more about the refitting of the 1st Division [after First Ypres] from talking to individual officers and men than from the official returns which are sent me."[34] Haldane commented in 1916 on the need to supervise everything, and be far fussier than would have been sensible before the war, since the army had so many inexperienced junior officers now.[35] Visits also complemented commanders' meetings at divisional and brigade headquarters. The corps commander would go to see the troops – marching, practicing an attack or any one of a substantial number of other activities (see Appendix 3 for a list) – to establish how well the brigade, divisional and corps staffs were doing their jobs, and raise any issues on the next visit to the divisional HQ. Haldane had a policy of going round the line without divisional commanders, since bringing them with him would have reduced the number of visits received by units. Instead, he went with brigadiers, and told them and division if he found anything wrong.[36].

The need to supervise more closely than in the pre-war army may be borne out by the greater frequency of specifically pre-battle inspections and pep talks early in the war, Rawlinson going round the troops on the day before Neuve Chapelle (while these were regular divisions, their staffs had suffered heavy losses in 1914), and Aubers, though not, curiously, before Loos.[37] Hunter-Weston saw all his brigadiers and almost all of the 52 battalions – especially the New Army ones – in his corps before the Somme and Haldane addressed several battalions before the Battle of Arras in 1917.[38] He did not do this before Cambrai or in 1918, which, while reflecting greater awareness of the need for secrecy before attacks, also indicates that there was less need by then for such close supervision of lower staffs by corps, especially in the Hundred Days. It is interesting that 151 of the 153 days on which Haldane conducted inspections in 1918 were before 16th August 1918; once his corps was involved in heavy fighting (from 20th August) he apparently relied much more on HQ visits and battlefield performance as indicators of its efficiency.

Corps commanders' visits to and encouragement of sports, from battalion level upwards, and at horse shows also served useful functions. The playing of sport was highly valued in the British army, not least in building character and team work which might stand a man in good stead on the battlefield. It was also important in fostering good officer-other ranks relations and morale.[39] Haldane even went so far as to provide a baseball trophy to the 26th Canadian Battalion.[40] Hunter-Weston's corps horse show in August 1918 has been held up to ridicule – Travers observes that it was organised at a time of heavy fighting on the Western Front, though he does not also point out that VIII Corps was not involved in this.[41] However, another observer felt that "Horse shows, in which all the transport units of a formation competed, were common to all good formations, and were a first class stimulus in animal care and management."[42] Both Haldane and Hunter-Weston recorded having made speeches at sports and horse shows. The idea of generals speechifying to troops is one likely to provoke ridicule in the modern context – the shadow of *Oh, What a Lovely War!* is long. However, Frank Maxwell VC, when a battalion commander, felt that the men liked being talked to, and commented on the way they would swarm round the prize-giving at sports events to listen to the speaker.[43] So although it is tempting to dismiss Hunter-Weston as simply a windbag, and even the rather more sensible Haldane as wasting his breath, the words of a figure of authority presumably carried some weight with ordinary soldiers in the early 20th Century.

Notwithstanding the traditional view of Great War generals as being securely ensconced in their châteaux and never going forward, corps commanders had to visit their trench lines. It was necessary to go to both front and support lines to ensure that the defensive arrangements of the corps were satisfactory. Consequently, there was usually a flurry of activity when the corps commander felt the need to review his defences on his taking over the corps or it moving to a new sector. After almost two months in command of VI Corps Haldane observed that he had been up to the front line 18 times, and gone along almost all of it three times (its length was 18,000 yards), as well as going up 15 of the 32 communication trenches leading to the front line.[44] Hunter-Weston was also keen to ensure that the trenches were maintained to the standard he expected, additionally going to the forward area to discuss the siting of strongpoints or machine-gun positions with his subordinates.[45] Rawlinson rarely explained the reasons for his visits but occasional comments reveal that he did keep an eye on how units were maintaining their sectors and also carried out reconnaissance.[46] Similarly, Wilson did not usually inform his diary of the purpose of his visits, though he did record the distance covered – nine miles walking in trenches on one occasion.[47] However, this level of activity did not stop him losing a portion of his line near Vimy Ridge in May 1916, which caused some him some embarrassment and led to friction with Army. Visiting forward areas was not without its hazards for the corps commanders themselves. On one occasion Congreve cut across the open and lost his hand to a German shell.[48] His diary entry is terse to a degree:

> Fine and hot. Out with Crinks [his ADC] to see the Oppy side of our line and whilst walking across the open to battalion headquarters on the Arleux Rd. a shell came down and cut off my left hand all but some bits. Crinks escaped and got a stretcher and so by that, walking and R.A. motor I got to St. Catherine's dressing station from where I went on to No. 19 C.C.S. by ambulance and by 1.30 my operation was over and I felt little the worse save for a bad ache in the missing hand.

In addition, Wilson came under rifle fire when doing much the same on one of his trench visits.[49] And Haldane and Wilson were shelled more than once, the former on one occasion being knocked over by the blast and the latter having to shelter in a dugout for a while.[50]

It is evident that these corps commanders followed what was considered sound practice at the time, in that they regularly visited not just their subordinates' HQs but also the front line, the troops themselves, and numerous back area units. In this way they could check to see whether all staffs, whether 'G', 'Q' or 'A', or corps, divisional or brigade, were doing their jobs. Especially until late 1917, it is likely that they felt the need to address the problems posed by inexperienced troops and staffs through closer supervision than would have been necessary before the war. All this conforms entirely to the Braithwaite Report's view of how *FSR II* should be applied. In addition, the visits of corps commanders to the front line go some way towards dispelling the myth of château generalship.

Meetings

The necessity of holding meetings to ensure good communications within the BEF has been referred to earlier. After inspections and visits, attending meetings or conferences was corps commanders' most frequent activity. In terms of *FSR II*, they can be seen as furthering the corps commander's

189

pursuit of the "efficiency of his command, and for the control and direction of the duties allotted to him", as indeed they were for his subordinates and superiors. In the BEF of 1915-17 especially, they would also help staffs get to know each other, promoting smoother staff work, as the Staff Manual pointed out. And these meetings covered all aspects of the work of the corps. Meetings with divisional or Army commanders might deal with routine aspects of the efficiency of the corps or be part of the planning process for operations. The same was true for meetings a corps commander would have with his BGGS, GOCRA, CHA, CRE or other staff officers, according to their specialisation. In addition, liaison with Allied formations and their commanders provided necessary lubrication to the mechanism of coalition warfare.

However, in only a minority of cases did corps commanders record what was discussed; most of their meetings with divisional and brigade commanders and their staffs, and a substantial proportion of those with Army commanders and theirs, were not minuted. This implies that these were routine gatherings, and not sufficiently out of the ordinary for corps commanders to record what went on. All the corps commanders studied here usually held more meetings than usual with individual divisions and brigades before offensives (sometimes going round as many as six brigade or divisional HQs in a day), in addition to having more conferences, with several divisional or brigade commanders at a time. It is not unreasonable to speculate that these could have been discussions of problems faced by divisions and what corps could do to help them get over them. Hunter-Weston rather vaguely observed just before the start of the Battle of the Somme that, "Many problems have to be dealt with, and I have been round all my Divisional Commanders talking over the situation with them,"[51] and he earlier recorded that he "went into the question of artillery lifts with Gen. de Lisle [GOC 29th Division]"[52] In addition, Haldane's practice of calling on divisions and telling them if he had found problems in inspections has been mentioned earlier.

On first taking the corps over, its new commander would go round his divisions to meet their commanders and staff. In general, this was a sensible enough activity since working relations would obviously be better if the corps commander had taken the trouble to meet his subordinates. However, Haldane found himself in the slightly awkward position that one of his divisional commanders, Maj.-Gen. C.L. Woollcombe (GOC 11th Division) was senior to him, but the latter was "quite pleasant" about it.[53] Similarly, on new divisions coming into a corps, its commander would either summon or visit the GOCs. Haldane held a conference on 14th March 1917 of brigade commanders (two) and battalion COs (eight) so that they and corps could get to know one another. This was intended as the first of a series and the idea ties in well with the Staff Manual's point about units working together more effectively when staffs and commanders knew one another.[54] Hunter-Weston, something of a sentimentalist about certain units, was always keen to go to divisions to say goodbye as they left the corps, especially if they had served with him at Gallipoli.[55] He also was careful to do the same with his Army commanders, moving Army more often than any of the other corps commanders in this group.[56]No introductory meetings between army and corps were recorded, which indicates that Army commanders seemed less concerned to see their corps commanders on taking up a command. In any case, they were likely to have known each other in the pre-war army or to have met earlier in the war.

Meetings between corps commanders, other than at Army conferences, were uncommon. Nevertheless, they did take place, being justified on the grounds that it was common sense to get to know one's neighbour, for example if one corps relieved another in the line. Hunter-Weston had several meetings with Godley of XXII Corps in 1917 when VIII Corps took over from the latter, and earlier in the year with the commanders of II, XIV, XVIII and XIX Corps when they took over from him.[57] Corps commanders would also meet if one decided to make himself acquainted with his neighbours on taking command. Haldane did this when he took over VI Corps and Wilson called on Fergusson of XVII Corps when the latter took over his command.[58] Meetings would also occur if they were planning joint operations, such as when Wilson discussed with both his neighbours ideas to retake the line near Vimy he lost in May 1916, and Hunter-Weston met both of his before the start of the Somme.[59]

Plainly the efficient conduct of operations was a crucial part of the corps commander's job. As has been discussed in earlier chapters, meetings were held between GHQ and Army; Army and corps; and corps and divisions to communicate the intentions of the high command and to discuss plans. This provides the most obvious instance of the C-in-C's orders cascading down the chain of command, as prescribed by *FSR II*. If a senior commander needed to talk only to one of his subordinates, a meeting was held at either HQ, but conferences where the discussion involved several subordinate officers were usually held at Army HQ if it were an Army conference and Corps HQ if a corps conference of divisions. Haldane recorded one (possibly three; the diary's wording is unclear) divisional conference in 1916, when the main action of the year was elsewhere, nine in 1917 and 12 in 1918. This appears to reflect his predilection for visiting his divisions. Hunter-Weston had 18 in 1916, 10 in 1917 and 13 in 1918; the difference between the yearly figures reflects how much fighting VIII Corps did in each year. In contrast, Haig held one conference as the 1914 campaign began (on 20th August), then he seems to have preferred to give orders in person (on 24th August he had seen five divisions or brigades by 4am!) and did not hold another until December. Wilson had 11 conferences between December 1915 and December 1916. Rawlinson recorded only one in 1914, on 17th December, and 11 in 1915. In addition, he held several specifically artillery meetings in 1915 – at this stage of the war his BGRA did not have the authority later acquired by the GOCRA, so Rawlinson may have felt the need to co-ordinate matters more himself. He also did not trust his then BGRA.[60] Since the corps commanders who held quieter sectors (Hunter-Weston and Wilson) appear to have had more conferences than those who did not (especially Haig and Haldane) it is evident that not all corps-divisional conferences were to discuss major operations.

Though one might expect paperwork associated with operational planning to take up a significant proportion of corps commanders' time, none of the diaries consulted for this chapter gives details of how the corps commanders produced their plans of attack or defence. Unsurprisingly, their burden of paperwork rose as they had to plan operations, as did the number of meetings with their own staff, Army or divisions.[61] Rawlinson commented not long before Loos that he was working after dinner on modified proposals, since he had seen Haig that day and been told that the French insisted on the British attack taking place on 25th September, whether the wind was right for the use of gas or not.[62] Haldane recorded doing paperwork only once in the first three months of 1917, on 28th March, which was "Studying Artillery programme etc.," for the Battle of Arras. That said, of eight occasions on which he recorded doing paperwork in 1918, five were reports or despatches on recent operations, which may indicate that these were more difficult to produce than orders; perhaps the latter could more easily be delegated to the staff.[63] Rawlinson in 1915 gave the Neuve Chapelle despatch to his BGGS to write, but had to take the job over from him.[64] The only other paperwork recorded, apart from letter-writing, which was by far the most common variety, was producing recommendations for decorations and awards, which did exercise these officers somewhat, not least if they felt passed over for promotion themselves.[65]

Though the number of Army conferences with corps commanders increased before major offensives, operational planning was not their only function. Obviously there was a requirement for all generals to disseminate information from their superiors down to their subordinates, who could hardly be expected to act in accordance with the C-in-C's intentions if they were kept in the dark as to the overall situation. During the March Retreat in 1918 (in which Second Army was not involved) Plumer had almost daily conferences at 9am to brief his corps commanders, after which Hunter-Weston often held a conference of divisions to pass the news on. The Army conferences abruptly stopped after 10th April, as the local situation made them redundant.[66] There was no direct correlation between the number of Army conferences a corps commander recorded attending and the amount of fighting his corps did. Wilson (whose diary is at a similar level of detail to Hunter-Weston's) recorded more Army conferences in 1916 than Hunter-Weston, who was involved in the Somme offensive and might have been thought likely to have attended more. Congreve, Haldane and Hunter-Weston all saw the proportion of Army conferences to other meetings with Army fall in 1918 compared to 1917. More revealing is that Haldane saw a steep rise in visits by Army to his HQ – from 19 in 1917 to 44 in 1918. Since VI Corps was busy with offensive action from mid-August 1918 onwards, Byng came to see him rather than take him away from his HQ too often during a battle or the planning of the next one. Twenty-four of the year's 44 meetings at Haldane's HQ were in the Hundred Days; had they been evenly distributed over the year, one might have expected 14 or 15. Sometimes during battles Army even held their conferences at corps HQs rather than their own.[67]

It was plainly in the interests of the efficiency of the corps for all interested officers to attend meetings. Therefore corps conferences to discuss plans of attack or schemes for raids might be attended not only by divisional commanders and their GSO1s, but their CRAs as well.[68] In addition, if defences were the topic of the meeting, CREs could be present.[69] Haldane walked his defences with either Byng or the Army CRE nine times between 14th January and 30th April 1918, and Hunter-Weston was out with either the Fourth Army CRE, the MGGS or the Army commander six times between 6th January and 19th March 1918, as well as at one point having all his divisional CREs to dinner.[70] Other specialists might also come to meetings on an ad hoc basis. Hence, Hunter-Weston held a conference in August 1916 attended by his divisional GOCs, and their GSO1s, CRAs, Divisional Signals Officers, CHAs, plus the Corps Heavy Artillery Signal Officer, Heavy Artillery Group commanders and Field Artillery brigade commanders, "to discuss the question of the use and abuse of telephones in the front line."[71] On another occasion, a German attack was expected, so Corps and Divisional Gas Officers were included.[72] The captain acting as Instructor of Army Catering even attended one of Hunter-Weston's divisional conferences.[73] On taking over his corps, Wilson wrote that "My mind is travelling this way; – that the thing of first importance is to make safe our Line, and the thing of next importance is the education and training of officers. I mean to fasten on to these two things."[74] It is therefore unsurprising to see him holding a conference within a fortnight which dealt with defence and schools.[75]

A variety of other meetings could take place, all broadly justified in terms of *FSR II* in the interests of improving efficiency by better communications. Army sometimes held conferences on the lessons of recent fighting, such as one attended by Haldane in May 1918, after which he confided to his diary that he thought Byng's views on the use of machine-guns were "heresies". He held a conference of divisions the next day to transmit the outcome of these discussions with Army.[76] An interesting variation of this sort of meeting was one Byng had with Haldane in early

1918, in which he dilated upon the possible spread of revolutionary ideas amongst the troops, especially those from seaports like the Tyne or the Clyde. He alleged that there were many such in the 34th Division (who at least originally were largely from Tyneside). Therefore it was incumbent upon Haldane to keep these men, when in rest, "amused and distracted from such harmful ideas."[77] The next day, Haldane saw the division's GOC (Maj.-Gen. C.L. Nicholson) and repeated the message.

Presumably in order to reward virtue and thus motivate their subordinates, senior commanders sometimes visited corps to bestow praise. In early April 1918 Byng came to thank Haldane for what VI Corps had done during the recent German offensive, and "He said that he had told the C-in-C that the late battle had been a Corps C[ommande]rs['] battle."[78] Later in the year, Haig visited him three times during the Hundred Days and observed that he was pleased with the work of the corps.[79] Hunter-Weston made his maiden speech in the Commons on 24th January 1918, on the Manpower Bill. Some days later, "the Army Commander came here and had a talk. He was very enthusiastic about my speech and said he hoped I would often go over and give such another."[80] Hard though it is for the early 21st Century sensibility to take Hunter-Weston seriously, there is no reason to think that Rawlinson was being flippant; the Daily Sketch had a headline describing it as the "Greatest War Speech of the War."[81]

Obviously, corps commanders needed to hold internal meetings with their own staff, though of this group, only Haldane and Hunter-Weston recorded any such conferences.[82] In Rawlinson's typical day he had an office hour between 8am and 9 which would seem a likely slot for routine meetings. Although both FSR II and the Staff Manual stressed the need for the staff to function smoothly, commanders sometimes experienced difficulty in achieving this. On taking his corps over, Haldane announced that he would institute a nightly staff conference, as he had done when commanding his division, so that the various branches of the staff might co-operate the better.[83] However, the system did not work quite as planned:

> I find... great difficulty in getting the staff to keep me fully informed of what is going on. Except the BGGS, I get little information out of the remainder unless I ask direct questions. The nightly conference has become a farce. Intended to keep all informed of what other branches are doing, all sit on their knowledge and have nothing to say at the conference. They do their work well but live in pigeon holes.[84]

In his submission to the Braithwaite committee, Lord Cavan observed that such conferences also enabled him to get to know his staff officers intimately, so that "it was easy to pick the sheep from the goats."[85]

As the chief of the operations branch of the staff, and (in theory) *primus inter pares* of the heads of the three branches of the staff, the BGGS was the officer with whom the GOC of a corps worked most closely.[86] Relations were not, however, invariably harmonious. Lord Loch, BGGS of VI Corps from May 1915 to July 1917, took a patronising attitude to his superiors, who, however, failed sometimes to grasp problems well enough to take his advice.[87] Indeed, he claimed that Haldane and the Army commander were too liable to get excited and needed to be calmed down, Haldane's particular problem being that "he has no brain but a good memory."[88] It is unsurprising that Haldane commented to his diary on taking command of the corps that "I gather that Loch has been de facto [underlined in original] commander of the VIth [sic] Corps, which must go on no longer."[89] Under the circumstances it appears strange that Loch retained his job for another 11 months before leaving to take command of a brigade, though Haldane did later describe him as "an excellent staff officer."[90] Rawlinson's first BGGS, Br.-Gen. R.A.K. Montgomery did not suit him, since he did not run his staff well and muddled things.[91] At the end of December 1914, Montgomery, who was apparently "broken hearted", went to be BGRA at I Corps.[92] His replacement, Br.-Gen. A.G. Dallas, also failed to satisfy Sir Henry and after the latter had arranged things with First Army and then had a "painful interview" with Dallas, the BGGS departed in August 1915.[93] Finally, Rawlinson got Archie Montgomery, who remained as his COS virtually for the rest of the war.[94] Haig fared considerably better, and removed none of his staff between the start of war and the formation of Armies at the end of 1914. However, in 1915-7 inexperience of staff officers put a heavier burden on corps commanders than they might have expected before the war.[95]

Corps commanders dealt with their other senior staff officers less frequently, but the smooth functioning of the staff and of the corps dictated that some contact was both necessary and desirable. Discussions of defence lines with CREs have already been mentioned. Haig used his CRE as a sort of general factotum in 1914, despatching him on liaison missions to the French, for example.[96] As mentioned earlier, Rawlinson ignored his BGRA, Br.-Gen. Hussey, when planning the Loos offensive. Instead he relied on Br.-Gen. C.E.D. Budworth, the CRA of 1st Division, who became IV Corps BGRA on 10th October 1915 and later became Rawlinson's MGRA at Fourth Army. Haldane complained that his GOCRA (Br.-Gen. J.G. Rotton) never gave him any information, thinking himself too clever to communicate with lay people.[97] Nevertheless, Rotton retained his job to the end of the war, unlike his predecessor, whom Haldane, on taking over VI Corps, had to advise to resign his post on grounds of ill-health since Allenby intended to sack him.[98] Haldane also made the general point that "The RA, and RE, on staff of armies and corps are given to working direct with each other and also RA, and RE, staff of divisions. I am endeavouring to stop this as it takes the command of the artillery, at any rate, very much out of one's hands."[99] Cavan suggested to the Braithwaite committee that the GOCRA revert to the status of an advisor since he was otherwise prone to act independently of the corps commander, which bears out Haldane's concerns.[100] Haldane seems to have been rather unlucky with his staff, since Allenby also warned him that his DA&QMG (Br.-Gen. E.R.O. Ludlow) drank and had an "attraction" in Paris and later another Army staff officer told Haldane that the Commandant of his Corps School drank too much too.[101] He also lamented that "I find that I am kept by my staff in the dark of some things which I hear when going to Div. HQ's e.g. orders from Army for something to be done, this having been communicated to a division and not mentioned to me. I have never yet had an SO, who kept me fully informed of all essential matters, and if one worries them in consequence they put it about that one fusses…"[102]

Another way of losing staff was to have them poached by higher formations. The reasoning behind this presumably was that the higher the level of the formation, the more important it was, and the more necessary for the successful prosecution of the C-in-C's plans (in accordance with *FSR II*) that the GOC should have his choice of staff officers. On one occasion, Hunter-Weston went to see his dentist in Boulogne, and on his return found that his GOCRA, Br.-Gen. T.A. Tancred, had gone to the Reserve Army, being swapped with their artillery commander, Br.-Gen. W. Strong.[103] Wilson complained in early 1916 that "I have now lost my Br. Gen. G.S., my 2nd Grade G.S., my CRA and my C[R]E and my Camp Comm[andant] – not bad!"[104] In this case, Fourth Army were the culprits, Rawlinson asset-stripping his old corps to benefit his Army staff. Indeed, the unfortunate Wilson later found that his divisions were also losing staff to corps in Fourth Army, 2nd Division's GSO1, Louis Vaughan, being taken to be BGGS of XV Corps in April 1916.[105] However, IV Corps was at the time in a quiet sector, whereas Rawlinson's Army was gearing up for the biggest British offensive of the war so far. In any case, corps were not above rearranging divisional staffs themselves. In March 1916 31st Division, fresh from Egypt, arrived in VIII Corps. It was apparent to Hunter-Weston that it needed a GSO1 who was experienced on the Western Front, so he made what he called a "suggestion" to the GOC 48th Division that his GSO1 swap with 31st Division's and had the 48th Division GSO1 (Lt.-Col. J.S.J. Baumgartner) to dinner, presumably to sweeten the pill.[106]

Meetings with representatives of the Associated and Allied powers were not specified anywhere in *FSR II* but common sense would have suggested that it was wise to maintain good relations. This applied especially to the French and Belgians, on both of whose territory the BEF was stationed. Hunter-Weston was in the line next to the latter in late 1916 and early 1917 and frequently visited Belgian divisional and corps HQs, occasionally even venturing to Belgian GQG. He also went round the Belgian lines and took the King of the Belgians round the British positions, doubtless feeling well rewarded with both French and Belgian honours, the insignia of which he described in detail to his wife.[107] Rawlinson's corps was in the line next to the French in 1915, meeting the corps commanders in question (Generals Maistre and Curé, of XXI and IX Corps respectively) not infrequently and borrowing artillery from them twice.[108] Haig in 1914 undertook a good deal of liaison with the French, especially during First Ypres, when they were at times on both his flanks. Haldane's contact with French troops was more limited, and he viewed them as rather unreliable.[109] Wilson, however, was the only corps commander who saw the French for pleasure alone, being a friend of General Foch and a noted Francophile.

Good relations with allied civil authorities and politicians were also important; the greater the degree of inter-allied goodwill, the more smoothly the alliance would operate. Haldane organised Christmas cards for the children of the village in which his HQ was, throwing large parties for them (79 boys and 77 girls on New Year's Day 1917), and Hunter-Weston was a good host to the gentry upon whom he chose to billet himself. It seems likely that his superiors viewed him as a good pair of hands for entertaining the great and the good, being something of a *grand seigneur* himself. He was careful to include the King of the Belgians on his Christmas card list, and obviously enjoyed having the Apostolic Delegate and Doyen of Ypres to dinner, upon whose purple attire, gold chain, cross and ring he commented approvingly.[110] He also had President Poincaré to lunch and twice in late 1918 accompanied him on visits to newly liberated towns and villages.[111] Perhaps his finest hour was the visit to the Front of the Portuguese President Machado in October 1917. Hunter-Weston laid on a Guard of Honour, two bands, and a four-course lunch for 20, with a different wine for each course. Afterwards, he and his staff took the president and his entourage to part of the line captured at the Battle of Messines, to show them the front and provide an opportunity for them to find some souvenirs, taking care to have the ground seeded with interesting items beforehand! Other guests at various times at VIII Corps were the Siamese, Italian and Romanian Military Attachés.[112] Alarmingly, on 4th January 1918, at 8.15 am the full Pipe Band of the 2nd Argylls paraded and played for an hour since General Green of the US Army (then staying at VIII Corps) had expressed a desire to hear them. Luckily, Congreve had no dealings with the Americans: "Oh damn them, how I hate and despise them – they are far lower than the Bosch who has [sic] some virtues, beastly though they are."[113] Nevertheless, dealing with Allies was a political necessity and though not always obviously to do with *FSR II*, was a useful activity.

It can be seen that corps commanders held or attended a wide variety of meetings with numerous different people. What was common to all was that they were deemed essential to ensure good communications within the corps, without which its efficiency would be impaired. The shortcomings of Hunter-Weston's meetings with subordinate commanders before the Somme (see Chapter 2), in particular the lack of discussion of the corps plan, show what could go wrong if operational meetings were mishandled.

Fighting Battles

If a corps commander was chosen to play an active part in operations (and if the Germans attacked, they might be the ones doing the choosing) it was essential that he handled his corps to the best of his ability. In terms of *FSR II* this could be seen very much as playing his part in the execution of the C-in-C's plan, whether it be the successful prosecution of an attack or series of attacks, or withstanding a German offensive. The corps commander had to await news of how the fighting was going and co-ordinate the activities of his divisions accordingly, providing resources where necessary. This required holding conferences, visits to chivvy divisional commanders into greater efforts and personal reconnaissance.

Of the diaries examined, Haldane's and Hunter-Weston's provide the most extensive records of what corps commanders did when their corps were fighting. In the former's case, this covers the Battles of Arras and Cambrai in 1917 and the March Retreat and Hundred Days in 1918. Hunter-Weston's corps saw action at the very start of the Battle of the Somme and in the Final Advance. Congreve's diary is too slight to reveal much about what he did during battles, and Rawlinson was not very forthcoming about what he did then, while Wilson fought no battles. Haig's diary shows I Corps acting as a clearing house for information and a juggler of reserves; he did not usually differentiate between his role and his staff's, though on the critical days of First Ypres he did. On 31st October 1914 he was very busy and rode forward to organise stragglers in person, an act which has attracted some controversy.[114] On 11th November he was frantically sending officers out to keep in touch with what was happening and trying to organise a reserve.

The GOCs of VI and VIII Corps demonstrated very different styles of command. Haldane took every chance he could to get forward and badger his subordinates to greater efforts. Hunter-Weston, in contrast, intended to be so hands-off as to be almost absent from the battle. Any reputation he has acquired since as a 'thruster' should be replaced with the image of a general drifting forwards with the steady plod of a sleepwalker.[115] On the night before the attack on the Somme, he noted that he was entirely content that he and his staff had done everything possible to ensure success, and all was down to the men. He would have nothing to do but rest until well after the attack, and indeed, expected to be getting up at the actual time of assault. Then he would take a quiet breakfast and await reports of success or failure (he appeared indifferent to their relative proportions) from his staff – "Very different from the idea of an old-fashioned General with battles on a small scale where the Commander was looking at the little battlefield himself."[116] Obviously he viewed this somnolent approach as the modern way. Nevertheless, he was "very busy" on 1st and 2nd July, as he attempted to salvage something from the disaster which had befallen his corps.[117]

However, the one resemblance between Hunter-Weston's and Haldane's approaches was that they needed at the start of an attack to wait at their HQ for reports to come in. In 1917 Haldane found it more frustrating than in 1918, noting on 10th April 1917 his regret that it was impossible to get to the front line on the first day of a battle, whereas in August 1918 he passed the time in reading.[118] Once the reports came in he became altogether more active, moving up reserves and artillery support where necessary and sending his CRE forward to ensure that roads were cleared. By the evening of 9th April 1917 he was beginning to move field artillery up too.[119] However, he felt the next day that the vital position of Monchy had not been taken through want of initiative on the part of the troops there, and had he been able to get forward he could have pressed the attack harder. On 10th April, he was desperate to instil a sense of urgency into his subordinates, ordering one of his divisional commanders to sack a brigadier if the latter would not carry out orders rapidly, issuing orders (via his staff) at 9.45 for an attack at noon and organising getting artillery forward to support it. In the afternoon he tried to get to Monchy but was prevented by hostile fire.[120] The next day he was again "gingering up" divisional commanders and telling them that they, staff, brigadiers and battalion COs should be close up to push things on. Impatience led him to take things in hand even more when "The 14th Div., on right of my Corps, is not pushing on. Shall go forward again myself to look after matters."[121] However, as the battle bogged down, so Haldane's level of activity fell, only to rise and then fall again during the course of the Second Battle of the Scarpe (23rd-24th April 1917) and subsequent operations. A clue as to how busy VI Corps HQ was on 9th April is that the Corps Signals Office dealt with 3,522 telegrams in the course of the day.[122]

Haldane operated in much the same way during VI Corps' attacks in the Hundred Days as he had in 1917. He held conferences, toured divisional HQs to check their plans, launched attacks and waited for information, then pressing his subordinates always to press on if possible. For example, on 23rd August he found that 52nd Division was consolidating, and told them to push on. Later he discovered that 2nd Division were not taking two locations he had told them to, so he sent a GSO2 to tell them to get on with it, if necessary by moonlight.[123] Second Division became something of a thorn in his side over the coming weeks, and he criticised the GOC (Maj.-Gen. C.E. Pereira) in his diary several times. Eventually he told Pereira that if he did not improve he would be sent home, which presumably had the desired effect, since the latter stayed on to the Armistice.[124]

The fighting in the Hundred Days also illustrated other points about the corps commander's job in battle. One was reconnaissance for future operations; Haldane undertook one for an attack on Havrincourt (near Cambrai) and his diary entry regarding the direction of the attack and the number of divisions required is impressively lucid. He then, as *SS135, 1918* said he should, suggested the next operation if the Havrincourt attack succeeded; Army gave its approval to this.[125] Hunter-Weston also regularly reconnoitred his front as VIII Corps advanced.[126] The corps commander also laid down the policy under which divisions attacked – Haldane's was to keep divisions (he had four, with two attacking and two behind at any time) attacking on a brigade front so that they would each fight for three or four days and then be relieved by the division behind.[127] There was also the problem of friction with other corps. Haldane frequently fulminated to his diary about the shortcomings (whether real or perceived) of Lt.-Gen. Sir G.M. Harper, GOC IV Corps, on his right flank. He complained that Harper was like his friend Wilson and looked only for personal advancement, and also that he was overly cautious in pushing IV Corps forward, so that it slowed VI Corps down. Haldane even got Byng (his Army commander) involved in pressing Harper not to consolidate but to push on in late September. Byng assured him that IV Corps were making progress, at which Haldane confided to his diary that "I should 'progress' by sending Harper to the rear."[128]

The corps commander had different problems when fighting on the defensive. Much of the problem was to regain the initiative which the attacker initially held. On 21st March 1918 Haldane had to await reports as usual, and then decide how to cope with the onslaught. Hard decisions had to be made as to what ground – fought over so bitterly in 1917 – should be given up, and it was necessary to establish where the blow would fall hardest and get reinforcements to that point. This sort of fighting was tiring for commanders and staffs (as well as the troops, of course), since meetings with divisions were often held at night, and there might be time only to snatch a few hours' sleep.[129] Even then, on the night of 24th March, Haldane's BGGS woke him up to warn him of a dangerous situation on his right flank, so he had to get up, take steps to stabilise things and go to bed later. Congestion on the roads made a simple task like visiting the divisions in the corps, which Haldane liked to do daily, take four hours.[130] However, communications with divisions and the passing back of reports to Army were essential. This could become very difficult, as when telephone communication with 3rd Division failed just as the Germans attacked.[131] Otherwise his role was to feed in dribs and drabs of reserves as they were allocated to him by Army.

Only a very few references to the strain of command were made in these diaries, and it is not surprising that these were made during active operations. However, corps commanders' reactions to the stresses of their job varied. Congreve confessed to losing sleep the night before an attack, since he had been warned that the German wire possibly remained uncut.[132] On the night of 21st March 1918, Haldane confessed that he had hardly eaten all day because of anxiety, and also commented on the need to keep such emotions concealed, presumably lest his staff and subordinates lose confidence because of it. He too went on to sleep badly.[133] In contrast, and notwithstanding the difficulties he faced in early July 1916, Hunter-Weston said he had been so well beforehand that "I did not feel the strain in any way."[134] Similarly, Wilson's almost complete inexperience as a commander did not seem to trouble him in the slightest, though he never had to fight a battle.[135] All the corps commanders whose diaries were examined for this chapter were regular churchgoers, this not being a sign of any sort of religious fanaticism but merely a reflection of the routine religiosity of a more devout age. It would be surprising if they did not derive some spiritual sustenance from this; indeed, in Haig's case it is well-known.[136]

Irrespective of the style in which it was done, it appears that corps commanders fighting a battle did not exert direct control over their troops but over divisional generals and made a difference by chivvying their subordinates and by allocation of resources – infantry, RE and RA – and in controlling which divisions were in the line and which not. They were also an essential conduit for information between the front line and Army.

Meals with other people and entertaining visitors

Meals fulfilled a number of roles for corps commanders in addition to providing physical sustenance. While they do not obviously fall into the range of activities which *FSR II* would prescribe for a commander, under a loose interpretation they could, nevertheless, be seen as assisting in the "decentralization of responsibility among subordinates" necessary to advance the C-in-C's strategy.[137] Put more bluntly, GHQ had numerous important visitors and it was necessary not only to entertain them there, but to pass them down the chain of command to corps, so that they might be shown that portion of the forward area which it was deemed desirable they should see. Therefore corps commanders had a diplomatic as well as a military role and meals were used to supplement the meetings with allies already discussed. In addition, they needed to liaise with other British officers and their staffs. To summarise their functions, meals also provided opportunities (1) to entertain or do business with Allies; (2) to enable the corps commander to get to know new subordinates (either staff or from lower formations) or to liaise with ones already known to him; (3) to enable the corps commander to get to know a new Army commander (or his MGGS) or to liaise with one already known to him; (4) to enable him to liaise with other corps commanders; (5) to provide an opportunity to chat or gossip with old friends, especially from another area of the front; and (6) to serve as a meeting for planning operations.

Predictably, the French and Belgians were the allies whom corps commanders entertained most often, and vice versa. Hunter-Weston had a M. Henri Bérenger, a Senator and journalist sent to him by GHQ, in order for Hunter-Weston to assuage French concerns over British staff organisation and give him tea and Lady Grace's plum cake.[138] This reinforces the view that irrespective of his military merits, GHQ perceived him as a social asset. He several times had the Comte and Comtesse who owned his billet (and were now living in a sub-section of their property while Hunter-Weston made himself comfortable in the rest) to dinner. This was usually on occasions when he had a band playing, occasionally supplemented by other performers.[139] He was also careful to entertain Belgian generals and their staffs to lunch or dinner, together with officers from the British mission to Belgian GQG and British divisional commanders.[140] The Belgians returned the hospitality, and he took lunch with not only his opposite number in the Belgian Army, and (at different times) various Belgian divisional commanders, but also the Prime Minister.[141] Similarly, when VIII Corps was on the verge of moving to the French Fourth Army in May 1918, Hunter-Weston had several lunches and dinners with its commander and other officers, including General Pétain.[142] Rawlinson arranged his corps boundary with General Maistre, his neighbour, over tea. Taking tea with the King of the Belgians provided Congreve with the opportunity to meet the Portuguese C-in-C, a General Constandun, "a big fellow, very sallow, very untidy and old and they say useless."[143] And Hunter-Weston had to tea in 1917 a group of American civilians, from both Congress and the press.[144] Haig saw the French more often when he was a corps commander than any of the other five with whom this chapter is concerned, conducting liaison with them frequently and, indeed, daily from 1st to 11th November 1914. However, at no time in 1914 did he record eating with them (though he did lunch with the Empress Eugénie, Napoleon III's widow, in London in late November).[145]

Entertaining visitors from Britain and the Empire was a burden which again apparently fell more heavily on Hunter-Weston than the other corps commanders. In this context the visitors were being treated as allies rather than subjects and their entertainment was part of the process of ensuring their co-operation. In the case of the Prime Minister of Newfoundland and representatives of its government, the choice of Hunter-Weston was unsurprising, since the Newfoundland Regiment had been under his command when it suffered appalling losses on the first day of the Somme.[146] GHQ astutely sent Sir Abe Bailey, the South African entrepreneur and philanthropist, to VIII Corps for lunch, at which he and Hunter-Weston renewed an acquaintanceship dating back to the South African War.[147] Hunter-Weston wrote to Haig's Private Secretary to express his thanks that he had been given the opportunity to meet Bailey again, and that "You know how strongly I feel that you and I and all the others of us, who have interests outside the Army as well as in it, should preach the gospel of confidence in our leaders. I, therefore, availed myself of the opportunity given me by Abe Bailey's visit to continue that propaganda, for he is in the way of seeing many important people both in England and South Africa."[148] This neatly demonstrates the way in which such visits were used by GHQ and politically connected generals like Hunter-Weston.

In fact, all the corps commanders examined in this chapter entertained a wide variety of visitors in the interests of spreading propaganda, or at least disseminating their own view of the war. Rawlinson took visitors round safe trenches after providing lunch and was himself given lunch by the French and then taken round part of their line, with the editor of Le Temps.[149] He entertained King George V to lunch in late 1914, being joined later by Joffre and the French President.[150] This may reflect his good connections, since when other corps commanders met the King he was usually a guest of their Army commander or GHQ. Hunter-Weston also specialised in taking British politicians to an observation post on Hill 63 to see the battlefield, with lunch included as part of the trip.[151] Haldane tended to have fewer aristocratic visitors than Rawlinson and Hunter-Weston (though it should be noted that the latter showed a Trade Union leader round Arras).[152] He specialised in having members of religious organisations, from the Catholic Bishop of Arras to a gentleman from the Church Army, either to dinner or lunch.[153] Artists tended to come to stay with him too, the sculptor John Tweed staying in early 1918 and again in the summer; the painters Sargent and Tonks dined at around the same time.[154] In addition, his guests included Spenser Wilkinson, the military historian, and one Brantling, leader of the Swedish Socialist Party.[155] Wilson's guest list was spread more widely between politicians and others, including the Anglican Primate of Ireland, the Archbishop of Canterbury, seven South African MPs, and Lord Derby to lunch, and, unusually, a breakfast engagement, with Clemenceau.[156] It should also be noted that Wilson, Hunter-Weston and Haldane all entertained members of the press, from Lord Northcliffe downwards, from time to time.[157]

Corps commanders needed to get to know their closest subordinates best, as well as introducing officers from different divisions to one another. Therefore they sometimes invited their subordinates to meals en masse and at other times one by one. As well as the team-building function, it was not unreasonable for corps to offer these gentlemen some entertainment as a relief from the stress of their jobs. Though Hunter-Weston did not offer his battalion commanders hospitality before the Somme, later in the year, he had on one day 26 COs (presumably with some other officers to get above the establishment of 24 battalions) from 38th and 55th Divisions to lunch and tea, and both GOCs and ADCs plus four Br.-Gens. and staffs to tea, saying "a few words to them afterwards."[158] Similarly, Haldane had several battalion COs to dinner before the Battle of Arras.[159] GOCs of divisions or brigades, with staff officers, were often invited to dinner on the day they joined a corps, and certainly at some time or times during their stay, often with other divisional commanders. On their moving to another corps the corps commander would throw a farewell dinner too.[160] Dinners with commanders or staff officers from divisions and brigades accounted for the largest subset of the dinners held by corps commanders. This is hardly surprising since these were the corps commanders' closest subordinates. One of the few corps staff officers to have written his memoirs (Lt.-Col. W.N. Nicholson) commented that when he was on a divisional staff no corps commander ever ate with them, and that corps were too distant from their divisions. It is apparent that this is not a fair criticism of the corps commanders discussed in this chapter, under two of whose corps Nicholson served.[161] Nevertheless, Haldane did not record any dinners with divisions and brigades between 16th August and 10th November 1918, apparently only having five of any kind in that period. Since he was reasonably conscientious about recording events in his diary, it seems likely that at the very least, he cut back on entertaining during the Hundred Days. New members of the corps staff could also expect to be invited to dine, such as Hunter-Weston's new APM in late 1917 and Haldane's Counter-Battery Staff Colonel earlier in the year. This officer, named Fawcett, was a famed Amazon explorer, and it seems, teller of tales. His corps commander found these "wonderful experiences, which no one in my Mess seems to believe but myself" very interesting, including one when Fawcett claimed to have killed a 65-foot-long anaconda.[162] Lord Loch, his BGGS, was more dubious.[163] Longer-established senior members of the staff were, according to Hunter-Weston, members of his 'A' Mess and so ate with him every day. Less senior staff officers were in 'B' Mess and junior officers were in 'C' Mess.[164]

Details of meals corps commanders had with Army commanders are scant, but it appears that they served as opportunities for confidential private discussions which were not possible at the usual conferences. Wilson told Horne that Count Gleichen (GOC 37th Division) was useless and should be sacked over lunch, and it was over breakfast that Monro told Wilson that Br.-Gen. John Charteris (Haig's Chief of Intelligence) had found his staff to be despondent.[165] Hunter-Weston discussed forthcoming operations over lunch with Rawlinson (then an Army commander) in April 1916, and Rawlinson found himself introduced to Willcocks of the Indian Corps over dinner at First Army when Haig was its GOC.[166] Haldane at one point in 1917 thought he was going to be sent to the Ypres Salient and had the Third Army DA&QMG to lunch so that they could discuss arrangements about the things the Corps would leave behind, such as the cinema, the school and the laundry."[167]

As with Army commanders, details of meals with other corps commanders are not very numerous. Haig's introduction of Willcocks to Rawlinson has been noted. Some discussions of operations took place over meals (see below) but apart from that, handing over part of the line to each other or social calls were the burden of most corps-corps liaison. Hence, Wilson and Byng had lunch when the latter handed over the troublesome Vimy sector to the IV Corps commander.[168] Hunter-Weston's meetings with various other corps when he went out of the line on May 1917 have been discussed; in addition he had to dinner on successive nights the GOCs XVIII and XIV Corps and their senior staff officers. Obviously feeling the need to be thorough, he had Cavan and his BGGS to lunch the day after as well.[169] Social calls included Hunter-Weston's lunch at VI Corps when he went on a day trip to see what was happening in the Battle of Arras, and Congreve calling at XIX Corps, where he "lunched with Watts very well and had a gin and vermouth cocktail" when things were quiet for both of them.[170]

Meals where the corps commanders met old friends are recorded more often and in more detail than, for example, corps-corps meetings, presumably because they were not routine. They provided an opportunity to exchange gossip about the conduct of the war and other officers, and acted as a safety valve, either party being able to let off steam about other generals with whom they might be having problems. Wilson, a notorious intriguer, had a nose for gossip and he and his favourites, such as 'Uncle' Harper, would meet, eat and criticise others.[171] He would also dine with officers who had been fighting on the Somme, to find out first-hand what was going on there.[172] Both Haldane and Congreve had dinner with Br.-Gen. Frank Maxwell VC, whom presumably they knew from South Africa, where he had been on Lord Kitchener's staff, just after the Somme (where he had acquitted himself well) and also in 1917.[173] Hunter-Weston liked formal occasions, such as a Wellingtonian dinner (he was an old boy of Wellington) and another he held for all senior RE officers in his corps (he was also an old boy of Woolwich).[174] So these meals provided a useful opportunity to find out what lay behind the official communiqués coming from other sectors.

From time to time, informal discussions of planned operations took place over, or around, meals, though operational planning was usually done via meetings and conferences. In early 1915, Rawlinson noted "Yesterday I teaed [sic] with Haking to discuss his plan of attack – I like mine better. Today I had tea with Putty [Lt.-Gen. Sir William Pulteney, GOC III Corps] and he told me what he was going to do..."[175] And Wilson: "Holland, Budworth, Archie [Montgomery] and Longridge [J.A. Longridge, GSO1 1st Division] talked over, after tea, all the details of the coming enterprise ag[ainst] 14 bis [a location in the German lines]."[176]

Though it is not, as stated earlier, possible very often to determine the function of a given meal, it is evident that meals were occasions of some significance for corps commanders, helping them maintain relations with allies, keep visitors informed about the progress of the war according to the view GHQ wanted presented and ensuring that they got to know and kept in touch with fellow officers, especially those below them. All of this conduced to the efficiency of their commands.

Exercise

Physical fitness was considered essential for any soldier – moral and physical strength were viewed as going hand-in-hand by officers of this generation.[177] In addition, all the officers with whom this chapter deals would have known of the fate of the famously overweight and unfit Sir James Grierson, who died of a heart attack on the train when on his way to take command of II Corps in 1914. Unlike Grierson, they took regular exercise, even bearing in mind that their diaries may well omit routine daily rides such as Rawlinson referred to in the typical day quoted earlier. Walking and riding seem to have been preferred; no sport was played except for two games of tennis mentioned by Wilson.[178] Sometimes walks or rides were taken for their own sake, but they were also taken on the way to or from the majority of the visits and inspections that these officers undertook. Even if they drove to the event they would often send a horse on ahead and then ride it during the inspection or parade and back home. When walking in the trenches Hunter-Weston took pride in his brisk pace and was always pleased if he had reduced one of his divisional or brigade commanders, or even his ADCs, to a state of sweating collapse, or at the very least made them puff with exertion.[179] On occasion he outpaced his companions to the extent that he lost them completely. Wilson was the most active, riding 50 miles in one day and later riding 15 one day and walking fast 11 miles the next.[180]

Exercise brought with it health benefits, and none of these officers appears overweight in photographs. Hunter-Weston wrote to his wife that, once he had settled into his quiet sector in August 1916, his work was very healthy, since he had a large area to cover and so he was out much of the time. "I have, therefore, to do a great deal of motoring, a considerable amount of walking, and some riding. I have... plenty of good wholesome exercise and am consequently in very good health and spirits. I do not think I have ever been better or fitter."[181] Indeed, on one occasion when he found his entire retinue struggling to keep up with him, the worst affected was a battalion commander aged about 35, who was pouring with sweat and could hardly speak in reply to the 52-year old general's queries; "I impressed upon this poor dear the necessity of keeping himself physically fit."[182] However, as an asthmatic, Walter Congreve was in a different position to the others, and his health prevented him from exercising sometimes.[183]

Exercise and meetings were sometimes combined, usually in the form of taking the Army commander or a member of his staff round the line, or doing the same with a divisional commander.[184] Towards the end of 1915, Rawlinson twice went for a ride with Haig and they discussed his promotion prospects on both.[185] In the Final Advance in late 1918 commanders needed to keep in touch with the positions their divisions held, which at one point necessitated Hunter-Weston climbing into a fort using a rope ladder.[186]

It is evident that exercise was one of the corps commanders' most common activities. The several functions it served – generating physical fitness, providing an example to others, a means of getting to and around inspections and trench visits, and even occasionally as a meeting itself, were beneficial to the exercise of corps command. In terms of *FSR II* it can be viewed, therefore, as contributing to the efficiency of the corps.

Leave, sick leave and under-employment

At first glance, it might seem that not working was hardly the best thing for a corps commander to do in order to advance the war effort. However, this was not always the case; from 1916 onwards there were more corps HQs than were needed to cover the front line. The majority could be left there, with whichever Army commander who was conducting an offensive getting the corps he thought best suited to the job, and others rested or put into reserve. If this happened, the corps might be a corps HQ looking after divisions which were also in reserve or just a corps HQ with no divisions and, effectively, nothing to do. Especially under the latter circumstances, the corps commander might find he too was at a loose end. In addition, like all officers, corps commanders were entitled to take leave, and sick leave if they were unwell.

All six corps commanders considered in this chapter took leave when it was due to them, which was not unreasonable. Hunter-Weston was in a better position to take leave than the others, owing to his Parliamentary duties and he had over three weeks at home when preparing for and delivering his maiden speech in the House of Commons.

Name	1914	1915	1916	1917	1918
Congreve				20 (229)	8
Haldane			10	39 (18)	14
Hunter-Weston			18	48	22
Rawlinson	0	24			
Wilson			37		

The table above shows the time taken as leave for each general during his tenure as a corps commander. Haig is omitted since he took none. Sick leave is shown in parentheses and was in addition to the main leave figure. Congreve took a great deal of time off because of losing his hand in June 1917, though he had already had 22 days on sick leave in Paris and the south of France owing to asthma leading to an attack of influenza early in the year. While Wilson and Rawlinson spent their leaves in England meeting politicians and royalty, Congreve dined in Paris with the novelist Elinor Glyn (who demonstrated 'psychic' powers with which he was unimpressed) and had tea with the American playboy Gordon Bennett.[187] Haldane went to a play and afterwards to Gladys Cooper's dressing room when in London on leave, though this was not a habit.[188] Hunter-Weston's maiden speech has been referred to; in addition, he had to ask Plumer's permission to go home in March 1917 for the Home Rule debate.[189] He was untroubled by ill-health, apart from the occasional cold, which circumstance afforded him at least one moment of self-congratulation; that said, self-congratulation was one of his favourite activities.

Hunter-Weston, Congreve and Wilson all found themselves with time on their hands when their corps were in reserve. All took advantage of the opportunity to meet their wives or friends in Paris, go shopping, visit other friends, lunch at the Ritz and go for scenic drives.[190] That these officers were effectively unemployed might appear wasteful, but it would seem that by 1916 there was a policy of letting the Army commander in charge of an offensive have his choice of corps commanders. Therefore Hunter-Weston handed over his sector to Maxse, Cavan, Watts and Jacob in May 1917 because Hubert Gough wanted them for the forthcoming offensive rather than the VIII Corps commander, whose efforts on the Somme had been signally unsuccessful. That just over three corps (Jacob only took over a small portion of the VIII Corps sector) occupied the line previously held by one demonstrates the higher density of troops on an active, compared to a quiet, sector. Wilson was unlikely to be chosen for an active sector, given his inexperience in command, and in late 1916 IV Corps held no line at all, having taken over a holding area behind the Somme sector for divisions resting, training or simply passing through, to or from the battle. By April-May 1918, when Congreve found himself with less and less to do, there were too many corps HQs for the reduced establishment of the BEF. Although he was far more able than Hunter-Weston, the competition for active sectors was too great, especially given his health record, and he was sent home sick, despite protesting his good health.

Another interest of these corps commanders was battlefield tourism. The focus was mainly on their activities earlier in the war, especially in 1914. Haldane and Sir Thomas Snow went together in 1917 to some of the places they had passed through in the Retreat from Mons, which provided Haldane with an opportunity to make the brutal remark that "Though he [Snow] is an old friend of mine I have never felt the same towards him since that time[,] when he showed what a poor spirited man he was when troublous times were upon us."[191] Haldane also visited the Somme battlefield, where his division had been heavily engaged, and despite his workload in the Final Advance, found time to take his servant, who had been with him in 1914, for more 1914 tourism.[192] Hunter-Weston dropped in on a farmer and his wife, in whose house he had his HQ at one point in 1914; "They were overwhelmed with joy at seeing me and almost fell upon my neck. For a very modest [sic] man like myself, it was quite embarrassing."[193] He also found time during the Final Advance to revisit the battlefield of Le Cateau and pat his younger self on the back for his handling of 11th Brigade there in 1914.[194] Congreve went further back, visiting the battlefield of Crécy, and seeing a cross erected in memory of the "kind king of Bohemia." Since the gentleman in question was famously blind, this is evidently a typographical error in the diary.[195]

Though corps commanders had much more leave than private soldiers, it can be argued that their greater responsibilities entitled these officers to longer periods of rest. Certainly sickness or injury entitled them to treatment as much as anyone else. When their corps were in reserve, it was because (in the eyes of GHQ, at least) the best corps commanders held the active sectors. Consequently, periods when corps commanders were not very busy or on leave can be seen not to have detracted from the efficiency of the BEF as a whole.

The corps commanders considered in this chapter are not intended to be a fully representative sample but do exhibit a broad spectrum of experience of corps command on the western front. It can be seen that they followed the principles laid down in *FSR II* and the Staff Manual. This encompassed a wide range of activities, the most common of which were to get out and see troops, in order to assess how corps and divisional staffs were doing their jobs, and to attend or hold meetings with a wide variety of people in order to communicate (or be told by higher authority) matters of importance or interest. As the role of corps expanded during the war, so did the scope of their commanders' activities, and all of these officers were busy men. This was exacerbated in 1915-17 especially as the BEF increased in size while lacking experience, and so corps commanders had to supervise more closely than in 1914. On taking over VI Corps in August 1916,

Haldane told his BGGS that when he had been a divisional commander he had been in a corps whose commander took responsibility neither for the front line nor the rear areas, leaving divisions entirely to their own devices and doing nothing to ensure continuity of work.[196] However, he took the view that "The Corps was the proper unit to supervise, and was no longer to be merely a Post Office."[197] He would take responsibility for the front line work and his administrative staff would deal with the rear areas and billets, which he would from time to time inspect. This broadly reflects the changes in the role of corps in general and the terminology he employed echoes the argument made earlier in this book regarding the increase in importance of the role of corps from its beginnings as a post office. It would be most informative for further research to be undertaken into the division-brigade relationship and into how generals at these levels did their daily work. It is tempting to speculate that they did much the same as corps commanders, but with fewer visits from dignitaries and more emphasis on local detail. In addition, their artillery responsibilities would have been different and would have changed over the course of the war.

It cannot, however, be over-emphasised that having a well-run corps along the lines of *FSR II* did not by any means guarantee operational success. None of Rawlinson's attacks as a corps commander gained more than an initial break-in (and some not even that); Hunter-Weston's attack on 1st July 1916 was a disaster; and Wilson lost part of his line in an important sector. A well-run corps with a bad attack plan or without the hardware and experience to get into the German position would advance no further than a poorly run one. Following *FSR II* in the absence of the conditions to attain superiority of firepower and those other prerequisites for a successful attack laid down in *FSR I* was not going to win the war. But that said, if the conditions in terms of *FSR I* were right, a well-organised corps like VI Corps on 9th April 1917 or in the Hundred Days could achieve a great deal.

NOTES

1 Terraine, *Douglas Haig, The Educated Soldier*, 73-124, De Groot, *Douglas Haig*, 155-168.

2 Farrar-Hockley, *Goughie*, 165-6.

3 Powell, *Plumer – The Soldier's General*, 106.

4 GOC XIII Corps 15th November 1915-17th June 1917, VII Corps 3rd January-13th April 1918 and X Corps 15th April-24th May 1918.

5 GOC I Corps 5th August-26th December 1914.

6 GOC VI Corps 8th August 1916-11th November 1918 (for the purposes of this chapter; Haldane actually took the corps into the army of occupation in Germany after the Armistice).

7 GOC VIII Corps 18th March 1916-11th November 1918. He had the job at Gallipoli but that is not germane to this study, and took over XVIII Corps on 22nd June 1918, but it was renamed as VIII Corps on 2nd July.

8 GOC IV Corps 5th October 1914-22nd December 1915.

9 GOC IV Corps 22nd December 1915-1st December 1916.

10 These figures were arrived at by referring to the durations of battles in James, *A Record of the Battles and Engagements of the British Armies in France and Flanders, 1914-1918* and comparing them with Becke's *Order of Battle* Part 4 to see how long a given corps was involved in a battle. The figures do not reflect time spent on preliminary planning.

11 Hynes, Samuel L, *A War Imagined. The First World War and English Culture* (London: The Bodley Head, 1990), 47. Hunter-Weston commented on 30th June 1916 that "Tomorrow is the great day, & by this time tomorrow another great page in History will be turned."

12 Sheffield, Gary and Bourne, John (eds.) *Douglas Haig: War Diaries and Letters 1914-1918* (London: Weidenfeld and Nicholson, 2005), 3-4.

13 Bourne and Sheffield, *Haig*, 7. The typescript was the version consulted for this chapter.

14 See Haldane Diary MS 20249, National Library of Scotland (NLS), for early July 1917 – the 4th and 5th are in the wrong sequence, with the comment for the 4th "I have typed 5th in wrong place." A clue as to when they were typed is given by the annotation to the entry for 10th April 1918 (Haldane Diary MS 20250) that Cameron Shute died in 1936.

15 The former is the diary at Churchill College Cambridge (henceforth CCC) and the latter at the National Army Museum (henceforth NAM).

16 Bourne and Sheffield, *Haig*, 2-10.

17 Ash, Bernard, *The Lost Dictator. A Biography of Field-Marshal Sir Henry Wilson* (London: Cassell, 1968), 51-2. Cited in Gardner, Nikolas, *Trial by Fire. Command and the British Expeditionary Force in 1914* (Westport, Connecticut and London: Praeger, 2003), 12.

18 Compare, for example, Hunter-Weston's diary entry for 14th June 1917 with letter of the same date, and also 5th February 1918.

19 Rawlinson NAM Diary, 20th January 1915.

20 Rawlinson NAM Diary, 18th March 1915.

21 Rawlinson CCC Diary, 29th April 1915.

22 Strachan, Hew, 'The British Army, its General Staff and the Continental Commitment, 1904-14' in French, David and Holden Reid, Brian (eds.) *The British General Staff: Reform and Innovation c.1890-1939* (London and Portland, Oregon: Frank Cass, 2002), 90.

23 *FSR II*, 23.

24 *FSR II*, 24.

25 *FSR II*, 25.

26 *FSR II*, 29.

27 Bourne and Sheffield, *Haig*, 178.

28 *War Office 121/Staff/5883 (S.D.2)*, 30th December 1918. TNA:PRO, WO 32/5153. Henceforth *Braithwaite Report*.

29 *Braithwaite Report*, point 3.

30 *Braithwaite Report*, point 17.

31 The OED offers the definition: "Good sound practical sense; combined tact and readiness in dealing with the every-day affairs of life; general sagacity."
32 These were Br.-Gen. A.A. Montgomery, BGGS IV Corps 19th August 1915-4th February 1916 (previously GSO1 4th Division from 4th September 1914) and Br.-Gen. H.D. De Pree, BGGS IV Corps 5th February 1916-18th March 1918 (previously GSO1 various divisions from 5th January 1915).
33 French, David, *Military Identities. The Regimental System, the British Army, and the British People, c. 1870-2000* (Oxford: Oxford University Press, 2005), 100-101.
34 Haig diary 2nd December 1914.
35 Haldane diary 4th September 1916.
36 Haldane diary 29th August 1916.
37 Rawlinson NAM diary 9th March and 8th May 1915.
38 Hunter-Weston diary 26th June 1916; letter to his wife 30th June. Haldane diary 14th and 30th March 1917.
39 Sheffield, Gary, *Leadership in the Trenches. Officer-Man Relations, Morale and Discipline in the British Army in the Era of the First World War* (London: Macmillan, 2000), 44-6.
40 Haldane diary 15th July 1918.
41 Travers, *How the War Was Won*, 5-6.
42 Nicholson, *Behind the Lines*, 110.
43 Maxwell, Charlotte, *Frank Maxwell. A Memoir and Some Letters, edited by his wife*, 172.
44 Haldane diary 3rd October 1916, by which time he had been in command of VI Corps for 57 days.
45 Hunter-Weston diary 12th May and 2nd August 1916.
46 Rawlinson NAM diary 2nd May, 11th and 30th July 1915.
47 Wilson diary 9th January 1916.
48 Congreve diary entry for 12th June 1917. Congreve Diary D/1057/O/5/1-4, Staffordshire County Record Office.
49 Wilson diary 30th December 1915.
50 Haldane diary 2nd and 11th August 1917, 22nd and 23rd July 1918. Wilson diary 10th January, 31st March and 13th August 1916.
51 Hunter-Weston letter to his wife 27th June 1916.
52 Hunter-Weston diary 20th June 1916.
53 Haldane diary, 12th August 1916. Haldane was commissioned in 1882, Woollcombe in 1876 and the latter was given a divisional command six years earlier than Haldane too.
54 Haldane diary, 14th March 1917.
55 Hunter-Weston letter to his wife, 7th October 1916. Diary, 8th March 1918.
56 Hunter-Weston diary 24th July 1916 and 26th August 1917.
57 Hunter-Weston diary 30th May, 1st, 11th, and 13th June, 28th August 1917.
58 Haldane diary 10th August 1916. Wilson diary 29th May 1916.
59 Wilson diary 19th April, 8th and 11th September 1916. Hunter-Weston diary 23rd and 27th June 1916.
60 Rawlinson CCC diary, 8th August 1915. His BGRA until 10th October 1915 was Br.-Gen. A.H. Hussey.
61 Rawlinson NAM diary 7th and 8th April, 25th August 1915.

62 Rawlinson NAM diary, 16th September 1915.
63 Haldane diary 13th-16th May, 15th September, 6th October 1918.
64 Rawlinson CCC Diary, 9th April 1915.
65 Congreve diary 2nd January 1917, Haldane diary 5th June 1917, 4th June 1918, 20th December 1917, 21st September 1918.
66 Hunter-Weston diary 22nd March-10th April 1918.
67 Hunter-Weston recorded Second Army conferences at I ANZAC Corps on 13th, 16th, 24th, and 29th October 1917 and at Canadian Corps on 3rd November. Haldane attended Third Army conferences at his own HQ on 16th and 27th April 1917 (and on 21st April he held a divisional conference at 29th Division's HQ).
68 For example, Haldane on 16th February, 19th March and 21st April 1917. Hunter-Weston diary 23rd, 26th and 29th May, 20th, 23rd and 30th June 1916, or Wilson 18th February 1916. For raids, see Hunter-Weston diary 23rd October 1916. For an example of the CRA attending, see Wilson 22nd May 1916.
69 For example, Hunter-Weston 16th July and 4th August 1916, Wilson 17th June 1916.
70 Hunter-Weston diary 4th January 1918.
71 Hunter-Weston diary, 29th August 1916.
72 Hunter-Weston diary, 31st March 1917.
73 Hunter-Weston diary, 27th October 1916.
74 Wilson diary 1st January 1916.
75 Wilson diary 13th January 1916.
76 Haldane diary 4th May 1918.
77 Haldane diary 5th February 1918.
78 Haldane diary 3rd April 1918.
79 Haldane diary 3rd September, 1st and 2nd October, 5th November 1918.
80 Hunter-Weston diary 5th February 1918.
81 Hunter-Weston diary, clipping pasted in.
82 For example, Haldane diary, 17th December 1916; Hunter-Weston diary 11th April 1917.
83 Haldane diary, 7th August 1916.
84 Haldane diary, 2nd June 1917.
85 GHQ Italy *G.156/1.*, 13th January 1919. TNA:PRO, WO 32/5153.
86 The three branches were the General Staff (for operations), the Adjutant-General's branch (administration) and the Quartermaster-General's branch (logistics, etc.).
87 Letter of 7th March 1917. Loch Papers, IWM, 1/3/22.
88 Letters of 20th March, 4th and 7th May 1917, Loch Papers 1/3/22 and 1/3/24.
89 Haldane diary, 11th August 1916.
90 Haldane diary, 30th December 1917.
91 Rawlinson CCC diary 8th December 1914.
92 Rawlinson CCC diary, 30th December 1914.
93 Rawlinson NAM diary, 9th August 1915, CCC diary 10th August 1915.
94 Rawlinson NAM diary 1st October 1915.
95 Robbins, *British Generalship on the Western Front*, 44-5.

96 Haig diary, 5th September 1914. TNA:PRO WO 256/1.

97 Haldane diary, 11th March, 18th June 1917.

98 Haldane diary, 7th August 1916.

99 Haldane diary, 16th November 1916.

100 GHQ Italy *G.156/1.*, 13th January 1919. TNA:PRO, WO 32/5153.

101 Haldane diary, 3rd November 1916 and 4th March 1918.

102 Haldane diary 26th June 1917.

103 Hunter-Weston diary, 13th July 1916.

104 Wilson diary 24th March 1916.

105 Wilson diary 11th April 1916.

106 Hunter-Weston diary, 23rd March 1916.

107 Hunter-Weston letters to his wife 29th September, 12th and 20th November 1916.

108 Rawlinson NAM diary 23rd June and 20th November 1915.

109 Haldane diary 20th September 1918.

110 Hunter-Weston diary 22nd December 1916, 16th April 1917.

111 Hunter-Weston diary 21st October and 10th November 1918.

112 Hunter-Weston diary 28th November 1917, 15th December 1917 and 6th September 1918, respectively.

113 Congreve diary 1st March 1917.

114 See Beckett, Ian F.W., *Ypres: The First Battle, 1914* (Harlow: Pearson Education, 2004), 139-40.

115 See Beckett, *Ypres: The First Battle, 1914,* 70.

116 Hunter-Weston letter to his wife 30th June 1916.

117 O.H., 1916 Volume 1, 445-9. Hunter-Weston letter to his wife 3rd July 1916.

118 Haldane diary 10th April 1917 and 21st August 1918.

119 Haldane diary 9th April 1917.

120 Haldane diary 10th April 1917.

121 Haldane diary 11th April 1917.

122 Haldane diary 28th April 1917.

123 Haldane diary 23rd March 1918.

124 Haldane diary 24th and 27th October 1918.

125 Haldane diary 7th September 1918.

126 Hunter-Weston diary 5th October-5th November 1918, passim.

127 Haldane diary 25th August 1918.

128 Haldane diary 3rd and 22nd-28th September 1918, passim.

129 Haldane diary 23rd March 1918.

130 Haldane diary 24th March 1918.

131 Haldane diary 28th March 1918.

132 Congreve diary 23rd April 1917.

133 Haldane diary 21st March 1918.

134 Hunter-Weston letter to his wife, 3rd July 1916.

135 Wilson diary 23rd December 1915.

136 Sheffield and Bourne (eds.) *Douglas Haig...* 12-13.

137 *FSR II,* 24.

138 Hunter-Weston letter to his wife 19th July 1916.

139 Hunter-Weston diary, 27th May 1917. See also 26th and 28th November 1916.

140 Hunter-Weston diary 16th September 1916, 16th and 28th April 1917.

141 Hunter-Weston diary 26th November 1916, 8th, 14th and 15th April 1917, 4th April 1918.

142 Hunter-Weston diary 18th, 19th and 21st-26th May 1918.

143 Congreve diary 17th May 1917.

144 Hunter-Weston diary 8th December 1917.

145 Haig diary 25th November 1914.

146 Hunter-Weston diary 20th-23rd July 1916.

147 Hunter-Weston diary 14th December 1917.

148 Hunter-Weston letter to Philip Sassoon, 15th December 1917.

149 Rawlinson NAM diary 18th September and 22nd July 1915.

150 Rawlinson NAM diary 1st December 1914.

151 Hunter-Weston letter to his wife, 3rd October 1917, diary 16th September, 12th and 6th October.

152 Hunter-Weston diary 28th September 1918.

153 Haldane diary 28th and 29th June 1917, 29th July 1916, 3rd February 1918. A Church Army Commissioner was attached to each Army. Messenger, *Call to Arms*, 453.

154 Haldane diary 13th January, 18th July, 1st, 6th and 12th August 1918.

155 Haldane diary 1st June 1917, 7th March and 15th July 1918.

156 Wilson diary, 1st February, 20th May, 20th July, 5th September and 5th May 1916.

157 Hunter-Weston diary 6th August 1916, 26th October 1917 and 23rd September 1918. Wilson diary 29th September and 4th November 1916. Haldane diary 19th June 1918, 31st December 1916.

158 Hunter-Weston diary 12th October 1916.

159 Haldane diary 28th March 1917 et seq.

160 For example, Hunter-Weston diary 11th and 18th May 1916, 18th July 1916, 13th August 1917. Wilson diary 17th July 1916, Haldane diary 22nd September 1916.

161 Nicholson, *Behind the Lines*, 127. He served under 15 different corps when on divisional staffs: I Corps, IV Corps, Indian Corps, X Corps, XIII Corps, IX Corps, XV Corps, VII Corps, II Corps, VI Corps, XVIII Corps, XVII Corps, XIV Corps, XIX Corps and V Corps.

162 Hunter-Weston diary 22nd November 1917, Haldane diary 27th March and 14th August 1917.

163 Letter of 28th March 1917, Loch Papers 1/3/22. Paddy Griffith recounts an amusing anecdote about Fawcett (of uncertain provenance) Griffith, *Battle Tactics…*,152.

164 Hunter-Weston letter to his wife, 28th December 1916.

165 Wilson diary 30th May, 14th October 1916.

166 Hunter-Weston diary 10th April 1916, Rawlinson NAM diary 11th January 1915.

167 Haldane diary 23rd June 1917.

168 Wilson diary 19th May 1916.

169 Hunter-Weston diary 28th-30th May 1917.

170 Hunter-Weston diary 22nd April 1917, Congreve diary 30th January 1917.

171 Wilson diary 22nd March 1916; for other examples, 18th June, 14th, 15th and

20th August 1916.

172 Wilson diary 13th and 15th August 1916.

173 Haldane diary 12th November 1916, 2nd and 5th September 1917; Congreve diary 27th May 1917.

174 Hunter-Weston diary 2nd January 1917, 19th December 1916.

175 Rawlinson CCC diary 22nd April 1915.

176 Wilson diary 7th January 1916.

177 See *Drill and Field Training* (John Murray, 1915), 1-3.

178 Wilson diary 18th May and 12th August 1916.

179 Hunter-Weston diary 18th November 1916; letter to his wife 18th October 1917.

180 Wilson diary 19th March and 28th-29th October 1916.

181 Hunter-Weston letter to his wife 16th August 1916.

182 Hunter-Weston letter to his wife 5th December 1916 (incorrectly dated 5th November in original).

183 Congreve diary 18th April and 8th May 1918.

184 For example, Haldane diary, 27th November 1916 and 16th September 1917; Hunter-Weston diary 2nd January and 6th February 1918.

185 Rawlinson NAM diary 9th and 13th November 1915.

186 Hunter-Weston diary 1st November 1918.

187 Congreve diary 8th January 1917 and May 1918, passim.

188 Haldane diary 3rd November 1917.

189 Hunter-Weston diary 4th March 1917.

190 Hunter-Weston diary June 1918, passim. Wilson diary 18th October 1916 for shopping in Amiens, 7th November 1916 elsewhere. Congreve diary May 1918, passim.

191 Haldane diary 10th November 1917.

192 Haldane diary 19th August 1917, 15th and 27th October 1918.

193 Hunter-Weston letter to his wife 7th October 1916.

194 Hunter-Weston letter to his wife 11th October 1918.

195 Congreve diary 16th April 1918.

196 This was V Corps, in which 3rd Division served from 31st May 1915 to 17th June 1916, and whose commander, Lt.-Gen. H.D. Fanshawe, was sacked in July 1916.

197 Haldane diary, 11th August 1916.

Conclusion

As the Introduction to this book stated, it is concerned with the operational role of British corps command on the Western Front. However, before coming to a conclusion about British corps, it is useful to address the issue of the 'colonial supermen'. The elite status of the Australian and Canadian Corps has been assumed by their partisans, and the OH backs this up.[1] Edmonds felt that the fact that divisions were not rotated through these corps but kept permanently with them led to staffs being more used to working together, and Sir Ivor Maxse was also critical of the British system.[2] The two Dominion corps were viewed as having a higher esprit de corps as a result. However, Peter Simkins has demonstrated that in the Hundred Days, British divisions were generally as successful as their Colonial counterparts, and sometimes more so, and the performance of British divisions does not seems to have been affected by their being rotated through different corps.[3] Edmonds, as a regular officer, was inclined to play down the success of the New Armies, and especially their junior officers. Bearing Simkins' views in mind, it is interesting that Schreiber ascribes the successes of the Canadians (the most successful corps in the Hundred Days, he contends) not only to the factors above but also to the ability of their commander, Sir Arthur Currie, "to exercise a *de facto* veto over what Haig or British Army commanders could or could not ask the Canadians to do."[4] Since Currie would not, presumably, undertake operations which he felt were likely to fail, this can be seen as contributing to the theory of Canadian superiority. Schreiber also asserts that the corps staff had more control over doctrine and tactics than their British counterparts. However, this book has demonstrated that doctrine (not that the word was used) and tactics were widely and successfully disseminated across all corps via the SS pamphlets, after-action reports and informal communications between commanders. Strangely, Schreiber also asserts that the Canadian Corps was better because its GOCRA acted as an artillery commander, while

British corps GOCRAs were merely advisers; again, this study has demonstrated that not to be the case. As regards command style, it is apparent that Currie did exercise a more hands-on style than was generally the case for British corps commanders.[5] However, evidently it did not make too much difference to the results.

John Millar, in his work on the Australian Corps, asserts that corps commanders in general were fettered by the hierarchy in which they operated, by their social background and by technical and resource constraints. He therefore concludes that Birdwood, GOC of the Australian Corps from December 1914 to May 1918, was powerless to act at all freely outside the realm of 'personality,' and the same is true of (for example) Hunter-Weston or Maxse.[6] This seems to reduce corps commanders to showmen or nonentities, and ignores their influence in operational planning and in day-to-day inspections and the like. Curiously, Millar does refer to Birdwood's prominence in the planning of the Battle of the Menin Road and subsequent operations in August and September 1917, but he stresses that Plumer's hands-off style permitted Birdwood to blossom as a commander.[7] His successor, Monash, would appear not to have had an especially prescriptive command style either.[8] One of the strengths of Bill Rawling's work on the Canadians is that he does not treat them in isolation from the rest of the British Armies in France and brings out that the learning curve was a process of learning for British as well as Canadian troops.[9] It is important to note that the basis for this at the corps level, be it British, Australian or Canadian, was the foundation laid in the principles of *FSR I*. The associated manuals merely had to be updated and, especially after the Somme, they were, by production of the *SS* series of publications. It must be concluded that the colonial corps were not as different from their British counterparts as their apologists would like; it was, after all, a British corps which stormed the Hindenburg Line when the Australians were held up.

The table which follows is intended to show how the tempo of the BEF's operations changed, by giving a selection of major attacks during the war and their preparation times. The latter are not always easy to establish precisely, so the start of planning has generally been taken as the date upon which it can be established from the OH or some other source that GHQ gave the go-ahead for planning to begin. If this is not obvious, the date used is that upon which an Army commander held a conference after which planning appears to have begun, or (if the plan was definitely initiated by Army) the date upon which the first draft was submitted to GHQ for the operation to be approved (such as for the Battle of Amiens). Since the table in any case serves as an indicator of trends rather than a precise comparison, it is hoped that any errors which may have crept in are not significant.

Name of Battle	Start Date of Battle	Date Planning Began	Diff'nce (Days)	Army	No. Corps	No. Inf. Divs.
Mons	23rd August 1914	22nd August 1914	1	BEF	2	4
Le Cateau	26th August 1914	26th August 1914	0	BEF	1	3
Aisne	13th September 1914	12th September 1914	1	BEF	3	5
Neuve Chapelle	10th March 1915	6th February 1915	32	First	2	4
Aubers Ridge	9th May 1915	14th March 1915	56	First	3	6
Festubert	15th May 1915	10th May 1915	5	First	2	6
Loos	25th September 1915	3rd July 1915	83	First	3	11
Albert	1st July 1916	7th March 1916	115	Fourth	5	12
Bazentin	14th July 1916	3rd July 1916	11	Fourth	3	7
Flers-Courcelette	15th September 1916	19th August 1916	26	Fourth	3	9
				Fifth	1	2
Morval	25th September 1916	18th September 1916	7	Fourth	3	10
Vimy	9th April 1917	2nd January 1917	95	First	2	5
First Scarpe	9th April 1917	28th December 1916	101	Third	3	10
Second Scarpe	23rd April 1917	16th April 1917	7	Third	4	9
Messines	7th June 1917	30th January 1917	127	Second	3	12

Name of Battle	Start Date of Battle	Date Planning Began	Diff'nce (Days)	Army	No. Corps	No. Inf. Divs.
Pilckem Ridge	31st July 1917	1st June 1917	60	Second	3	5
				Fifth	4	12
Langemarck	16th August 1917	1st August 1917	15	Fifth	4	9
Menin Road	20th September 1917	27th August 1917	24	Second	3	6
				Fifth	3	5
Cambrai	20th November 1917	16th September 1917	74	Third	2	6
Amiens	8th August 1918	13th July 1918	26	Fourth	3	11
Albert	21st August 1918	13th August 1918	8	Third	3	13
Albert	23rd August 1918	22nd August 1918	1	Third	3	10
Drocourt-Quéant	2nd September 1918	28th August 1918	5	First	2	5
Havrincourt	12th September 1918	9th September 1918	3	Third	2	3
Epéhy	18th September 1918	12th September 1918	6	Third	1	3
				Fourth	3	7
Canal du Nord	27th September 1918	15th September 1918	12	First	2	5
				Third	4	8
St. Quentin Canal	29th September 1918	18th September 1918	11	Third	1	2
				Fourth	3	10
Ypres	28th September 1918	16th September 1918	12	Second	4	10
Beaurevoir	3rd October 1918	2nd October 1918	1	Third	1	1
				Fourth	3	4

Name of Battle	Start Date of Battle	Date Planning Began	Diff'nce (Days)	Army	No. Corps	No. Inf. Divs.
Cambrai	8th October 1918	5th October 1918	3	Third	4	8
				Fourth	4	9
Selle	17th October 1918	11th October 1918	6	Fourth	3	7
Sambre	4th November 1918	29th October 1918	6	Third	4	8
				Fourth	2	6

The differences in the time taken to prepare attacks reflects (amongst other factors) the changing role of corps and the corps learning curve over course of the war. The brief preparation required for the 1914 battles reflected that staffs, even if relatively hastily put together apart from I Corps', consisted of experienced officers; that the technology used was limited to the existing artillery establishments of divisions; and for corps staffs, that the demands upon them were largely limited to transmitting GHQ's orders. Corps were only put in place on the outbreak of war in order to assist the C-in-C in running the four infantry divisions of the BEF, this being thought too many for one man to command. This is not to say that they were mere ciphers; Haig's handling of his reserves at First Ypres made his reputation as a field commander. But their role in planning and executing operations was limited.

By the time of Neuve Chapelle, however, the importance of artillery was beginning to be realised, and ammunition shortage slowed tempo down, since it took time to build up stocks, even for the limited bombardment envisaged. However, corps' role was still restricted to allocating artillery delegated by Army to them (from the HAR Groups formed over the winter of 1914-15) to divisions. The same was true of Aubers, conceived as a follow-up to Neuve Chapelle, but delayed by the need to send ammunition to Gallipoli.[10] As at Aubers, operations at Festubert suffered not only from a shortage of ammunition, but also of artillery owing to the Second Battle of Ypres raging to the north. However, enough stocks were available to launch the Festubert attack soon after Aubers, but not to prolong it for more than 12 days.[11]

After Festubert, corps' importance began to increase, since at that battle problems had been caused by one divisional CRA being given command of far more artillery than he could handle, and the decision was made that for the next attack the corps BGRA should have a larger staff and co-ordinate all the artillery in the corps. Tempo, however, still suffered from the need to assemble the necessary munitions, hence the delay before the

Battle of Loos, which even caused the French to postpone their own offensive to co-ordinate with the British.[12] It should be noted that after Aubers the BEF's policy was not one of high tempo but of the massing of resources for a deliberate attack, irrespective of the time it took (within reason; the French would not wait forever). At the same time, divisional staffs in particular were still very inexperienced, leading to an increasing degree of centralisation of planning by corps. Indeed, Sir Henry Rawlinson had to lend the 51st Division his BGGS in June 1915, and dissatisfaction with his BGRA led Rawlinson to sideline him and instead entrust the artillery planning for IV Corps to the CRA of 1st Division.[13]

It is unsurprising, given the emphasis on careful and deliberate operations, that the Battle of Albert took so long to prepare (it would have taken still longer had it not been for French pressure).[14] The infrastructure for Fourth Army had to be constructed, including water supplies, new roads and the like, as well as amassing stocks of ammunition and artillery and moving troops up. Again, tempo was not an issue in the planning. Corps staffs also had plenty of time to make their plans in conjunction with Army, providing the parameters within which divisions did their own planning. Corps plans were comprehensive and detailed, since they now played a far more important role than before, by virtue of their command of all the artillery in the corps and of associated RFC resources. As the battle went on, the tempo generally increased. For example, the 11 day preparation time for the Battle of Bazentin reflected that though much of the artillery needed to be brought up across the old front line, for example, the distances over which roads needed to be cleared and repaired were not great. Time also had to be allowed for the preliminary bombardment, of course, and the capture of positions on the flanks of the attack. Though the battle literally bogged down later, the time to organise attacks was necessarily reduced by corps' relative immobility, so that their local knowledge could be passed on to new divisions as they arrived to make new attacks, and they also provided continuity of artillery control.

The Vimy and First Scarpe operations took a substantial time to organise, unsurprisingly since they both were very artillery-intensive, and preparations on the ground, such as road-building, had to contend with winter weather. They were highly structured attacks, reflecting the lessons of the Somme. At the operational level, these were encapsulated in the pamphlet *SS135*, which (in various editions) had a crucial influence on how corps conducted operations for the rest of the war. It established beyond doubt what the respective spheres of Army, corps and divisions were in the planning process, and also made up for the difficulties of inexperienced staff (who were far fewer in number by now) by standardising it. Given the leap forward in artillery techniques in these attacks, the corps role was even more important than before, since within the principles set out by Army they devised the artillery plan and allocated all guns to their (now specialised) tasks within it, and divisions, with whom the plans were discussed, had to state their specific requirements to corps, even for their own artillery. That said, moves towards a flexible degree of decentralisation were made, so once the attack had begun, division regained control of some artillery. This was in part because more was now available, so these extra guns could be 'superimposed' on the main barrages. However, once the initial, carefully planned phase of the Arras offensive was over, though tempo rose, the effectiveness of operations did not, since the Germans were able to respond as least as fast, much as on the Somme.

Messines was a still more structured affair than Arras, not least because 19 mines, some of which had taken years to dig, were integral to the plan. It unsurprising that the tempo of preparation was slow and very deliberate, though only when the Arras offensive was closed down was sufficient artillery available for the attack, arriving in the middle two weeks of May.[15] Corps again followed *SS135*, but with some changes because of lessons learnt at Arras. Artillery control was somewhat decentralised, in that corps set out the timetable of the attack but left it to divisions to arrange the details within that framework, and Heavy Artillery Groups were linked to specific divisions and not just handled through corps. Counterbattery fire (the staff for which had been established at corps level during the Somme) was improved by tying specific RFC units to the relevant heavy artillery. At a tactical level, machine-guns (and their barrages) fell under the control of the Corps Machine-Gun Officers. While all this contributed to the great success at Messines, it was not an operation designed with high tempo in mind. The next step of the Flanders campaign was to the north, although not far.

The break between the end of the Battle of Messines on 14th June 1917 and the Battle of Pilckem Ridge on 31st July has been criticised as being too long, but in reality, the Messines front needed to be consolidated, with new roads, tramlines and other logistic infrastructure put in place, lest it be vulnerable to counterattack. Then the new battlefield to the north had to be prepared in the usual way.[16] Only then might it be possible to raise the tempo of operations. From the point of the learning curve for corps, little changed from Messines, except that the artillery plan became still more complex. However, the attack plans themselves had become considerably slimmer documents than in 1916, presumably since experience and the *SS* series of pamphlets had helped standardise the approach. Indeed, it was apparent that corps was now the level of command which organised the attack, within guidelines set by Army. Notwithstanding that, any chance of raising the tempo of operations was lost in the rain and mud which attended the initial assault and subsequent days. Once the ground had dried somewhat in September, corps developed a more or less stereotyped style of attack, based around their being issued with a map by Army showing the objectives, and leaving it up to them how these were to be attained. Hence, the Battle of the Menin Road Ridge took place on 20th September, Polygon Wood on 26th September, Broodseinde on 4th October, Poelcappelle on 9th October and First Passchendaele on 12th October.[17] Though these operations were conducted with increasing frequency, they became steadily less successful as the Second Army advanced into a salient and the ground got worse, so again it was not possible to sustain a tempo higher than the enemy's.[18] However, the set-piece attack, organised by corps, had been fully developed.

There is relatively little to say about the 1917 Battle of Cambrai in this context. It was revolutionary in that it was the first British offensive where surprise was achieved by omitting the preliminary bombardment, tanks being used to crush the German wire and help the infantry forward. Valuable lessons were learned in open warfare, but in terms of planning at the corps level it was largely conventional. Like the other offensives of 1917, a promising start where higher tempo than the Germans' was achieved degenerated into a slogging match. Nevertheless, the experience gained bore fruit in the British offensives of 1918.

Plainly, the pace of operations in the Hundred Days was much faster than in earlier years; though the preparation times for the Battles of Bazentin, Morval and the Second Battle of the Scarpe and the battles in Third Ypres from the Menin Road Ridge onwards were small, they began in positions close to those for the previous attacks, and so the movement of material was far smaller than that in 1918. It should also be noted that the planning times before the Battles of the Selle and Sambre were extended by the need for the BEF to wait for heavy artillery and ammunition to come up.

The question of how this increased tempo was attained arises. Perhaps the most important factor was that by the middle of 1918, the BEF finally had enough artillery and ammunition for it to conduct large-scale operations at more than one point on its front – the table shows that four or more major battles could be conducted in one month by two or more Armies.[19] By comparison, it should be noted that for the bombardment before the Battle of Pilckem Ridge, Fifth Army had to borrow more than half of Second Army's artillery and significant quantities from First and Third Armies too.[20] There was obviously a substantial logistical overhead in moving over 1,500 artillery pieces from these other sectors to the Fifth Army front, but, more importantly, it took time as well as denuding other areas of artillery, if not completely, at least in sufficient quantities for a large-scale attack not to be possible elsewhere than Ypres. In addition, the sustained bombardments before the attacks in 1916 and 1917 were not generally required in 1918 (though three days were spent on the preliminary bombardment in front of the Hindenburg Main Position), when intense, hurricane bombardments were more commonly employed. The second factor, which ties in with the availability of artillery and ammunition, was that the BEF had the logistic base necessary to support the material-based offensives which characterised the Hundred Days.[21] Indeed, Brown points out that in this respect – the tying of operational aspirations to logistic necessity – the British showed a better grasp of the reality of fighting on the Western Front than the Germans had in the spring. Surprise played a greater part in operations than at any other period in the war, and this too helped maintain the tempo.

The role of corps in preparing for the set-piece operations in very short times was vitally important, given their share in organising the artillery. A new edition of *SS135* in early 1918 demonstrated that the lessons of 1917 in both attack and defence and set-piece and open warfare had been learnt. Haldane's analysis and proposal for an attack on Havrincourt in September 1918 has been touched upon in the last chapter; that he also suggested the operation after was precisely as laid down in the new *SS135*. It might be argued that the German successes in early 1918 demonstrated that for the defence the BEF had arrived at the wrong conclusions, but in reality the March Retreat (in particular) was more the result of shortage of manpower than defensive errors, though undoubtedly some were made. In any case, the retreats of March and April also provided valuable experience in mobile warfare. The Hundred Days saw the BEF's technique of attack brought to its highest point. Planning was decentralised from Army to corps; corps only centralised for set-pieces, and otherwise devolved control of artillery and operational planning to divisions as far as possible, only acting in a co-ordinating role (such as laying down the policy for leapfrogging divisions) when necessary for larger mobile operations. In effect, they acted like the clutch in a car, intervening when a change of gear was necessary, either taking control of artillery if the pace slowed for a set-piece, or releasing it when a faster advance was required.

As the role of corps changed, so did that of the corps commander. At the start of the war it was limited to passing Army orders to divisions and organising them and the reserves. By mid-1915 Rawlinson (for example) held frequent conferences with his chosen artillery expert in order to plan forthcoming attacks. On taking over his corps in 1916, Haldane reflected that he would "require now to know much more about [artillery matters] than when in command of a division."[22] Unlike Haig in 1914, who, *in extremis* rode forward from his HQ to see what could be done on the spot, corps commanders by 1916-18 acknowledged the need to be at the centre of their communications network – that is, at their HQ – at the start of a battle. It was the best place to receive reports from subordinate formations and the corps RFC squadron and act accordingly. Only later could they go forward and chivvy divisional and brigade commanders. However, the commonest activities of corps commanders – inspecting or otherwise visiting troops and meeting divisional and brigade commanders – were carried out throughout the war. There was no need to change from the practice of 1914-15 when it served its purpose perfectly well, though the range of formations which needed to be visited rose as corps took on more responsibilities and organised anything from schools to laundries.

This book attempts to assess how important the corps level of command on the Western Front was, and to establish what did British corps did, and how. Though corps began the war as just an administrative body, as the army expanded in 1915 and its artillery complement grew, so did the influence of corps. From 1916 onwards, corps was the highest level of command in the BEF concerned with the detail of operations, and success was crucially dependent on the planning of corps staffs. Corps became central to the planning and execution of operations. And as resources, especially artillery, became more plentiful, so it was possible for corps, when appropriate, to decentralise back down to divisions, as the principles of *FSR I* required. The importance of corps' role continued into the next war, despite declining as some of the lessons taught in the learning curve were forgotten in the desert campaign in 1941-2. Only before Second Alamein was British artillery centralised at division and corps when necessary; corps fireplans were drawn up, effective counter-battery techniques put in place by corps, and corps wireless networks created.[23] Western Front veterans – by 1942 senior officers – were able to draw upon the experiences of 1918 when organising the set-piece battle of October 1942 with more modern resources, and this continued into the North-West Europe campaign of 1944-5.[24]

NOTES

1 O.H., 1918 Volume 5, 179.

2 *Note by a member of the* [Cambrai] *Court of Enquiry*, Maxse Papers, IWM. 69/53/11, 40.

3 Simkins, Peter, 'Co-Stars or Supporting Cast? British Divisions in the 'Hundred Days,' 1918' in Griffith, Paddy (ed.) *British Fighting Methods in the Great War* (Frank Cass, 1996).

4 Schreiber, *Shock Army of the British Empire*, 19.

5 Schreiber, *Shock Army...*, 73.

6 Millar, *A Study in the Limitations of Command: General Sir William Birdwood and the AIF, 1914-1918*, 202-3.

7 Millar, *A Study in the Limitations of Command...*, 179, 183.

8 Serle, Geoffrey, *John Monash. A Biography* (Melbourne University Press, 1982), 341, 353, 358.

9 For example, Rawling, *Surviving Trench Warfare...*, 5-6, 167-87.

10 Brown, *British Logistics...*, 90.

11 O.H., 1915 Volume 2, 77.

12 O.H., 1915 Volume 2, 118-9.

13 Rawlinson CCC diary, 11/6/15.

14 Prior and Wilson, *The Somme*, 31.

15 O.H., 1917 Volume 2, 41.

16 Brown, *British Logistics...*, 164.

17 Note that all these bar the first are omitted from the table since Plumer's scheme for all these attacks was drawn up before the Menin Road Ridge, so the planning time here is not simply the time elapsed between battles. See Prior and Wilson, *Passchendaele...*, 113.

18 Prior and Wilson, *Passchendaele...*, 138-9.

19 O.H., 1918 Volume 5, 595-6. Griffith, *Battle Tactics...*, 147.

20 O.H., 1917 Volume 2, 108.

21 Brown, *British Logistics...*, 198-204.

22 Haldane diary 7/8/16.

23 Barr, Niall, *Pendulum of War. The Three Battles of El Alamein.* (Jonathan Cape, 2004), 183, 287, 292-4.

24 Barr, *Pendulum...*, 190, 261, Bidwell and Graham, *Fire-Power*, 290.

APPENDIX 1

Corps Commanders on the Western Front

This list is of corps commanders in corps sequence, and within that it is chronological. Consequently, the same officer may appear more than once.

Some corps commanders' tenures were interrupted by other officers taking over acting or temporary command, usually if the normal corps commander went on leave or fell sick or wounded. These periods are counted into the latter's tenure.

XXII Corps is omitted since Lt-Gen. Sir A.J. Godley, like Currie, Monash and Birdwood, was in an atypical position, in his case because of his responsibilities towards the New Zealand Government.

Name	Corps	Start	End	Duration (days)
Allenby E.H.H.	Cavalry	10/04/14	06/05/15	391
Byng J.H.G.	Cavalry	07/05/15	15/08/15	100
Bingham C.E.	Cavalry	23/10/15	12/03/16	141
Kavanagh C.T.McM.	Cavalry	04/09/16	11/11/18	798
Haig D.	I	05/08/14	25/12/14	142
Monro C.C.	I	26/12/14	12/07/15	198
Gough H. de la P.	I	13/07/15	31/03/16	262
Kavanagh C.T.McM.	I	01/04/16	03/09/16	155
Anderson C.A.	I	30/09/16	10/02/17	133
Holland A.E.A.	I	19/02/17	11/11/18	630
Smith-Dorrien H.L.	II	21/08/14	31/12/14	132
Fergusson C.	II	01/01/15	27/05/16	512

Jacob C.	II	28/05/16	11/11/18	897
Pulteney W.P.	III	05/08/14	25/02/18	1300
Butler R.H.K.	III	26/02/18	11/11/18	258
Rawlinson H.S.	IV	05/10/14	21/12/15	442
Wilson H.H.	IV	22/12/15	30/11/16	344
Woollcombe C.L.	IV	01/12/16	10/03/18	464
Harper G.M.	IV	11/03/18	11/11/18	245
Plumer H.C.O.	V	08/01/15	07/05/15	119
Allenby E.H.H.	V	08/05/15	22/10/15	167
Fanshawe H.D.	V	23/10/15	04/07/16	255
Fanshawe E.A.	V	05/07/16	27/04/18	661
Shute C.D.	V	28/04/18	11/11/18	197
Keir J.L.	VI	27/05/15	07/08/16	438
Haldane J.A.L.	VI	08/08/16	11/11/18	825
Snow T.D'O.	VII	15/07/15	02/01/18	902
Congreve W.N.	VII	03/01/18	12/04/18	99
Hunter-Weston A.G.	VIII	18/03/16	11/11/18	968
Hamilton Gordon A.	IX	20/06/16	12/09/18	814
Braithwaite W.P.	IX	13/09/18	11/11/18	59
Morland T.L.N.	X	15/07/15	14/04/18	1004
Peyton W.E.	X	24/05/18	02/07/18	39
Stephens R.B.	X	03/07/18	11/11/18	131
Haking R.C.B.	XI	04/09/15	11/11/18	1164
Congreve W.N.	XIII	15/11/15	16/06/17	579
McCracken F.W.N.	XIII	17/06/17	12/03/18	268
De Lisle H. de B.	XIII	13/03/18	11/04/18	29
Morland T.L.N.	XIII	12/04/18	11/11/18	213
Cavan Earl of	XIV	11/01/16	29/10/17	657
Horne H.S.	XV	22/04/16	28/09/16	159
Du Cane J.P.	XV	29/09/16	11/04/18	559
De Lisle H. de B.	XV	12/04/18	11/11/18	213
Anderson C.A.	XVII	09/12/15	12/02/16	65
Byng J.H.G.	XVII	27/02/16	24/05/16	87
Fergusson C.	XVII	25/05/16	11/11/18	900
Maxse F.I.	XVIII	15/01/17	21/06/18	522
Watts H.E.	XIX	04/02/17	11/11/18	645

APPENDIX 2:

Composition of Corps Headquarters in the BEF, 1914-18

Composition on Mobilization in 1914 (note that when the Mobilization Tables were compiled the term 'Army' was used for corps):[1]

GOC and 1 ADC to GOC

GS Branch

BGGS
GSO1
GSO2 (Operations)
GSO2 (Intelligence)
GSO3

A&QMG's Branch

Deputy A&QMG
Assistant A&QMG
Assistant QMG
Deputy Assistant A&QMG

Administrative Services and Depts.

"Officer i/c Army [sic] Signals"
"Medical Officer"
Assistant Director of Postal Services

Special Appointments

Assistant Provost Marshal
Camp Commandant

Attached to Headquarters, 1st Army [sic]

Brigadier-General, RA
Colonel, RE

Composition in June 1916:[2]

GOC and 2 ADCs to GOC (3 ADCs in Canadian Corps)

GS Branch

BGGS
GSO2 (2xGSO2 in Canadian Corps)
2xGSO3 (1xGSO3 in Canadian Corps)

A&QMG's Branch

Deputy A&QMG
Assistant QMG
Deputy Assistant A&QMG

Administrative Services and Depts.

Assistant Director of Signals
Deputy Director of Medical Services
Deputy-Assistant Director of Medical Services
Assistant Director of Ordnance Services
Deputy-Assistant Director of Army Postal Services

Special Appointments

Assistant Provost Marshal
Camp Commandant

Headquarters, Artillery of the Corps

Commander
ADC to Commander
Staff Officer

Headquarters, Corps Heavy Artillery

Commander
Brigade Major
Staff Captain

Attached

Appendix 2

Chief Engineer (CRE)

ANZAC Corps had same composition as British.

Composition in June 1917:

GOC and 2 ADCs to GOC (3 ADCs in Canadian Corps)

GS Branch

BGGS
GSO2 (Operations)
GSO2 (Intelligence)
GSO2 (2xGSO2 in Canadian Corps)
GSO3

A&QMG's Branch

Deputy A&QMG
Assistant QMG
Deputy Assistant AG
Deputy Assistant A&QMG

Administrative Services and Depts. (no change from 1916)

Assistant Director of Signals
Deputy Director of Medical Services
Deputy-Assistant Director of Medical Services
Assistant Director of Ordnance Services
Deputy-Assistant Director of Army Postal Services

Special Appointments

Assistant Provost Marshal
Camp Commandant (and Staff Captain in Canadian Corps)
Corps MGO *(only in Order of Battle tables June-August inclusive)*

Headquarters, Artillery of the Corps

Commander
Staff Officer
Staff Captain
Staff Officer for Reconnaissance
Lt.-Col., RA, attached, for Counter-Battery work (CBSO)
Orderly Officer for Counter-Battery work (May and June only)

Headquarters, Corps Heavy Artillery

Commander
Brigade Major
Staff Captain
Staff Officer for Reconnaissance (May and June only)

Attached

Chief Engineer (CRE)
Staff Officer to CRE
Commanding Royal Engineer, Corps Troops (temp. Lt.-Col., RE)
Adjutant, Royal Engineer, Corps Troops (temp. Lt., RE)

ANZAC Corps had same composition as British.

Composition at 11th November 1918:

GOC and 2 ADCs to GOC

GS Branch

BGGS
2xGSO2
2xGSO3
(Some corps have 3xGSO2 and 1xGSO3)

A&QMG's Branch

Deputy A&QMG
Assistant QMG
Deputy Assistant AG
Deputy Assistant A&QMG
Staff Captain

Administrative Services and Depts.

Assistant Director of Signals
Deputy Assistant Director of Roads
Labour Commandant
Assistant to Labour Commandant
Deputy Director of Medical Services
Deputy-Assistant Director of Medical Services
Assistant Director of Ordnance Services
Assistant Director of Veterinary Services
Deputy-Assistant Director of Army Postal Services

Special Appointments

Assistant Provost Marshal
Camp Commandant (and Staff Captain in Canadian Corps)
Corps MGO

Headquarters, Artillery of the Corps

GOC
GSO2
Staff Captain
Captain attached for Intelligence Duties
Lt.-Col., RA, attached, for Counter-Battery work

Headquarters, Corps Heavy Artillery (no change from 1916)

Commander
Brigade Major
Staff Captain

Attached (no change from 1917)

Chief Engineer (CRE)
Staff Officer to CRE
Commanding Royal Engineer, Corps Troops (temp. Lt.-Col., RE)
Adjutant, Royal Engineer, Corps Troops (temp. Lt., RE)

XXII Corps was as above, but had in addition "For Special Duties in Connection
with the New Zealand Expeditionary Force" Godley as GOC with an AAG
and a DAAG. The Australian Corps was as the British but the artillery HQ was
as in 1917. The Canadian Corps was as the British but had more GSOs on the
strength.

NOTES

1 From file TNA:PRO, WO 33/611 (Mobilization Tables).
2 Hereafter from Hunter-Weston Papers, BL, no. 48362, unless italicised, in which
   case from Orders of Battle in Maxse Papers, IWM, 69/53/14.

APPENDIX 3

List of Corps Commanders' Visits, Inspections, etc.

The number of different places and functions that a corps commander might attend was large. The commonest were:

Visiting or inspecting troops, including medal and other parades (this usually involved addressing the troops as well).

Visiting and/or addressing schools (their own, divisional or Army).

Inspecting trenches, defence lines or artillery positions, and visits to tunnel systems with mining experts. Visiting or inspecting machine-gun emplacements.

Attending demonstrations, such as tanks on their own, tanks and infantry, Fuze 106, the machine-gun barrage, sound-ranging, camouflage and flamethrowers.

Attending sporting events (football, rugby, boxing and even baseball, or just 'sports' in general) or horse shows (corps, divisional or lower) and presenting prizes.

Attending concerts given usually by divisional troupes (though Haldane established a Corps Theatrical Company).

Attending lectures, both on military (such as tanks, gas, the legendary Major Campbell on the bayonet) and non-military topics (the US and the war; what Japan has done in the war; Haldane showed a particular interest in medical lectures[1]).

Less frequent according to the diary entries (but see Rawlinson's diary entry quoted early in Chapter 8, which implies a daily, routine hospital visit) were:

Visits to hospitals or dressing stations or other medical facilities.

Visits to or inspection of other corps facilities, e.g. laundry, Corps Club, Corps Cinema, Corps Ranges, workshops etc.

Visits to or inspection of divisional facilities, e.g. laundry, baths, Divisional Ammunition Column.

Very occasional visits, such as to salvage dumps, prisoners' cage, light railways, balloon squadrons or to inspect the roads (with the corps CRE).

Since visits to troops were by far the most frequent, it is useful further to subdivide them by formation and activity:

Battalions or brigades doing practice attacks (this might include US Troops in 1918).

Battalions or brigades doing practice raids (and to compliment the raiders if successful).

Battalions or brigades (or, rarely, divisions) training (this might include US Troops in 1918).

Training with tanks (less common).

Battalions or brigades on the march.[2]

Battalions or brigades on parade. As well as their own, corps commanders attended Army medal parades and also occasionally those conducted by visiting foreign generals.

Address battalion(s) – Hunter-Weston was very fond of this; Haldane did more in 1918 than before, presumably owing to his and Byng's fears of poor morale.

Machine-gun companies.

Artillery, both heavy and field, and their positions and horse lines.

Trench Mortar batteries.

Corps troops (cyclists, cavalry) training or inspection or even occasionally a medal parade.

Corps RFC/RAF Squadron.

Inspecting the billets of any formation.

The record for the number of visits in a day was probably held by Hunter-Weston, who on 28/7/18 went round his rear areas and visited and inspected railhead supplies, a 12-inch gun, 20th Divisional Motor Transport Company, the Corps Troops Reception Camp, a Veterinary Evacuation Station, and the Corps Farm. He stopped for lunch, afterwards going on to 318 Road Construction Company, 195 and 718 Labour Companies, 20th Divisional baths, three dumps of unspecified type and finally to the salvage dump, Motor Transport refuelling point, and the Corps Ordnance depot.[3]

NOTES

1 See, for example, Haldane diary 6/9/16, 12/11/16.

2 James Jack considered that watching troops marching, apart from being good for discipline, permitted officers to assess the "general form of their troops". Terraine, John (ed.), *General Jack's Diary* (Eyre and Spottiswoode, 1964), 265-6.

3 Hunter-Weston diary 27th July 1918.

Bibliography

Unpublished Primary Sources

The National Archives (Public Record Office), Kew

Departmental Papers

Cabinet:
CAB 45/114, 115, 116, 118, 120-125, 129, 132-138, 140, 141, 182, 183, 184-199
CAB 103/115

War Office:
WO 32/4731
WO 33/9, 11, 606, 660
WO 95/3-22, 25, 91-95, 148, 154-160, 168-170, 268-277, 360-375, 431-440, 518-522, 588-592, 619, 620, 706-712, 728, 729, 743-752, 756, 757, 760, 804-808, 811-813, 815, 820-822, 824, 825, 827, 835-837, 841, 842, 844, 850-854, 862-867, 872, 895-897, 901-903, 910-913, 915-917, 918, 934-6, 942-944, 946, 951-953, 955, 956
WO 158/17-20, 38, 40, 52-55, 79, 181, 182, 207-212, 215, 223, 233-237, 242, 243, 245-249, 258, 291, 298, 304-307, 311, 314, 316-321, 327-331, 345, 351, 376, 378-384, 396, 415, 419, 420
WO 163/9
WO 279/18, 48
Field Marshal the Earl of Cavan (WO 79/66)
Field Marshal Earl Haig (WO 256/1-38)

British Library, Department of Manuscripts

General Sir Aylmer Hunter-Weston Papers

Churchill College, Cambridge

Field Marshal Lord Rawlinson Papers

Durham County Record Office, Durham

Lt.-Col. Sir Cuthbert Headlam Papers

Imperial War Museum, Department of Documents

Fourth Army Papers
General Lord Horne Papers
Maj.-Gen. Lord Loch Papers
General Sir Ivor Maxse Papers
General Sir Thomas Morland Papers
Field Marshal Sir Henry Wilson Papers

Liddell Hart Centre for Military Archives, King's College London

Br.-Gen. John Charteris Papers
Br.-Gen. Sir James Edmonds MSS
Sir Basil Liddell Hart MSS
Br.-Gen. Philip Howell Papers

National Army Museum

Field Marshal Lord Rawlinson Papers

National Library of Scotland

General Sir Aylmer Haldane Papers

Staffordshire County Record Office, Stafford

General Sir Walter Congreve Papers

West Sussex County Record Office, Chichester

General Sir Ivor Maxse Papers

Published Primary Sources

Official Publications

General Staff, *Field Service Regulations, Part I, Operations (1909)* (London, 1909)

—, *SS 109 Training of Divisions for Offensive Action.* (May, 1916)

—, *SS 135 Instructions for the Training of Divisions for Offensive Action.* (December 1916. Reprinted with Amendments August 1917)

—, *SS 135 The Training and Employment of Divisions, 1918.* (January 1918)

—, *SS 148 Forward Inter-Communication in Battle.* (March 1917. Reprinted with Amendments September 1917)

—, *SS 158 Notes on Recent Operations on the Front of First, Third, Fourth and Fifth Armies.* (May 1917)

—, *SS 192 The Tactical Employment of Machine Guns.* (Undated)

—, *SS 210 The Division in Defence.* (May 1918)

Published Primary Sources, Memoirs etc. (place of publication is London unless otherwise stated)

Birdwood, Field Marshal Lord, *Khaki and Gown* (Ward, Lock 1941).

Blake, Robert (ed.) *The Private Papers of Douglas Haig, 1914-1919* (Eyre & Spottiswoode, 1952).

Bond, Brian and Robbins, Simon (eds.) *Staff Officer. The Diaries of Walter Guinness (First Lord Moyne) 1914-1918* (Leo Cooper, 1987).

Boraston, Lt.-Col. J.H. (ed.), *Sir Douglas Haig's Despatches (December 1915 – April 1919)* (Dent, 1919).

Carrington, Charles, *Soldier From the Wars Returning* (Hutchinson, 1965).

Dunn, Captain J.C., *The War the Infantry Knew* (Jane's, 1987).

Eden, Anthony, *Another World* (Allen Lane, 1976).

Ferris, John (ed.), *The British Army and Signals Intelligence During the First World War* (Army Records Society, 1992).

Fraser, David (ed.), *In Good Company: The First World War letters and diaries of the Hon. William Fraser* (Salisbury, Wilts.: Michael Russell, 1990).

Gough, General Sir Hubert, *Soldiering On* (Arthur Barker, 1954).

Haldane, Sir Aylmer, *A Soldier's Saga* (Edinburgh and London: William Blackwood and Sons, 1948).

Lloyd George, David, *War Memoirs* (Odhams, 1938).

Maxwell, Charlotte, *Frank Maxwell. A Memoir and Some Letters, edited by his wife* (John Murray, 1921).

Nicholson, Col. W.N., *Behind the Lines* (Stevenage, Herts.: The Strong Oak Press with Tom Donovan Publishing, undated).

Woodward, D.R. (ed.), *The Military Correspondence of Field-Marshal Sir William Robertson, Chief of the Imperial General Staff, December 1915-February 1918* (Army Records Society, 1989).

Published Secondary Sources (place of publication is London unless otherwise stated)

Anon, *59th Division 1915-1918* (Chesterfield: Wilfred Edmunds, 1928).

Anon, *The Work of the Royal Engineers in the European War, 1914-19. Bridging*

(Chatham: W & J Mackay & Co., 1921).

Atteridge, A. Hilliard, *History of the 17th (Northern) Division* (Glasgow: Robert Maclehose & Co., 1929).

Barr, Niall, *Pendulum of War. The Three Battles of El Alamein.* (Jonathan Cape, 2004).

Baynes, Sir John, *Far From a Donkey: The Life of General Sir Ivor Maxse* (London and Washington: Brassey's, 1995).

Beach, James Michael, 'British Intelligence and the German Army, 1914-1918.' (Ph. D. thesis, University of London, 2005).

Becke, Major A.F., *History of the Great War: Order of Battle of Divisions*, 6 parts (HMSO 1935-45).

Beckett, Ian F.W., and Simpson, Keith (eds.), *A Nation in Arms* (Manchester: MUP, 1985).

Beckett, Ian F.W., *Johnnie Gough, VC* (Tom Donovan, 1989).

Beckett, Ian F.W., *Ypres. The First Battle, 1914* (Harlow: Pearson Education, 2004).

Berton, Pierre, *Vimy* (Toronto: Penguin Books Canada, 1987).

Bewsher, Major F.W., *The History of the 51st (Highland) Division 1914-1918* (Edinburgh and London: William Blackwood and Sons, 1921).

Bidwell, Shelford and Graham, Dominick, *Fire-Power. British Army Weapons and Theories of War 1904-1945* (Allen and Unwin, 1982).

Blaxland, Gregory, *Amiens: 1918* (Frederick Muller, 1968).

Bond, Brian (ed.), *The First World War and British Military History* (Oxford: Clarendon, 1991).

Brown, Ian Malcolm, *British Logistics on the Western Front 1914-1919* (Westport, Connecticut and London: Praeger, 1998).

Brown, Ian M., 'Not Glamorous, But Effective: The Canadian Corps and the Set-Piece Attack, 1917-1918.' *Journal of Military History*, Volume 58 (July 1994), 421-44.

Charteris, Br.-Gen. John, *Field-Marshal Earl Haig* (Cassell, 1929).

Childs, D.J., 'British Tanks 1915-18, Manufacture and Employment' (Ph.D. thesis, Glasgow University, 1996).

Childs, David J., A Peripheral Weapon? The Production and Employment of British Tanks in the First World War (Westport, Connecticut: Greenwood Press, 1999).

Clark, Alan, *The Donkeys* (Hutchinson, 1961).

Coop, Rev. J.O., *The Story of the 55th (West Lancashire) Division* (Liverpool: Liverpool Daily Post, 1919).

Danchev, Alex, *Alchemist of War. The Life of Basil Liddell Hart* (Phoenix, 1998).

Davies, Frank and Maddocks, Graham, *Bloody Red Tabs* (Leo Cooper, 1995).

De Groot, Gerard, *Douglas Haig, 1861-1928* (Unwin Hyman, 1988).

Denman, Terence, *Ireland's Unknown Soldiers. The 16th (Irish) Division in the Great War, 1914-1918* (Dublin: Irish Academic Press, 1992).

Duff Cooper, Alfred, *Haig* (Faber and Faber, 1935).

Edmonds, Sir James E. and others, *History of the Great War: Military Operations, France and Belgium 1914-18*, 14 volumes plus appendices and maps (Macmillan and HMSO, 1922-48).

Essame, H., *The Battle for Europe 1918* (B.T. Batsford, 1972).

Ewing, John, *The History of the 9th (Scottish) Division 1914-1919* (John Murray, 1921).

Falls, Cyril, *The History of the 36th (Ulster) Division* (Belfast and London: McCaw, Stevenson & Orr, 1922).

Farndale, General Sir Martin, *History of the Royal Regiment of Artillery: Western Front 1914-18* (RA Institution, 1986).

Farrar-Hockley, Anthony, *Goughie* (Hart-Davis MacGibbon, 1975).

Farrar-Hockley, Anthony, *The Somme* (Pan, 1966).

Fothergill, R.A., *Private Chronicles. A Study of English Diaries* (Oxford: OUP, 1974).

French, David, *Military Identities. The Regimental System, the British Army, and the British People, c. 1870-2000* (Oxford: Oxford University Press, 2005).

French, David and Holden Reid, Brian (eds.) *The British General Staff: Reform and Innovation c.1890-1939* (London and Portland, Oregon: Frank Cass, 2002).

Gardner, Brian, *Allenby* (Cassell, 1965).

Gardner, Nikolas, 'Command in Crisis: the BEF and the Forest of Mormal, August 1914.' *War and Society* Vol. 16 No.2 (October 1998), 13-32.

Gardner, Nikolas, *Trial by Fire. Command and the British Expeditionary Force in 1914* (Westport, Connecticut and London: Praeger, 2003).

Gat, Azar, *British Armour Theory and the Rise of the Panzer Arm* (Macmillan, 2000).

Gooch, John, 'Military Doctrine and Military History' in Gooch, John (ed.) *The Origins of Contemporary Doctrine* (The Strategic and Combat Studies Institute. The Occasional, No. 30, September 1997), 5-7.

Gough, General Sir Hubert, *The Fifth Army* (Hodder and Stoughton, 1931).

Graham, Dominick and Bidwell, Shelford, *Coalitions, Politicians and Generals* (London and New York: Brassey's, 1993).

Green, Andrew, *Writing the Great War. Sir James Edmonds and the Official Histories, 1915-1948* (London and Portland, Oregon: Frank Cass, 2003).

Griffith, Paddy, *Battle Tactics of the Western Front* (New Haven and London: Yale University Press, 1994).

Griffith, Paddy (ed.) *British Fighting Methods in the Great War* (London and Portland, Oregon: Frank Cass, 1996).

Handy, Charles, *Understanding Organisations* (Penguin, 1993).

Harington, General Sir Charles, *Plumer of Messines* (John Murray, 1935).

Harris, J.P., *Men, ideas and tanks* (Manchester and New York: MUP, 1995).

Harris, J.P., with Barr, Niall, *Amiens to the Armistice. The BEF in the Hundred Days' Campaign, 8 August-11 November 1918* (London and Washington: Brassey's 1998).

Headlam, Lt.-Col. C., *History of the Guards Division in the Great War, 1915-1918* (John Murray, 1924).

Henniker, Col. A.M., *Transportation on the Western Front* (HMSO, 1937).

Hynes, Samuel L, *A War Imagined. The First World War and English Culture* (The Bodley Head, 1990).

James, Captain E.A., *A Record of the Battles and Engagements of the British Armies in France and Flanders, 1914-1918* (London Stamp Exchange, 1990).

James, Lawrence, *Imperial Warrior* (Weidenfeld and Nicholson, 1993).

Jerrold, Douglas, *The Royal Naval Division* (Hutchinson, 1923).

Jones, H.A., *The War in the Air, Vol. VI* (Oxford: Clarendon, 1937).

Kincaid-Smith, M., *The 25th Division in France and Flanders* (Harrison and Sons, undated).

Kiszely, John 'Achieving High Tempo – New Challenges', *Journal of the Royal*

United Services Institute for Defence Studies, Volume 144 No. 6 (December 1999), 47-53.

Liddell Hart, B.H., *The Real War 1914-1918* (Faber and Faber, 1930).

Liddell Hart, B.H., *The Tanks. Volume I 1914-1939* (Cassell, 1959).

Liddle, Peter H. (ed.) *Passchendaele in Perspective* (Leo Cooper, 1997).

Longworth, Philip, *The Unending Vigil* (Leo Cooper, 1985).

Marble, William Sanders, 'The Infantry cannot do with a gun less: the place of artillery in the BEF, 1914-1918.' (Ph.D. thesis, University of London, 1998).

Macleod, R., 'Sight and Sound on the Western Front. Surveyors, Scientists and the 'Battlefield Laboratory' 1914-1918.' *War and Society* Vol. 18 No.1 (May 2000), 23-46.

Marden, Maj.-Gen. T.O., *A Short History of the 6th Division, Aug. 1914-March 1919* (Hugh Rees Ltd., 1920).

Martinson, Deborah *In the Presence of Audience: the Self in Diaries and Fiction* (Columbus: Ohio State University Press, 2003).

Maude, A.H. (ed.) *The 47th (London) Division 1914-1919* (Amalgamated Press, 1922).

Maurice, Maj.-Gen. Sir F., *The Last Four Months. The End of the War in the West* (Cassell, 1919).

McCarthy, Chris, *The Somme: The Day-by-Day Account* (Arms and Armour Press, 1993).

McCarthy, Chris, *Passchendaele: The Day-by-Day Account* (Arms and Armour Press, 1995).

McKee, Alexander, *Vimy Ridge* (Souvenir Press, 1966).

Mearsheimer, John J., *Liddell Hart and the Weight of History* (Ithaca, New York, and London: Cornell University Press, 1988).

Messenger, Charles, *Call to Arms. The British Army 1914-18* (Weidenfeld and Nicholson, 2005).

Middlebrook, Martin, *The Kaiser's Battle* (Penguin, 1983).

Millar, John Dermot, 'A Study in the Limitations of Command: General Sir William Birdwood and the AIF, 1914-1918' (Ph.D. thesis, University of New South Wales, 1993).

Montgomery, Maj.-Gen. Sir Archibald, *The Story of the Fourth Army in the Battles of the Hundred Days, August 8th to November 11th, 1918* (Hodder and Stoughton, 1919).

Montgomery of Alamein, Field-Marshal Viscount, *A History of Warfare* (Collins, 1968).

Moreman, T.R., 'The Dawn Assault – Friday 14th July 1916', *Journal of the Society for Army Historical Research*, LXXI (Autumn 1993), 180-204.

Munby, Lt.-Col. J.E. (ed.), *A History of the 38th (Welsh) Division* (Hugh Rees Ltd., 1920).

Nichols, Captain G.H.F., *The 18th Division in the Great War* (Edinburgh and London: William Blackwood and Sons, 1922).

Nicholls, Jonathan, *Cheerful Sacrifice* (Leo Cooper, 1990).

Palazzo, Albert, *Seeking Victory on the Western Front. The British Army and Chemical Warfare in World War I* (Lincoln, Nebraska and London: University of Nebraska Press, 2000).

Pidgeon, Trevor, *The Tanks at Flers* (Cobham, Surrey: Fairmile Books, 1995).

Pitt, Barrie, *1918 – The Last Act* (Reprint Society, 1964).

Powell, Geoffrey, *Plumer – The Soldier's General* (Leo Cooper, 1990).

Priestley, R.E., *The Signal Service in the European War of 1914 to 1918 (France)* (Chatham: W & J Mackay & Co., 1921).

Prior, Robin, and Wilson, Trevor, *Command on the Western Front* (Oxford and Cambridge Massachusetts: Blackwell, 1992).

Prior, Robin and Wilson, Trevor, *Passchendaele: The Untold Story* (New Haven and London: Yale University Press, 1996).

Prior, Robin and Wilson, Trevor, *The Somme* (New Haven and London: Yale University Press, 2005).

Rawling, Bill, *Surviving Trench Warfare: Technology and the Canadian Corps 1914-1918* (Toronto, Buffalo and London: University of Toronto Press, 1992).

Richter, Donald, *Chemical Soldiers. British Gas Warfare in World War I* (Leo Cooper, 1994).

Reid, Brian Holden (ed.) *Military Power. Land Warfare in Theory and Practice* (London and Portland, Oregon: Frank Cass, 1997).

Reid, Brian Holden, 'War Fighting Doctrine and the British Army' in Reid, Brian Holden, *A Doctrinal Perspective 1988-1998* (The Strategic and Combat Studies Institute. The Occasional, No. 33, May 1998), 12-28.

Robbins, Simon, *British Generalship on the Western Front, 1914-18: Defeat into Victory* (London and Portland, Oregon: Frank Cass, 2004).

Sambrook, James, *With the Rank and Pay of a Sapper: the 216th (Nuneaton) Army Troops Company, Royal Engineers, in the Great War* (Nuneaton, Warwicks.: Paddy Griffith Associates, 1998).

Samuels, Martin, *Command or Control: Command, Training and Tactics in the British and German Armies, 1888-1918* (London and Portland, Oregon: Frank Cass, 1995).

Samuels, Martin, *Doctrine and Dogma. German and British Infantry Tactics in the First World War* (New York, Westport, Connecticut and London: Greenwood Press, 1992).

Savage, Raymond, *Allenby of Armageddon* (Hodder and Stoughton, 1925).

Scott, Maj.-Gen. Sir Arthur B. (ed.), *History of the 12th (Eastern) Division in the Great War, 1914-1918* (Nisbet and Co., 1923).

Schreiber, Shane B., *Shock Army of the British Empire. The Canadian Corps in the Last 100 Days of the Great War* (Westport, Connecticut and London: Praeger, 1997).

Serle, Geoffrey, *John Monash. A Biography* (Carlton, Victoria: Melbourne University Press, 1982).

Shakespear, Lt.-Col. J., *The Thirty-Fourth Division 1915-1919* (H.F. and G. Witherby, 1921).

Sheffield, Gary, 'British High Command in the First World War: An Overview,' in Sheffield, Gary and Till, Geoffrey (eds.), *Challenges of High Command in the Twentieth Century* (The Strategic and Combat Studies Institute. The Occasional, No. 38, December 1999), 15-25.

Sheffield, Gary, *Forgotten Victory. The First World War: Myths and Realities* (Headline, 2001).

Sheffield, Gary, *Leadership in the Trenches. Officer-Man Relations, Morale and Discipline in the British Army in the Era of the First World War* (Macmillan, 2000).

Sheffield, Gary, *The Somme* (Cassell, 2003).

Sheffield, Gary and Bourne, John (eds.), *Douglas Haig: War Diaries and Letters 1914-1918* (Weidenfeld and Nicholson, 2005).

Sheffield, Gary and Todman, Dan (eds.), *Command and Control on the Western Front* (Staplehurst: Spellmount, 2004).

Simons, Judy, *Diaries and Journals of Literary Women from Fanny Burney to Virginia Woolf* (Macmillan, 1990).

Simpson, Andy, *The Evolution of Victory* (Tom Donovan, 1995).

Sixsmith, Maj.-Gen. E.K.G., *British Generalship in the Twentieth Century* (Arms and Armour Press, 1970).

Stewart, Lt.-Col.. J. and Buchan, John, *The Fifteenth (Scottish) Division 1914-1919* (Edinburgh and London: William Blackwood and Sons, 1926).

Terraine, John, *Douglas Haig, The Educated Soldier* (Hutchinson, 1963).

Terraine, John (ed.), *General Jack's Diary* (Eyre and Spottiswoode, 1964).

Terraine, John., *To Win a War: 1918, The Year of Victory* (Sidgwick and Jackson, 1978).

Tosh, John, *The Pursuit of History* (3rd ed., Longman, 2002).

Thornton, Lt.-Col. L.H and Fraser, Pamela, *The Congreves, Father and Son* (John Murray, 1930).

Travers, T.H.E., 'Command and Leadership Styles in the British Army; The 1915 Gallipoli Model', *Journal of Contemporary History*, Vol. 29 (1994), 403-441.

Travers, T.H.E., *How the War Was Won. Command and Technology in the British Army on the Western Front 1917-1918* (London and New York: Routledge, 1992).

Travers, T.H.E., 'Learning and Decision-Making on the Western Front 1915-1916: the British Example', *Canadian Journal of History*, Vol. 18 (1983), 87-97.

Travers, T.H.E., 'Technology, Tactics and Morale: Jean de Bloch, the Boer War and British Military Theory, 1900-1914', *Journal of Modern History*, Vol. 51 (1979), 264-86.

Travers, T.H.E., 'The Hidden Army: Structural Problems in the British Officer Corps, 1900-1918', *Journal of Contemporary History*, Vol. 17 (1982), 523-44.

Travers, T.H.E., *The Killing Ground: The British Army, the Western Front and the Emergence of Modern Warfare 1900-1918* (Allen and Unwin, 1987).

Travers, T.H.E., 'The Offensive and the Problem of Innovation in British Military Thought, 1870-1915', *Journal of Contemporary History*, Vol. 13 (1978), 531-53.

Turner, John, *British Politics and the Great War* (New Haven and London: Yale University Press, 1992).

Walker, Jonathan, *The Blood Tub. General Gough and the Battle of Bullecourt 1917* (Staplehurst: Spellmount, 1998).

Whitton, Lt.-Col. F.E., *History of the 40th Division* (Aldershot, Hants.: Gale and Polden, 1926).

Williams, Jeffrey, *Byng of Vimy. General and Governor General* (Leo Cooper, 1983).

Wolff, Leon, *In Flanders Fields* (London, New York, Toronto: Longmans, Green, 1958).

Wynne, Captain G.C., *If Germany Attacks: The Battle in Depth in the West* (Faber and Faber, 1940).

Wyrall, Everard, *The History of the 19th Division 1914-1918* (Edward Arnold, n.d.).

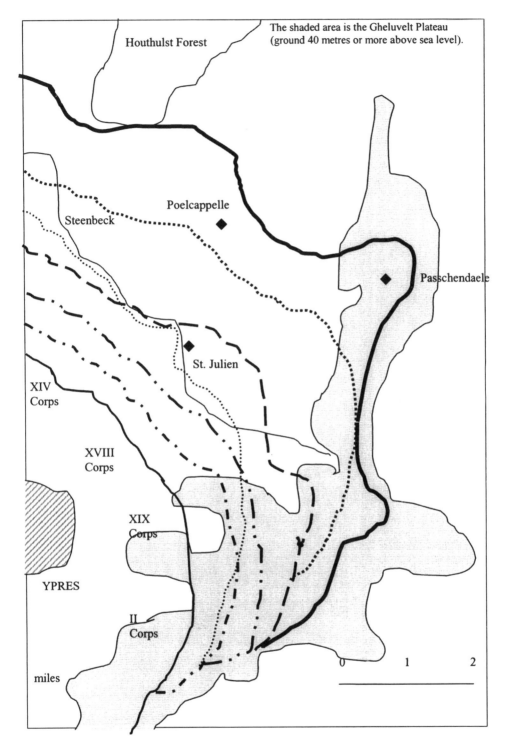

Houthulst Forest

The shaded area is the Gheluvelt Plateau
(ground 40 metres or more above sea level).

Poelcappelle

Steenbeck

Passchendaele

St. Julien

XIV
Corps

XVIII
Corps

XIX
Corps

YPRES

II
Corps

miles

0   1   2

Sketch map of Fifth Army operations on 31st July 1917.

———————	British Front Line before the attack	———————	Front line on 7th December
— · — · —	Blue Line (1st Objective)	— · · — · · —	Black Line (2nd Objective)
— — — —	Green Line (3rd Objective)	·············	Red Line (4th Objective)
···············	Line gained on 31st July		

Index

Note that officers' ranks are generally given as they were at the time of the index reference, with exceptions such as Haig or Army commanders, where the highest wartime rank is given.